MW00609346

AL GRAY
MARINE

THE EARLY YEARS
1950-1967

VOLUME 1

BY SCOTT LAIDIG

FOREWORD BY: GENERAL TONY ZINNI, US MARINE CORPS (RET)
PREFACE BY: DR. JOHN F. GUILMARTIN, LIEUTENANT COLONEL, US AIR FORCE (RET)

POTOMAC INSTITUTE PRESS

Published by Potomac Institute Press
Potomac Institute for Policy Studies
ISBN: 978-0-9852483-0-7 (Hardback) Vol. 1

USMC Eagle, Globe & Anchor, image courtesy of the USMC. Neither the USMC nor any other component of the Department of Defense has approved, endorsed, or authorized this product.
Cover images From General Gray's private collection.
Cover Design: Patrick Worcester, Editorial Assistant: Dan Degerman

Publisher's Cataloging-in-Publication Data

Laidig, Scott.

Al Gray, Marine : the early years, 1950-1967 / by Scott Laidig ; foreword by: General Tony Zinni ; preface by: Dr. John F. Guilmartin. Arlington, VA : Potomac Institute Press, c2012.

p. ; cm.

ISBN: 978-0-9852483-0-7 (v. 1, cloth) ;
978-0-9852483-4-5 (v. 1, ebk.) ; 978-0-9852483-6-9 (v. 1, ebk. : Kindle ed.)
Includes bibliographical references and index.
Summary: volume 1 of a proposed set telling the story of General Gray's years as an enlisted Marine, junior officer and field grade officer. The author also reviews the Vietnam War: the politics surrounding it, the reporting of it, and them military decisions made in Saigon and Washington.--Publisher.
Contents: In the wrong line -- A brief early history of Vietnam -- Take any assignment and make the best of it -- Vietnam history, 1955-1961 -- Captain Gray goes to Washington -- Vietnam history, 1961-1963 -- First Marine ground combat unit enters Vietnam -- Southeast Asia heats up -- Back to combat arms -- Major American combat units arrive in South Vietnam -- Gray commands at Gio Linh Outpost -- SIGINT again -- Vietnam War, 1967 -- Bibliography -- Appendix -- Index.

1. Gray, Alfred M. 2. United States. Marine Corps--Officers--Biography. 3. United States. Marine Corps--History--20th century. 4. Generals--United States--Biography. 5. Vietnam War, 1961-1975--United States. 6. United States--Military policy. 7. United States--Military relations--Vietnam. 8. Vietnam--Military relations--United States. I. Title.

VE25.G73 L35 2012

359.9/6092--dc23   1211

Notes on formatting and usage: With respect for those who serve, capitalization has been applied to named ranks and titles throughout this work. Military terminology can vary depending on the scope, tenor, and context of usage, and every effort has been made to maintain authenticity of usage while ensuring clarity. Given myriad service acronyms, an acronym/abbreviations listing has been included in the appendix for each volume.

POTOMAC INSTITUTE FOR POLICY STUDIES
901 N. Stuart St, Suite 200
Arlington, VA, 22203
www.potomacinstitute.org
Telephone: 703.525.0770; Fax: 703.525.0299
Email: webmaster@potomacinstitute.org

This book is dedicated to Sergeant Ronald S. Earle, United States Marine Corps; Sergeant Daniel D. Jones, United States Marine Corps; and Sergeant Robert R. Jones, United States Marine Corps; and all the other wounded warriors from all the military services who have come home mentally or physically scarred as a result of their duties in Iraq and Afghanistan; and to the families of all those warriors who made the supreme sacrifice.

To those who have served honorably, often multiple times, in the war zones of Iraq, Afghanistan, and elsewhere around the globe, we extend our most heartfelt thanks, and say welcome home!

All the net proceeds from this book will be donated to the Injured Marine Semper Fi Fund. The Injured Marine Semper Fi Fund is a 501(c)(3) nonprofit set up to provide immediate financial support for injured or critically ill members of United States Armed Forces and their families. The Injured Marine Semper Fi Fund directs urgently needed resources to Marines and Sailors, as well as members of the Army, Air Force or Coast Guard who serve in support of Marine forces.

More information about the Injured Marine Semper Fi Fund can be found at: http://www.semperfifund.org

ACKNOWLEDGEMENTS

There were many, many Marines who contributed to the writing of this book, and others who encouraged me to get the project completed. Many of those are mentioned in the text, but many more others will go unnamed. To each and every one of you I owe a significant debt of gratitude; you are too numerous to mention but I sincerely hope that you all know who you are and that you are content with this outcome.

The genesis of this book occurred during a late night discussion I had with an old friend and former colleague, Terry Collins, who loved hearing my stories about General Al Gray and encouraged me to write a book. The idea was relatively easy to finally try to implement. Getting General Gray's approval and cooperation was an entirely different matter. We finally succeeded only after pointing out that a book about him might be a successful fundraiser for the Injured Marine Semper Fi Fund, and that perhaps current and future Marines might learn from his story.

After we got started, Lawrence Bowdish, PhD, not only guided me through the intricacies of word processing but also made many contributions to the text. My friend Bill Sinclair read the initial drafts and my sister, Betty Earle, did much of the final proofreading. The publisher provided wonderful assistance in the form of James Giordano, PhD, and Sherry Loveless, and their counsel to a new author was very significant. To each, thank you. Of course, any errors remain my responsibility.

My business partner and boss for most of my career, Cliff Cooke, Jr., made it possible for us to retire at a relatively young age. Cliff's dad was a great Marine who served at Guadalcanal and throughout the Pacific in World War II. Much of Cliff, Sr., rubbed off on his children. Thanks, Cliff.

Dr. Paul Otte is the President Emeritus of Franklin University of Ohio, and currently heads the Leadership Center at that University. He is General Gray's co-author of the book, *The Conflicted Leader and Vantage Leadership*. That Paul had gone through the process of writing a book with the General made my own journey much easier; thanks for everything, Paul.

Dr. John F. (Joe) Guilmartin, Jr., of The Ohio State University's Department of History has become a close friend and esteemed mentor. Joe is a war hero in his own right, having earned two Silver Stars, and he was present as the senior United

States Air Force H-53 Jolly Green pilot and detachment commander during the evacuation of Saigon, where his path and Colonel Al Gray's crossed. Special thanks for your many contributions to the text, Joe, and for helping to make my knowledge of the war more complete. I hope your new Vietnam War book is soon finished.

My beautiful wife Susan has been my closest friend for more than 30 years. But in this instance she has another quality that made her especially useful: she is my best editor! And since she has absolutely no knowledge of the Marine Corps except what she has read herein, she has tried keeping me from falling into the trap of using too much military jargon. Thanks, honey, you're the best.

Many people know Jan Gray as the Commandant's gracious lady from when she and General Gray occupied the residence at Marine Barracks, Washington, D.C. Others may recall her for her tireless efforts related to the funerals of the Marines and Sailors lost as a result of the Beirut bombing incident. And a few recall her days with General Gray's mother, Emily. She is surely the perfect complement to the General. She grew up in a military family; her dad was a bomber pilot who retired as an Air Force Lieutenant Colonel after having been a German Prisoner of War during World War II. Jan well understood military protocol and manners, and she also understood it was Al Gray, not she, who wore the stars in the family. Jan's assistance to me during this time has been simply essential. I can never thank you enough, Jan, for putting up with me for these past years and for always having the guest room ready!

And finally I need to acknowledge my debt to General Gray for permitting me to tell this story. It is one worthy of a much more accomplished author. That the General allowed me the access, that he shared portions of his private papers, his pictures, and all the various notes and letters that he has kept over the years is something I could never have imagined when I first met this fine man; it is humbling to have had this honor.

Thank you, sir, for the privilege of sharing the story of your life as a Marine.

–Scott Laidig

AL GRAY, MARINE

THE EARLY YEARS

1950-1967

VOLUME 1

CONTENTS

FOREWORD

Every organization or institution that has a long successful history is marked by a number of legendary leaders who have shaped that success and built its reputation. The United States Marine Corps is no exception. Our remarkable history is replete with leaders whose courage, innovation, skill, and charisma made our Corps into an elite military organization steeped in pride and respect for the extraordinary service we have given to our nation. The list of these legendary leaders over our two plus centuries of dedicated service include names such as Henderson, Lejeune, Puller, Wilson, Barrow, and many others from our officer and enlisted ranks. One of these superb leaders from our more recent history is General Alfred M. Gray.

I first met General Gray in 1972 when he was a Lieutenant Colonel. At the time I was a Captain commanding a rifle company in the 2nd Marine Division at Camp Lejeune, North Carolina. A good friend and fellow company commander, Captain (later General) Jack Sheehan, kept telling me about his extraordinary battalion commander, a decorated Vietnam veteran named Al Gray. He invited me to have dinner with the two of them at the Officers' Club one evening. I quickly saw why Jack had such high regard and admiration for General Gray. That began a relationship that has lasted to this day and one that I truly cherish. General Gray became a mentor and role model for me. Despite coming from another battalion, he took me under his wing, as he did many other officers in whom he saw promise. Here was a rare senior officer who could talk the nitty-gritty of tactics and leadership issues at our level with a depth of knowledge and understanding that was far greater than his peers. He immediately connected to us junior officers because of his passion for our profession and his clear understanding of what we did. I would have the honor to serve under him several times after that. I was also able to seek his advice and counsel when I didn't. As I rose through the ranks over the remaining three decades of my military career, I knew I could call on General Gray for advice or to bounce thoughts and ideas off of him. Most impressive to me, he always sought me out, as he did many others, to ensure I was doing OK or to share his thoughts and ideas.

General Gray's legacy to our Corps is rich and varied. He is renowned for his charismatic mentoring of junior leaders; his exceptional operational skills; his dynamic approach to leader education and development; his organizational and doctrinal innovations; and his strategic vision for the role of our service in defense of our nation.

He drew young leaders to him like a powerful magnet with his approachable and personable character. They were also drawn to him by his clear understanding of their world and his common sense brilliance about every aspect of their mission and tasks. He talked fire team tactics or strategic planning with a degree of insight and detail that few other senior leaders could. His ability to communicate to, and connect to, privates as well as presidents attracted a following of loyal junior and senior leaders seeking his valuable counsel.

General Gray is credited with forging a renaissance in thinking about our profession of arms. He changed the outdated and constipated approaches to war fighting and the operational art that had evolved and were reflected in our training, organization, concepts, and doctrine. He encouraged out of the box thinking and challenges to our operational concepts and fathered the *Maneuver Warfare* conceptual basis for campaigning.

Without question he is considered the foremost leader in leader education and development in the history of our Corps. He created the Marine Corps University, Research Center, Training and Education Command, and other organizations dedicated to building strong, creative leadership. These institutions significantly changed our service by developing an officer and NCO corps with a competence and skill level fully capable to meet the challenges of 21st century.

Arguably, General Gray's greatest contribution to our Corps was his vision for how our service best met our mission to win our country's battles. His saw a much more expansive role for us. A role that did not encroach on the roles of other services but complemented them because of the flexibility, readiness, adaptability, deployability, interoperability, and expeditionary nature of our organization. He saw the Marine Corps as a "reservoir of combat capability" that can be shaped, organized, and tasked to meet the missions assigned in the most effective and efficient manner. He did not believe in rigid structures or dogmatic organizational designs. He saw a unique contribution from our service that required the flexible and creative organization and leadership he intended to build and promote in our revitalized leader development and operational concepts.

For all of us who were fortunate enough to learn at the knee of General Gray, he provided us with an exciting environment that was intellectually challenging and invited our participation in the development and decision making that shaped our service. Sergeants and Generals had a voice. His enthusiasm was infectious. His challenges were stimulating. Most of all, his total dedication and love of our Corps were inspiring.

To many, General Gray is best known for the remarkable things he accomplished as a general officer. For those of us who knew him well before he rose to flag rank, we witnessed and benefited from his exceptional talents well before that time. Scott Laidig has superbly captured that time in this excellent book. Typical of General Gray is his, Scott Laidig's, and the publisher's request that all proceeds from this book go to the Semper Fi Fund to benefit our Marines.

-General Anthony C. Zinni
US Marine Corps (Ret)
Former Commander-in-Chief, US Central Command

PREFACE

General Alfred M. Gray, Jr., holds a special place among Commandants of the Marine Corps. Serving as the 29th Commandant from 1987 to 1991, he is widely regarded as having had a transformative influence on his service, notably in re-invigorating the Corps' warrior ethos and in replacing the existing attritional warfighting paradigm with one of maneuver warfare. That the maneuver warfare paradigm undergirded spectacular battlefield success in *Operation Desert Storm* and the initial stages of *Operation Iraqi Freedom* and proved adaptable to the challenges of asymmetrical warfare in a counter-insurgent role in Iraq and Afghanistan both underlined the thoroughness of the transformation and added lustre to the Corps' reputation.

Al Gray – as he styled himself and was widely referred to by Marines of all ranks, and to a remarkable degree still is – assumed the Commandancy at yet another difficult and challenging period in the Corps' long history. In four years he guided the Corps through what might be termed an intellectual renaissance, centerpieces of which include the publication of Fleet Marine Force Manual 1, *Warfighting*, which expounds the theory and practice of maneuver warfare based on the encouragement of low-level initiative and innovation, and on the establishment of the Marine Corps University and Marine Corps Combat Development Command. An important ingredient in Gray's transformational success was the degree to which he was perceived by field Marines as "looking out for them." Simply put, Gray inspired a remarkable degree of loyalty, not least of all among the junior officer and enlisted ranks. The degree to which he fostered this ethos and the degree to which it simply happened is open to question, but he was clearly aware of it. As evidence, consider Gray's adoption of "Papa Bear" as his personal radio callsign as the Ground Force Commander during the Saigon evacuation.

As former Marine Staff NCO-turned historian Earl Cantagnus has pointed out, what General Gray did as Commandant is generally well established.[1] The how and why of his accomplishments as Commandant are much less clear and here the volume at hand has a great deal to offer. Clearly, Al Gray's take on the profession of arms and on the proper role of the Marine Corps within it was heavily influenced by his experience in the Cold War and in Vietnam… and we should remember that the two cannot be cleanly separated. Indeed, the Vietnam War can be considered a major "hot" campaign waged within the strategic context of the Cold War. With that in mind, it is perhaps less than coincidental that the benefits of Gray's transformational impact on the Marine Corps took effect in the wake of the collapse of the Soviet Union and proved remarkably well tailored to the new strategic challenges that emerged.

Plainly his belief in the warrior ethos and his unbounded faith in Marines that accompanied General Al Gray into the Commandancy were heavily shaped by his experience in Vietnam. It is to that experience that Scott Laidig, who saw combat in Vietnam as a company grade Marine infantry officer before serving in intelligence billets, turns in the pages that follow. Above and beyond Vietnam's shaping influence on Al Gray, what Laidig has to say is of considerable interest in its own right, for Gray saw the Vietnam War "up close and personal" as few Americans did. He was there in 1964, close to the beginning of the United States' overt military commitment to South Vietnam, commanding a Special Operations and Intelligence unit in northern I Corps that included a Marine infantry company, the first American line infantry to see combat in that country. He was there at the bitter end as a regimental commander, heavily – and critically – involved in the planning for *Operation Frequent Wind*, the helicopter evacuation of Saigon, and commanding the ground security force that secured the landing zones from which Marine and Air Force helicopters took evacuees, and eventually the ground security force, out to the ships of Navy Task Force 76.

In between, Gray served in a remarkable array of billets, serving as a regimental operations officer and unofficial intelligence advisor to high level Marine commanders (though not by that name; despite his extensive experience in the field, particularly as a cryptologist, Gray was never actually an intelligence officer); as an artillery battalion commander in a particularly difficult situation; and serving in what amounted to a corps-level intelligence billet during the run-up to the 1968 *Tết Offensive*. In between, he commanded an infantry battalion and infantry regiment in the 2nd Marine Division, and an infantry regiment (the 4th Marines) along with Camp Hansen, on Okinawa. As America's commitment to Vietnam was winding down, he found himself dealing with a host of problems involving demoralization, drugs, and race and leadership issues that plagued all the military services. His draconian prescriptions, including mandatory high school education for those lacking one, proved remarkably successful and helped point the way to a better Corps.

It is worth noting at this point that Gray's career pattern, one that exposed him to a remarkably wide range of issues and problems, would have been impossible in any other service. Testimony to the mission orientation and flexibility of the Marine Corps, he was not shoe-horned into the career progression ladder of a weapons system community (Navy), arms branch (Army) or weapons system identifier (Air Force). Although he was honored by the National Security Agency for his professional skills related to cryptology, he was never an intelligence officer *per se* but rather had extensive experience in the combat arms.

Al Gray had a colorful personality with seemingly contradictory facets. Unusual among general officers, he served as a sergeant in an elite amphibious reconnaissance unit that included duty aboard a submarine. He was regarded by some as an intellectual and had a flair for languages (he became fluent in Japanese and spoke some colloquial Korean, Chinese and Vietnamese as well as other Asian dialects without benefit of formal instruction), but applied for and received his college degree only after his promotion to Lieutenant General. Although not a teetotaler, he eschewed alcohol while overseas but was an inveterate tobacco chewer. Beyond his cryptologic talents, he proved to be a virtuoso artillery commander and shrewd tactician. Unusual among American officers who were not advisors, he developed close personal and professional relations with many of the South Vietnamese officers with whom he served. Committed to the Corps, he remained a bachelor until he had attained flag rank. The constants in his professional life were frightening competence, a competence on which many of his superiors commented; a willingness to take on challenging tasks; an ability to think "out of the box"; loyalty to the Corps; and always – particularly as he moved upward in rank – "his Marines."

In the pages that follow, Laidig uses Al Gray and his experience in Vietnam as an analytical lens through which to examine the Vietnam War and America's role in that war. In the process, he gives us a richer understanding of just what that war was about, interweaving the twists and turns of Gray's career with those of American politics, Vietnamese politics, the shifting strategic balance, debates within our national leadership as to how the war should be prosecuted and the news media's coverage of the war. *Al Gray, Marine: The Early Years* is more than the biography of an important figure in the history of the Marine Corps, though it is certainly that; it is an analytical examination of an institution under challenges at a critical time in its history and that of our nation, one that demonstrates that an individual can make a difference.

-John F. Guilmartin, Jr.
The Ohio State University
Columbus, Ohio

1. Stories detailing the experiences of Marines who met Gray abound on the internet and are frequent in conversations with Marines [who served] in the "Gray years," Earl Cantagnus, Jr., "Intellectual Warrior: General Alfred M. Gray's Transformational Commandancy, 1987-1991" (Annapolis, Maryland, 2009 U.S. Naval Academy Naval History Symposium Conference Paper), cited with permission.

PRELUDE: TO VOLUMES I & II

There was no historical precedent for the events of April 30, 1975.

Never in the history of the United States of America had it lost a war. Never in history had an ally of the United States, fighting for its independence with American military support, been forced to surrender.

Never in the modern era had a Congress and a President turned their backs on friends, allies, and comrades-in-arms. During the days leading up to April 30, 1975, for the first time in American history, they had.

The People's Republic of Vietnam (North Vietnam) had been continuously attacking the Republic of Vietnam (South Vietnam) since at least 1960. The circumstances that in 1955 had created North and South Vietnam were complex and confusing, but no more so than those that established North and South Korea, or East and West Germany. America did not sanction East German attacks against West Germany, and America fought a war to stop North Korean aggression against South Korea. And for a long while, and at great cost in national treasure and in the lives of its best young men and women, America had stood with South Vietnam, though the American military always fought with at least one arm tied behind its back. On April 30, 1975, the American commitment to South Vietnam died a painful death, and with it expired freedom for the citizens of the Republic of Vietnam and the lives of many of their patriots.

After the Paris Peace Accords had been signed in 1973, which ended the active participation of the United States in the war, the American Ambassador to South Vietnam had hoped against all hope that the country could be saved. The South Vietnamese President, buoyed by innumerable promises of endless financial and military support made by two successive American Presidents, was incapable of making the tough decisions that might have saved his nascent nation. Reality was, that without American military aid and financial resources, South Vietnam's fight against communist aggression faced extremely long odds and was almost surely doomed to failure. The North was, after all, sustained, abetted and encouraged by the two largest communist powers on Earth, the Soviet Union and China. As recently as 1972, during what was dubbed the *Easter Offensive*, South Vietnam – aided substantially by American air power and military assistance – had drubbed the invaders and inflicted tremendous casualties on the attackers. But by the end of 1974 and early 1975, the American Congress had lost its resolve to assist the South, and the American Presidency, weakened by the events of Watergate, could not push back against the Congress with the will to do what was right – to defend a free people fighting for freedom.

Many Americans and other allies had remained in Saigon in April 1975, and they needed to be rescued. Three large columns of communist forces had overwhelmed the South Vietnamese defenders, who by that time lacked sufficient amounts of bullets, bandages and bombs to put up a good resistance. There were also numerous, near countless, South Vietnamese who had worked for America, and they faced certain death in the event of a communist takeover. They, too, needed rescuing, and many were.

The American commander of the ground forces that saved the Ambassador and about 8,000 others sat in the rearmost seat of a large helicopter, one that he thought was the last helicopter out of Saigon. Gazing out the open rear hatch as the aircraft flew eastward in the darkness, he felt a great sense of personal loss. After all, he had been operating and fighting in and for South Vietnam during parts of eight of the past 13 years, and he had great admiration for the South Vietnamese people as they waged their struggle to be free from communist oppression. He had observed first hand the North Vietnamese Army and Viet Cong forces carry out barbarous terrorist tactics and other atrocities against the Vietnamese people in hamlets and villages. Looking back at the events of April 29-30, 1975, Colonel Al Gray knew that the Sailors, Airmen, and Marines had performed brilliantly. His men had landed, carried out their mission flawlessly for over 26 hours, and now they were returning to their amphibious ships lying 50 miles off the Vietnamese coast. The loss of two Embassy Marines and two helicopter pilots, though grievous, was far from what casualties might have been. Like many veterans of the long conflict, he wondered how their loyal South Vietnamese military and civilian personnel left behind would survive in the future. Gray was tired from not having slept for nearly 48 hours, but he remained alert, thinking.

He was thinking mostly about the future, because that is how Al Gray lives – looking ahead. In an hour there would be a new dawn of a new day and new challenges. Nevertheless, it was impossible for the Marine not to ponder the innumerable events, twists and turns that brought him to this day, April 30, 1975.

CHAPTER I

IN THE WRONG LINE
A BRIEF EARLY HISTORY OF VIETNAM

IN THE WRONG LINE

Al Gray stood near the end of the seemingly interminable line. He appeared bored, though as anyone who ever knew him would testify, he was taking in everything that was happening. Gray never rushed to the front of crowds, preferring to hang back and carefully survey the scene, loath to attract attention to himself. He was at Camp Pendleton, California, one of the largest Marine Corps bases on the West Coast of the United States. Quickly promoted to sergeant, he had been a Marine for little more than two years, having enlisted when the war came to Korea in 1950. Gray had found the experience everything he had expected, and more. After graduating from boot camp at Parris Island, completing an extended tour of mess duty in San Diego, and while enrolled at the basic Field Radio Operator's Course in California, he had volunteered for and been accepted into an elite amphibious reconnaissance unit; he then had spent more than a year doing all sorts of things interesting to and typical of recon Marines.[1] Gray was challenged by his current duties and motivated by his recon comrades-in-arms. However, there was a war raging in Korea, and the young sergeant had volunteered to serve there.

The line he stood in was the first step in transferring overseas to the combat zone. Gray patiently waited his turn to reach the assignment table, where an officer and several staff non-commissioned officers reviewed records and formed the volunteers into drafts that would travel together across the Pacific aboard Navy transport ships.

Sergeant Gray was working on a chew of tobacco, his omnipresent accessory, when he was surprised to hear a staff non-commissioned officer whom he knew calling his name. "Gray, get over here, you're in the wrong line," yelled Staff Sergeant Shirley. Al Gray was trying to figure out what his mistake could possibly have been when the more senior man pointed to another column, one much shorter, off to the side. Gray ambled over and his quizzical look led to a further explanation, "You've been assigned to Officer Selection Screening Course at Quantico, Sergeant Gray."

Instead of being off to war in Korea, the 22-year-old non-commissioned officer was heading to Virginia and officer training. No one could have predicted the future profession of the young sergeant, least of all him.

BEFORE THE MARINES

Alfred Mason Gray was a great fit with the many personalities that populated the Marine Corps in the 1950s. He had left Lafayette College in eastern Pennsylvania for financial reasons. Lafayette was not far from Point Pleasant Beach, New Jersey, where Gray grew up and was the local sports star. Aside from his sports stardom, Gray was a good student who graduated from high school at 17, despite deciding to attend an extra year to take additional courses, play sports and work part-time at various jobs. Al Gray was on pace to graduate in 1945, but many local citizens wanted him to remain in school for another year. World War II was winding down, and his parents would not sign the papers needed to permit him to enlist. In addition to the school principal, the football coach (who doubled as the baseball coach), the basketball coach, and the President of the Board of Education all joined to persuade him to stay at Point Pleasant Beach High School an extra year. An alternative would have been to attend college or a college preparatory school for a year, but that was cost prohibitive.

While growing up in both Rahway and Point Pleasant Beach, Gray was two or even three years younger than his classmates and those heavily involved in sports. However, he learned much from the older lads who befriended him and he frequently held his own. By the time he was a sophomore, Gray was starting in three sports, all the while continuing to work an assortment of part-time jobs. Working was something Gray had done since he was eleven and obtained his Social Security number. Called "Peanuts" by his older friends and pals, he was widely respected as a hard worker by his peers. He packed fish at the docks at night, delivered mail and ice in the summer, worked as a scallop fisherman and on a dredge in the early years. Charles A. (Charlie) Bertalotus, Peter Dunn, Frank Martin, George Martin, Al Pearce, Earl Sprague and Tom Wilson were among the many teammates and friends who were older than Gray and went off to war, but not before setting a good example for the youngster growing up during World War II.[2]

Charlie had been the quarterback before Gray took over that position in 1944. Then, by going fishing instead of taking his final English examination, Gray returned for the school year that ended in 1946. He earned all-state accolades in football, baseball and basketball both his junior and senior years, while captaining all three teams. Younger players especially looked up to Gray, not only because of the respect with which he treated them, but also because of the encouragement he gave. Although only a year separated Al Gray and Don McIntyre in age, the latter was a freshman when Gray was a junior. McIntyre grew into one of Point Pleasant Beach's greatest athletes. A skilled basketball player, Don was a deadly set shooter who later played on the All-Army team after enlisting. He tells the story that Al Gray had broken his right forearm during basketball season, but continued to practice alone with his arm in a cast. Gray, the team captain, amazed his teammates by returning to play in the state championship game, his arm still in a cast. Despite that, Gray made several baskets shooting one-handed set shots, and Point Pleasant Beach almost won the game. McIntyre, who loves basketball as a lifelong player and fan, noted that Al Gray was the first person he had ever seen shoot in such a way.[3]

Years later, teammates like Gene Ritchings would remark that "Al Gray was their leader off and on the field." In 1984, his high school coach, Mr. Joe Pagano wrote a letter to Gray saying, "To me, you will always be 'Peanuts,' who lacked the size, but who had fierce determination to succeed, and that you did... Whatever success I had in football, you were the most important experiment, and why I chose you a T Q-back was what I saw in you, a competitor, shy but able to motivate your friends. You were a leader then, and now."

Gray finally went off to college in 1946 with a partial athletic scholarship; he was intent on majoring in mathematics while playing baseball and football. In high school, Al Gray had been a T-formation quarterback on one of the first high school teams that converted to the modern offense. Most schools ran the old single-wing formation, as did Lafayette the first year Gray was there; as a result, Gray concentrated on playing defensive back and running back, though as one of the youngest

Figure 1.1
The 1945 Point Pleasant Beach Gulls starting backfield, at one of their reunions several years after General Gray's retirement: Bob Moore, Al Gray, Joe Miller and Lloyd "Bucky" Johnson. Along with teammates like Jim Cherry, Dick Wilson, Don Deter, Gene Ritchings, Bob Farr, Don McIntyre, George Martin and Charlie Apter, the Gulls remained a close-knit group. Al Gray takes great pride in his friends, all good family men who did well.[4]

players on the team, he did not have much playing time his freshman year. He did see enough action to get injured, and dealt with water-on-the knee the rest of that year.

Lafayette, in the late 1940s, participated in big-time athletics; the Leopards' schedule included then national powerhouses Army, Navy and Penn. Gray, at 5'8 ½" and 168 pounds was an average sized running back. He was also a good outfielder who batted and threw left-handed, and he could pull an inside fastball. While he had enjoyed sports since being a youngster playing on the diamonds and fields around Point Pleasant Beach, football and baseball at Lafayette gave Gray something he had not planned on receiving – exposure to many veterans returned home from World War II.

Figure 1.2
Al Gray and Walt Germusa, halfbacks at Lafayette. Germusa was an Army veteran of World War II and a rugged player from football-rich Pennsylvania.[5]

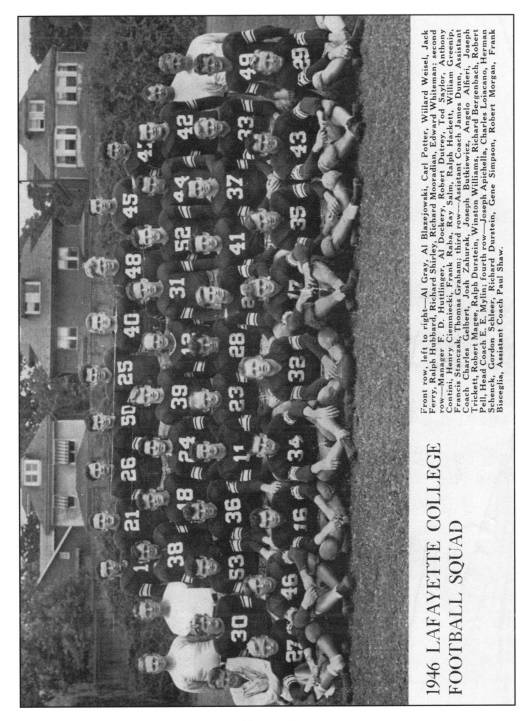

1946 LAFAYETTE COLLEGE FOOTBALL SQUAD

Front row, left to right—Al Gray, Al Blazejowski, Carl Potter, Willard Weisel, Jack Ferry, Ralph Hubbard, Richard Shirley, Richard Mooradian, Edward Whiteman; second row—Manager F. D. Huttlinger, Al Dockery, Robert Dutrey, Tod Saylor, Anthony Contini, Henry Ciemniecki, Frank Raba, Ray Salm, Ralph Hackett, William Greenip, Francis Stanczak, Thomas Graham; third row—Assistant Coach James Dunn, Assistant Coach Charles Gelbert, Josh Zahurak, Joseph Butkiewicz, Angelo Alfieri, Joseph Trickett, Robert Magee, Ralph Durstein, Winston Williams, Richard Bergenbach, Robert Pell, Head Coach E. E. Mylin; fourth row—Joseph Apichella, Charles Loiacano, Herman Schenck, Gordon Schleer, Richard Durstein, Gene Simpson, Robert Morgan, Frank Bisceglia, Assistant Coach Paul Shaw.

Figure 1.3
The 1946 Lafayette Leopards. Al Gray is seated on the left of the first row.
Reprinted with permission, The Melange.[6]

Figure 1.4
Three of Lafayette's outfielders in 1947; John Tierney, Al Gray, and Wally Berger.[7]

Typical of the men on the 1946 Leopards' football team were Leo Swayze, Bill Greenip, Richard Perrotty, Anthony Contini, and the luckiest of the all, Gordon Schleer. A total of 34 military veterans appeared on the team roster that showed only 42 players. Only nine players were 18 or 19 years old – and one of the 19-year-olds had two years in the Navy; the others ranged up to 25. Gray was a boy playing among men. Leo Swayze was a B-29 pilot who flew 35 missions over Japan and earned a Distinguished Flying Cross. Bill Greenip was a Marine for nearly three years and served on Iwo Jima and Okinawa. Dick Perrotty had been the regular right tackle on Lafayette's 1942 team, but went off to the Navy and served 14 months in the Pacific, including the Okinawa campaign. Tony Contini was also a letterman returned from the 1942 team, but he then spent 29 months in the Marines and saw action on Peleliu and Okinawa. Gordon Schleer, however, had the best war stories. A patrol boat Sailor, Schleer survived twice being sunk – once by the Japanese and once by friendly fire. Through their example the veterans had a huge effect on the young back at the Jersey shore.

Though he enjoyed his varsity football experience, Al Gray really loved baseball. One of Gray's best friends at Lafayette was another superb athlete from New Jersey, John Tierney. Tierney's football activities ended his freshman year, but he continued to play baseball and basketball for the Leopards. Gray's friends tended to be fellow athletes and he remained close to men like Marty Zipple, a fellow baseball player and Lafayette College Hall of Fame basketball star; George Davidson, another basketball Hall of Famer and a Marine; John Bird, Jack McVeigh and Billy Killenger, all fellow baseball teammates; and basketball star Norman "Whitey" Carlson.

The spring of 1948 saw the pinnacle of Al Gray's athletic career at Lafayette – and it also marked a highlight in the college's long athletic history. Gray had had a great season as a power hitting outfielder who managed to get on base consistently, leading the team in getting hit by a pitch while also batting over .300. The Leopards were district champions but had a difficult path to the college world series.[8] After beating the University of North Carolina, then Illinois and Navy, Gray and his teammates advanced to play powerful Yale. The talented Eli team included a tall first baseman home from the war, George H.W. Bush.[9] Late in the game, with the potential winning runs on second and third, Gray smashed a hard hit ball to left-center field; unhappily for the Leopards, the Eli outfielder made a shoestring catch and then doubled the Lafayette runner off second. That ended the Leopards' run, and also closed Gray's participation in Leopard sports as he could no longer afford to be a full-time student. He left college to return to Point Pleasant Beach and work in construction and variety of other jobs.

His education and his experiences at Lafayette, along with what he learned from his peers, were instrumental in shaping his views for later life. To this day, he is grateful for having become a man at Lafayette, and he treasures the Honorary Doctorate Degree that the college awarded him in 1988.

During the summers when he was home from college, Gray would join Bertalotus, Sprague and others – all home safely from the war – playing baseball for the local semi-pro team. After he left college, Gray also continued to play for the semi-pro Point Pleasant Pelicans, the Jersey Shore Football League Champions in 1949. The baseball team was also very good, and played many games against the old Negro League teams, like the New York Black Yankees, the House of David and others. It was really good baseball and Al Gray loved the game. Other teammates included Al "J.P." Morgan. Morgan was an African-American whose father was a great friend of Al Gray, Sr.; the younger Morgan was a great athlete from arch-rival Manasqun

PELICAN POUNDER

Figure 1.5

This picture of Al Gray playing for the semi-pro "Pelicans" was put in the local paper, The Leader, and in their later years it provided lots of ammunition for his buddies to ride Gray about his "stance." In the early 1950s the New York Yankees had a new star, Mickey Mantle, whose picture in a similar stance became widely publicized. Gray's friends accused him being Mickey Mantle before anyone knew Mickey Mantle. Image and caption reprinted with permission, Ocean Star, Point Pleasant Beach, NJ.[10]

There's plenty of power in that bat perched on **Al Gray's** shoulder. For proof positive trek down to Clayton Field one of these Tuesday or Thursday nights and watch the ex-Garnet Gull ace as he patrols the outfield for the **Point Pleasant Pelicans.**   Photo by Tupper

High School who attended Morgan State University. Another high school rival was Tom Olsen, who captained the Manasqun football team in 1946. Olsen and Gray remained good friends through the years and still correspond. Gray has fond memories of the men he grew up with in New Jersey and is proud they turned out to be fine, family-oriented, hard working and successful adults. Throughout his life they have remained close and many attended his promotion to Lieutenant General in 1984 and subsequently visited him in the Commandant's House during his last tour on active duty.

When the Korean War broke out, Gray decided to join the Marines. He had been working construction, cleaning Bell Telephone trucks at night and taking courses at what was then Monmouth Junior College. In fact, Gray became the college's first informal baseball coach; he was a playing-coach for a good collection of athletes then attending night courses.[11] Undoubtedly the stories he heard from his high school and college teammates made his choice of branch of service easy, though he also respected his father's and uncles' tales of the World War I Navy.

In a lifetime that was marked by a long series of relationships with famous Marines, fortuitous for Gray was the fact that his recruiting officer was Major Louis H. Wilson, Jr. As a Captain, Wilson had earned a Medal of Honor while leading a rifle company on Guam in World War II. Over the years, he watched Gray's professional accomplishments unfold to successive heights. When Wilson was the 26th Commandant of the Marine Corps, he promoted Al Gray to Brigadier General. Later, in retirement, General Wilson proudly observed as his former Marine recruit, Alfred Mason Gray, Jr. became the 29th Commandant of the Marine Corps.[12] In October 1950, Al Gray became Al Gray, Marine.

Most of Al Gray's time as an enlisted man was spent serving with a cream of the crop reconnaissance element, the Amphibious Reconnaissance Platoon – the forerunner of the Force Reconnaissance Company. Tough, charismatic, highly motivated professionals whose leadership techniques and traits were among the best the Marine Corps had to offer surrounded him. A quick study, and dedicated to his craft, Gray very quickly rose to the rank of Sergeant. Gray learned and applied those leadership lessons very early on after joining recon. In addition to his communications responsibilities, after his promotion to sergeant Gray frequently served as the right guide for the platoon despite being the junior sergeant. The right guide was responsible for keeping the unit supplied and its gear maintained, and the senior Staff NCOs (staff non-commissioned officers) quickly realized that Gray did that better than anyone. Of course, Gray was also, at various times, a squad leader and when the unit started training in rubber boats, Gray quickly earned the

Figure 1.6
Cpl Al Gray, recon Marine and field radio operator.[13]

Figure 1.7
This picture shows three of the stalwarts of the 1ˢᵗ Marine Division's Reconnaissance
Company following the landing at Inchon in September 1950. The Company Commander,
Capt Kenny Houghton, is shown in the foreground, with Gy Sgt Ernie DeFazio (with
helmet) to his left, and 1ˢᵗ Sgt John Slagle in the background. In early 1951, the Company
was rotated back to the U.S., where Slagle, DeFazio and another recon sergeant, Dave
Kendricks, formed the nucleus of the Amphibious Recon Platoon, which PFC Al Gray soon
joined. Photo courtesy of: Harry Ransom Center, The University of Texas at Austin. [14]

portside bow position, where his powerful left-handed stroke was a valuable asset. Gray became the unit's jack-of-all-trades, go-to guy.

Gray's days in reconnaissance were particularly important in molding the young Marine. One of his mentors, Gunnery Sergeant Ernest DeFazio, became a well-known officer in his own right, serving as the Executive Officer to Lieutenant Colonel (and future 28ᵗʰ Commandant of the Marine Corps) P.X. Kelley in the 2ⁿᵈ Battalion, 4ᵗʰ Marines (2/4) in Vietnam. DeFazio himself retired as a lieutenant colonel.[15] The unit's 1ˢᵗ Sergeant, John Slagle, was commissioned and later retired as a captain. One of the staff sergeants, Neal B. King, later served as the Sergeant Major of Marine Barracks, Washington, D.C., and the right guide of the platoon, Sergeant David Kendricks, also became a Sergeant Major prior to his retirement.

Figure 1.8
S Sgt Dave Kendricks, 1ˢᵗ Lt Ernie DeFazio, Sgt Al Gray.
Kendricks retired as a Sergeant Major and DeFazio as a Lieutenant Colonel.[16]

All four men, and many others, profoundly influenced Gray. Their toughness, their professionalism and especially their treatment of the troops provided Gray with exceptional leadership models that he was quick to emulate; they were the epitome of Marine Staff NCOs. Gray also closely watched, and learned, how the unit's Captain, future Colonel Francis "Bull" Kraince, properly used and relied upon staff Staff NCOs and NCOs (non-commissioned officers). Plus, Gray was exposed to the leadership skills of future Major General Kenneth Houghton; Houghton had been DeFazio and Slagle's company commander in Korea. The company served during and after the Inchon landings. Both Houghton and DeFazio were wounded during operations that preceded the Chosin Reservoir campaign. Captain Houghton often returned to meet with his former comrades-in-arms. Then Captain James Flood also was around the troops on many occasions, providing another fine example of strong officer leadership. Then, after Gray made sergeant, Slagle and DeFazio would take "Sam" to the Staff NCO club, and show him that aspect of their lives.

When Al Gray first reported to the unit, he was with another graduate of the Field Radio Operator's Course. That Marine, when asked Private First Class Gray's name at check-in (Gray was elsewhere for the moment), responded that it was "Sam Gray." Obviously, the young Marine, who shortly left the platoon, had no knack for remembering names; and so it was that as long as Al Gray knew any of his former recon friends, they called him "Sam."[17]

"Sam" Gray could not have asked for a better experience during his first two years in the Marine Corps.

Figure 1.9
Cpl Al Gray goes for a run on the beach.[18]

The Amphibious Reconnaissance Platoon was a rough and cocky unit, though the Marine Corps was not sure exactly what to do with them. Only they wore the camouflaged (brown side, green side) utilities left from World War II. Both their uniforms and their training attracted much high-level attention, and while they were never committed as a unit to the war in Korea, they had stories to tell, nonetheless.

It was not unusual for the recon platoon to be used as aggressors during field exercises. During one such event at Camp Pendleton, the Assistant Division Commander, Brigadier General Lewis B. (Chesty) Puller, was serving as a Brigade Commander. When the recon Marines attacked and captured Puller's Command Post, well, suffice it to say that the General was not happy. Puller had been watching from overhead while flying around in a small, two-man helicopter – one of the early models that the Marine Corps was evaluating. The General's aircraft landed and he ordered an Officers Call. The recon troops took that as their chance to withdraw to a nearby tree line to watch what unfolded. Chesty started by lighting into his junior officers for their inattention to detail; by the time he reached the colonels, Puller was really fired up. Young Sergeant Al Gray and his cohort had a front row seat to the episode and got to see how a Marine legend handled such a situation.

In late spring of 1951, the Amphibious Reconnaissance Platoon and the USS *Perch* (ASSP 313) received classified orders to proceed to Korea. Not much was known about the future operations that the platoon would conduct, though they were well quali-fied to both perform reconnaissance and conduct raids. On the way to the war zone, *Perch* conducted a practice raid on the historic World War II island of Midway before continuing on to another World War II battleground, Guam. Conditions for everyone were tight aboard the converted submarine. Although the torpedo rooms had been converted to troop living spaces, "hot racking" was still the order of the day. Corporal Gray, being a NCO, was assigned a berth amidships, where he shared a bunk with two Sailors. Hot racking got its name from the fact that when one person was asleep, the others were standing watch. Then when the sleeper arose, one of the people who shared the rack had to climb in, and of course found "hot" sheets – thus, the term "hot racking." Simply put, there were far fewer bunks aboard *Perch* than there were people, so each bunk had to be fully utilized. Officers, especially the boat's Commanding and Executive Officers, seldom, if ever, encountered a "hot racking" situation, but for Gray and his enlisted brethren it was part of the deal in being in recon.

Other aspects of recon provided more hair-raising issues. Indeed, at least once Gray had serious doubts about living to see the next morning. As an amphibious

Figure 1.10
The Amphibious Recon Platoon spent over six months aboard the USS Perch going and coming from Korea in 1950. Space was at a premium. Here Gy Sgt DeFazio goes over an operational map with several of the recon Marines. Cpl Gray is standing, the second from the right.[19]

recon unit, landings from submarines were an important aspect of the training regimen. At the stop in Guam, the plan was for Gunny DeFazio and Corporal Gray to lead a beach reconnaissance of the area near Aggana Point. Unfortunately, the submarine crew mistook a radar scan of a reef for the beach and landed the pair several miles from the planned debarkation position. Adding to their problems, the water was unusually warm, which further debilitated the swimmers as they struggled toward the beach. Happily, the men were in excellent condition and both were very strong swimmers. DeFazio, however, experienced severe cramps on the way in and Gray patiently waited nearby until the rugged Gunny worked through his condition. Although exhausted after eight hours in the water, they were able to make landfall near the point, but were horrified to find that they had come ashore exactly where both the American forces and the locals dumped their trash. Needless to say, had DeFazio and Gray known they were swimming through seas where sharks were looking to feed on garbage, their experience would have been even worse. As it was, the incident served to bind the men even more closely while providing each with a great story, not that either was inclined to discuss it – or any other professional achievement.

While on Guam, the recon platoon again served as an aggressor force for the Navy personnel charged with protecting various facilities. During one such exercise the importance of troop safety was driven home on the young Marine in a very personalized way. After the recon team had captured several of the Sailors, and while in the midst of transferring them to a different location, one of the captives unexpectedly fired his weapon. Even though blanks were used for the exercise, the accidental discharge hit Gray in the torso, causing a painful scar that provided a lifelong reminder about safety. Following their training exercises on Guam, the USS *Perch* and her platoon of Marines continued on to the Far East. But there never was the opportunity to employ the recon element and so after about a month the *Perch* and her cargo returned to the United States.

On the way back to the United States, the *Perch* stopped for repairs and upkeep in Hawaii and that permitted the Marines to utilize the training facilities on the island to get in more training in submarine safety, including their introduction to the Momsen Lung. Also during their short stay the platoon was able to use new scuba gear in a pool, a welcomed diversion from the cold waters of the Pacific.

After completing repairs, *Perch* continued on to the mainland. The platoon was off-loaded at Long Beach onto trucks for the journey down to San Diego and home. But the date is forever burned into Al Gray's memory. On October 3, 1951, shortly before 1 P.M. local time, Gray's truck had made a stop for gas. The troops piled out of the back of the vehicle and were treated to a radio playing inside the gas station. It was tuned to the National League championship game between Gray's beloved New York Giants and the hated Brooklyn Dodgers. As the Marines gathered to hear the goings on, after all Willie Mays was in the on deck circle, Bobby Thomson hit *the shot heard round the world*.[20] For lifelong Giants fans like Al Gray, Sr. and Jr., Thomson's home run was a unforgettable occasion. For the recon platoon, it was back to training at Camp Pendleton and fulfilling other duties as assigned.

Figure 1.11
The USS Perch *and embarked recon platoon leaving Pearl Harbor, November 21, 1951.*
Al Gray is third from left of the third rank (hands on hips).[21]

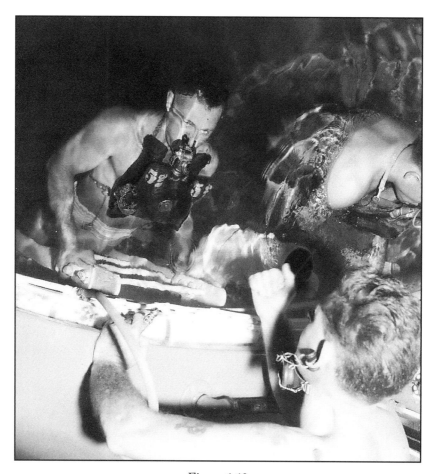

Figure 1.12
Cpl Gray, in the water on the right, undergoing submarine
escape training using a Momsen Lung. [22]

The platoon was often used as guinea pigs for testing new gear, including one time a device that was supposed to keep the rubber boats from broaching in the surf near the beach and then capsizing. Needless to say, on that occasion "Sam" Gray and his cohort, not yet equipped with exposure suits, got to experience how really cold the Pacific can be in late fall. It was almost enough to make Al Gray give up chewing tobacco, since the Marines were dumped into the angry surf and had trouble breathing. While gurgling and gasping for air, Gray vowed that orange juice would become his only vice; it was a resolution soon forgotten.

Around that time, then Brigadier General Lewis B. (Chesty) Puller had been reassigned to the Landing Force Training Command at Coronado. There, he often watched as the recon Marines honed their rubber boat skills. Chesty being Chesty, it was only a matter of time before General Puller decided that he ought to find out first hand what the young Marines in cammie uniforms were doing. He decided to accompany the platoon onto their dedicated training platform, the submarine USS *Perch*, and then make a nighttime landing. As luck would have it, Corporal Al Gray's boat was assigned the task of getting the General safely, and as important – dryly, to shore.

Corporal Gray was a strong boatman and, being left-handed, was always assigned to the portside front position on the boat. General Puller sat in the middle of the boat and watched keenly as the six rubber crafts approached the beach in a lazy "W" formation. The surf was high and plunging, and the first couple boat crews had the misfortune to flip during their final approach to the beach. Puller growled to Corporal Gray something to the effect that "if I get wet, you'll be a private for the rest of your time in the Marines!" Sure enough, and happily for the young Corporal from the New Jersey shore, they caught a wave just right and rode well up onto the beach. General Puller stepped ashore, thanked the recon team on its successful landing, and quickly departed; obviously the General had other, more important duties that evening. Al Gray would meet General Chesty Puller face-to-face again a little later during his service, and under better circumstances for the younger man.

The recon unit returned to Camp Pendleton and participated in a series of interesting affairs that provided training lessons galore. In addition to its many activities on and around Coronado Island, the recon platoon operated an escape and evasion school for pilots at March Field, northeast of Camp Pendleton, California. But Al Gray did not join the Marine Corps to train in California, he joined because there was a war going on and he wanted to serve. Thus, he volunteered for assignment to Korea.

During his time in the platoon, Gray had plenty of opportunities to impress the Staff NCOs and officers. Before his nomination for promotion to corporal and then sergeant, he faced a grueling informal examination by the unit's senior leadership – First Sergeant Slagle, Gunnery Sergeant DeFazio, and Staff Sergeant King. They were an imposing group, and tough. In later years General Al Gray would joke to crowds of enlisted men that he could not pass the examination to staff sergeant, and as a result the Marine Corps made him a 2nd Lieutenant. Given the descriptions of Slagle and what is known about DeFazio and King, he might not have been jesting.

After getting his proper orders to report to the Officer Selection Screening Course at the Crossroads of the Marine Corps, the base at Quantico, Virginia, Gray returned to the platoon area. He was, after all, uncertain about many things, including whether he was capable of becoming an officer. His platoon commander, Captain Bull Kraince, took the time to explain that good Marine officers had to be able to spend time in the mud with the troops during the day and then at night put on dress whites and get along with the ladies – inferring that officers needed to be gentlemen. Kraince thought that Gray demonstrated those traits, and that he already knew a lot about taking care of his troops, that Gray did not do a lot of drinking or getting out of hand – so he would do just fine as an officer. And it did not matter to Kraince that Al Gray had not yet decided to stay in the Marine Corps; he encouraged the younger man to go to Quantico.

Kraince's letter recommending Sergeant Gray for a commission is interesting. Aside from the normal things that one might expect to find in a recommendation for commissioning an enlisted Marine, Kraince also noted, "He [Gray] possesses in an outstanding way the ability to never deviate from his mission no matter how difficult the attainment of final success is."[23] Throughout Gray's professional life, his focus on the successful completion of his mission never wavered. Kraince's reassurance was sufficient for Gray to make the attempt, and he agreed to go to Quantico.

Al Gray set about traveling to the East Coast in February 1952. He had been to March Field (now Air Force Base), California, several times while in the recon unit, and he figured that he might be able to find an air force transport going east. He successfully boarded one that dropped him off him near Valdosta, Georgia.

Gray's father and uncle were conductors on the Pennsylvania Railroad, and Gray knew that if he could find a train terminal, he could get home. Learning where the railroad station was from a couple of local fisherman, Gray easily hiked the five miles or so needed to reach the station, though he arrived in the middle of the night long before the ticket counter was opened. Finding a comfortable place to pass a couple hours was no hardship for the young recon Marine, and soon he had a ticket to Savannah and on to the District of Columbia. That suited Gray just fine, because his father and his Uncle Charlie alternated working the express from New York City to Washington, and he was sure either one or the other would be there to accompany him home. Sure enough, Al, Sr., arrived in the capital a few hours after Gray had, and together, seeing each other for the first time in almost two years, they rode home. After a relaxing weekend in New Jersey, Gray drove his pickup truck down to Quantico and reported to the Officer Selection Screening Course.

Sergeant Gray thought the Officer Selection Screening Course was rather routine; after all, he was in terrific physical condition and had learned the elements of his profession from some of the Marine Corps' finest. But of the 79 Staff NCOs and NCOs who attended the screening course with Sergeant Gray, only 39 were commissioned. The course evidently was a little more demanding than the Sergeant's standards might have suggested. Upon graduation in April, newly commissioned

2nd Lieutenant Gray found he had some time on his hands. His class would not start The Basic School until the Naval Academy and Naval Reserve Officer Training Corps midshipmen graduated in June. True to the form he exhibited throughout his time in the Marine Corps, Gray did not let grass grow under his feet.

In the early 1950s athletics were a very big part of the peacetime military services and, even with the war in Korea, the major bases fielded competitive athletic teams. The Quantico Marines played a football schedule against major college programs, and often players of some note led the Marines. Gray, assigned to The Basic School but having not yet started training, helped coach the The Basic School baseball team and played centerfield. While coaching, he met another Marine officer, just back from Korea, who played shortstop and who had been a great Little All-American quarterback at the College of the Pacific; his exploits were well known to Gray, who played in college at the same time. The two spent long hours talking together about the war in Korea and about football. As they threw the ball around together, the more senior Lieutenant told Gray that he was upset when his orders to Hawaii were changed to Quantico in order that he could play football. Although he spoke of staying in the Marines, he told the service that if he were going to play ball, it would be professionally a little further up the street. True to his word, Eddie LeBaron resigned his commission and went on to become a legendary quarterback for the Redskins, playing for Washington well into the 1960s.

While awaiting The Basic School to start, in the summer of 1952, Lieutenant Gray also attended the last Horse & Mule School ever held for officers. Those animals, of course, had been a key component in moving supplies for Marines throughout the period of the Banana Wars. Not until Korea did the helicopter (a Marine Corps innovation) begin to replace pack animals to move supplies. Horses and mules toiled – often heroically – throughought the war. However, one horse, "Sergeant Reckless," was the most famous of those animals. Lieutenant Gray and his cohort had the opportunity to observe Sergeant Reckless as she carried supplies and ammunition to the combat outposts. The little Mongolian mare was a real morale booster for the Marines.[24]

Neither coaching baseball nor attending Horse & Mule School was an important achievement for junior officers (though under-estimating the appeal that sports had for some Marine generals of that era could easily be done). It was Gray's completion of an Administrative Course for Officers, taken by correspondence, which would prove to be a significant educational milestone in his professional development. It would pay big dividends in the very near future, as Gray commanded several units while still a lieutenant.

Gray's personality changed not at all after he became an officer. Don McIntyre had joined the Army during the Korean War and was assigned to Ft. Belvoir, Virginia. After being commissioned at Quantico, Gray would often travel to New Jersey and the two athletes would often return together to Northern Virginia via train after weekends at home. McIntyre initially wondered if the fact that Gray was now a Marine officer would change their relationship; he soon concluded it would not. In fact, McIntyre reported that Gray often sought out others from Point Pleasant Beach who had enlisted in various services in order to encourage them and determine if they needed any type of assistance. It reflected what would become a hallmark of Gray's professionalism: he never changed no matter how high he rose in the military.

Al Gray, Marine, had already been introduced to one future Commandant (Wilson) when he enlisted; at Quantico he met two more legends of the Corps, General Lemuel C. Shepherd and then Colonel David M. Shoup. Gray did well at The Basic School and he came to the attention of the school's Commanding Officer, Colonel Shoup. Shoup had earned a Medal of Honor while leading a regiment on bloody Tarawa in World War II. But Colonel Shoup was much more than a war hero; he was sharp and kept track of impressive young officers. Upon graduation, Shoup recommended Gray for a Regular Commission; it was approved and conferred by General Shepherd, the 20th Commandant of the Marine Corps, who also met with the young Lieutenant for a short personal visit. Following the The Basic School graduation ceremony, both Shepherd and Shoup sought out Gray's parents to tell them how well their only son was doing as a young Marine. Al Gray, Sr., a World War I troop transport Sailor, was impressed that such high-ranking officers would take time to meet with him and Mrs. Gray, and the example the senior Marines provided was never lost on the young Lieutenant.

While a Regular Commission was a coveted prize for young officers, Gray's subsequent assignment to artillery was not his first choice. Infantry would have been his selection all other things being equal, but his appeals to change his assignment were unsuccessful. His letter, which was the only one from his class forwarded recommending approval, was denied; the Marine Corps needed artillery officers, particularly forward observers. As Gray was to learn time and time again, the needs of the service always trumped personal preference. The Lieutenant also found out early on that taking what you get and making what you want was a good way to manage a life.

Fortunately for 2nd Lieutenant Gray, the war in Korea had largely stabilized, and while it was still the primary factor in personnel assignments, the situation was not so critical that he had to report directly there. Instead, he first was ordered to attend the Army's Artillery Officer's Basic Course at Ft. Sill, Oklahoma. While in school, Gray forfeited his Christmas leave period in order to stay and learn advanced topics. In February 1953, Gray left Ft. Sill and proceeded to Camp Pendleton to command a draft that was being sent to Korea. Almost a year after first standing in line to ship out as a sergeant, he now led 70 or so men as a 2nd Lieutenant. He was more than ready to go. The artillery course was widely recognized as one of the very best professional schools for officers, and it taught Lieutenant Gray important lessons that he put to use immediately upon his arrival in Korea.

KOREA JUNE 1950–APRIL 1953

The Korean War began in June 1950, when North Korea launched an all-out blitzkrieg against the Republic of Korea. The Allies, led by the Americans but including British, Turkish, Australian and many others, came to the defense of South Korea, otherwise known as the Republic of Korea. Most of the famous battles of the war occurred in the first seven months. The enemy gained control of almost the entire Korean Peninsula before battering themselves against the last Allied position – the Pusan Perimeter, located in the far southeast of the country. There, U. S. Army forces, the remaining Republic of Korea units and a hastily organized Provisional U.S. Marine Brigade (nicknamed the "Fire Brigade") made a desperate stand. The Marine Brigade arrived just in time to play a critical, essential role in stopping the North Korean onslaught.

In September 1950, General of the Army Douglas MacArthur, in perhaps his finest moment as a Soldier, ordered the Marines to conduct an amphibious operation against the western flank of the enemy at Inchon, the seaport that serves as Seoul's port of entry.

MacArthur had divided his forces between the 8th Army under Lieutenant General Walton (Johnny) Walker, which pushed north from Pusan, and the 10th Army Corps under Major General Edward (Ned) Almond. The 1st Marine Division was part of Almond's 10th Army Corps, and it was that famous Marine unit that conducted the amphibious assault at Inchon. The North Koreans were caught by complete surprise and though they fought with determination and commitment, soon both 8th Army and 10th Army Corps were pushing north, well into North Korea.

By late fall (October-early November 1950) the Americans and Republic of Korea forces had pushed the North Koreans back almost to the Yalu River, the dividing line between North Korea and China. By then, the North Koreans were largely defeated as a fighting force. MacArthur pushed Generals Walker and Almond into a frantic rush toward the Yalu. China was not part the early calculus associated with the war; in any event, MacArthur was quite confident that Chinese communists would not enter the war.

Despite what the General of the Army thought, in the late fall and early winter of 1950-1951, massive Chinese forces quietly infiltrated into positions in the northern mountains on the Korean side of the Yalu River. Indeed, in late November 1950, even when many Americans, particularly the Marines, were reporting Chinese troops to their front, MacArthur and especially Almond were dismissive of the news. Only because Major General Oliver Prince Smith, the Commanding General of the 1st Marine Division, whose studious, quiet demeanor masked his extensive warrior experience, purposefully slowed the advance of his division is the "Chosin Resevoir" revered in Marine Corps lore. By assuming mostly defensive positions, in direct contradiction of his Corps Commander's (Almond) orders, the Marines were better prepared to meet the Red Chinese counter-offensive. MacArthur visited the 8th Army front on November 24th, urging General Johnny Walker and his forces forward. Two days later, 8th Army and 10th Army Corps were in a precipitous retreat southward. The Red Chinese had announced their presence in a forceful, overpowering way.

The 1st Marine Division did not retreat, according to Colonel Lewis B. (Chesty) Puller the irrepressible commander of the 1st Marine Regiment. No, the Marines attacked in a different direction, back towards their lifeline to the sea at the port of Hungnam. The resulting epic, the Battle of the Chosin Reservoir, is among the most famous, the most written about battles in Marine Corps history. It was surely the most noteworthy battle during the Korean War and was the topic of countless news articles in the United States. Most people today do not realize that Chosin occurred within the first year of the war that would last over three years.

The year 1951 was spent trying to stabilize the war against the overwhelming hordes of Chinese. The Americans did that with a new Commanding General, Matthew B. Ridgeway. General MacArthur had been fired by President Harry S. Truman; despite MacArthur's brilliant strategic move at Inchon, his actions prior to and after the amphibious landing were questionable at best. Throughout 1951 and into 1952, there took place a series of bloody attacks and counter-attacks from both combatant forces, during which time ground was gained and lost though neither side able to achieve ascendancy.

The 1st Marine Division had been moved from the western part of the battle line to a position north and slightly east of Seoul. It was along that axis that the Allied high command thought the Chinese most likely to try to attack the South Korean capital. By 1952, the portion of the Main Line of Resistance occupied by the Marines

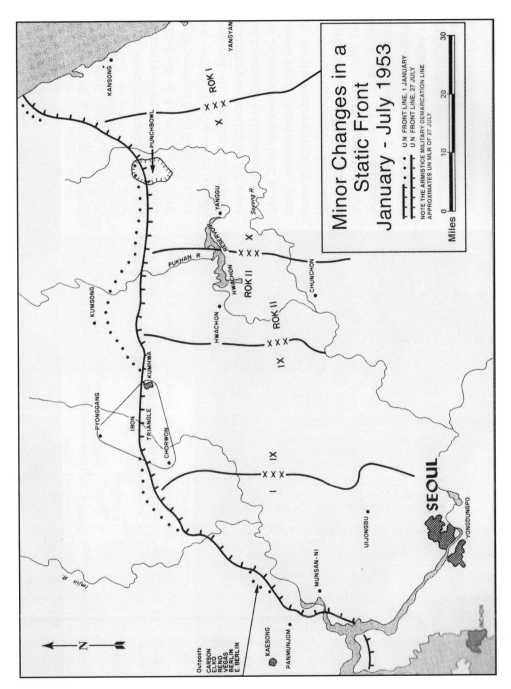

Map 1.1

During 1952 the Main Line of Resistance stabilized. The 1st Marine Division, part of First Corps, was placed on the far eastern portion of the line, where the 8th Army thought the most likely Chinese attacks toward Seoul would occur. On the Marines left, the Korean Marine Brigade covered the waterways west of Munsan-ni, while the Turkish Brigade was to the Marines right. Note the location of Pammunjom, the site of the truce talks that continued from 1951 until the Armistice on July 27, 1953. Map reproduced from U.S. Marines in the Korean War, Charles R. Smith, editor. History Division; Washington, D.C. 2007.

Figure 1.13
Al Gray in perhaps his most typical pose. This picture is a
favorite of the General's from his early days in Korea.[25]

included another significant and confusing obstacle. There were on-again, off-again peace talks were being held in the North Korean/Chinese sector at Pammunjom, and a "peace corridor" was established to expedite the flow of participants. Marine artillery could not fire into the peace corridor, though the outposts and positions along the Main Line of Resistance were often subjected to heavy enemy fire and attacks. It was just another complication the Division Commanding General, now Edwin A. Pollock, had to deal with. Thus, while there were no division-sized engagements that caught the attention of the nation, there were numerous, extremely bloody small unit engagements across the entire Main Line of Resistance. Fighting in an around the combat outposts that were spread across the front of the Main Line of Resistance was often even more intense. It became bunker warfare at its worst. The weather, especially the extremely cold Korean winters, combined with the tenacious fighting qualities of the enemy, made Korea a miserable, too often deadly place to fight.

By the time Lieutenant Gray arrived, though the fighting remained intense, the Main Line of Resistance was largely fixed. Lethal small unit actions continued to dominate the activity on both sides.

KOREA, 1953

In April 1953, Al Gray made it to the combat zone. While his arrival was largely undistinguished from that of any other young officer, something he saw made an indelible impression on him. There had been a series of tent fires caused by careless-ness, and a very large poster overhanging the entrance into the 1st Marine Division's processing center read, "Through these tents pass the finest men ever seen, but you'll look like hell as a barbequed Marine. Be safe." Gray never forgot the banner or its admonition.

Assigned to the Fox (now Foxtrot) Battery, 2nd Battalion, 11th Marines (2/11), Gray had to first find his way to his new unit located along the Main Line of Resistance.[26] Since there was no regular transportation system for new arrivals, getting to his unit took Gray the better part of an entire day, and he turned up about 1800 (6 PM) local time. The Battery Commanding Officer was not present that night, as he had become ill. So 2nd Lieutenant Gray reported to the Executive Officer, who never got out of his bunk to welcome the new arrival. Gray soon learned that the Executive Officer would be leaving within hours for a much-sought-after period of rest and recuperation. Al Gray chose to ignore the rather frosty welcome that circumstances had conspired to give him and, as was his norm, decided to walk around and see what was happening. As soon as he stored his gear in the officers' billet, the Lieutenant went to visit the motor pool, where he learned the status of

Figure 1.14
Lt George Shelly, T/Sgt Ewell, and Lt Al Gray. The two officers had
been commissioned together and trained together at Ft. Sill, Oklahoma,
where all Army and Marine artillery training occurs. [27]

the Battery's vehicles. He then visited each of the Battery's gun pits and introduced himself to the six different crews. From there, he made his way to the Fire
Direction Center (FDC) where he found the very capable Staff Sergeant Woods
had things well under control. After watching as the Battery fired a few rounds, he
left, checked with the perimeter security, and grabbed a bite at the mess hall before
returning to his "quarters" sometime after midnight.

No sooner had he gotten to sleep when a call from Staff Sergeant Woods awak-
ened him. The Staff Sergeant reported that Gray was the only officer present, and
that the Battery had been ordered to move immediately to a new position about 20
miles distant. The Chinese had broken through the Main Line of Resistance well
to the east of the Marine positions, and the Battery was needed to provide supporting fires for a counter-attack. Thus, Gray, on his first night on the lines and for the
first time in combat commanding Marines, whom he had just met, quickly issued
a Close Station March Order directing the unit to move to the Central Sector.
The young Lieutenant relied on both Staff Sergeant Woods and another Marine
from the FDC, Corporal Calloway, to provide important leadership roles during
the movement and subsequent establishment of new firing positions. As those who
have known Gray might have predicted, the movement to the new position, the

deployment of the guns and firing in support, and the return to the original site on the Main Line of Resistance all went without any problem or issues.

Lieutenant Gray was subsequently assigned as a forward observer in support of Baker (now Bravo) Company, 1st Battalion, 7th Marines. Forward observer, after all, was the normal assignment for new artillery lieutenants. But even the expected was not quite usual in Gray's case.

By spring 1953, late in the war, the 1st Marine Division held a line nearly 26 miles long. Each infantry company was responsible for nearly 1,000 yards of frontage. Those numbers far exceeded what Marine tacticians would have considered normal in 1953. Gray's mission was to support the infantry by directing artillery fire against targets as they presented themselves. As the forward observer, he had direct communications back to the Battalion's FDC as well as to Staff Sergeant Woods at the Battery's FDC. That was all customary and to be expected; but what Gray found unusual, and discomforting, was that he was the only officer along the front lines in his section. The company had no officers as platoon leaders and the company commander remained in a bunker well down the reverse slope of the Main Line of Resistance. That Gray had to go down to see and brief the company commander daily, leaving no officer on the line, was a source of concern and represented a style of leadership with which Gray was unfamiliar. At night, the artillery lieutenant spent time in either Combat Outpost 9 or 11. After all, he had been taught that officers share dangers with their men while providing direct, personal leadership. That no officers were located along the front lines had an impact on the young forward observer – a negative one. Gray was a quick study, and very much like a sponge when it came to learning the lessons of good leadership. But he also learned to recognize, and often ignore or correct, deficiencies when he encountered them.

During the time spent on the Main Line of Resistance, Gray viewed several interesting events. Active attacks by the Chinese though resulted in prolonged, major combat towards the end of the war. Of course, having the Chinese take random, but well-aimed shots with their 76mm pack howitzers provided sufficient excitement along the line to satisfy many Marines in 1953. The Chinese guns were hidden deep in caves; they would be run out, take a pot shot and return to the sanctity of the cave in mere moments. The Marines countered those tactics by bringing tanks up to the Main Line of Resistance. They would patiently watch as Chinese soldiers would appear in the mouth of the cave, toss out the dirt that had filled their bucket, and go back inside. Sooner or later the howitzer would appear, ready to fire off a quick shot. It was a deadly game of cat and mouse; the Marine tank would try to fire before the Chinese could get back inside. There were casualties on both sides, though the

Chinese really hated being in front of the Marines. It was later learned that any shirkers, malcontents or disciplinary problems within the Chinese ranks were sent to the Marines' neighborhood as punishment.

In June, President Rhee of South Korea turned loose 25,000 North Korean prisoners. While some stayed in the south, others wanted to return north. The Marines were on high alert for any suspicious activity. One night, Lieutenant Gray, who at the time prided himself on being quite a proficient scout – being recon trained, having good hearing and excellent eyesight, etc. – was seated on top a bunker on guard for any passing North Koreans. Gray was also confident that he could smell both the Chinese and the Koreans, the latter because of their all-embracing use of garlic in their foods. During a rainstorm, he heard a rustling noise behind his position. Sure enough, four members of the Korean Service Corps were right behind him in the trench, trying to find shelter from the rain.[28] It was a humbling lesson for the great scout – being snuck up on by four weary workers looking to find someplace dry to wait out the storm.

When the 1st Marine Division was relieved by U.S. Army units and sent into reserve, the artillery units remained on the line. As a result, Gray had the opportunity to serve as a forward observer for the Turkish Brigade. When the new units failed to patrol properly and permitted the Chinese to place mines close to the American positions, the Marines returned. His unit fired continuously against a major attack against the "Berlin Outpost," when just before the Armistice the Chinese made one last push to realign their forward positions. It was an intense engagement.

On July 27, 1953, the Korean Armistice was signed, and the guns fell silent for the first time in over three years. The day after the Armistice was signed, the Chinese to the front of the Marines danced with joy, under the wary eyes of their recent combatants. On the American side, there was no pandemonium or jumping for joy. The Marine reaction to the Armistice, at least in Lieutenant Gray's area, was silent thankfulness that the shooting was over.

In August 1953, Al Gray was promoted to 1st Lieutenant and made the Executive Officer of the battery. The Executive Officer of an artillery battery is responsible for the total performance of the battery and its equipment. Signing for the equipment the first time is usually a sobering experience for any lieutenant; what will happen if the unit loses something? No sooner had Gray completed taking inventory of his new realm than 1/7 and its supporting battery, F/2/11 were ordered to participate in a Marine Landing Exercise in October 1953. After some time aboard ship, the amphibious exercise was held one of the small Korean islands, Tokchok-To. Gray's battery, F/2/11, was embarked aboard an Landing Ship Tank and was using

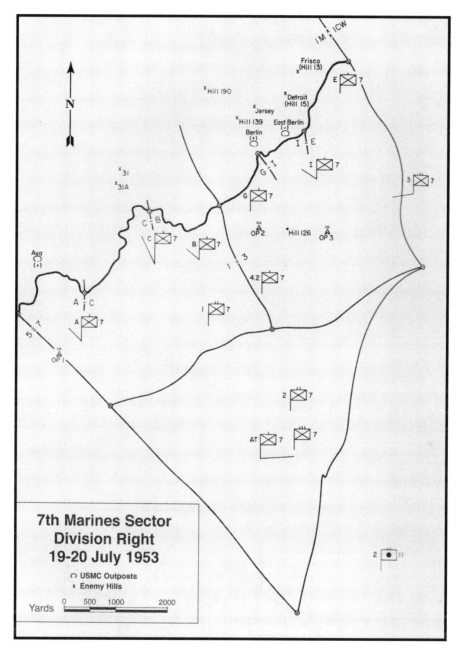

Map 1.2

This map shows the final positions occupied by the 7th Marines, on the far right of the 1st Marine Division's portion of the Main Line of Resistance, just before the Armistice of 27 July 1953. During the final months of the war, Lieutenant Gray was assigned as the forward observer with B/1/7 (near the center of the line), and his battery, Fox/2/11, normally fired in support of 1/7. However, during the final weeks of the war, artillery fire was often massed to defend against repeated, determined Chinese attacks against the Marine outposts. In the weeks before the Armistice, Chinese assaults against the Berlin Outpost were very heavy. Marine artillery also supported the Turks, located east of the 7th Marines. Reproduced from U.S. Marines in the Korean War, Charles R. Smith, editor. History Division; Washington, D.C. 2007.

Figure 1.15
A last chew on the Main Line of Resistance, Korea,
27 July 1953 after the Armistice was signed.[29]

DUKWs (pronounced "Duck"), a six-wheel drive amphibious vehicle left over from World War II, to offload the battery's howitzers. Everything went smoothly until Howitzer #6 (of 6) and the DUKW that carried it rolled down the ramp of the Landing Ship Tank. The DUKW splashed into the water, never to be seen again. Gray and others were able to save the men, but he was left with the aiming stakes and little else of the equipment. The paperwork required explaining the loss kept Gray busy for more than a little while. It was another learning experience for the young artilleryman.

Surviving the loss of a howitzer, Gray was subsequently assigned as the Artillery Liaison Officer to the 1st Battalion, 7th Marines (1/7). The assignment was a plum for the young officer, giving him more opportunity to be closer to where he really wanted to be – with the infantry on the front lines. It was during his time with 1/7 that perhaps the most unlikely episode in Gray's time as a Marine officer occurred.

Al Gray's first priority as both an enlisted man and as a Marine officer was to be a professional. Gray's attitude manifested itself in many ways: his constant study of various manuals and plans, his unending curiosity with all facets of his assignments, and his denial of alcohol whenever stationed outside the United States. But there was also another thing that went hand-in-hand with his professionalism: his sense of humor. It was during his time as liaison to 1/7 that Gray procured what was surely his most infamous cohort ever – Mike the Monkey! Mike provided comic relief from the daily drudgery of combat. Although Mike "belonged" to 2/11, no one objected when Gray took him to the infantry battalion. Regrettably, some unforeseen acts of destruction caused Gray to have to choose between loyalty to Mike and his future as an officer.

The Battalion's Operations Officer, Major Frank Seabeck, was not amused when Mike ripped the transistors from Seabeck's beloved Zenith Trans-Oceanic radio set. Seabeck threatened to banish Gray to someplace far away, perhaps Siberia. Knowing where his bread was buttered, Lieutenant Gray was able to trade Mike to a British officer in return for a German 9mm Luger that the Brit claimed came from Normandy. Even though Mike did not last long, a sense of humor remained one of Gray's constant traits.

Upon his return to 2/11, Gray was assigned as Commanding Officer of the Service Battery of the 2nd Battalion, 11th Marines. Gray had been slated to command a firing battery but the Battalion S-4 (logistics) officer went on emergency leave and, therefore, he was assigned to the Service Battery and the S-4 billet. Gray was also tasked as the ammunition officer and given other sundry duties, evidently based on the theory that if an officer is busy, assign him even more duties to make sure he stays

Figure 1.16
Lt Gray and Mike the Monkey. [30]

active. But being the S-4 caused Gray to learn logistics, something about which most lieutenants know little, and care less. The staff assignment also taught Gray to work with truck drivers, supply clerks and others outside the mainstream of infantry or artillery operations. He also was fortunate that the hard-nosed Executive Officer of the Battalion, then Major Herman Poggemeyer, Jr., developed a liking for the young Lieutenant. Gray came into contact with Poggemeyer many times before that officer retired in 1977 as a Major General.

In April 1954, Gray decided to extend his tour in Korea and requested an assignment to the infantry. One had to admire his persistence; at every opportunity since reporting to the Replacement Battalion at Camp Pendleton, Gray listed infantry duty with the 1ˢᵗ Division as his first choice for future duty. Predictably, his artillery commanders usually recommended his continued assignment with the "cannon cockers" (as they are known within the service). There was an exception; one Battalion Commander, Lieutenant Colonel Gordon H. West, recommended that

Figure 1.17
Artillery Shoot, Korea, 1954.[31]

Figure 1.18
Al Gray has had a continuous relationship with dogs dating back to his time in Korea. This is perhaps the first photographic evidence; it shows him holding "Taps" and "Reveille."[32]

Gray's choice be applied. It would not be the last time that Colonel West provided professional planning advice to Lieutenant Gray. Of course, as many familiar with the service might expect, the Marine Corps paid no more attention to Colonel West's endorsement than it did to Lieutenant Gray's repeated requests. Only by extending and staying in Korea had Gray achieved his long-time goal of service with the infantry.

Thus, in a most unusual move, Gray went from being a battery commanding officer to an assignment as an infantry platoon leader. While some may have viewed that as a step backwards, leading infantry Marines was what he longed to do, and Al Gray enthusiastically welcomed the professional change. After two months as commander of the 1st Platoon, Gray was assigned to be the Executive Officer. Then six weeks later he became the Commanding Officer, Able (now Alpha) Company, 1st Battalion, 7th Marines (1/7). His first battalion commander in 1/7 was Lieutenant Colonel Michael P. Ryan, an officer who rose to become a Major General. Ryan had earned a Navy Cross on Tarawa in World War II when he commanded the only one of then Colonel Shoup's force to make any headway inland.

Able was a good company, one Gray fondly remembered. From its position near Hill 495 on the Kansas Line, Gray had a commanding view of the entire region all the way to Panmunjom, the site of the Armistice talks. Gray also had plenty of time to read and reflect while in Korea. Though he had not yet established his custom of traveling with a book-filled footlocker, he nonetheless read everything he could get his hands on. One book, *The Koreans and Their Culture*, provided Gray with detailed information about how Korean villages are constructed, why their houses are L-shaped, how their hooches are built to capture the breeze, and how they had been historically treated by the Japanese. In addition, Gray took the time to learn the basics of his first Asian language. Having learned an affinity for languages from his grandfather, he became familiar with the Korean tongue quite readily. He never missed an opportunity to speak Korean with the laborers who attended the Marines or with his counter-parts in the Korean Marine Corps. Since the Republic of Korea Marines were on the left-flank of the 1st Marine Division, Gray saw them often. Between his reading and his self-taught language efforts, Lieutenant Al Gray developed a healthy respect for the country and its people.

While Gray was serving as the Company Commander of Able Company, there were several noteworthy situations and events that caused his Battalion Commander, Lieutenant Colonel Ryan, to take note. First, Gray's company seemed to always be doing physical exercise. When called upon to work to improve defenses along the old Main Line of Resistance, which was now manned as a security barrier against the North Koreans, Able Company usually jogged up the hill to go to work. Ryan liked that Able was in great shape. Second, when Ryan had Marines who had received non-judicial punishment or courts-martial, he sent them to Able Company. He liked the personal attention that Lieutenant Gray gave such men, which frequently resulted in their rehabilitation as good Marines. But more than being in good shape, and well led, Able was a confident group that could get the job done.

Another 1st Lieutenant, Al LaPorte, had joined the company as Gray's Executive Officer. LaPorte was a brilliant, highly self-confident officer, but he had little troop-leading experience. Shortly after his arrival, another 1st Division amphibious exercise held on the eastern side of the Korean Peninsula near Sokcho. Gray's men were the lead for the entire column that went ashore. They pushed some 20 miles inland before the exercise was terminated. During the event, Gray took the unusual step of declaring himself a casualty, leaving LaPorte in command of the Company. Gray's action was not overlooked by either his troops or the battalion's senior officers. The Company, of course, provided the support that Lieutenant LaPorte needed to get through the experience, and the new Executive Officer learned a valuable lesson – sometimes the troops, the NCOs and the Staff NCOs can help an inexperienced officer get his mission accomplished. All benefitted from the incident, and Gray had trained a newly competent #2 officer. LaPorte went on to a distinguished career and retired a Colonel of Marines.

While near Hill 495 in 1954, 1/7 celebrated the Marine Corps Birthday on November 10; the Birthday celebration is a ritualistic event no matter where Marines are or what Marines are doing. The lieutenants of the battalion, being lieutenants, were a little rowdy and making noise, and had begun to party soon after the celebration began.[33] At the appointed time, someone read the Commandant's Message, as is custom. Then, Gray recalled Colonel Ryan's Birthday speech as the shortest one he ever heard. It went something like, "When I was a young officer like you, I thought this birthday ball business was a bunch of malarkey. And then one day on Tarawa, in two minutes, it all made sense." Ryan then sat down to somber silence, and no one said another word.

A week or so after the Birthday celebration, Lieutenant Colonel Frazier West, another fine officer, replaced Ryan as the Commanding Officer. And in about a month, it was time for Al Gray to rotate home.

Without any unusual or exceptional incidents, but rather with experience common to thousands of Marines who manned the Main Line of Resistance during those years, Gray returned to the United States near the end of December 1954. His time in the infantry was well spent. Ryan, and several other officers, remarked upon Gray's exceptional leadership abilities. Indeed, outstanding leadership was Gray's forte as far as most of his reporting seniors were concerned; his leadership abilities were consistently lauded. And his performance resulted in the first of what would become many personal awards, a letter of appreciation from the Commanding General.[34] Michael Ryan, with whom Al Gray would cross paths several times, remained one of the officers whom Gray most respected. He also gained the respect of Lieutenant Colonel West, who would remain an admirer throughout Gray's career and visited him in the Commandant's House during Gray's final tour.

Gray left Korea fully qualified as both an artillery and infantry officer. He had been in both command and staff positions, and he had served under some celebrated Marine officers – as well as some not so good. And he learned other lessons that were tucked away in his memory for later use. One of the stories that fascinated him was the fact that the old-timers suggested that the Marine Corps knew there were Chinese around the Chosin Reservoir long before Generals Willoughby or MacArthur realized it.[35] Gray heard stories about how linguists accompanying the 1st Division reported hearing Chinese on the radio circuits. But the senior Army generals rejected that information, saying it was simply the North Koreans speaking Chinese. Gray filed away these reports, but never forgot where they were stored.

Predictably, when Gray was transferred back to the United States and the 2nd Marine Division, he again requested that his primary Military Occupational Specialty (MOS) be changed to 0302 (Infantry). The Marine Corps agreed to go as far as giving him a secondary 0302, and so it was 1st Lieutenant Alfred M. Gray, Jr., USMC, 0802/0302 who reported to Camp Lejeune, North Carolina in December 1954.

CAMP LEJEUNE, NORTH CAROLINA, 1954

Despite his artillery MOS, upon his arrival at Camp Lejeune, North Carolina, Gray was assigned to the 8th Marine Regiment, an infantry unit. His hopes of an assignment to an infantry battalion remained alive. However, he had not even reported officially when he was spotted by Major Frank Seabeck, the same officer who in Korea had made Gray cut his ties with Mike the Monkey.

Seabeck was the Regimental Operations Officer (S-3), and he knew that the 8th Marines needed a commanding officer for its troubled 4.2 Mortar Company. Seabeck intervened and Gray was designated for that billet. Again, in what had by now become a recurring theme, the needs of the service trumped the Lieutenant's personal desire for infantry battalion duty. And once again, the assignment would have significant future benefits for Gray.

The Marine Corps did away with 4.2 mortars (pronounced "4 deuce" within the service) in the late 1960s, but when Gray assumed command, a mortar company was part of each infantry regiment, reporting directly to the Regimental Commander. While again being a commanding officer made Gray very happy, there were aspects of the assignment that were particularly daunting. Soon after his arrival, in January 1955, the regiment deployed to the Caribbean to participate in Atlantic Training Exercise III-55; the exercise lasted until May. But for Lieutenant Gray the excitement started during the live fire drills on Vieques, Puerto Rico. The drills provided Gray with disappointing, first-hand knowledge of the poor state of training in his company.

In order to save money on ammunition, and using the initiative loved by Marine commanders, a warrant officer in the regiment had developed a way to insert a 60mm mortar tube into the larger 4.2 (107mm) mortar, thereby permitting the 4.2 to fire 60mm mortar ammunition. There were limitless tons of 60mm rounds left over from World War II and Korea, and each round cost considerably less than a 4.2 round. Thus, for practice firings, the project was an accountant's nirvana, but for an artillerist it was problematic – at best. Despite the money-savings aspect of the modification, there was a major shortcoming. The 60mm ammunition was so old and unreliable that it caused countless hang-fires.[36]

The first time a hang-fire occurred, the mortar crew quickly exited the firing pit, fearing for their safety in the event of an unexpected explosion – a misfire. Gray, who was watching nearby, was stunned by their reaction; he quickly entered the pit and called some of the men back to assist him. He then personally cleared the malfunctioning round from the tube. During the course of the exercise, he subsequently cleared what seemed to be hundreds more hang-fires, all the while training his crews in the proper techniques needed to safely operate the mortars. There was no yelling or screaming, no lectures or orders given from afar; Lieutenant Gray led by example and demonstrated repeatedly to his men precisely how to clear the faulty rounds.

But there was more to life on Vieques than clearing hang-fires. The waters off the island were home to countless creatures of the sea, and given its crystal clear purity, Gray and many Marines found lobstering and spear-fishing welcomed diversions from their training. Gray had always prided himself on his ability in and around the water, and the all-expenses paid cruise to Vieques permitted him time to enjoy one of his favorite pastimes.

During the return to the United States from the Caribbean, Al Gray was Commanding Officer of Troops aboard the Navy amphibious ship, a Landing Ship Tank that carried his company. A brief liberty stop in Miami proved a big hit among the troops, and many beaming Marines were delivered back to the ship in expensive cars driven by attractive young women. It seemed both the local population and the

Marines had enjoyed the port visit. On the way out of the harbor, however, an incident happened that, over the years, surely added to Gray's legacy among the troops.

One of Gray's Marines, Otto Lebeck, received a telegram that his father was dying and his return home on emergency leave was requested. With the ship already underway and in the channel out of the port area, and with most Marines thinking that no way would the Landing Ship Tank's commanding officer turn around for a Marine enlisted man, Gray approached the Captain with that very request. When the ship indeed stopped to permit Lebeck to be dropped off onto a small patrol craft, Gray's already lofty status, and his personal legend, grew. "You should have seen how our lieutenant told that captain to stop the ship or else," became the way the story would be told. One thing is certain; had Lieutenant Gray not requested such action, surely the Marine would not have left on emergency leave on a timely basis.

Within a month of the 8th Marines landing at Morehead City and returning home to Camp Lejeune, the 10th Marines (the division's artillery regiment) were off for summer exercises at Ft. Bragg, North Carolina. The large Army base had better ranges for firing artillery, and the 10th Marines usually stayed there for 4-6 weeks each summer. Invited to participate were each of the 4.2 Mortar Companies from the division's three infantry regiments – the 2nd, 6th and 8th. Gray's men, now a sharp, close-knit unit went out to fire with the real cannon cockers, to surprising and very gratifying results.

By mid-summer, Lieutenant Gray was quite proud of his company. Many had attended artillery schools to learn fire direction procedures and other technical details used by the artillerymen. Over the course of just a few months, under Gray's leadership, they had thrown out the normal procedures for the firing of 4.2 mortars, and instead adopted the same procedures, commands and aiming points used for 105mm (pronounced "1-oh-5") howitzers. While the 4.2 could not fire as far as the 105s (only about 4,000 yards as opposed to 11,000 yards) the company could deliver massed fires with the artillery (within limits of the mortars), and they more than impressed their commanding general.

When then Major General Edward Snedeker asked Gray if his unit could hit a target of opportunity equally well as they hit planned targets, Gray rose to the challenge and asked the General to pick one. The General pointed to a tank out in the middle of the range, and, sure enough, Gray's Marines were all over it on the first volley. Luck? Perhaps, but it was enough to make a good impression on the General. It was obvious which regiment had the best mortar company.

It was while serving with the 8th Marines that then 1st Lieutenant Al Gray again encountered then Major General Chesty Puller, the new commanding general. Soon after the artillery exercise, the Marine legend came to the 2nd Division; it was Puller's style to meet once a month with officers, and during one such occasion he met and recalled previously meeting Lieutenant Gray. General Puller also needed an aide. Gray was sent to interview for the assignment; during the course of his conversation with the General both recalled the night they had paddled ashore on North Island during the recon platoon's training exercise. But Al Gray knew he did not want to be an aide, even for so famous a general as Puller. The Lieutenant was pleased that General Puller honored his preference and returned him to the 8th Marines and his mortar company. It would be the last face-to-face encounter that Gray had with the General until long after Puller's retirement on November 1, 1955.

Prior to shaping up his mortar company, Gray made a significant change to his personal life. A lifelong animal lover, in particular Labrador Retrievers, Gray purchased his first dog, Lucky, during Christmas leave. Lucky was a large, 120-pound Retriever from the Barnegat Bay New Jersey line; his mother was from an English line. Little did the breeder know that his puppy would end up accompanying Gray to duty stations across the United States and even across the Pacific, to several Asian countries. Lucky would be the first of many Labs that served with Gray during the years leading to his final assignment in Washington. But in early 1955, Gray thought that he and Lucky would be at Camp Lejeune for at least a couple years. That would not be the case.

The Regimental Commander, who also had personally seen Lieutenant Gray in action on many occasions, was Colonel Marlow C. Williams. Gray had no indication of the very high regard Colonel Williams had for him, until a few years down the line when Colonel Williams's respect became evident. But there was little the Regimental Commander could do when in late July 1955 his mortar company commander received Permanent Change of Station orders which required Gray to attend the Communications Officer Course at Quantico.

A BRIEF EARLY HISTORY OF VIETNAM

INDOCHINA SUMMARY, TO 1946

Vietnam's recorded history predates that of the United States of America by more than 1,000 years; actually, it is closer to 2,000 years. For most of that time, China controlled the whole region that Americans have come to call Southeast Asia. Thus, long before Columbus discovered the New World, Vietnam celebrated its heroes and heroines who fought for the country's independence. Moreover, it is important, when discussing Vietnam, not to think that independence was a goal only recently adopted and turned against the French; rather, the fire of independence had burned brightly for two millennia.

What is now considered Vietnam, Laos and parts of Cambodia, had been a French colony for many decades. French hegemony began in the 1860s; and long before that, the area had been invaded and occupied by the Chinese from the time before Christ. Indeed, among the most revered Vietnamese heroines were the Trung sisters, who led the war against the Chinese in the period 43-39 BCE. Another Vietnamese woman, Trieu An, led another failed rebellion against the Chinese during the 2nd century AD. While many, including the French, have lumped together most of the people of Southeast Asia, there are ethnic, social and linguistic differences amongst those indigenous to what is now Vietnam, Laos, and Cambodia – all of which combined to form the French colony of Indochina.

Not widely reported in the literature surrounding Vietnam is the fact that within that country itself there are linguistic and social differences among the Vietnamese people. The north, Tonkin, and south, Cochinchina, have long been understood to be distinctive, but the middle of the country, Annam, that area just to the immediate north and south of what would become the De-Militarized Zone (DMZ), also has language and cultural variations. Those three areas combined are called Vietnam. In addition, the area changes from the sea to the mountains, and the peoples inhabiting the mountains are much different from the others. The coastal plain includes the area along National Route 1, which ran from Hanoi to Saigon. The coastal plain is where most of the rice is grown. It is a very rich agricultural region, and it holds by far the largest population. Inland, there is the Piedmont, an area of hills that connect the mountains with the coast. Less thickly populated and not as fertile for rice growing, the Piedmont was the scene of many military actions during the war. People who are not Vietnamese populate the mountains. A variety of ethnic tribes, commonly called Montagnards, but collectively known as the Degar, inhabit the region. The Vietnamese historically have maltreated these people. Throughout the war the Montagnards fought well and bravely, usually on the side of the French or Americans. In the final analysis, it can be said that for a relatively small region Vietnamese geography is as complex as the makeup of its population.

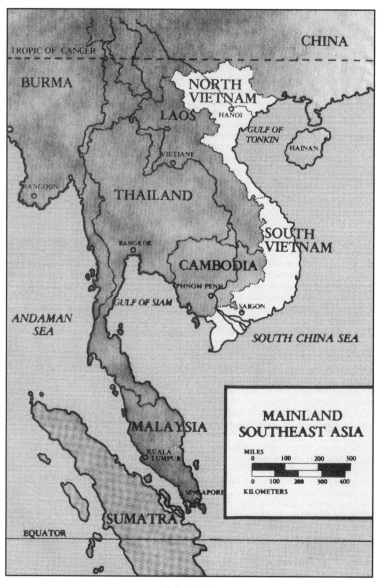

Map 1.3
Southeast Asia Overview. Reproduced from History and Museums Division,
Headquarters, Marine Corps, Marine Corps Series, U.S. Marines in Vietnam, 1964.

World War II and its aftermath created political confusion in many areas of the globe, but nowhere more than in Southeast Asia. Nationalism has proven to be a strong force around the world, including Southeast Asia. Among the well-educated and well-to-do Vietnamese the desire for independence was persistent, pervasive and, for at least the group led by Ho Chi Minh, well-organized. The French, however, were looking to regain their power, influence and especially their prestige following their defeat early in World War II, and they did not give up their colony easily.

As colonial masters, the French were largely even-handed and even did some good throughout Indochina, having created a system of roads, laws, and improved infrastructure throughout the area that helped to maintain a relative peace. But even before the onset of the global war, nationalism was on the rise, and the colonial era was fast closing; it simply took the French a little longer to accept that fact. The consequence of World War II was chaos in Vietnam, with various sides changing positions politically, changing partners, and no single person emerging as the clear leader, though Ho Chi Minh came closest. Ho, however, was virulently opposed by the small but influential Catholic faction throughout the country.[37]

By 1946, Ho's Vietminh was in open rebellion against the French, who had finally returned in force to the area after deciding to restore its empire (both the British in Saigon and the Chinese in and around Hanoi were occupying Vietnamese territory after the armistice with Japan was signed).[38] The French had propped up the Emperor Bao Dai before the war, hoping he would agree to grant them a protectorate over the country. But Bao Dai was a weak playboy much more interested in the vestiges of power rather than actually leading his country. His presence was just another complication is the scheme of things following the Japanese defeat.

The American involvement in Southeast Asia started just before the end of World War II. The Japanese had overrun almost the entire area of Indochina and, of course, the Americans and their allies were looking for any assistance they could muster to do harm to the invaders. Not surprisingly, among the first partners the Americans agents reached out to was a nationalist leader, Ho Chi Minh. An American major, Archimedes Patti, who worked for the Office of Strategic Services – the forerunner of the Central Intelligence Agency (CIA) – had contacted Ho and later stood by his side when Ho proclaimed Vietnamese independence on 22 September 1945. There is some reason to think that America's acceptance of Ho led to an increase in his popularity among Vietnamese nationalists; and some historians point out that Ho played Patti like a violin, completely out-maneuvering the American. Ho, who had changed his name in order to hide his communist affiliations, was also surely a nationalist. Even had he openly admitted being a full-fledged communist, the Americans would probably have still sought his support to oppose the enemy. After all, there were no bigger communists than those in Moscow, who were vital allies in the war against Germany. The American attitude toward communism was largely ambivalent immediately following World War II, so aligning with Ho would not have been surprising. It was not until President Harry S. Truman's policy of "Containment" was announced in 1948 that communism became a very dirty word in the United States. Of course, the civil war going on in China pitted the communists against Chiang Kai-shek. But far more important than even the Chinese civil war, the Korean War, 1950-1953, would soon change the ambivalence toward communism among American diplomats, and significantly, the American public. Strong opposition to communist expansion became a major, and recurring, theme in American politics during the 1950s, the 1960s and even into the 1980s.

But in 1945, Southeast Asia was just a murky backwater of the war, and it held little significance to those who formulated and implemented the foreign policy of the United States of America. Significantly, it is doubtful that even 10% of American public could have found Vietnam on a map. It was out of sight, and certainly out of mind.

Nevertheless, while Al Gray attended high school in Point Pleasant Beach and college at Lafayette, the events that would dominate his life two decades later were taking shape in Southeast Asia.

THE FRENCH WAR, 1946-1954

By 1954, while Americans cheered the end of the Korean War, most Americans old enough to read were also aware of the French military defeat at Dien Bien Phu in May. Unfortunately, few Americans, including even the military leaders of the day, understood how and why the French came to lose their colony in Indochina.

Perhaps the primary cause of the French defeat was simply that the nationalist movement overwhelmed the French military and its local allies. Many ethnic tribes who lived in the mountainous region between the Piedmont and the Laotian and Cambodian plains were closely allied with the French. These peoples, collectively called the Montagnards, were long-time enemies of the Vietnamese. French officers and Staff NCOs led these local forces, however.

The French did not lose because of the failure of their troops to fight well. Throughout the war, most elements of the French military fought bravely and tenaciously. Nonetheless, except for a brief two-year period from late 1950 until early 1952 when General Jean de Lattre de Tassigny, easily France's best commander, led the effort, the French lacked both purpose and commitment. Indeed, other than during the interval when de Lattre commanded, the French had essentially no strategy for winning. Adding to the French internal strategic difficulties, as the war progressed the Vietminh received the increased support from Mao Tse-Tung's communists after that Chinese leader arrived at the border with Vietnam. Mao, who soon threw the American-backed Chinese Nationalists of Chiang Kai-shek off the Asian mainland, provided his Vietminh friends with secure bases and American-made arms and equipment – all captured from the Chinese Nationalists. With bases secure from French interdiction, the Vietminh could regroup, resupply and rest without fear, protected by their Chinese communist neighbors.

Surprisingly, the French colonial administration did not take advantage of the presence of a strong and highly influential minority – the Catholics. Most native Catholics preferred French rule to that of the Vietminh. They considered Ho Chi Minh a godless communist; still, there was no significant government push to expand Catholicism or even to use locals as officers. As a result, the two sources of local support – the Catholics and the non-Vietnamese mountain tribes – were squandered. In the end, the fact that the French could not and did not protect the local peasants, regardless of their religion, from the deprivations and physical assaults made by the Vietminh led to their downfall.

Security, that is simply being left alone to cultivate his fields and protect his family, was by far the most important motivation to the average Vietnamese peasant. While it may have been chic for Vietnamese intellectuals to discuss nationalism, the peasants in the countryside had simple wants and desires. They cared little about who ruled in Hanoi or Saigon so long as their families and the product of their fields, invariably rice, were protected. The French never learned the counter-insurgency lessons of the British in Malaya or the Americans in the Philippines. Unfortunately, most Americans, including the policy makers in Washington, also failed to learn that lesson when confronted by it a decade later.

For the French, Dien Bien Phu was the culmination of a decade of poor decisions. The then overall French commander, Lieutenant General Henri Navarre, had decided to flush out the Vietminh so that he could pummel them with his (supposedly) superior firepower.[39] However, the General's faith in the superiority of his army's weaponry was a cruel myth. The French did not have sufficient air power to bomb the Vietminh into submission, and by 1954 the insurgent Vietminh had at least matched the French in artillery. Indeed, when Navarre ordered Colonel Christian de Castries and the crème de la crème of French troops into northwest Vietnam, with the goal of attacking the extended Vietminh supply lines that supported the communist offensive toward Laos, Navarre was confident that Castries would not encounter strong enemy forces. If he did, reasoned Navarre, then the more potent French firepower would overwhelm their enemy. At least that was Navarre's plan – a plan universally rejected by his subordinates. Thus, by the time it was apparent to all the French that Navarre was challenging the Vietminh military leader, Senior General Vo Nguyen Giap, to a major confrontation, it was too late to turn back.

Until 1954, the only strategy that had provided success to the French military was based upon the results of the Battle of Na San, which led to the development of the "hedgehog" concept. Each hedgehog was to be a strong fortified position constructed around an airfield. At Na San, the Vietminh attacked in great numbers, only to suffer high casualties. The French wanted to implement that same approach at Dien Bien Phu, only on a much larger scale.

Following the French script, the military commander of the Vietminh, General Giap, pounced on the French force shortly after it arrived. He ordered several of his major maneuver elements to attack, while the French tried to dig into what was a nearly indefensible position. By occupying the reverse slope of the hills that ringed the French position, the Vietminh were able to hit the de Castries forces with artillery from all directions, while themselves being relatively safe from counter-battery fire. For direct fire, the Vietminh burrowed their artillery into bunkers deep into the sides of the mountains; the only thing the French could see was the muzzle flash. While the French artillery was excellent, and well used, the French commanders were stunned by the amount of ammunition Giap got to the battle and the accuracy of the fire to which they were subjected.[40]

Navarre reinforced his cavalier on-scene commander by almost immediately committing additional forces to the battle. Though the French fought bravely and well in most cases, the insurgents finally overwhelmed the colonialists.

While Dien Bien Phu is remembered as the culminating battle of the war, simultaneously with the siege there, a French Mobile Task Force operating in the central highlands near Pleiku was also decimated. Near simultaneously, in the Red River Delta an inexorable flood of insurgents moved into position. The simple fact is, even if a miracle had occurred and Colonel de Castries could have escaped Giap's grip, the French forces throughout Indochina were being out-gunned and out maneuvered. Colonial France's control of Indochina was surely at an end.

The torrent of American air power and other war materials that had been transferred to the French earlier in 1954 proved to be too little too late. Indeed, it is not clear that the Eisenhower administration paid any attention to the conflict until it was apparent the French were going to lose and that a vacuum would be created in the region. Given that American interests in China had been lost when Chiang

Kai-shek was expelled from the mainland, and American foreign policy in 1954 was based on "containing communism," Ho Chi Minh's rise to power was alarming. But not too alarming. After all, Eisenhower, his forceful Secretary of State, John Foster Dulles and Eisenhower's entire defense establishment was focused on the Soviet Union and the possibility of nuclear war. Furthermore, having just ended the Korean War, Ike was in no hurry to become involved in another Asian conflict. In fact, avoiding another land war in Asia was as much a principal tenet of American policy as the containment of communism.

Ho Chi Minh had won the war against the French, though strangely he did far less well with the Geneva Accords, the 1954 peace treaty that dissolved French Indochina. True, Ho was given complete control of the north, but the French were permitted to retain the Emperor Bao Dai in the south. The Accords called for national elections in 1955-1956, and so, probably and realistically, Ho was content to take control of Tonkin, assured that he would soon get all of Vietnam.

As it turned out, when 1956 ended, Ho had not achieved the goal that he had been fighting for over the previous decade. But no matter how complex the situation in Vietnam was in 1956, it was about to become even more confusing, and in the end, two decades into the future, much more frustrating for the Americans.

NOTES AND REFERENCES

1. General Al Gray videotaped interview, 4 May 2009.
2. Not only did Gray's friends provide a role model for him, but also they enlisted during the war and contributed significantly to effort. Bertalotus was seagoing Marine aboard the carrier USS *Bon Homme Richard*; Pearce was seriously wounded fighting with the 1st Marine Division at Peleliu; Dunn and Frank Martin served as a Marines in the Pacific; and Sprague joined the Navy and survived the kamikaze attacks against the U.S. Fleet during the Battle for Okinawa; Tom Wilson served aboard merchant ships as armed guard and made many trips to Murmansk, Russia. Yes, the Point Pleasant Beach boys did their fair share and more.
3. Author interview with Don McIntyre, 2012. It is hard to believe when watching the modern game, but as late as the 1940s and early 1950s, everyone shot the ball with two hands while standing flat-footed on the floor – it was called a "set shot." There were no one-handed, jump shots like those common to the game today. That Gray, with his arm in a cast, was able to score shooting one-handed was so noteworthy it was mentioned in the local newspaper account of the game. The article also mentioned he made a "hook shot."
4. From General Gray's private collection.
5. From General Gray's private collection.
6. *The Melange*, the Annual Publication of the Students of Lafayette College, 1947. Special Collections and College Archives, David Bishop Skillman Library, Lafayette College.
7. From General Gray's private collection.
8. The college world series was different in the 1940s. District champions faced off in brackets until the final two teams played the "College World Series." That is far different than the current format.

9. Years later, Vice President and then President George H.W. Bush and the Commandant of the Marine Corps, Al Gray, often reminiscenced about their college baseball days. General Gray holds President Bush in the highest possible esteem.
10. From General Gray's private collection.
11. Years later it became Monmouth College and today it is Monmouth University. General Gray was awarded an Honorary Doctorate in 1990, and then after his retirement, he served on the University's Board of Directors for eight years.
12. The author had the privilege to interview Mrs. Jane Wilson by telephone in early 2010, and she reported this story about General Wilson after he had retired, "Every time that Louis heard Al Gray mentioned, he would say, 'I recruited that boy off the streets of New York.'"
13. From General Gray's private collection. Gray was promoted to Private First Class as the honor man in his basic training platoon, and was promoted to corporal and to sergeant while serving in the Amphibious Reconnaissance Platoon.
14. Photograph courtesy of Harry Ransom Center, The University of Texas at Austin. Photograph by David Douglas Duncan, a well known independent combat photographer whose pictures of Marines in Korea and Vietnam were widely used in various news magazines, including *Life*. Used with Mr. Duncan's express permission.
15. Major Ernie DeFazio was serving as the Executive Officer when the author reported for duty with 2nd Battalion 4th Marines (2/4) at Chu Lai in February 1966. In the author's opinion, Major DeFazio was a man whose good side any Marine wanted to stay on; he seemed as though he could eat nails, and probably did.
16. From General Gray's private collection. Dennis K. Jenkins letter to General Al Gray, dated July 1987. General Gray received a letter from Jenkins that included the photo. A retired police officer in Phoenix, his letter was addressed: "Dear Commandant ------ Sam". Jenkins had served in the Amphibious Recon Platoon and recalled his admiration for Sam Gray, who after some research on his part, determined was the new Commandant. His letter is quite poignant and expressive as he called his days with then Sergeant Gray."
17. Around 2005, General Gray spoke to the 5th Marine Division reunion in Phoenix, AZ. Lieutenant Colonel Ernie DeFazio's widow, Mrs. Peggy DeFazio, heard about the occasion and had her daughter drive her from New Mexico to attend the General's speech. General Gray immediately recognized her, and they had a warm embrace, during which Mrs. DeFazio rejoiced at being able to see "Sam." The nickname stuck, at least among the old recon community.
18. From General Gray's private collection.
19. From General Gray's private collection.
20. The fact that the game was broadcast on Armed Forces Radio and it was heard by the troops in Korea, literally around the world from New York, was probably inspiration for the *shot heard round the world* comment.
21. From General Gray's private collection.
22. From General Gray's private collection.
23. Captain F.R. Kraince, USMC, letter dated 21 December 1951, Recommendation for promotion to 2nd Lieutenant, case of Sergeant Alfred M. Gray, Jr., 1157125/2531 USMC. From General Gray's private collection.
24. The website dedicated to Sergeant Reckless is available at: http://www.sgtreckless.com.
25. From General Gray's private collection.
26. The United States Marine Corps is much, much smaller than the United States Army, or indeed any of the other American military services. There are only three active duty Marine divisions supported by one reserve division. The basic unit to which most Marines form an attachment is the battalion. During the Korean and Vietnam Wars, a Marine battalion consisted of roughly 45 officers and about 1,000 men, though it usually fielded far fewer than that number. Most officers in the battalion are Marines, but there are also a chaplain, a surgeon or maybe two, and sometimes a dentist, all naval

officers. Hospital Corpsmen from the U.S. Navy provide approximately 40 enlisted men for the battalion. Any Marine combat veteran will tell you that the corpsmen (universally known as "docs") are perhaps the most important men in the unit. The battalion is designated infantry or artillery by the regiment to which it is attached. The 1st Marine Regiment through the 9th Marine Regiment are all infantry. In the reserves, the 22nd through 24th Marine Regiments are infantry. Thus, then someone says they are in the 7th Marines, the reader can assume that an infantry regiment is being discussed. If someone is identified as being in 1/7, that means the 1st Battalion, 7th Marines is referenced – an infantry battalion in an infantry regiment. The 10th through 12th Marines are the active-duty artillery regiments. Thus, 2/11 identifies an artillery battalion. If the reader sees a reference to the 3rd Marines, that would refer to a regiment. If discussing a division, the unit would be indentified as the 3rd Marine Division or 3rd Division. Battalions that are neither infantry nor artillery are identified by a number and the type unit they are; for example, the 1st Radio Battalion, or sometimes just 1st Radio, or 3rd Engineers, or 2nd Tanks all denote separate battalions. The "Marines" designation is used only when the unit is a regiment. Usually three or more battalions comprise a regiment, and three infantry regiments, an artillery regiment, plus additional separate battalions, form a Marine division. A "Force" such as Fleet Marine Force, Pacific, or III Marine Amphibious Force (MAF), implies a unit composed of a division or perhaps two, and air wing and a logistics unit, plus additional separate battalions.

27. From General Gray's private collection. After the Marines, Shelly became a Chinese linguist and taught for many years at Norwich University. It was he who first introduced General Gray to that University, where he served many years on the Board after having been awarded an Honorary Doctorate in 1988. Gray also worked with General P.X. Kelley to bring the NROTC (Naval Reserve Officer Training Corps) to Norwich University.

28. The Korean Service Corps performed a variety of duties for the Allies, including digging trenches and bunkers, carrying supplies and the like. They were not soldiers.

29. From General Gray's private collection.

30. From General Gray's private collection.

31. From General Gray's private collection.

32. From General Gray's private collection.

33. The lieutenants certainly became loud and boisterous, but there was no alcohol available. General Gray comments. From General Gray's private collection.

34. 1st Marine Division Letter of Appreciation dated 15 December 1954 signed by Major General Robert Hogaboom, endorsed for delivery to 1st Lieutenant Gray in the 8th Marines by Major General Lewis B. (Chesty) Puller, and copied to Lieutenant Colonel Michael P. Ryan, Commanding Officer of 1st Battalion, 7th Marines. Part of General Gray's private collection.

35. General of the Army Douglas MacArthur was the Allied Commander in Korea. Major General Charles A. Willoughby, U.S. Army, was MacArthur's long-time Chief of Intelligence, dating back to World War II. Neither Willoughby nor MacArthur got wind of the Chinese attack at Chosin until well after it happened. Even after they had made substantial attacks against U.S. Army units, MacArthur and Willoughby continued to deny that the Chinese had a large presence in Korea. Had not Major General O.P. Smith, the 1st Marine Division's Commanding General, acting on his own intelligence reports and initiative, slowed his division's movement north and assumed a defensible position near the reservoir, the outcome of the battle would have probably been much different and decidedly worse for the Marines.

36. A "hang fire" occurs when the round is placed into the tube and allowed to drop, but the firing mechanism mis-fires and instead of the round being fired out of the tube, it remains in the tube. Mortar rounds are usually safe until fired, the rotation of the round "arms" the fuse after it leaves the tube. Hang-fires, then, are presumed to be safe so long as they are properly (and very carefully) extracted from the tube. The procedure involves

one man lifting the tube and sliding the round out, while another catches it with both hands and then re-inserts the safety pin. Repeatedly performing the procedure is tedious at best and always potentially life-threatening should another malfunction arise.

37. French missionaries converted large numbers of Vietnamese during the 17th century. While Catholics numbered about 10% of the population, their numbers did not expand significantly during French colonial rule, 1860s through 1954.

38. The period 1930 through 1946 is much too complicated to be covered here. For an excellent summary of events and personalities that dominated this time in Vietnam, see John F. Guilmartin's *America in Vietnam: The Fifteen Year War*. Stanley Karnow gives a more detailed account of this time in his *Vietnam: A History*.

39. Unfortunately for France, though there is little likelihood his presence would have altered the outcome, General Jean de Lattre de Tassigny had returned to his homeland in late 1951, having fallen ill to an advanced cancer. He died only a few weeks later on January 11, 1952.

40. While his theory is unproven, Dr. Guilmartin, an expert on the battle, speculates that the Vietminh ammunition supplies were augmented in a timely fashion by a most unexpected source – the French airdrops that fell into Vietminh hands. Both sides used American 105mm howitzers, and in 1954 the accuracy of airdropping supplies was still problematic. Thus, the pre-battle French assessment of the amount of artillery ammunition Giap's troops might have were probably wrong on two counts – the under-estimation of the Vietminh tremendously impressive internal supply efforts, and two, the amount they received from the French themselves.

CHAPTER 2

TAKE ANY ASSIGNMENT AND MAKE THE BEST OF IT
VIETNAM HISTORY, 1955-1961

TAKE ANY ASSIGNMENT AND MAKE THE BEST OF IT

Captain Al Gray faced a challenge. From the super secret Naval Security Group Activity, Kami Seya, Japan, where he was now assigned, he had been sent to Sakato, in northwest Honshu, to open a new base near the shores of the Sea of Japan. Gray was responsible for erecting antenna farms, refurbishing buildings, establishing messing operation; in other words, creating a naval base where before none existed. Even before he rebuilt the physical plant, he was to start conducting live operations. Moreover, the work was classified and the mission of the new base could not be revealed to the Japanese civilians who were employed in a variety of positions helping the Americans.

Al Gray's capabilities as a problem solver were becoming well known and highly respected by the naval officers to whom he reported, and he certainly needed every skill at his present assignment. Gray first earned the cooperation of the local Japanese at Sakata; but in the end, he earned far more – their esteem. His U.S. Navy seniors were stunned at his achievements and the professionalism that marked all his efforts there. Combining a few of his Marines with many more American Sailors and Japanese civilians, the new naval base was quickly and efficiently created. And when budget shortfalls nearly closed the facility before it became operational, Captain Gray personally intervened and won a reclama that kept the base operational.

Gray became a celebrity whose status within the area around Sakata lasted more than a decade. His professional reputation for getting things done, already off to a great start, grew, especially within the intelligence community.

COMMUNICATIONS OFFICER SCHOOL, QUANTICO, VIRGINIA, 1955

It was in late fall of 1955 that Al Gray had a major professional transformation, and it had nothing to do with his exceptional qualities as a 4.2 mortar company commander or his experience in combat arms. He had arrived at Camp Lejeune less than a year previously, but again the needs of the service beckoned. After the end of the Korean War, the Marine Corps had found itself short of both communications and supply officers; thus, many Regular officers in the major combat arms MOSs were sent to professional schools and then on to assignments for a temporary two-year tour in those support MOSs.[1] Normally, they then returned to their primary field. Gray, along with 48 other Marine and Allied officers received orders to the Communication Officer Course.

Gray wanted to stay in combat arms; he had worked tirelessly to become a professional in a field he loved, and thus was hesitant to move to the communications field. While in Washington visiting Headquarters Marine Corps (HQMC) in order to fill out paperwork necessary to obtain high-level security clearances, he had a chance encounter with an officer whom he knew and respected highly. He received advice that he followed for the rest of his time in the Marine Corps. Colonel Gordon H. West had been Gray's artillery battalion commander in Korea when Gray had been the battalion S-4 and commanded the service battery. West told Gray, "We can probably get the assignment changed, but I think it is best for Marine officers to accept any assignment they are given and make the best of it." Colonel West was then serving as the Commandant's military secretary, a position from which he undoubtedly could have influenced the assignment of the young lieutenant.[2] Gray needed little further encouragement and made his way down to Quantico to the Communications Officer Course.

The Communications Officer Course in the 1950s closely paralleled the Junior School (Amphibious Warfare School), which was designed to give officers the professional skills needed to function as field grade officers in the Fleet Marine Force.[3] The instruction included some 196 hours of tactics and 96 hours of staff functions. Emphasis was on amphibious operations and their inherent communications requirements.

Shortly before Gray went to Quantico, in 1954, the Marine Corps turned to one of its finest officers, Major General Robert E. Hogaboom, to lead a long-range study of the future needs of the Corps. Hogaboom's study had wide ranging implications.[4] As a result of that study, a fourth rifle company was added to each battalion; such addition was the result of then Lieutenant Colonel W.K. Jones's observation of Finnish tactics during the Russo-Finnish War of 1939.[5] The Hogaboom study had other recommendations that were partially implemented or planned; one led to a Force Reconnaissance Company being assigned to each Fleet Marine Force and added a Reconnaissance Battalion to each division. Other ideas included the need for Counter-Intelligence Teams and Interrogator-Translator Teams. But a proposal for what Hogaboom called "Composite Radio Reconnaissance Companies" at the division and force level had not been implemented. Even though the companies were not manned; nonetheless, their need was identified.

Nearly simultaneously with the Hogaboom study, Admiral Arleigh "31-Knot" Burke, the Chief of Naval Operations and former hard-charging World War II destroyer commander, had a problem that he shared with General Randolph McCall Pate, the Commandant of the Marine Corps. The Navy was short about 1,000 men in its Naval

Security Group (NSG), the organization that provided cryptologic and special communications capabilities to both the Fleet and the National Security Agency, (NSA). The NSA coordinated all the United States' efforts related to Signals Intelligence (SIGINT), and Communications Security (COMSEC). Unless Pate could make some Marines available, Burke was going to have to use civilians to make up the shortfall. Pate agreed to provide the 1,000 men over a three-year period, but only with provisos. The primary one was that, in the event of unseen contingencies, the Marine Corps could withdraw up to one-third the number to meet its own special requirements for direct support of their Fleet Marine Forces. Burke agreed and the Marine Corps set about building the requisite capability.

Thus, while Gray was in residence at the Communications School, the wheels had been put into motion to establish Marine cryptologic units. The resulting plan included having Marines working beside Sailors of the NSG at locations (Activities) around the world; and, of course, officers were needed to populate the new unit. The Commandant approved the initial arrangement that would assign a small number of Marines for duty in the European region at Bremerhaven, Germany. This first step would result in about 100 Marines going off to Europe. All the officers and Staff NCOs chosen had solid communications backgrounds, though none had the required special clearances and none had ever worked in SIGINT. General Pate insisted that those selected to command have, first and foremost, experience as unit commanders. Pate wanted to ensure that the officers would have the requisite troop-leading experience and administrative knowledge needed to handle both the leadership and organizational challenges that would surely test Marine officers on independent duty with the Navy. The Marine commanders would be reporting directly to HQMC, and thus they would not have support from various intermediate Marine commands.

Consequently, selection to communication course was not the event that most affected Al Gray's future. Rather, it is what happened when he heard about the need for two communicators who would be selected by a team of officers from HQMC, sent in response to Commandant Pate's instructions. When the prospective volunteers asked what the assignments might entail, they were told it was for "duty that was to be described at a later date." Because of the high security clearance associated with the duty, it is unlikely that even the officers making the selection knew exactly what the secretive work entailed.

Gray, thinking that the unknown might be more exciting than a straightforward Marine communications billet, decided to volunteer even though he was a relative novice in his new occupational specialty. In fact, it turned out that 12 of the officers attending the course had come from outside the communications field. They, as a group, decided that volunteering for an unknown, perhaps exotic, assignment was something all should do. Of course, they also felt that the likelihood of any of them being selected was miniscule; they were, after all, not seasoned communicators. But in one case, they were wrong.

Despite being a 1st Lieutenant, Gray's experience as a commander was unusual for an officer of his rank. He had commanded an artillery unit and a rifle company in Korea as well as a 4.2 Mortar Company at Camp Lejeune. Moreover, he had honed his leadership skills during both combat and peacetime assignments, and of course, he had taken the Administration Course as a brand new 2nd Lieutenant, before he even attended The Basic School. He had been selected for Captain but not yet promoted. Except for being so junior in rank, he met the Commandant's selection guidance.

NAVAL COMMUNICATIONS STATION, IMPERIAL BEACH, CALIFORNIA, 1956

As luck would have it, Gray was the first officer selected, though he still did not know what position he would hold. While still at Quantico he was called to the Pentagon to meet with two old sages. They were both colonels who might be able to shed some light on his assignment. He entered a room that had a big conference table covered by a green felt cloth. The colonels told him to stand-by while they finished their work. Gray watched intently as Colonel Bradshaw, an expert on COMSEC, and Colonel Boyd, an officer who had helped draft the Orange War Plan, hunched over the table moving various templates around on the green felt cloth. Gray thought that perhaps these officers were planning an amphibious operation. After all, from the formations indicated the templates might represent the outer transport area and the inner transport area typical of World War II-era amphibious operations. "This might be good," reflected Lieutenant Gray regarding the situation. Bradshaw and Boyd kept moving objects and mumbling, sometimes excitedly, for nearly 15 minutes before motioning Gray to join them. Instead of working on amphibious operations, Gray discovered that they were planning a forthcoming cocktail party. Their admonition to Lieutenant Gray, "We can't tell you what you'll be doing since you aren't cleared yet." Gray smiled to himself; he had heard that before! The colonels also said that he would receive more detailed instructions in the future. As he started to leave, Colonel Boyd said, "One more thing, Gray, the Commandant wants one unit to go to the Pacific; he wants the first one to be sent to the Far East. Since you're a bachelor, you're going to Japan." The detailed instructions? As of 2012, those have not yet arrived.

Al Gray and his colleagues graduated from Communications School and he was ordered to California for additional training. 1st Lieutenant Gray reported to Imperial Beach, California, an NSG facility south of San Diego. He found 120 enlisted Marines, eight Staff NCOs, and five other officers who joined him there; the enlisted men were training as intercept operators and given other cryptologic skills.[6] The Staff NCOs and officers received a shorter, four-week introductory course. Their orders initially included their subsequent assignment to Bremerhaven, Germany. All the men, formed into two platoons were going to Germany; however, a subsequent decision determined that the 1st Special Communications Platoon would go to Japan, while only the 2nd Platoon went to Bremerhaven.

The new orders indicated that the senior officer, an older, mustang Captain would take 2nd Platoon, while 1st Lieutenant Al Gray would take the 1st. However, the junior enlisted men were not assigned to their duty station.

Throughout the time at Imperial Beach (March-April 1956) Gray again proved to be a successful leader, forging close though demanding relationships with his men. Gray participated in all the training, and soon knew all the men; he knew their circumstances, whether or not they were married, their capabilities, etc. Meanwhile, the senior captain was involved very little. Nearing the end of the training, and without orders about who to send where, Gray went over to the Marine Corps Recruit Depot at San Diego and asked them to send a speed-letter to HQMC requesting that orders be issued to the men for duty in Japan or Germany.[7] Gray soon had his answer. "You decide," retorted the usually all-knowing Headquarters.

When deciding about how to divide the men between the two duty stations, his initial attempt was to identify who would go to Japan by simply asking for volunteers to take one step forward if they wanted to go to Japan. No one responded; practically no Marine ever got to go to an assignment in Germany or even Europe for that matter, except on a Mediterranean cruise from Camp Lejeune. And here were 120 Marines who had a 50-50 chance of going there, or to Japan, where thousands of Marines go each year to Okinawa. He then asked who wanted to go to Germany; again, no one stepped forward. After a moment, someone in the back of the formation asked, "Where are you going, sir?" When Gray replied that he would be going to Japan, all but two Marines stepped forward.

And Gray had learned yet another leadership lesson. Young Marines are quick to realize which officers are interested in them and their mission, and which officers are not. By never participating in their training, the older captain had tipped his attitude. What Marine would not rather serve with an officer who seemed to care about them,

Figure 2.1
Lucky and T/Sgt Walter F. Hunter, Jr. aboard ship on way to Japan.[8]

who understood at least a little the challenges associated with their work, and who had taken the time to learn their names and some things about them?[9]

Needing to divide the force, Gray then resorted to a more traditional approach, and made the personnel decisions himself. All the married men went to Japan with him, because the other captain did not want the problems associated with dependents. A couple Marines had relatives serving in Germany, so Gray directed them to the 2nd Platoon. Gray also decided to take the two African-Americans with him, and then selected every other man in the formation to go to Japan.

With 60-odd newly trained cryptologists, two lieutenant assistants, and his beloved, very large black Labrador Retriever, Lucky, he set about getting his men to Japan. But there was a trend developing; he received very little assistance from HQMC. Gray found his one-sided relationship with HQMC and its modus operandi challenging but also a very interesting way to operate. He was being given "mission-type" orders long before that phrase came into usage.

Drawing on the procedures outlined in the Landing Force Manual, Gray already ensured that both platoons were properly prepared for overseas deployment. In addition to being issued individual equipment, qualifying on the rifle range, and given 10 days leave, each Marine was briefed on the special responsibilities being entrusted to the unit.

With the unit prepared for overseas duty, Gray went over to the San Diego Naval Headquarters on 32nd Street and made arrangements for his command to be airlifted to Oakland where they would embark aboard a naval vessel for movement to Yokosuka, Japan.

One of Gray's first tasks was to ensure that he could get Lucky to San Francisco and Japan. The troops and their leader would be traveling by air transport and taking the dog would have been highly problematic. Fortunately, Gray's second in command, 1st Lieutenant Joseph C. Hedrick, his wife, Betty, and their infant daughter were driving up the coast to Oakland, the unit's embarkation point. Hedrick was serving as the Platoon's advance party and his responsibility was to make the initial liaison with the ship. Betty had been looking forward to a pleasant trip and was slightly put off at the prospect of sharing their small car with such a big, imposing Lab. Thankfully, both the Hedricks and Lucky proved adaptable and they all arrived without any difficulties. Lieutenant Hedrick also had another mission immediately upon his arrival – get the ship's commanding officer to approve taking Lucky aboard. It would be the first of many assignments that Hedrick handled perfectly for his new boss.

But as newly promoted Captain Gray walked his companion up the gangway to go aboard the ship that would take them across the Pacific, the ship's Executive Officer, a Navy Commander, bellowed down from the bridge words to the effect, "Keep that bleepin' dog off my ship!" Unfortunately, neither Hedrick nor the Commanding Officer had thought to alert the Executive Officer to the decision. Al Gray knew he had received permission for Lucky to make the trip, and so he kept on walking toward the Quarterdeck where he could explain the situation. Within mere days of boarding, however, Lucky's primary shipboard benefactor, and the person who spent the most time with the very sociable dog, was, as might be guessed, the Executive Officer!

NAVAL COMMUNICATIONS STATION, KAMI SEYA, JAPAN, 1956

Al Gray entered the secretive and largely unknown (even to most general and flag officers in 1956) world of SIGINT when he arrived in Japan. How his assignment was handled administratively reflected the highly classified nature of his work. Attached to the then Naval Communications Station, Kami Seya, his Navy-reporting senior was the Commanding Officer. Also, serving aboard the Communications Station was a Naval Security Group Activity. It was to the NSG unit that Gray's Marines provided most of their technical support, and it was with the NSG officers that he most worked. His unit designation was 1st Special Communications Platoon, Casual Company, Headquarters Battalion, HQMC.[10] That designation was later changed to Detachment, "G" Company, Headquarters Battalion, HQMC, Washington, D.C. Obviously the Marine Corps had little interest in sharing even where Captain Gray and his men were physically assigned. In addition, there was very little hint of the exact nature of his duties. Some referred to "Naval Security Group" duties, but there were very few Marines in 1956 who had any idea what the "Naval Security Group" was or, more importantly, what it did.

To say that he was out of the mainstream of typical Marine officer assignments, especially for one who had so fervently and without exception desired service in combat arms, is to grossly understate the situation. His tour of duty in Japan would reflect the very essence of his belief that a Marine *should take what he gets and make what he wants.*

In his initial discussions at Kami Seya, Commander Carlin White, USN, told Gray that his two officers had the necessary experience to work in the communications center and that all the Marines would be employed "down in the tunnel" where the intercept operations took place. However, White continued, the NSG officers were at a loss about "what they should do with an infantry/artillery officer?" Gray, noting that the Navy was using a four-section watch, replied that he wanted all his Marines on one watch for unit cohesion. He further said that he would take care of his Marines and try "to learn what he could about operations."

Interestingly, within a few weeks, Gray was put in charge of a large 600 man intercept division for two months as a temporary measure awaiting the arrival of a lieutenant commander. In short order, he got to know all the officers, Chief Petty Officers and many other senior petty officers. Many of the Security Group contingent were superb cryptologists and some were even legendary within the community. They were the best of mentors and the ever-curious Gray became a serious student. He found he could learn a lot from 1st Class Petty Officers.

The diversity of assignments given Gray in Japan ranged from tasks traditionally given to Marines serving with the Navy, such as organizing and training the base security force, to duties that would be unusual for any naval cryptologist, much less a Marine captain new to the occupation. Gray knew he could rely on the very capable Lieutenant Hedrick to run the administrative aspects of the platoon. As a sergeant, Joe Hedrick had been a Forward Air Controller during the 1ˢᵗ Marine Division's epic struggle at the Chosin Reservoir in Korea; he would go on to a very successful calling as a Marine officer, including a stint as the commander of the Marine Security Guard detachment at Camp David during the Johnson Administration. With Hedrick available, Gray was free to accept any project that came along, even those that required long absences away from Kami Seya. Both Hedrick and the other officer, 1ˢᵗ Lieutenant Tom Bowling, went straight to work in the special communications center. Gray was left with the freedom to move around and learn. And learn he did. Indeed, with a group of 60 highly intelligent, well-motivated Marines, there were no disciplinary issues and no other distractions that called for his continued presence.

Perhaps the measures that Gray took when assigned to coordinate the Navy Emergency Ground Defense Force explained why the senior Navy officers came to hold him in high regard. Kami Seya was home to both a Naval Communications Station and a Naval Security Group Activity. There was always a rivalry between the two separate Navy units, and the Marines tended to serve as a buffer. Instead of simply permitting the Marines to be used as the security detail, Gray suggested to the Executive Officer that his Marines would serve as instructors and leaders for the Sailors assigned to the unit. Drawing some 200 Sailors from each of four watch sections, Gray had his Marines teach their naval counterparts concepts such as patrolling, establishing fields of fire, proper use of crew-served weapons, basic marksmanship and other skills the defense force would require. It gave the Marines a chance to hone their own skills and soon all the Sailors involved enjoyed acting like Marines – at least during training exercises. Instead of having separate and distinct units (Navy and Marine), the emergency security was fully integrated and served as a morale booster.

In September 1956, Gray got his first independent tasking as a cryptologist. He was assigned a detachment and ordered to conduct a Research and Development mission on Paengnyong Do (White Wing) Island, just off the coast of South Korea. Gray's detachment included an assortment of military and civilian technical specialists and linguists; the motley group had never worked together before and it was headed by a Marine with no cryptologic experience. But before they could begin operations, they had to survive a challenging voyage aboard a World War II-era Landing Ship Tank that had been given to the Japanese Merchant Marine Service and was manned by eight civilians. The old 100-class ship made only 6 knots in tumultuous seas while passing through the Tsushima Straits and around the tip of Korea into the China Sea. The grand finale of the trip occurred when a violent tempest literally blew the Landing

Figure 2.2
Gray received his promotion orders while traveling to Japan aboard ship.[11]

Ship Tank into the port of Inchon, where it remained for safety until the storm had passed. Finally making their way to White Wing Island, the detachment disembarked and established operations on a hilltop overlooking North Korea.

On the island, Gray was reunited with his old mentor from the Amphibious Recon Platoon, Captain John Slagle, who was an advisor to the South Korean Marines on White Wing. Gray also helped the South Koreans get started with their new 4.2 mortars as well as performing other activities he still refuses to discuss. It was and still is a crucial outpost off North Korea, and it was in the news in 2011 when the

Figure 2.3
Capt Gray with his friend and mentor, Capt John Slagle, taken
while on Temporary Additional Duty to Korea, 1956.[12]

Figure 2.4
Two of Al Gray's favorites, Capt John Slagle and Lucky, Paengnyong Do, 1956. In
a Marine Corps populated by many hard and tough men, Slagle stood in the first rank.[13]

North fired artillery at the island killing several South Korean civilians. Paengnyong Do's position makes it a crucial asset in monitoring North Korean military activity, though as the recent (2011) fire fight demonstrated, it can also be dangerous. Gray and his detachment's 1956 assignment lasted until almost Christmas, and was quite successful. The detachment's accomplishments resulted in the Navy officers having more confidence in the young Marine, which soon resulted in more duties away from Kami Seya.

Soon after his return to Kami Seya at the end of December 1956, Al Gray embarked on perhaps his most challenging and professionally rewarding experience while assigned to Japan. From January through September 1957, he was assigned as Special Project Officer and Commander for Construction and Activation of the United States Navy Electronic Intelligence Activity at Sakata, a city of about 100,000 people on the island of Honshu in northwest Japan. In addition to the relatively mundane though technically challenging tasks of building and refurbishing buildings or constructing antennae needed for operations, Gray was presented with a far more demanding confrontation – dealing with local Japanese politicians and authorities. He was on

Figure 2.5
Al Gray attended many quasi-social functions while building the base at Sakata,
where there had been few Americans previously. Here on Gray's immedi-
ate left is Mrs. Toshi Nakayama, his chief interpreter. On Toshi's left is LCDR
Kirby Robinson, while the base Chief Petty Officer is to Gray's right.[14]

Figure 2.6
Gray spent lots of time with children at Sakata. He gave away lots of candy and chocolates,
and they remembered him because of it. They all needed warm clothes because
the winter of 1956–1957 saw the worst blizzard in Sakata since 1936.[15]

independent duty essentially, over 400 miles from his nominal Commanding Officer at Kami Seya.

Gray had been given an assignment to construct and man a base, using a diverse group of Sailors and a single Marine that would be augmented by Japanese nationals, who would not have any access to the classified materials. No one had anticipated the socio-political negotiations that would be required.

The Japanese had a considerable range of questions about why the Americans needed the local site, and what they would be doing there. Mr. Mitsui Kudo, Gray's interpreter (and language teacher) helped the Marine through the maze of Japanese culture and politics. Given the secret nature of the mission, it was impossible for Gray to say exactly what the American intentions were, nor was there a Japanese Self-Defense Force unit nearby to run interference. His goal became getting Japanese cooperation while being very vague about the mission. In addition to the basic give and take, there were additional fascinating, and very complicating, factors that added more than a little spice to the drama. First, communists, led by the mayor, dominated the local government; and, second, the leaders of the newly created police and fire departments were, respectively, a former Japanese admiral and a former Imperial Army general.[16] The Yamagata Prefecture (State) government was also socialist, and no particular friend to America.

Both the admiral and general had served in northern Asia, where Japanese military and naval units were largely undefeated during the war. Neither they, nor the communists, displayed any degree of subservience toward the young Marine Captain; the eager-to-please attitude that generally characterized Japanese manners toward Marines in other areas of Japan was simply not present at Sakata.[17] In the end, however, everything at Sakata worked as envisioned, though not without a series of trials and tribulations.

The 40 plus acres that the new base encompassed were made ready for operations, and the locals, for the most part, stayed away from the new or reconstructed structures. Captain Gray's loyal companion Lucky very ably augmented the base security force. Lucky had developed a sense of who belonged and who did not, and he would roam around within the fence that bordered the perimeter, ready to challenge intruders. Since Sakata was located just south of Akita Prefecture, where the Japanese national dogs, the "Akita" originated, the people respected big, black dogs that guarded property, and Lucky certainly filled that bill. He was almost twice the size of large Akitas, and while friendly when under the command of his master, Lucky's 120-pound frame posed a real threat to potential trespassers. Still, everyone who knew Lucky loved him, and Captain Gray never wanted for volunteers to take care of the big dog during Gray's numerous absences. "Lucky-san" was appropriately named, though the Japanese could not pronounce the "L," and thus the large Retriever had to learn to respond to "Rucky-san."

At Sakata, Al Gray had turned in a remarkable performance. First and foremost, in the manner that characterized his leadership, Gray earned the respect of his men. Whatever the task, from carrying heating coal into buildings to testing or installing equipment, whatever the men were required to do, Gray would be found working just as hard and just as long. He not only led and directed, he participated in the dirty work. That Captain Gray was able to build a diverse group of men – Sailors, a single enlisted Marine and Japanese – into a well-functioning team was the source of wonder to the Navy captain for whom he worked. And no aspect of the assignment escaped Gray's personal attention.

A Navy Chief Petty Officer, who was an antenna expert, and Captain Gray were the two who climbed high to install the yagi antennae that the facility needed.[18] On northern Honshu, in the midst of winter, doing anything outside is difficult. Climbing well into the air and then attaching the wiring to an antenna is doubly difficult. Gray and the Chief would have to use their bodies to shield the wind while

Figure 2.7
Lucky earned some relaxation, and more, at Sakata.[19]

Figure 2.8
Local dignitaries often visited the American base. Here Al Gray is shown seated
beside the President of the local chemical company, who became a friend. Evenings
Gray would teach him English and he would teach the Marine Japanese.[20]

working without gloves to ensure connections were properly made; certainly climbing up to redo the work was the last thing either man desired. But doing the dirty
things and the difficult stuff had lots to do with why the men followed Al Gray
and would try to run through walls for him. After all, there must be something very
attractive on the other side. As soon as the antennae and equipment were installed,
the Command started conducting operations.

In addition to his normal duties, Gray also spent countless hours learning and
practicing the Japanese language, an accomplishment that bore gigantic dividends a
few years down the road – and not just in Japan. Gray had begun to study Japanese
immediately upon his arrival in the country, and his attempt to speak the native
tongue, unusual for Americans, undoubtedly made negotiations and discussions
with the local politicians much more productive. By the time he left Japan, his
spoken Japanese vocabulary was quite extensive. He also had learned to differenti-
ate among and mimic the various dialects of the country, particularly the one used
on northern Honshu and Hokkaido.

Initially, the Navy intended to assign only bachelors to Sakata, thereby minimizing the need to provide various services that dependents require – housing, medical, educational, and dietary. But when that decision was reversed in mid-stream, it fell to Captain Gray to ensure that not only was the base ready to handle its classified mission, but also that dependents could live comfortably in the area. The inspection of the area's medical facilities resulted in some interesting tales, but none more so than Gray, a bachelor officer, being invited to observe a hysterectomy at one of the local hospitals. It was part of his mission to determine if the hospital's doctors could handle emergencies that might arise among the civilian women. Education for the children was easily provided for; the American children would attend local schools where they could help the Japanese learn English, while they were exposed to the Japanese language as well as local music and art. The children would have their instruction supplemented by correspondence courses from the Calvert School of Baltimore, a leading American school of that type.

Of course, Gray had been living in Japanese housing – hotels – and eating the local food so he knew those areas would pose few little problems – indeed, he considered the local rice the best in Asia. By complementing the local foodstuffs with American "B" Rations, Gray thought the civilians would do just fine.[21] But the food issue provided the impetus for the Navy commander to see another side of Al Gray. It happened at a meeting in Kami Seya at which Gray briefed all the details associated with medical care, education, housing and food. All the items except food had been approved. The supply officer, whom Gray considered to be an arrogant, condescending bureaucrat, objected to providing B Rations to Sakata on the grounds that, for example, a 10-pound can of peanut butter could not be divided among families. Captain Gray, having very patiently explained the whys and wherefores of all the dependent-related services, had had enough. He declared the meeting over.

Al Gray took very seriously his old recon platoon leader Bull Kraince's admonition to take care of his men. By 1957, having been commissioned almost five years, Gray had studied General John A. Lejeune's writings that officers' relationships with enlisted men was like that of a teacher to a student. Thus, if anyone was trying to learn their profession, or needed help accomplishing their mission, then Al Gray had almost infinite patience and a caring, supportive attitude. But Gray had little tolerance for military officers who did not know their profession or who constructed specious barriers where none should exist. Toward such people Gray could be cold, even ruthless. He told the base commander that he expected B Rations to be made available in order that families could go to Sakata, and they were. As a side benefit, Gray never encountered further problems with the more senior supply officer.

Among Gray's friends at Kami Seya was a Navy Chief Warrant Officer, Julian (Pat) Wilder and his wife Lois, whom everyone called Ned. The Wilders had four children, two older sons and younger daughters. After he left Sakata, the two Wilder boys spent two weeks with Gray in the Basic Overnight Quarters (BOQ) at Kami Seya. They accompanied the Marine everywhere he went, and they were amazed that he knew everyone they encountered – from maids to enlisted Sailors to local fishermen.[22] It had a lifelong effect on the boys, especially the older son, Patrick. More than 56 years after the event, Lieutenant Colonel Patrick D. Wilder sent a letter to his old mentor, General Al Gray. It recounts the time the Wilder boys spent in Sakata and Kami Seya with "Captain Gray." The letter says, in part:[23]

> *"Then you, Uncle Al, came into my life at Sakata, Japan with a big handle bar moustache, great smile, terrific wit and a large black Labrador Retriever named Lucky. I won't say I was ready for your vision as a young boy but looking back now you and others certainly helped prepare me to make good choices in my life.*
>
> *I want to share some memories I have of you, your words and the impact you made during my youth that still help me today.*
>
> *I read everything I can and the newspaper every day and only believe in the sports section and the funny pages. When I see what might be a UFO in the sky I look for shape, color, speed and direction. Your words helped expand my world. (My brother) Mike and I shined your shoes in Sakata and you put 100 Yen pieces in your shoes as payment. Big money in those days. My first job was shining shoes in Homestead FL at a barber shop for 25 cents afterwards. I am still employed today. (My sisters) Becky, Nancy and I bathed Lucky and tried to brush his teeth when we could catch him. Nancy loved Lucky and he was a great friend to all of us. When we couldn't find him for 3 days in Sakata we're now sure there is a lot of Lucky in Yamagata Prefecture. I named my first dog Lucky and kept him on a leash. Mike and I spent two weeks in your BOQ rooms and had a terrific time. You knew everyone by name and took us trout fishing. We ate them in the Officer's Club and then didn't want to return home. Trout is still our favorite meal. You gave us wooden models from the bottom drawer of your dresser to keep us busy before we (our dad) got transferred to Homestead FL. You were always thinking ahead. It was a big adventure for two young boys in a foreign country without their parents. (My wife)*

Linda and I invite our family kids to Camp Nonnie Nana in our home each summer without their parents. Everyone gets a project to work on when they leave and they all look forward to coming back. Great memories they all pass forward…

You inspired a young boy and helped shape a young man to become a Marine and good citizen. I know you'll say you're not worthy of this recognition but without you and others like you my life would be different.

You're a special person and the reason I'm proud to wear the emblem and uniform as a Marine Officer. It is my privilege, honor and pleasure to serve our country in our United States Marine Corp with you."

Having succeeded in building the Sakata base and hiring the required labor, Gray's efforts in Sakata almost came to naught for a reason that has ended many projects – budget cuts. In the late 1950s, reduced funding within the Department of Defense (DoD) and especially the NSG Command made continuing operations at Sakata highly problematic, even though the base had only recently been activated. President Eisenhower and his administration had decided that the nation's nuclear deterrent deserved the great bulk of the DoD money. Thus, places like Sakata were reduced or eliminated in spite of operational requirements. Having put his personal reputation on the line during the negotiations about construction and the wide ranging personnel issues, Gray was alarmed to learn that budget cuts would adversely affect, indeed ruin, the contracts and formal agreements that had been settled with the Japanese. Besides destroying the contracts, the more than 40 Japanese hired for the base would face uncertain futures if the cuts were made. For Captain Gray, far more than pride was at stake.

Adding significantly to the issue was the fact that the work rules that had been established for the Japanese meant that laying off the workers would be just as expensive as keeping them on the job. Al Gray sought a meeting with the Prefecture Governor, a graduate of the University of Massachusetts. During their discussion, the Governor never spoke English and the Marine Captain never spoke Japanese. During the time the translators were doing their work, each participant had time to frame his answer. It would not be Al Gray's last meeting with high level Japanese politicians, though the next one would occur more three decades in the future, and there would be no translators. As a result of the encounter with the Governor, the American officer decided on an unusual course of action.

Al Gray obtained individual travel orders to go to the District of Columbia so that he could personally discuss the potential problems that not funding the new base would have for American-Japanese relations, particularly at Sakata. Gray called upon those who were influential in the budget process. His efforts resulted in a reclama to the planned fiscal reductions, thus keeping the base open. The NSG was used to having "captains" dramatically affect its budgetary decisions, just not Marine Corps captains with less than two years in grade![24]

When Al Gray returned to Sakata in 1957, opened the base and turned it over to its permanent detachment, he announced that he would be leaving to return to duties at Kami Seya, far to the south. He had been living in a hotel downtown, about three miles from the base. The morning of his departure arrived and to the 28-year-old Captain's amazement, hundreds of people were outside the hotel and at the train station, ready to bid adieu to "Gray-san." His months of negotiating with local officials, of handing out hundreds of candy bars to local children, of walking throughout the town with his well-known large black dog, of eating in local restaurants and getting haircuts at local barbershops, all the while speaking and learning more Japanese, had a very positive effect on the populace. Despite the strong presence of communists and the socialists, and the largely anti-American feelings present in the city and throughout the prefecture, Captain Gray was well-liked. The people showered him with going-away gifts, enough to fill a boxcar. Gray was startled by the reaction. At least for a few moments in 1957, the anti-American sentiment had been subdued, if not eliminated.

As a result of his efforts, Al Gray was cited for his "inspirational leadership, sound judgment in the use of both money and materials and his skillful diplomacy in dealing with the people of Sakata and the officials of Yamagata Prefecture, thereby assuring their continuous cooperation."[25] But Gray's handling of the Sakata situation earned him something far more important than the citation and the friendship of the Japanese people – his reputation within the cryptologic community grew immensely.

After leaving Sakata, Gray was tasked to conduct additional special activities on the northern tip of Hokkaido at Wakkanai and Nemuro. It was as close as he could get to the Soviet-held Sakhalin Islands without getting his feet wet. He also served as Special Projects and Supplementary Detachments coordinator, which required him to lead installations of SIGINT equipment aboard various Pacific Fleet ships and submarines. Gray's skill, and the Navy's respect for him, grew to the point that he was assigned duties normally given only to professional cryptologists.

Figure 2.9
Capt Gray leaves Sakata.[26]

Figure 2.10
LT (jg) Jack Daly sits at the bar with the club manager
watching Lucky and Al Gray pour drinks for them.[27]

Captain Gray became the go-to guy for almost any special tasking. Whether the project was installing special equipment on ships, submarines or aircraft, or building more experimental antennae, Gray was given the work. He recalled that installing electronic equipment on submarines, using Japanese labor, often resulted in strange circumstances. Once, using a collection of wiring diagrams marked "Confidential" he was surprised to find that the Japanese technicians had the same book, but without any classified marking. On another occation, he was tasked to install the new Mark 8 A Periscope on a submarine, then conduct testing in Tokyo Bay. But getting the assignment done was always Gray's focus, and countless senior officers have commented officially and unofficially about his highly focused resolve to accomplish a mission, no matter how tough or how complicated.

In 1957, one of Al Gray's men, Corporal Edgar Kitt, a manual Morse intercept operator, became the first Marine to deploy aboard U.S. Pacific Fleet submarines during missions against the Soviet Union. In those days, the fact that Marines were serving aboard submarines as cryptologists was so closely held that Corporal Kitt wore a navy uniform when aboard. From Kitt's humble start, Marines would become a routine part of cryptologic detachments aboard Pacific Fleet submarines.[28]

Of the many naval officers who crossed paths with Gray, one was then Lieutenant Commander John K. (Slim) Everson, U.S. Navy. Captain Gray's performance was so outstanding, and his approaches to his craft so unusual, especially for a Marine, that Everson, who as a giant in the naval cryptologic community and had served behind the lines in China during World War II as part of the "Rice Paddy Navy," told Gray that he "would either retire a captain or become Commandant of the Marine Corps." Everson was perhaps as fine a cryptologist as the Navy as ever produced, though his ability as a soothsayer was not fully appreciated until 30 years later.[29]

Gray's work with antennae continued at Kami Seya and he learned much from a young engineer from the NSA, Louis Tordella. The two men created a mutual admiration society that benefitted both. Tordella rose through the ranks to become the longest serving Deputy Director in NSA history, while Gray advanced to the summit of the Marine Corps. Gray could thank Tordella for the solid support that NSA extended to the burgeoning cryptologic efforts in the 1960s and 1970s, while Tordella was sure that the Marines would do exactly what Al Gray said they would do.

While earning the respect of senior naval officers was important to Gray, it was his relationship with his men that truly characterized his time in Japan and throughout his 41 years in the service. Some four decades after the fact, former Corporal Doug Marcy related this story about travelling to Iwakuni, Japan with Gray:

"The next thing I remember is transferring from the train to the ferry boat and there was Captain Gray. I remember going to lunch with Captain Gray. We sat in a booth for four, Don B. [Don Behnke] and I on one side and Captain Gray on the other. The aisle seat was open and an elderly Japanese man took the open seat. He was obviously not from the highest socio-economic group of Japanese people. Captain Gray immediately started a conversation with the man. I remember being impressed at how much Japanese Captain Gray knew. They talked for a minute or two and then Captain Gray said he was asking what was good to eat on the ferry. About that time our order was taken and Captain Gray ordered the same as the Japanese man. I can't remember what Don B and I had, but when they brought Captain Gray his fish head soup, he had kind of a funny grin on his face, then looked at the older man who had taken his chopsticks, picked up his bowl and started slurping the soup and flipping in the meat. Captain Gray followed his lead but did not eat all of the fish heads. Don B. and I looked at each other and just grinned." [30]

His men never tire of telling stories about him and the warmth and respect that comes through is obvious for all to see. Then Sergeant (and later financial company Chief Executive Officer) Larry Bangs provided this insight into Gray and his leadership methods when he wrote:

"General Gray was not a looming presence...not one that the troops were intimidated by. Instead, he was very approachable and a good listener. He was always around and one never knew when he might come strolling into the squad bay or the mess hall. He had a sharp wit and great sense of humor. If you passed him on the sidewalk he would of course return the salute and then usually stop for a word. In fact what he was doing was managing by wandering around. I recall him saying to Jim Flatters as we passed him, 'hey Flatters, you'd better lay off the chow, your ass is getting wider than your shoulders!' He set very high standards but did not impose them in a heavy-handed manner. He expected us to always be personally squared away, our quarters spotless, our weapons cleaned and boots polished. No one wanted to disappoint him by failing to live up to those standards (which he himself always exhibited). He used his Staff NCOs very effectively. When he wanted something changed or improved, they were the ones to get it done and therefore he was never seen to be involved directly in any 'corrective action.'

He kept his distance, certainly never sought to be one of the guys, but it was clear to us that he respected us and did not look down on us as enlisted men. He wanted above all for us to be the best Marines he could make us. He insisted that we be Marines first, and technicians second. Our days off were frequently filled with close order drill (we had our own very good drill team), platoon maneuvers with full combat gear out in the boonies, classes on military subjects, etc. He required (or should I say strongly encouraged) us to take correspondence courses from the University of Maryland, which we all did. Finally, he did everything he could possibly do to put us (not himself) in the limelight. We were volunteered for all manner of things...parade inspections with visiting dignitaries, etc.

In summary, he was special and we knew it, and he thought we were special, and that was the ultimate compliment he could have paid us."[31]

While in Japan, Gray read everything he could on the subject of cryptology. Demonstrating one of the many traits that would characterize his professional attitude, Gray believed officers had to understand fully the background and history of their profession, and in this case it meant learning everything he could about the military application of cryptology. It helped him tremendously that Slim Everson was his boss. Everson could trace his lineage directly to the on-the-roof gang of Sailors and Marines whose efforts were so important to American success in the Pacific against the Japanese. Gray learned everything he could from the older naval officer and from the many Chief Petty Officers with whom he served. He did not sit in the company office awaiting assignment; he was out and about and learning, questioning, and doing.

In late 1957 Captain Gray received a surprising visitor from HQMC. Colonel Raymond G. Davis was part of the G-2 section at HQMC where he worked for Brigadier General James M. Masters. Colonel Davis was well known among Marines, having been awarded the Medal of Honor during the 1st Marine Division's breakout from the Chosin Reservoir in Korea after having earned a Navy Cross on Peleliu in World War II. Davis's trip was in response to General Masters's orders to create a SIGINT capability for the Marine Corps. Davis had previously traveled to Europe to investigate issues associated with the 2nd Special Communications Platoon at Bremerhaven, Germany. When Colonel Davis stopped in London to meet with the Director, Naval Security Group, Europe, Captain John Lehman, USN, he was told by Captain Lehman that if he wanted to see how Marines did things right, he should visit Captain Gray in Japan. That was the impetus for Davis's trip.

Figure 2.11
1ˢᵗ Special Communications Platoon, Naval Security Group Activity, Kami Seya, Japan (1956).
Capt Gray is seated in the front row, fourth from the left.[32]

Figure 2.12
The men of the 1ˢᵗ Special Communications Platoon have remained a close-knit group, with many
belonging to the Marine Corps Cryptologic Association, where General Al Gray is Member #1.[33]

Figure 2.13
Al Gray as a Captain of Marines at Sakata, Japan.[34]

Colonel Davis and Captain Gray had dinner at the Camp Zama Officer's Club. Camp Zama was a U.S. Army facility not far from Kami Seya. That location permitted the two Marines an uninterrupted conversation that would not have been possible at the Naval Communications Station Officer's Club, where the relatively small officer contingent would have wanted to be introduced to the visitor, especially one so well known as the highly decorated Ray Davis.

Colonel Davis was nicknamed "the Razor" because of his keen intellect and natural curiosity. Though the visiting colonel had no practical experience related to special intelligence, he spent the night probing and questioning the younger officer's views and opinions about cryptology as it applied to the Marine Corps. By then, Gray had been become an energetic disciple of cryptology, and he happily recounted his experiences while also giving his opinions regarding what Marine Corps needed to do in the future. It was the first meeting of the two men who would each become a legend within the service; it was by no means their last.

Gray's two and a half years in Japan flew by, and were very rewarding both personally and professionally. Professionally, he had mastered a new craft, SIGINT, and earned a wide reputation as a result. The senior naval officers were amazed that a young Marine officer, with no experience in cryptology, could so rapidly become so proficient in such a wide range of operational issues. Personally, he had mastered a new language (Japanese) and learned a smattering of others (Russian, Chinese, Thai and Tagalog) while getting to brush up on some Korean he had learned while serving in that war. For Gray, it was most important that his men were also highly successful. They proved that Marines could be effective cryptologists while conducting themselves with pride and decorum. During his tour at Kami Seya, all the Marines in Gray's command completed Marine Corps required correspondence courses and qualified for Good Conduct Medals, and most completed multiple college courses. Their performance was a testament to their professionalism, and a tribute to their leader.

Joe Hedrick, Gray's Executive Officer, commenting with the advantage of hindsight, recalled that Gray was also highly respected by his naval contemporaries, officers who had little in common with the plain spoken, tobacco-chewing Marine. Indeed, Hedrick thought that of all Al Gray's accomplishments, earning the respect and admiration of the junior naval officers had to be high on the list.

It was only fitting that in 1958, while on Temporary Additional Duty conducting a field operation in Thailand, supporting police in the Golden Triangle area, Al Gray received orders to report without delay to Kaneohe Bay, Hawaii, to form and activate the 1st Composite Radio Company there. While it was called a radio company, its mission was to be SIGINT, electronic warfare (EW), and signals security (SIGSEC). Gray quickly called Japan to have his personal effects and his pal Lucky shipped to Hawaii, and then he jumped on a military air transport to cross the Pacific.

FORMING 1ST COMPOSITE RADIO COMPANY, KANEOHE, HAWAII, SEPTEMBER 1958

During World War II the Marine Corps had a SIGINT capability. But the post-war drawdown saw that capability sacrificed. The Force Radio Company remained on the books at Camp Pendleton, but it was a shell of an organization. It had no linguists, no intercept equipment and really had nothing more than a modicum of counter-measures (jammers) assets. It was essentially useless for SIGINT. The company had not been used in Korea because it simply did not have the means to accomplish its mission. When, as a result of the General Hogaboom study and Commandant Pate's commitment to the Navy, the decision to form the Composite Radio Companies was made in 1958, the company at Camp Pendleton was sent to Camp Lejeune, there to become the 2nd Composite Radio Company. A new organization was to be constructed in Hawaii. The word "composite" was included in the name because a portion of the company was designed to support division operations, while another segment was intended to sustain higher level – force level – requirements.

When he was given the radio company assignment, Captain Gray had been told that he would be the Commanding Officer and that his mission included focusing on creating a Marine SIGINT and EW capability. His meeting with Colonel Ray Davis in Japan probably cemented the assignment for Gray; Davis's boss, the Marine Corps' G-2, Brigadier General James M. Masters, was tasked with re-building the SIGINT capability and the General was undoubtedly looking for officers to fill key positions. HQMC had sent Lieutenant Colonel John Reber to Hawaii as the Marine Corps representative to Naval Security Group, Pacific, and Major Charles Beale was assigned to the corresponding position in London at Naval Security Group, Europe. The Marines needed officers with operational experience to man the new radio companies, however, and that is where Gray entered the mosaic. An indication that Gray's orders were unusual was reflected by their urgency; he was given 48 hours to report.

However, as might be expected by those used to dealing with HQMC and the G-1 (Personnel) section, things happen, and they are often unintended. Very soon after Gray's arrival, two more senior captains joined the company. Though neither had any SIGINT experience, seniority dictated that he became the S-3, the Operations Officer. Among the first Staff NCOs to join the unit was Staff

Sergeant "Mouse" Green. Several years later Green would become well known in SIGINT circles as the man who transmitted the Critical Communications message that announced the North Vietnamese attack against the USS *Turner Joy*, the event that sparked President Johnson to expand the war in Vietnam.

With his usual diligence, creativity and professionalism, Al Gray set about to develop a SIGINT capability, permitting no stones to gather moss while building the 1st Composite Radio Company. It did not take Gray long to recognize the depth of the challenge that he faced. His quick personal evaluation of the issues he encountered provided far more questions than answers.

There were no office spaces or barracks for the nascent company. They were literally working out of a broom closet. However, when the Air Naval Gunfire Liaison Company left its offices to go on a month-long exercise, Gray seized the opportunity to move into the Company spaces. Of course, when that unit and its commanding officer, a lieutenant colonel, returned they sought to throw out the interlopers, but to no avail. Gray refused to budge until new quarters were found. The furor resulted in the Radio Company being sent across the island to Kaneohe Bay, and the lieutenant colonel and Gray soon reconciled to become professional friends; the more senior officer had admired Gray's chutzpah all the while he vented his anger about the situation. Although the company gained permanent spaces, there remained a multitude of challenges.

There were few men, most of whom had communications backgrounds but no SIGINT skills. There were no training aids like those he had been exposed to at Kami Seya, and there were no operating positions where the men's skills could be developed. There was some assorted equipment on hand, but it was not useful for field operations.

Perhaps the most daunting challenge was the new company's location in the middle of the Pacific Ocean. Hawaii was far, really far, from any potential adversaries; Gray had learned during his time in Japan how the American intelligence community located bases in proximity to likely targets; those locations permitted operators to hone their technical skills while monitoring live signals from potential adversaries. In addition, various SIGINT sites had a wealth of training aids and technical information available as reference materials for the technicians.

None of the advantages that Al Gray had seen in Japan were accessible to the Marines of 1st Composite Radio Company. There was a ton of work to do and no time to waste doing it. His new Company Commander and Executive Officer were quite content to give Gray great latitude in getting things done. Neither had a cryptologic background nor the professional confidence to deal with the senior officers who had little understanding of the company's mission or its needs. Following Gray's established modus operandi, he deflected credit from himself while protecting his commander and executive officer from criticism; he became the single spokesman for policy and operational matters within the company.

Even before the 1st Radio had its own offices and places to store its equipment, Gray undertook a project that he knew from his recent experience would be a prerequisite to future operations.[35]

Fleet Marine Force, Pacific, (FMFPAC) did not have its own Special Security Officer nor any equipment nor the personnel needed to undertake Special Security Officer operations. Consequently, FMFPAC had to depend on Commander-in-Chief, U.S. Pacific Fleet to send and receive its special communications.[36] Gray knew that if his efforts ever became successful, then FMFPAC would not want to continue the inefficiencies related to such an arrangement. Thus, his first action was to establish a Special Security Officer office within the FMFPAC Headquarters. But the absence of a Special Security Officer was not the only shortcoming at FMFPAC related to SIGINT operations.

The senior staff understood very little about the future mission of the 1st Composite Radio Company. There were, of course, senior officers who had special security clearances, but none of those men, there being no senior women Marines in those days, had detailed, practical knowledge of how special intelligence information was created or how it was processed. They simply knew there was something – or some unit – that "did stuff" to generate highly classified messages. Thus, in terms of assistance in SIGINT matters of any sort, Captain Gray was pretty much the Lone Ranger.

This became de facto another mission for Al Gray: training the various Marine staffs about cryptology, its advantages and why 1st Radio was essential to future success on the battlefield. Gray's mission of educating and indoctrinating other Marines about SIGINT was one that never ended during his long service, but it started in earnest on Hawaii in 1958.

Fortunately, many senior officers were supportive of the concept identified by General Hogaboom and implemented by Commandant Pate; such officers listened patiently to the requirements and then supported the growth of the cryptologic and special security capabilities. One was then Brigadier General Herman Nickerson, who was Fiscal Director and then Comptroller of the Marine Corps in the late 1950s who supported General Masters's initiatives fully; he was buying what Gray was selling.

While the senior officers at FMFPAC might not have had the background in SIGINT needed to assist Captain Gray in his assignment, they were a highly capable group and open to innovation, though they could also be strong-willed and often dogmatic until convinced that any innovation was worthwhile. Gray loved to use sports analogies, and he realized that the FMFPAC staff of 1958-1961 represented in the National Football League – they were pros.

Besides future Major General Kenny Houghton and Marlow Williams, both colonels that Gray knew from previous assignments, the FMFPAC staff included a galaxy of future generals. Future Lieutenant General Donn J. Robertson was the G-3; his assistant was future Major General Robert G. Owens, a Navy Cross recipient from World War II; the G-3 for Plans was future Assistant Commandant of the Marine Corps Samuel Jaskilka.[37] Prominent colonels, including Tom Fields, a General David M. Shoup confidante with whom Gray would later work at the HQMC, filled other staff positions. The G-1 was Colonel Chamberlain and the G-4 was Colonel Taplett; both were critical decision makers in carrying out Captain Gray's plans. The Communications-Electronics Officer was Lieutenant Colonel Bowman, and he too became a vital Gray supporter. Perhaps the most imposing of all was the old-time Chief of Staff, Colonel De Wolf (Dutch) Schatzel, with whom Gray would work very closely and from whom Gray would learn the intricacies of good staff work.

Almost as important as the support Gray received from the FMFPAC staff was the counsel and support he got from those on the Commander-in-Chief, Pacific Fleet, and even the Commander-in-Chief, Pacific staffs. Commander-in-Chief, Pacific Fleet was located down the hill in the Macalapa area while Commander-in-Chief, Pacific was with FMFPAC at Camp Smith, and both higher staffs included a number of Marines, and even more importantly, several U.S. Navy officers who had great knowledge of and a commitment to SIGINT/EW. Perhaps Gray's best support on the Fleet intelligence staff came from Major, and future Major General, H. Lloyd Wilkerson. Wilkerson's support for the Special Security Officer and other intelligence initiatives Gray put forth at 1st Radio was crucial.

When Gray first arrived in Hawaii, the 1st Radio had no practical equipment and one man. The Marines needed to organize the company soon arrived and so did some equipment. But nothing that really helped do SIGINT was available. Men needed more to do than wash trucks and clean typewriters if they were to become proficient in their cryptologic trade. Their location denied them the capability to intercept Very High Frequency (VHF) radiotelephone signals, and even hearing longer range High Frequency (HF) communications was problematic. So how could Marines learn to work against Russian, Chinese, Vietnamese, Korean or other foreign languages while idling away in paradise? It was left to Al Gray to come up with the answers.

It helped that the Radio Company, while eventually being located in the same area as the 4th Marine Regiment, part of the 1st Marine Brigade at Kaneohe Bay, reported not to the Brigade but to the FMFPAC Commanding General. In early 1958, however, the 1st Radio's site was the cause for concern. The Commanding Officer of the 4th Marines was a well-respected, highly aggressive officer who deemed anyone occupying facilities in "his" area to be part of "his" organization. Gray was determined not to let that happen, as it would highly complicate 1st Radio's future activities.

By taking the top deck of the barracks and turning it into a classified work and training area, 1st Radio could bar anyone without a proper clearance from entering. Thus, the perception of what was happening "behind the green door" was born. The green door depicted a classified area, and when combined with the numerous antennae that the unit had constructed on the roof, along with its own Special Security Officer activities, there was little chance that the domineering Commanding Officer of the 4th Marines could gain control of Gray's Company. 1st Radio was intended to be a Fleet Marine Force-level asset, and that it would remain.

Arguably Al Gray's finest and most challenging work during his entire professional life was reflected in many innovative and creative operational and training efforts related to SIGINT, EW, and SIGSEC that he instituted in the late 1950s. The training regime that Gray put into practice at 1st Radio continued into the 21st century. There was no previous example, no reference basis, no prior point of departure for the work Al Gray did on Hawaii; and without that work, which was later adopted at 2nd Composite Radio Company, there would have been no effective Marine SIGINT/EW capability in Vietnam.

The chain of command gave Gray direct access to the senior staff officers at FMFPAC. But there was no one to give the young Captain "guidance" about how to develop the budget needed to implement a professional training program for cryptology. Gray realized that his 1st Radio Marines would have to travel far and wide for both training and to gain operational experience, and travel was expensive.

Gray conceived a plan that would use four flyaway detachments, each focused on a different mission. The detachments would travel both back to the United States to receive technical training, and then deploy to various bases around the Pacific Rim. It was a concept unheard of in the Marine Corps, or any other service; but without travel funds Gray knew it could never be implemented. He began his missionary work of both convincing key FMFPAC staffers of the plan's viability and also the Marine Corps' need for well-qualified cryptologic technicians. And he let no grass grow while undertaking the effort.

The budget needed to support such training evolutions had to be created from nothing, yet Gray knew that he needed significantly more than any budget for any other Marine unit on Hawaii, or anywhere else for that matter. Indeed, obtaining approval of the 1st Composite Radio Company travel budget was a tremendous undertaking for the Marine Captain.

CREATING FLYAWAY DETACHMENTS, 1958-1961

Gray believed that if the Marine Corps wanted a cryptologic capability, then the service must also develop and support the training requirements needed for professional development. After he conceived the plan for creating flyaway detachments, he quietly worked up and began briefing the need for an annual travel budget of well over $125,000. It was an incredibly high figure for that time, and completely unprecedented – especially for an organization so small and so unknown to most Marines. Without travel monies, the entire plan was doomed to failure. Adding to the problem, skepticism within the FMFPAC Headquarters abounded.

Al Gray's missionary work related to educating the staff met with considerable success in some quarters, primarily the G-3 and G-5 sections. The officers on the staff who knew Gray and respected his work were more easily convinced that his goals were important. Chief among these may have the former commander of the Amphibious Recon Platoon, then Lieutenant Colonel and Assistant G-5 (Plans) Kenny Houghton, a man whose duties over the years intersected many times with Gray's.

But Gray developed other allies as well; for example, at the Naval Security Group, Pacific where Lieutenant Colonel Reber was assigned. Naval Security Group, Pacific provided technical direction to 1st Radio, Gray's broad initiative was enthusiastically endorsed by the Director, Captain Duane Whitlock, USN. Gray had heard stories about Captain Whitlock's expertise while serving at Kami Seya; he was among the top cryptologists in the country. The Marine Captain often sought out the older naval officer for advice and counsel, and Captain Whitlock was more than willing to provide whatever he could. Whitlock's boss in Hawaii was the Commander-in-Chief, Pacific Fleet N-2, Admiral Rufus Taylor. Admiral Taylor also liked what he heard from Al Gray. On the Commander-in-Chief, Pacific staff, Colonel John Morrison, USAF, became a key backer. Colonel Morrison was part of the NSA apparatus at the Pacific Headquarters, and only a few years in the future, Colonel (and later Major General) Morrison would have a significant role in another of Gray's operations.

Nonetheless, there was also wide skepticism and less than ringing approval from other quarters. For example, the G-2, Colonel William F. Prickett, thought that only a radio-telephone capability was needed, not the full range of duties required to support both the NSA and the NSG, which is what Commandant Pate had agreed to do, and for which Captain Gray's training program provided.

As Gray's efforts generated both interest and debate within the Headquarters, Colonel Schatzel called for a staff meeting chaired by the Commanding General, FMFPAC. Captain Gray was asked to explain and justify his wild financial necessities.

The discussion about Gray's proposal and request was wide ranging and opinions varied significantly. Despite the G-2's dissent, and the ambivalence of others, Gray had the support of several primary staff officers. While the G-2 had staff cognizance over cryptology, the G-3 had staff cognizance over EW, and the Force Communications-Electronic Officer had cognizance for the Radio's Companies tasking related to COMSEC. Thus, Gray had close working relationships throughout the staff, and he had fully briefed each component in advance of the meeting with the Force Commanding General.

After a prolonged discussion, Lieutenant General Thomas A. Wornham turned to Colonel Marlow C. Williams, the Force Comptroller, and asked his opinion. Williams replied, "Well, General, I know nothing about cryptology and understand very little of what Captain Gray is proposing, but when I knew Captain Gray at Camp Lejeune he was the best 4.2 Mortar Company Commander we ever saw, so I would be inclined to approve his request." The Commanding General was convinced.

Once again, and it would happen often during Gray's time as a Marine, doing good work in a position he did not seek (4.2 Mortar Company Commander) contributed to his success later in a professional field he had not wanted (communications-cryptology). Who knows whether Marine cryptology would have flourished like it did had not Colonel Williams known Captain Gray previously? Certainly Colonel Williams' comments were fortuitous, but there is also no doubt that Gray would have persisted in his efforts to establish meaningful training for his men. After all, his leadership philosophy did not change whether he commanded a platoon, a battalion or the Marine Corps: *do as much as you can, for as many as you can, for as long as you can.* That meant overcoming bureaucratic and administrative obstacles, prevailing over conflicting opinions, establishing unprecedented training methods, developing new operational procedures and capabilities, and finally, and perhaps most of all, freeing people to achieve as much as they can.

Gray's efforts resulted in the birth of the Flyaway Detachments. He had conceived, budgeted for and organized the four detachments; each consisted of two officers and 40 Marines who had a variety of technical capabilities. Having ensured the requests for dollars and other resources (for example, military air transportation) were successfully staffed through FMFPAC, Headquarters, Gray's plan went forward.

Each unit was placed in a cycle of basic and specialized training that started with a period of 45 to 60 days of Temporary Additional Duty at the NSA in Washington. After a couple weeks back in Hawaii, the detachment would then be assigned to forward SIGINT sites where the Marines would perform actual operations. Locations the Marines were assigned Temporary Additional Duty ranged from Gray's old stomping grounds at Kami Seya, to Okinawa, Korea, the Philippines, or Thailand. The host units were Naval Security Group Activities, Army Security Agency and Air Force Security Service installations. Early on, in 1959 or 1960, only collection and special communications functions were performed. However, as the expertise of the Marines increased, including the results of specialized on-the-job training, they also conducted analysis, crypto-analysis, processing and reporting. Thus, Marines soon were completing the whole gamut of technical tasks needed to contribute to the national intelligence effort.

Even just a collection mission, however, was sufficient for the Marines to earn a SIGINT designator, USN-414, and the detachment became 414J/K/L/M.[38] The number was always 414 but the letter denoted the type of mission each of the four detachments was assigned – be it Korea, China, Southeast Asia (Vietnam, Cambodia, Laos) or other (Indonesia, Singapore, Malaysia, Thailand). Over the years, as the Marine Corps capability grew, the personnel composition of each detachment changed to match its ultimate operational mission. For example, the linguists attached to each flyaway unit would reflect the operational site's mission; there was little reason to send Chinese linguists to sites that had missions directed toward Indonesia or Vietnam. All Marine cryptologists, however, had basic capabilities to operate against Soviet naval and air targets; that foe was ubiquitous.

Each training cycle culminated with the detachment providing direct support for major Fleet Marine Force exercises in the Western Pacific or on the West Coast. Direct support to the Marine operating forces, was, after all, the primary goal of the entire SIGINT/EW/SIGSEC program. Early on Gray had figured out that by having his men operate in close proximity to the staffs of the various high level commanders, several good things happened. First, the generals and their staffs got to know the Marines of the 1st Composite Radio Company. Second, slowly but surely those same officers came to rely more and more on the expertise that 1st Radio provided. And, of course, their presence permitted Gray at least two fundamental advantages regarding his professional education program; first, he was able to build the understanding the senior officer corps had for the capabilities and limitations of SIGINT/EW, and second, his close observation of how

Figure 2.14
Working as a cryptologist in the Philippines.[39]

to integrate the Radio Companies into the Force structure aided him in making improvements going forward.

Gray's frequent trips to NSA with various detachments permitted him to build relationships there, and one important one was with David W. Gaddy, the head of the North Vietnamese desk. Little did either man realize how intertwined their future activities would become. Gray also was able to renew his friendship with Dr. Louis Tordella, the NSA engineer with whom he had worked in Japan while learning new techniques related to constructing antennae. He also became friends with Dr. Milt Zaslow, who headed the Chinese Directorate and who made his people available to help the Marines. Zaslow, a legendary member of the NSA Cryptologic Wall of Honor, became an ardent supporter of the Marine Corps and their young pioneer.

Al Gray was a field Marine, always had been and, as it turned out, always would be. He knew that his cryptologic detachments had to first be exemplary Marines before they could be technicians. From the first group sent to the field to support other SIGINT units and other Marines, the flyaway teams from Hawaii were self-sufficient. The detachments were configured so that they could be carried anywhere in the Pacific by VR-21, the fleet logistics aircraft. They asked for very little if anything, and they worked hard to give information to those they were in proximity to. Thus, whether it was an Air Force Security Service installation in Korea or a Naval Security Group Activity on Okinawa, an Army Security Agency operation in the Philippines or a Marine Brigade Headquarters on a training exercise in Thailand, the SIGINT Marines provided all the support they could. Nevertheless, breakthroughs in the attitudes of senior Marines toward SIGINT came slowly, but they came.

While on a large Marine Expeditionary Force training exercise on Taiwan, a rubber boat full of recon Marines had been swept out to sea by a current that was far too strong for them to overcome. The Marine general in command of the exercise was vexed for days as extensive search and rescue operations came up empty-handed. But then Gray's SIGINT detachment picked up a Japanese trawler's radio transmission saying that it had plucked a boat full of Marines from the middle of the ocean, and the fishermen were taking the Marines to Yokohama. The flyaway detachment, collocated with the general aboard the flagship, was able to convey to him the good news, and SIGINT earned another advocate in the senior ranks. In this case it was Lieutenant General Wornham, the Commanding General of FMFPAC, who was also commanding the Landing Force in this exercise. General Wornham had probably not realized that his earlier approval of Gray's astonishingly large travel budget would be paid back in spades so soon. Indeed, it was a very, very happy General who heard of the safe recovery of his reconnaissance unit.

Al Gray realized that the Marine Corps would never have sufficient numbers of men to permit them to be highly specialized; consequently, he encouraged his men to cross-train as much as possible. Thus, it was not unusual for Marines to begin to pick up elementary language skills, to learn about other targets, and, especially, to show initiative. Captain Gray knew the men he led were among the finest, and often the brightest, in the Corps, and he set high standards for them. They never disappointed him while earning the respect of both the other services' cryptologic agencies and the Marine staffs with whom they deployed.

That Gray worked long hours was obvious in his performance at every stop during his 41 years of service. In Hawaii, Gray's habits were constantly on display. In addition to taking every Temporary Additional Duty opportunity that came to the Radio Company, his dedication to getting things done right was legendary. By being the detachment commander, Gray assured the men would receive the best training and best experience he could provide; further, it permitted him to train junior officers in how to conduct each aspect of the flyaway team's mission. He was seldom in Hawaii for extended periods of time. Gray's tour on the island paradise lasted 32 months; he actually was there nine.

Perhaps no one has a better Al Gray story of that era than Chief Warrant Officer - 4 Jim Wiese. Wiese, a former enlisted cryptologist, was serving as a new Warrant Officer - 1 in the Accountable Officer billet in 1st Radio; he was the guy charged with keeping track of all the equipment. Wiese relates this story of dealing with Captain Gray:

> *"One type of example was his disregard for 'working hours.' He was getting ready to go on one of his famous WestPac* [Western Pacific] *trips and as usual working late. He called me at my quarters* [at Kaneohe Bay] *about 0300* [3 A.M.] *and said 'Jim, what are you doing?' Still having my wits about me, I answered 'what did you think?' His response was, 'well, when you're done, come on in to work, we need to go over some stuff.' About 0730* [7:30 A.M.] *we finally finished up the necessary business, so he said, 'well, let's go home, take a shower and get into uniform and get back to work!!!!!!!!!!!!!!!!!' Typical of that guy."* [40]

Gray remained full of activity with a myriad of cryptologic efforts, though supporting the Fleet Marine Forces was always his highest priority.

As successful as Gray had been, the path had been fraught with controversy, strong disagreements about both substantive and financial issues, and some strong-willed officers opposed Gray's program at almost every step. Colonel Prickett, FMFPAC G-2, headed the skeptics.

Colonel William Prickett had been a young lieutenant when captured at Corregidor with the rest of the 4th Marines when the Japanese overran the Philippine Islands shortly after the start of World War II. In keeping with the policy then in effect, he received regular promotions during the war whenever his classmates were promoted. As a result, when he was repatriated in 1945, he was the one of the youngest colonels in the Marine Corps. By the time Al Gray arrived in Hawaii in 1957, Colonel Prickett was a grizzled veteran, and the very formidable G-2 at the highest Marine Headquarters in the Pacific. Formidable does not always have a good connotation, and unfortunately that was the case with Colonel Prickett. Make no mistake, however, Prickett was quite self-confident about his views; in fact, he was a regular contributor to the *Marine Corps Gazette* during the period 1949 through 1962. But Prickett also knew many sides to Al Gray.

During weeks that Gray found himself in Hawaii, he sometimes taught Sunday school classes at Pearl Harbor, where William Prickett was the head teacher. The two men had a congenial relationship, though Gray, who had as much practical experience in cryptology and serving with the NSG as any Marine officer then in service, found himself sometimes thwarted by the G-2.

Colonel Prickett questioned, frustrated, or even tried to foil Gray's efforts. The younger man was also tested in his ability to simply get along with the senior officer. By this time, several seniors had noted Gray's friendliness and the fact that he was a pleasant shipmate. But Colonel Prickett tested those opinions. During one animated exchange Prickett told Gray that he was being rude. Gray, bewildered at the charge, retorted that he had never been rude to anyone in his life. "Well," responded Prickett, "your voice is louder than mine." Listening in the next room, Prickett's deputy, Lieutenant Colonel Wesley Noren, USMC, fondly retold the tale throughout the Headquarters: "you will never guess what Al Gray did today," the story would start.

So while Colonel Prickett had staff cognizance over SIGINT matters, Lieutenant Colonel Reber exercised some technical control of the operations of the Radio Company as he was in the chain for the NSG. The major disagreements over matters such as training requirements, flyaway teams, and the need for extensive travel throughout the Pacific resulted in strong professional difference of opinion that eventually came to the notice of the General Masters in Washington. Reber thought the FMFPAC G-2 was throwing unnecessary roadblocks on the path of progress, and he was none too happy about it. Caught in the middle was the hard-working Captain who was the Operations Officer of the Radio Company and the de facto leader of the program.

General Masters became increasingly concerned by the cantankerous dispute in Hawaii. When Gray returned to HQMC to attend the annual Intelligence Symposium, the General asked Gray to stop by his office.[41] Gray arrived and was surprised to find himself in a meeting not only with General Masters, an impressive officer who wore a deep blue ribbon with a broad, vertical white center stripe denoting a Navy Cross, but also Colonel Ray Davis, his former dining companion at Camp Zama. It was heady company for the young Captain.

The senior duo asked that Captain Gray tell them exactly what was happening in Hawaii with respect to the ongoing dispute over intelligence matters, at least insofar as they affected the Radio Company's activities. Gray, never one to reveal private conversations to third parties, balked at speaking, even in confidence. But General Masters and Colonel Davis persisted; they were, it was clear, intent on learning Gray's view of what was happening between the two intelligence professionals. Gray very reluctantly revealed his analysis of the situation. Satisfied with his account, a pause in the conversation gave Gray reason to believe the interview had ended and he got up and asked permission to leave. "Where are you going?" asked the General. "I am going to turn in my letter to resign," answered Gray. That moment was one of the closest Al Gray ever came to resigning; he thought he had betrayed the special trust and confidence afforded officers by making critical remarks about senior officers, and resigning was the only way to make it right.

What followed was a highly charged conversation during which the two senior officers reiterated their concept of the "good of the service." But the two senior Marines went even farther. Gray was directed to return to Hawaii and continue to do exactly what he had been doing. No matter whom he had to go around, go over or go through, just get the mission done were Gray's marching orders. Predictably, neither General Masters nor Colonel Davis explained how a captain was supposed to accomplish that mission. Happily, the same coterie of officers who had supported Gray's efforts to implement the Company's training program also supported his efforts to successfully navigate the troubled waters surrounding the FMFPAC G-2.

Al Gray would soon learn of General Masters' high regard for him. Though it was extremely unusual, the G-2 of HQMC sent a personal letter directly to the Operations Officer of 1st Composite Radio Company. General Masters' admiration for Gray's efforts was reflected in the letter, which read in part:

*"I have just received the report of your specialized operational train-
ing at National Security Agency. I wish to express my deep pride in
your accomplishment and that of the men who composed the training
team. It is no mean task for a Marine to go to NSA and do so well,
particularly when we are new in the program. However, the reputation that the Marines have achieved at NSA is due primarily to the
effort expended by those like you and the men of your team.*

*It is not only the written reports… When someone such as Admiral
Kurtz makes a remark, even though partly in humor, 'that we are
now seeing a fourth cryptologic service,' it's an indication that even
the professionals in the business are impressed by the performance of
duty of the Marines that they have observed."* [42]

During their meeting, Gray had not known that General Masters recognized
very well exactly what Gray had been up to; Masters had been told by NSA about
the excellent work that the Hawaii Marines were doing to support the Agency and
to build a cryptologic organization. Colonel Ray Davis had shared with Gray that
General Masters desired to build a cryptologic program during their evening in
Japan, and what Gray had been working to implement in Hawaii was precisely what
General Masters needed done. That Gray would soon be a vital part of that project
at HQMC was still unforeseen, however, at least by Al Gray. There can be no doubt
that the energetic Captain was, as early as 1959, well known to many high level
decision makers, the officers charged with guiding SIGINT into the mainstream of
the Marine Corps.

In later years, Al Gray would often remind younger officers who were frustrated
by more senior bosses, "You sometimes do not work for people who know more than
you do; nevertheless, you have to get the mission done." Little ever got between Al
Gray and completing his assignment. Colonel Prickett was a tough case, though,
even for Al Gray. Nonetheless, Gray always maintained the highest respect and
admiration for the Colonel, who had courageously endured the long and brutal
captivity of the Japanese and who was dedicated to improving the Marine Corps
intelligence capabilities.

General Masters would assume an even bigger role in Al Gray's life in the not-
too-distant future. But the Captain's successes in Hawaii resulted in more than just
letters from faraway generals, however, and the fruits of the newly implemented

1st Radio training program and the expenditure of the large amounts of travel funds did not take long to ripen.

Perhaps the one detachment that most exemplified the efforts put forth by Gray's Marines occurred in the Philippines in the fall of 1959. Deployed in reaction to the developing situation in Southeast Asia, including Laos and Vietnam, and given a signal search and analysis mission by the NSA, the Marines set up their equipment in a field outside a U.S. Army Security Agency's permanent installation at Clark Field. The Marines, operating from tents, strung concertina wire for site security and made antennae for their operations. After a few weeks, Gray's unit was moved to Thailand, but not before the prodigious results turned in by Gray's men had greatly enhanced the intelligence production of the local Army unit, cementing Gray's reputation at the NSA.[43]

The expertise demonstrated by the detachment reflected the innovative training methods that Gray had utilized. By first learning all they could from the experts at the NSA, then maintaining their proficiency by listening to tapes of intercepted Morse and voice communications, as well as by using live traffic, Gray had trained his men to recognize signals from many target areas across the Pacific. When they arrived on the scene, they were ready to go to work and be productive.

By the time Gray departed Hawaii in 1961, and for the first time since World War II, Marine cryptologists, led by Captain Al Gray, participated in a series of operational exercises throughout the Pacific. Gray also prepared SIGINT annexes to various Pacific Fleet Operations Plans, something that had never before been done. During those years, 1958 through 1961, Gray and his men supported eight brigade-level and three Marine Expeditionary Force exercises throughout the Pacific, from California to Thailand. Gray not only led the cryptologic efforts, but also he taught the supported staffs about the use and exploitation of SIGINT, including the capabilities and limitations of his men and equipment. Throughout this period, Gray was the Company's primary interface with Fleet Marine Forces, Pacific. The many personal contacts made with brigade and force staffs during his time in Hawaii would stand Gray in good stead in the future.

Besides supporting operational exercises, Gray interacted with the staffs of various headquarters in other important ways. First, he worked to prepare detailed operational support plans for all contingency requirements in the Pacific, including coordinating instructions for all cryptologic installations in the area. Second, in conjunction with the NSA and Naval Security Group, Pacific, and Commander-in-Chief, Pacific Fleet, Gray planned for, developed and implemented the standard operating procedures for certified Special Intelligence/Special Security installations for the 1ˢᵗ Marine Division at Camp Pendleton, Air FMFPAC and the Marine Air Wings at El Toro, California, and Iwakuni, Japan; and FMFPAC in Honolulu. The consequence of those efforts was that Gray knew almost every intelligence, operations and communications officer and Staff NCO working in the Pacific, and, as importantly, they knew him. The installation of the Special Security Officer capabilities in each major headquarters was particularly noteworthy.

The Marine Corps was the first service to achieve its goal related to Special Security Officer systems; Gray's role was remarkable and brought him to the attention of many senior Marine commanders. More importantly, as a result of those efforts, the Marine commands all had special communications capabilities long before the other services did. At least in their garrison headquarters area that was true – it remained for Gray to address the issue of Special Communications and Special Intelligence for deployed Division, Wing or Brigade staffs at a later date.

THE LAOTIAN CRISIS, 1960

Dutch Schatzel, the FMFPAC Chief of Staff, was a Marine legend by the late 1950s. As a 2ⁿᵈ Lieutenant, Schatzel began his career in China and in 1939 he was the last commander of the Mounted (Horse) Detachment of the Legation Guard in Peking (now Beijing). Following World War II, as a Lieutenant Colonel, Schatzel had been part of the Chowder Society, the small group of Marine officers led by Brigadier General Merrill Twining, whose membership included then Lieutenant Colonel Victor (Brute) Krulak. The Chowder Society is generally credited with saving the Marine Corps from oblivion, a story told in General Victor Krulak's *First to Fight*, a must-read for any Marine. Schatzel then went on to write the *Marine Corps Staff Manual* while becoming its leading practitioner. On two occasions, Colonel Schatzel took the opportunity to laud Gray's leadership traits, professionalism, and ability to plan for the future.[44]

If the impressive FMFPAC team of officers provided Captain Gray with an informal Masters Degree in staff work, then during his last operation in the Pacific, supporting Major General Donald M. Weller's 3ʳᵈ Marine Division during the Laotian crisis, Captain Gray proved that he was an honor graduate.

It was 1960, and there was a major crisis brewing in Laos. President John F. Kennedy was highly agitated about developments there, and he passed his concerns down the chain of command.[45] Captain Gray was collocated on Okinawa with General Weller, providing the General's Special Security Officer capability as well as a SIGINT detachment, when his Commanding Officer from 1ˢᵗ Radio, Major Henry von der Heyde, came visiting.[46] The General received a very highly classified message from Commander-in-Chief, Pacific Fleet, Admiral Herbert G. Hopwood, in which the Admiral revealed that he had ordered the 1st Marine Division, already aboard ship for landing exercises, to steam north of Oahu under radio silence and proceed directly to Okinawa to be ready for operations in Southeast Asia. Only an enlisted Marine, who had labored to decrypt the communication, and Captain Gray saw the message before it was delivered personally to General Weller. Gray realized that the message indicated that two Marine divisions were preparing for operations in Laos; and he never forgot the dramatic wording Admiral Hopwood had used. It was very big stuff.

Major von der Heyde learned that something of significance had happened, but did not know exactly what. He asked Al Gray about any messages that might have been received, then became upset that Captain Gray refused to show him the communication in question. It did not take the Major too long before he realized that Gray, true to form, was simply doing what was required. It was, of course, General Weller's decision to release the contents of any classified message, not Captain Gray's. Major von der Heyde, despite his status as the Company Commander, had no reason to know the message's contents.

Gray and his men had been alerted to support possible operations in both Vientiane and Seno, Laos. In fact, the initial plans called for the Radio Company detachment to be committed ashore at L-Day minus 2 (i.e., two days before the assault elements would land). Given freedom of movement by his position and in keeping with his long-standing modus operandi, the Gray Ghost finagled a flight into Laos and moved around undercover in civilian clothes, continuing a practice that would last his entire career.[47] Gray believed in seeing and experiencing things for himself whenever possible. So while the American diplomats negotiated, and finally frittered away hegemony over most of Laos to the communists from Hanoi, Captain Gray was conducting a personal reconnaissance getting ready for action.

Almost always part of any Gray visit anywhere in the world was a stop at the American Embassy to speak with the Marine Security Guards. They could provide valuable information about the happenings on the ground in the area. By this time in his career (1960) he probably also knew the local representative of the CIA, or at least how to contact that person. His deployment to Thailand in 1957, while still stationed in Japan, most likely had been coordinated with the intelligence community. Between the Embassy Marines and whatever other sources he had, Captain Gray developed his own plans for his detachment, should it be committed to the operation. Gray's preparations would be based on recent, first-hand information. As it turned out, however, while on the ground in Vientiane, Gray was notified that the operation was cancelled. He returned to his unit on Okinawa with the 3rd Marine Division and Commander, Joint Task Force 116.

During the trip, Al Gray formulated an idea for something General Weller required, something that the time-consuming process of decrypting the Commander-in-Chief, Pacific Fleet message had reminded him to ask for in future operations.

At that time, when the Marine SIGINT units were operating in the field and aboard ship and they needed to communicate with the NSA, the process necessitated an operator and often an officer to encrypt and decrypt messages using offline crypto-equipment. This method was time-consuming and slow; indeed, painstakingly tedious would be the best way to describe the technique used. Just like he had installed for the Special Security Officer at the Headquarters of FMFPAC soon after his arrival, the embarked Marines needed automated machines for encryption and decryption. Such machines that would speed the process and permit the exchange of information needed to work against the enemy. Gray presented General Weller with an operational requirement for new special communications equipment for use during deployments. The General, who had so recently seen both the importance of and the need for rapid special communications, promptly signed and sent it forward before Gray had left Okinawa to return to Hawaii.

Of course, "operational requirements" from commanding generals of a Marine division weave a tortuous path before they reach the Commandant. There are many endorsements – approvals – required from intermediate commands, and at every level there is the possibility of the request being denied. But in this case, Captain Gray was fairly certain he knew how to grease the skids.

Above the 3rd Division in the chain of command was the headquarters of the FMFPAC, where the Chief of Staff, Colonel Schatzel, admired Captain Gray very much. FMFPAC would pose no issues. Gray, passing through Hawaii on his way to a Permanent Change of Station orders to HQMC, paused long enough to prepare the staff work that would gain Weller's requirement of a positive endorsement at Commander-in-Chief, Pacific Fleet. In that regard, he was aided by Admiral Taylor, the N-2; indeed, Admiral Taylor's concurrence meant the requirement received quick approval at Commander-in-Chief, Pacific. At both higher headquarters, the Marine Captain who personally accompanied the paperwork was well known, and his explanations for the requirement were accepted without any need for elaboration.

Gray, having taken the time to personally walk the requirement through the various staffs, thus ensured that it left Hawaii even before he gathered up his personal belongings, his new dog, Lucky II, and took his leave of the island.[48]

Al Gray was on his way to Washington. About the only bad thing that had happened on Hawaii was that big Lucky, everyone's favorite Labrador Retriever, had become the victim of heartworms. The big dog contracted the disease while in a long period of quarantine in Hawaii after his arrival from Japan. Al Gray buried Lucky on a hillside above Kaneohe overlooking the home of the 1st Composite Radio Company. Fortunately, the Captain had arranged to breed Lucky before losing him, and his new dog, Lucky II, was the 110-pound runt of the resulting litter; two littermates became seeing-eye dogs, and two others became drug-sniffing Labs. Lucky II's travel back to the United States was far less complicated than had been big Lucky's trip to Japan six years earlier.

It was a chance assignment to Communications Officer School that had led Captain Alfred Mason Gray, Jr. into the mysterious world of SIGINT, EW and SIGSEC. In the 1950-1970 Marine Corps, those fields were so secretive that many officers steadfastly avoided learning anything about them lest their careers in combat arms be adversely affected. But Gray embraced his new specialty. By 1961, he had become the Marine Corps' most proficient practitioner, its foremost advocate, and its most polished educator on matters related to SIGINT and ground-based EW. Gray was convinced that SIGINT would save Marine lives on the battlefield and he was determined to prove his beliefs to others.

VIETNAM HISTORY, 1955-1961

WASHINGTON, 1955-1961

The Eisenhower Administration had done little to assist the French in Indochina. There were several reasons. First and foremost, the American President did not believe that the Europeans should be maintaining "colonial empires." The British Empire was but a shadow of its former self, with India, Pakistan, Burma (now Myanmar), and Ceylon (now Sri Lanka) all gaining their independence within a couple of years after the end of World War II. The British opted to voluntarily loosen their ties to Empire. The French, on the other hand, stubbornly hung on until defeated in Algeria in 1962. Previously, in the mid-1950s, France had permitted Tunisia and Morocco to become independent only upon threat of armed insurrection. Thus, the loosening of empire strings by both France and Great Britain, combined with the unmitigated rise of Soviet expansionism and a full-fledged communist government in China, gave Washington more than a full diplomatic plate. Finally, and perhaps the biggest single factor in the Eisenhower view of Southeast Asia, was the Korean Conflict, which was winding down simultaneously with the French defeat in Indochina.

Containing communism had been a primary American goal since President Harry S. Truman's decision to keep Greece from falling to communists in 1948; however, the idea of "avoiding a land war in Asia" was also a dominant American military theme, stopping the spread of communism notwithstanding. Nonetheless, having lost mainland China and the whole of eastern Europe to what was then considered monolithic communism, no American President could stand aside passively and permit yet more of the globe to fall to such threats to freedom. While Eisenhower wavered over a course of action in the months leading up to Dien Bien Phu, one of the leaders of the U.S. Senate was among those politicians who argued forcefully against military intervention.[49] That person was the indefatigable Lyndon Baines Johnson, the senior senator from Texas. A decade later, it would be Johnson who was making the decisions about American involvement in Southeast Asia.

President Eisenhower had altered the entire United States military in order to meet a possible challenge from the Soviet Union. Part of his decision-making was to reduce the emphasis on conventional warfare in favor of building nuclear capabilities in all areas, from bombs that could be delivered from aircraft and ships to tactical nuclear shells that the artillery could fire. Intercontinental ballistic missiles were just becoming the rage, and their price tags consumed a major portion of the defense budget. Budget cuts to conventional forces were deep into the bones of the U.S. Army and Marine Corps.

On the other hand, the American military had an abundance of out-moded and obsolete weaponry that might be useful to the South Vietnamese. Thus, Eisenhower, without much fanfare or sense of commitment, permitted an American advisory group to be established in Saigon to train the South Vietnamese and supply them with discarded or unused American weapons. Unfortunately, it was lost on many Americans, especially politicians and reporters, that numerous officers and men in the Army of the Republic of Vietnam (ARVN) had much more experience fighting their enemy (the Viet Cong (VC) and the Vietminh before them) than did the Americans. Moreover, the Americans committed a cardinal error right from the start: instead of helping to create an army designed for the environment and culture found in Vietnam, the U.S. advisors tried to replicate the American Army of Korea and World War II. Consequently, instead of ARVN soldiers learning to live among the people and subsist on rice and local foods, like their VC counterparts, they lived in American-style barracks and went into the field carrying 80-pound backpacks that seemed nearly as large as they were.

Nonetheless the introduction of such weapons as T-28 trainer aircraft, reconfigured as attack planes, gave the South Vietnamese some air power, and M-113 armored personnel carriers (APCs) provided the ARVN with much needed mobility in the wet, marshy areas of the Mekong Delta. By 1959 there were 750 or so American advisors in South Vietnam. Many of them realized the complexities of the Saigon's political situation, but no one in Washington ever seemed to ask for their opinions. After all, everyone in Washington knew everything they needed to know – or so they believed.

SAIGON, 1955-1961

While Ho Chi Minh was the undisputed leader of what came to be known as North Vietnam, the leadership situation in the South was far cloudier, even murky. No one except a small minority wanted to retain the Emperor Bao Dai, but there was no charismatic figure stepping forward. The central candidate, however, was Bao Dai's Prime Minister, the devoutly Catholic Ngo Dinh Diem.

Ho Chi Minh and his movement had tried aggressively to recruit Ngo Dinh Diem into their ranks. Indeed, Ho came to view Diem as perhaps the only man who could realistically oppose his own goal to lead a unified country. That is, of course, surprising, since most Americans have come to the view that Diem was a corrupt, uninspiring, aloof and largely incompetent politician.

Nothing is further from the truth. Most Americans adopted the views of the American reporters in Saigon, and those American reporters' view of Diem was forever tarnished by the "elections" of 1955. That was the event Diem used to remove Bao Dai permanently, and marked the founding of the Republic of Vietnam (South Vietnam). It was surprising that reporters of the war, and those who later wrote histories about it, led by men like Stanley Karnow, Neil Sheehan, Peter Arnett, A.J. Langguth, David Halberstam and others, expected a country with absolutely no tradition in having any national elections, much less free elections, to have American-style voting processes and procedures.[50] When open elections were not forthcoming, the American reporters then used the events to charge criminal activity on the part of the local politicians, in this case Diem. (Such expectations were both unrealistic and bizarre, given that after more than 200 years of freedom, people in New York, Chicago, Detroit and other American cities and many states still encounter massive electoral frauds.)

Also interesting, when reviewing the Vietnam literature, is the pass that Ho Chi Minh is given by these same stalwarts of freedom. Ho had only ever held one election, which he used to identify and then liquidate his opponents, yet men like Karnow and Langguth consider him a true national leader while dismissing Diem.[51] A better explanation of the news coverage by these men is that these reporters developed a strong distaste for American involvement in Vietnam, and used whatever justification they could find – or fabricate – to attack the war. Certainly no objective observer, comparing the regimes of Ngo Dinh Diem and Ho Chi Minh, would find the latter preferable in any sense.

A much more even-handed analysis of Diem and his administration is found in Mark Moyar's book, *Triumph Forsaken*.[52] Moyar painstakingly refutes many of the conclusions drawn by Karnow, Sheehan and other early reporters of the war. In many cases, he uses their original reports to disprove their later conclusions.

What cannot be denied is that Diem put in a masterful performance as President of his nascent republic. A devout Catholic, from a large, influential and extended Catholic family, Diem was well regarded at an early age. Spurned by his only serious girlfriend, he lived a chaste existence when others around him, including his older brother who was a priest, dallied widely. Another brother, Ngo Dinh Khoi, had been the Regional Governor of Quangnam Province, the area south of Hué that encompasses Da Nang. When the communists murdered him and his son in 1945, the action crystallized Diem's opposition to the Vietminh (the forerunner to the VC). He used the event to explain personally to Ho Chi Minh his decision not join Ho's party.[53]

Diem's path to power went right through the Emperor Bao Dai, the very man he tossed out in the rigged election. They had met in France, where the latter was in exile until the Geneva Accords granted him South Vietnam. Being anything but a leader, Bao Dai turned to Ngo Dinh Diem as his prime minister. Interestingly, as the years went by the American anti-war movement claimed that the United States government had handpicked Diem. In fact, Bao Dai needed a premier with solid anti-communist credentials who had not overtly collaborated with the Japanese. Diem was essentially the only South Vietnamese of any stature who filled the bill.

Once appointed, Diem quickly moved to establish a power base within the newly created Army, and in doing so he astonished the local observers by quickly wielding the military to concentrate power, in the process eliminating militias loyal to various religious factions and the French. Moreover, by the end of 1956, Diem had dramatically reduced the influence of the communists in South Vietnam. In a rare propaganda victory, Diem successfully labeled the communist insurgents the "Viet Cong" – short for Vietnamese Communists. Given his powerbase of Catholics and land-owning peasants, opposition to the communists was wide-ranging throughout the country.

Another reason that the anti-communist movement gained strength was because of the unrestrained behavior demonstrated by Ho Chi Minh and his followers in North Vietnam in the years following the Geneva Accords (1954). More than a million peasants were put to death in the rice-rich Red River Delta. In addition, more than 800,000 Catholics and other non-communists fled south in early 1955, as the Accords gave Ho control of the north. The combination of executions and defections turned North Vietnam from one of the world's great rice producers to a country dependent on its allies for its basic food requirements. Whatever the intemperance that Diem might have shown in the south towards his enemies, who sought the violent overthrow of the internationally constituted government, it paled in comparison to the treatment of Ho Chi Minh toward his own people. But, according to the American reporters, Ho was the true nationalist, while Diem was characterized as corrupt, weak and unpopular. In recent years, other opinions have emerged that balance the picture.[54]

To be sure, there were excesses in Diem's rule. Most of these could be traced to his brother, Ngo Dinh Nhu, and his brother's flamboyant wife, Madame Nhu.[55] Nhu was in charge of his brother's security apparatus and propaganda. It was primarily due to Nhu's relentless and very aggressive counter-intelligence activities that the Vietminh, now re-labeled Viet Cong, were considerably reduced to a small cadre of only their most loyal followers by 1958 and 1959. So while the communists had been executing their enemies in the countryside for years, and would continue to do so during the entire war, it was Diem and especially Nhu who caught the wrath of the Americans – both the reporters and governmental officials. While assassination is never acceptable to Americans of any time or age, the communists were masters of that means of intimidation. Diem and even his brother never reached the same league. Although taking such extreme measures to rout out enemies was un-American and not the type of things done in a free society, it was not as though Diem had time to convert his adversaries through the more leisurely approach of political persuasion. Finally, the communists never willingly negotiated with their opponents, a fact lost – or simply ignored – in most the early histories of the Vietnam War.

While it is also true that the Eisenhower Administration had few, if any, alternatives to Diem, it is certainly accurate to state that Diem skillfully maneuvered through the minefield that was international politics. He made no secret that he wished to replace French support with that from the Americans, and, as described above, the Americans were actively looking for someone to support. Everyone from the intractable John Foster Dulles to foreign policy amateur Lyndon Johnson endorsed Diem, though none seemed to have high expectations for him or his government. That was especially true when it became evident to General J. Lawton Collins, the then (1955) ambassador, that Diem was much more likely to follow the advice of the Nhus than that of Collins. Regrettably, that turned out to be one of Diem's biggest mistakes. While he relied on the Americans for aid and American military advisors to train his army in a variety of new equipment and tactics (such as, for example, helicopter assaults), he could not simply suffer fools quietly; rather, he ignored them altogether. Not that all the Americans were fools.

Then Colonel Edward G. Lansdale, USAF and former member of the Office of Strategic Studies during World War II, arrived in Saigon in 1954. He was fresh from a successful tour in the Philippines, where he advised Ramon Magsaysay's defeat of the communist-led Hukbalahap rebels. Though Ambassador Collins and most Americans had little regard for Diem, Lansdale embraced the Vietnamese leader and proved to be a ruthless, resourceful and highly effective aide to the South Vietnamese President. Lansdale knew that the key to rooting out the insurgency was to separate the insurgents from the people, a concept that men such as Stanley Karnow later derisively characterized as "simple."[56] Lansdale helped Diem in many ways, and in many different areas, from domestic politics to psychological warfare to disruptions within the communist-controlled north. During Diem's climatic showdown against the French-backed Binh Xuyen sect in 1955, Lansdale's support was critical and Diem's resulting success surprised just about every other observer.

The event cemented Diem's regime, and the Americans rewarded him by sending a new Ambassador who pledged America's full support. Lansdale remained loyal to the Vietnamese leader even after he returned to the Pentagon in 1957. Unfortunately, despite Lansdale's recommendations to his superiors in Washington, his counter-insurgency plans were never implemented.[57]

Nonetheless, the years 1956 through 1961 had, by many measures, been fruitful for the South Vietnamese. Diem had addressed the VC aggressively, in part by establishing "Agrovilles." These were strong, fortified villages designed to separate the villagers from the insurgents. While the idea was good, oft times the implementation was spotty. And when Diem's cohort did not treat the locals with respect and tolerance, they bred support for the guerrillas. On the other hand, there was the beginning of support for Saigon, and Uncle Ho definitely was concerned about Diem, whom he continued to view as the only other viable leader of Vietnam. Even Stanley Karnow, perhaps grudgingly, accepted the North Vietnamese view of Diem.[58] Of course, Karnow – like many other journalists – was getting most of his information about the Diem government and its acceptance in the countryside from the communist agent turned *TIME* reporter, Pham Xuan An, thus coloring Karnow's understanding of local affairs.

In fact, Pham Xuan An's influence cannot be under-estimated. As John Guilmartin points out, almost all that reporters like Halberstam, Karnow, and Sheehan knew about the social and political dynamics of South Vietnam had been spoon fed to them by Pham Xuan An, a communist intelligence officer. The North Vietnamese Army (NVA) agent had started as a stringer for Reuters, but went on to become the *TIME* Bureau Chief in Saigon by the time the city fell in 1975. Among many misconceptions he created, Pham Xuan An convinced the American reporters that the Buddhists were a majority, which was utter hogwash. Perhaps a majority of the people observed some elements of Mayahana Buddhism, which is more a philosophy than a religion, but the percentage of practicing Therevada Buddhists never exceeded 15-20%.[59]

But Diem had bigger issues than peasants disaffected by his brother's aggressive management of the countryside. In 1960, the North Vietnamese decided to commit major numbers of forces to the south, and the cadres of VC who had fled north during the previous years, thereby escaping Diem's clutches, returned in force.

Traveling via the Ho Chi Minh Trail, well-trained, well-equipped and well-led VC battalions returned to all areas of South Vietnam, including the Mekong Delta.[60] By the end of 1959, Diem had beaten the insurrection by local communists; after 1960, he had to prove he could defeat an invasion.

As 1961 closed, the Diem government was in fairly good shape. The American press had not yet fully turned against him, and the support in Washington to not permit the communists to succeed was, in fact, growing, for whatever were the reasons.

NOTES AND REFERENCES

1. A "Regular" officer is denoted by "USMC" after his name and rank. A "reserve" officer is denoted by USMCR. The number of "Regular" officers in the service is fixed by law, and usually any officer desirous of making the military a profession seeks to become a "Regular" officer. There are, however, some reserve officers who remain on active duty through retirement. Graduates of the Naval Academy and some others start their profession as Regulars.
2. Colonel Gordon H. West went on to become the Marine Corps' official advisor to Hollywood, advising directors in matters related to Marines in the movies.
3. Junior School is now the Marine Expeditionary Warfare School, and "Fleet Marine Force" is now simply "Marine Force."
4. General Hogaboom was the Commanding General who awarded Al Gray a Letter of Appreciation when Gray left the 1st Marine Division in Korea. Al Gray had many personal reasons to respect General Hogaboom and his work.
5. William K. Jones retired as a Lieutenant General in command of Fleet Marine Forces, Pacific. His nephew, General James L. Jones was the 32nd Commandant of the Marine Corps, after having previously served as General Gray's Senior Aide and Military Secretary when General Gray was Commandant.
6. Intercept operators are usually associated with Morse Code, the old dit-da-dit form of communications. Radio-telephone operators are also commonly called intercept operators.
7. During the 1950s, only senior headquarters sent messages. When others wanted to communicate with HQMC, they sent formal, highly formatted "speed-letters" via the mail.
8. From General Gray's private collection.
9. Author interviews with various members of 1st Special Communications Platoon (2007-2010).
10. Dr. John Guilmartin provided this definition of "special." In military terms "special" usually means one of three things: (a) "We" don't want "them" to know what it is or does; (2) "we" don't know what it is or does; or (c) both the above.
11. From General Gray's private collection.
12. From General Gray's private collection.
13. From General Gray's private collection.
14. From General Gray's private collection.
15. Photograph courtesy of Captain George Carnako, USMC (Ret).
16. The Communist Party was very strong in Japan for a number of years following World War II, diminishing in strength only after the Japanese economy became robust in the 1960s.
17. As late as the 1960s, many Japanese would avoid eye contact with Marines when entering the passenger cars of trains or buses. However, units of the Japanese Imperial Army that were formed from the northern areas of that country ended up fighting their

Emperor's enemies in Northern Asia, where they were largely undefeated (and faced no American forces). Thus, when such soldiers returned to their homeland, they did not suffer from any demoralized sense of inferiority or insecurity. Captain Gray treated everyone with respect and honor, and thus established a long-term relationship formed on the basis of mutual respect and trust.

18. Yagi is a specific type of antenna design used often in military communications applications.
19. From General Gray's private collection.
20. From General Gray's private collection.
21. Military mess halls and dining facilities, even in the field, are provided "B" rations which came in large portions suitable for serving mass meals. B Rations were not designed to be given to individuals, though there was no reason families could not share them. As it turned out, they could and did.
22. Telephone interview with Lieutenant Colonel Patrick D. Wilder, 2012.
23. Letter to Alfred M. Gray from Patrick D. Wilder dated October 7, 2011. From General Gray's private collection.
24. Marine Corps officers often benefit from the fact that Navy captains hold the pay grade O-6, the rank just below admiral, while Marine captains are pay grade O-3, between 1st lieutenant and major. Many a Marine officer has worked the confusion to his advantage, calling, for example, for a staff car by identifying himself to a Navy enlisted person as "Captain Laidig," while forgetting to mention his branch of service.
25. Letter of Commendation, Naval Communications Facility dated 16 September 1957.
26. Some 13 years after Corporal Kitt's mission aboard USS *Wahoo*, the author led a team of 10 Marines (out of a total detachment of 14) on a similar mission. Security considerations remained important, however. During an unplanned stop in Adak, Alaska, on a different mission, the author went ashore disguised as a navy lieutenant in order not to create any interest as to why a Marine captain was serving on an attack submarine. Interestingly, both the mission during which Ed Kitt was embarked on the *Wahoo* and one of the author's are mentioned in Sherry Sontag's book *Blind Man's Bluff*.
27. From General Gray's private collection.
28. From General Gray's private collection.
29. Then Captain and later Vice Admiral Milton E. Miles, USN, led a group of Navy intelligence specialists who were completely immersed with the Chinese Nationalists of Chiang Kai-shek during World War II. The group operated against the Japanese and later assisted Chiang against the communists. It is a fascinating story told in the book *Rice Paddy Navy*, which Gray read from cover to cover while in Japan.
30. The members of the 1st Special Communications Platoon who served with General Gray remain a close-knit group, and a high percentage of those Marines are active members of the Marine Corps Cryptologic Association. As can be expected, General Gray has rock-star status with the group.
31. Email from Larry Bangs to author dated April 10, 2008.
32. From Larry Bangs' private collection.
33. From Edgar Kitt's private collection. Front row kneeling L to R: Donald Behnke, Larry Bangs, Richard Trok (in front with field jacket), Robert Payne. Middle row standing L to R: Kenneth Cogswell, Edgar Kitt (goofy look). 3rd Row standing L to R: Robert Page, Thomas Meyering, Michael Sullivan, Roger Egan (in Helmet), Lyle "Doug" Marcy (in the Sailors cover). 4th row L to R: Jerry Zembles, James Krueger, Oscar Smith, Ronald Jensen. Standing far rear center: Donald Jones.
34. From General Gray's private collection.
35. Within the service, abbreviations for units are commonplace, and they are used in this book. 1st Radio denotes the 1st Composite Radio Company or its successor unit, 1st Radio Battalion.
36. "Special Communications" involve a system completely separate from and often parallel to "normal" communications. Special Communications usually reflect very high-level

intelligence information that is protected from wide distribution or access. In the late 1950s and early 1960s, the Special Communications system was in its relative infancy and had a much more "secretive" status than it does in 2012.

37. This was the start of Gray's long professional relationship with General Jaskilka, a relationship that culminated when Gray was promoted to Brigadier General when Jaskilka was the Assistant Commandant of the Marine Corps.

38. SIGINT Designators are simply a shorthand way to identify each SIGNALS Intelligence operational unit. Instead of using "Naval Security Group Activity Kami Seya, Japan," the SIGINT designator for Kami Seya was USN-39 and that much shorter identification would be used in communications traffic. U.S. Army units use the prefix "USM" and Air Force units are designated "USF." Since the Marines are part of the Department of the Navy, Marine cryptologic units have the "USN" designator.

39. From General Gray's private collection.

40. Email from James Wiese to author dated March 20, 2008.

41. The Marine Corps Intelligence Symposium brought together intelligence professionals from units stationed around the world. It was a very big deal during the 1950s and early 1960s before the Vietnam War overwhelmed all other requirements.

42. Letter from Brigadier General James M. Masters, Sr. to Captain Alfred M. Gray dated 1 June 1959. From General Gray's private collection.

43. Email correspondence between former Deputy Director, NSA, Pacific, Harry T. Williams, and author, 2007-2008.

44. From General Gray's private papers.

45. For more about the diplomatic happenings in Laos in 1961, see Chapter 3.

46. Major Henry von der Hyde became the Commanding Officer of 1st Composite Radio Company in 1959.

47. In every task he was ever given, Gray made a habit of practicing the walking around leadership style that Larry Bangs first noted in Japan. Whether a captain of a cryptologic unit, or a major in the artillery, or the Commandant of the Marine Corps, Gray could be expected to show up in unusual places at surprising times, looking for information that would help him execute his duties or make conditions better for those serving in his command. His men came to call him the "Gray Ghost."

48. In 1961, the Commanding General, FMFPAC was a lieutenant general (3-stars) who commanded all Marines from (generally) California to Asia. Both the 1st Marine Division at Camp Pendleton, California; the 1st Air Wing at El Toro, California; and 3rd Marine Division on Okinawa and the 3rd Marine Air Wing in Japan reported to FMFPAC. The Commanding General FMFPAC reported to a Navy admiral (4-stars) who was Commander-in-Chief, Pacific Fleet (CINCPACFLT). That admiral reported to the Commander-in-Chief, Pacific (CINCPAC). CINCPAC was usually, but not always, a Navy admiral. Each of those headquarters had to endorse any operational requirement initiated by Commanding General, 3rd Marine Division. Of course, there were Marine officers at each echelon of command, and Gray knew them all very well.

49. See Karnow, p. 197.

50. Halberstam was perhaps the worst. President Kennedy is said to have religiously read whatever Halberstam wrote.

51. See Bernard Fall, *Two Viet Nams*. The "election" was held in 1946 and following it, Ho had essentially no remaining opposition in the North.

52. Moyar, *Triumph Forsaken*.

53. See Karnow, pp. 216-7.

54. See Mark Moyar's *Triumph Forsaken* or Edward G. Lansdale's *In the Midst of Wars*.

55. Madame Nhu was a glamorous, prominent and quite outspoken defender of her brother-in-law's regime. She much preferred French to Vietnamese as her language of choice, and her religious intolerance was surely a bad, and quite significant, influence on

the Diem Administration. Further, she was a magnet for the criticism leveled against Diem particularly by the Buddhists and other non-Catholic sects.

56. See Karnow, pp. 220-1.
57. For Lansdale's inside look at Ngo Dinh Diem, and one you will not find in any work written by American reporters, read Lansdale's memoir, *In the Midst of Wars: An American's Mission to Southeast Asia* (Paperback).
58. Karnow, 217.
59. David Halberstam, *The Making of a Quagmire*, etc.
60. Pribblenow, pp. 114-120.

CHAPTER 3

CAPTAIN GRAY GOES TO WASHINGTON
VIETNAM HISTORY, 1961-1963

CAPTAIN GRAY GOES TO WASHINGTON

The portly Lieutenant Colonel (there was no kinder adjective) and the spook Captain strode down the passageway together. The duo tried to walk in step, as Marines are wont to do, but most thought it impossible to stay in step with the Lieutenant Colonel. These were not picture-perfect models like those steely-eyed 6-footers who serve at the Marine Barracks, 8th & I, nor did they resemble the specimens seen in the Marine Corps' acclaimed television ads. Neither man was even 5'9" tall; in fact, the Lieutenant Colonel was barely 5'6". Neither strutted with an exaggerated swagger that would make a Marine drill instructor happy. No, the Captain seemingly jostled forward, more like a football player entering the huddle than a Marine on parade. Still, each man appeared confident, and no one at Headquarters Marine Corps would doubt their resolve, despite the circumstances.

Their circumstances were extraordinary; the Captain had been placed on report. Not a formal report based on poor performance or unauthorized behavior; no, his situation was more serious. The younger officer was accused of improperly exceeding his authority. The denizens who represented the combat arms within the Marine Corps had succeeded in having his alleged impropriety reviewed by the highest authority possible, General David M. Shoup, the Commandant of the Marine Corps. Shoup had earned a Medal of Honor in the Pacific during World War II and, as Commandant, his impatience with incompetence or sloth was legendary. The Captain had been a Marine for more than a decade, but this was the second time that he had been accused of doing something careless at Headquarters Marine Corps. The previous summons to General Shoup's office had turned out okay, and so the Captain had hopes this encounter would as well. The Lieutenant Colonel, his boss and friend, accompanied him simply as moral support. The bigger boss, a brigadier general who avoided the Commandant's office as though he might catch the plague there, was not going to be present. But others were in attendance, for the Captain and Lieutenant Colonel had not achieved unanimity amongst the staff for their goals.

The improbable reason the Captain was summoned to see the Commandant was at once both simple and complex: the Captain had been sending far too many Marines to foreign language schools. Most Marine officers consider the infantry to be the backbone of the Corps. And aviation and its concomitant manpower, as well as the other combat arms – artillery and tanks – were steadfastly supported within the Headquarters. But linguists? Why would Marines trained in such exotic languages as Urdu, Vietnamese, Thai, Serbian, Russian, Chinese, Korean, and Indonesian be needed? The Captain's protagonists viewed as unhealthy his scheme of siphoning riflemen and other combat-essential specialists into language billets. And they felt he surely had exceeded his authority. They waited with growing anticipation to see how the Commandant would give the young staff officer his comeuppance.

The Lieutenant Colonel was also a lawyer, renowned in the service for his skills, though on this day he knew his powers of advocacy would not be needed. Through years of practice, the Captain had become an impressive briefer, and the Commandant's office was territory well known to him. After all, he survived a previous encounter during his first weeks at the Headquarters. Moreover, the Captain had done his homework. He planned to explain in concise, easily understood, and well-reasoned terms exactly who, what, when, where and why Marines needed to learn languages, and how they would remain proficient while serving in duty stations throughout the world.

The encounter was over relatively quickly, and with none of the drama that the audience craved. The Commandant listened attentively to the Captain's briefing, and then, after only a few questions, opined, "I am very happy to hear that some officers in this Headquarters are not sitting on their butts, doing nothing!"[1]

With that, Lieutenant Colonel Charlie Beale led Captain Al Gray from the room. Beale had long thought that his subordinate was destined for great things as a Marine, but again surviving the Commandant's possible inquisition was a necessary prelude. Gray was confident that he had been right in stressing that the Marine Corps fill any language billet offered it and the Commandant had just totally reinforced that belief. Gray stopped in his office only long enough to drop off his charts, graphs, and other data before heading outside. He had started chewing tobacco, usually Red Man, while in college, and it remained his only observable vice. There were other times when he thought the simple pleasure of a chew was better deserved, or even more well-earned, but on this occasion Gray knew the Red Man would taste mighty good.

HEADQUARTERS MARINE CORPS, WASHINGTON, D.C., 1961

Spring is the most beautiful time of year in Washington. It is a metamorphosis; the abundance of cherry trees annually announces the changing season, to the delight of Washington's residents and many visitors. In 1961, a transformation was also afoot at both the White House and at Headquarters, United States Marine Corps. Some recall that the cherry blossoms were particularly beautiful that spring. Perhaps they were a harbinger of good things to come, at least for Marines.

The election of 1960 brought about many political changes to the government of the United States of America, and those changes had a dramatic effect on the U.S. military. Following the end of the Korean War in 1954, President Dwight D.

Eisenhower presided over a most welcomed, and perhaps the most tranquil, six-year period in American history; it was probably the most serene since the period before the Great War of 1917-1918. Lasting proof of the domestic calm of the Eisenhower years exists in the form of Ike's most memorable achievement – the Eisenhower Interstate Highway System.

In the background of the domestic tranquility of Eisenhower's last six years, however, was the inexorable rise in the "Cold War" between the United States and the Soviet Union. Military budgets on both sides were dominated by a nuclear buildup, as everything from bombs to artillery and rockets were outfitted with nuclear warheads. Moreover, the British and French soon joined the nuclear club, while during the next decade several other countries came crashing into the world's most elite membership. These included China, India, Pakistan and Brazil. The combination of the Cold War and the threat posed by nuclear weapons and their proliferation had, reasonably, a significant effect on Eisenhower's military policies.

Eisenhower was totally focused on nuclear weapons and nuclear deterrence, and his DoD continuously and persistently chipped away at both Marine Corps personnel and strength, the number of Soldiers or Marines on active duty, and the Marine Corps' budget generally. The U.S. Army was similarly affected, while United States Air Force and Navy budgets generally grew. Of course, Eisenhower was no particular friend of the Marines, having in legend said, "not one Marine would be permitted to participate in the Normandy invasion, lest the Marine Corps get credit for the entire operation." While it is doubtful that General Eisenhower ever said anything like that infamous quip, his disdain for all things Marine was not imaginary. Thus, the change in political leadership in 1960 also led to a shifting of priorities at the Pentagon, a welcomed difference indeed for the United States Marine Corps.

The new President, John Fitzgerald Kennedy, was interested in altering the shape of many things, and first among them was the nation's military policy. While maintaining Eisenhower's aggressiveness against the spread of communism, Kennedy and his national security advisors, led by his military advisor, General Maxwell D. Taylor, rejected a policy based so heavily on nuclear deterrence. Instead, they adopted a "flexible response" strategy based on the level of the threat, a course of action advocated by General Taylor. The new strategy gave hope to Marines that their years of increasingly bare bones budgets would end. Further, after the young President and his Secretary of Defense, Robert Strange McNamara, interviewed the relatively new Commandant of the Marine Corps, David M. Shoup, who had been only recently appointed by Eisenhower, both found they liked and respected the highly decorated General.

The period leading to the elections of 1960 was also a transition time at HQMC. General Shoup had been nominated to be Commandant in late 1959 by the outgoing administration, an act that clearly demonstrated the DoD's lack of confidence in the senior Marine Corps leadership. David Shoup had earned his status as a veritable Marine hero while serving as a regimental commander during an amphibious assault. But his appointment was largely unexpected; Shoup had been serving as a Major General, with six Lieutenant Generals and several Major Generals senior to him. Defense officials wanted to shake up the military, and perhaps the Marine Corps more than other services, so they recommended that Eisenhower, the hero of the war in Europe, go deep down into the general officer ranks to select the hero of Tarawa, Shoup. Change was also surely on Ike's mind; only a year after announcing Shoup's appointment, on the night before he ceded the presidency, Eisenhower gave his famous Farewell Address, which warned the United States against the growing Military – Industrial complex. Ike's speech is still cited by critics of the military establishment.[2]

David Shoup was bright, engaging and uncompromising. He came to the Headquarters determined to change the direction of the Marine Corps. A previous tour as the Budget Director while serving as a new Brigadier General gave Shoup a working knowledge of the administrative side of things, and reform of the Corps' archaic Quartermaster General supply system was one of his primary goals – and a significant challenge. The Quartermaster General bureaucracy was very well entrenched. Commandant Shoup also faced spirited opposition from some of his generals. His predecessor, General Randolph McCall Pate had been one of the "1st Division gang," a group of officers who had served together in that famous unit dating back to Guadalcanal. They held hegemony on Marine Corps leadership, with a lineage that ran through Pate back to the hero of Guadalcanal, General A.A. Vandergrift, and included Commandants Clifton B. Cates and Lemuel C. Shepherd, Jr. Commandant Shoup was a relative outsider despite his war-hero status. His appointment upset the Corps' internal political balance, creating a state of affairs that delighted officers who were not part of the old 1st Division team.

The new Commandant attacked HQMC with the same persistence and doggedness he displayed on the distant Pacific beach. For his Chief of Staff, Shoup adroitly selected Lieutenant General Wallace M. Greene, Jr., a consummate staff officer and a gifted planner, with a legendary reputation as such. Greene provided the balance and professionalism needed to keep the Headquarters functioning. Each month, General Greene required all the newly assigned officers and civilian employees to be present for his briefing. Gray recalled that the General emphasized, among other things, that the Marines needed to take advantage of the considerable expertise that civilians at HQMC had for the minutiae associated with their functions. It was advice the Captain never forgot, and it paid huge dividends when Al Gray needed something from Mr. Casey in Personnel, or Mr. Meade in Transportation, for example, or any of countless others who mostly labored in anonymity at the huge building at Henderson Hall.

Other general officer legends of the Marine Corps served in various capacities at the Headquarters in the early 1960s, including future Commandants Leonard F. Chapman, Jr. and Robert E. Cushman, Lieutenant Generals Henry Buse and Ormand R. Simpson, Colonel Mike Ryan – also a hero of Tarawa, General Herman Nickerson, and perhaps the best military tactician of them all, future General Ray Davis. Those officers helped change the course of the Corps, but not always harmoniously. Shoup was quick to criticize and had an acid tongue; what is more, he did not suffer fools gladly. Everyone and anyone could feel the heat of Shoup's glare; indeed, many general officers were not enthusiastic about having to appear before their Commandant.[3]

Commandant Shoup, let there be no doubt, was clearly in charge and very efficient, and there was much to accomplish to update the Marine Corps after nearly a decade of budgetary neglect in an environment of far-reaching technological change. The General was determined to bring his Corps in line with the best personnel and equipment standards of the time. The Fleet Marine Forces were emphasized and expanded, and they became more active than ever before. Jet aircraft were brought into the air arm; tanks, artillery, weaponry, vehicles and logistic systems were extensively updated. Moreover, Shoup was attentive to detail. In the areas of communications and signals intelligence, Shoup knew the Marine Corps needed considerable improvement.

Brigadier General James Marvin Masters, who learned of Al Gray's activities in the Pacific, was the Assistant Chief of Staff, Intelligence. Masters was the first general to hold that billet. The Intelligence Section, and its Head, was also commonly referred to as the "G-2." And within the Headquarters its designator was AO2. General Masters was a southerner whose younger brother, John Hillary (Bud), was also a Marine general, becoming the Quartermaster General in the early 1960s. One of Shoup's favorites, Bud Masters often traveled with his Commandant. But it fell to Jim Masters to improve the Corps' SIGINT and special communications capabilities.

For those assignments, and much more, Masters turned to a radar-turned-special-communications officer who had been recommended to him. That officer, Lieutenant Colonel Charles H. Beale, was returning from London for assignment, and Masters was determined to get him.

NAVAL SECURITY GROUP DETACHMENT, HEADQUARTERS MARINE CORPS, 1961

Lieutenant Colonel Charlie Beale was somewhat of a character, during an age when many Marine officers were characters. Beale's very short and stocky appearance belied his natural athletic ability, while his ubiquitous sense of humor endeared him to his many friends and bedeviled any potential adversaries. A native of Westmoreland County, Virginia, Beale attended William & Mary for three years, playing baseball for the college. But 1941 found him short of funds, and while in Farmville visiting friends and coaching kids, he was noticed by the President of Hampden-Sydney College. Their conversations led to Beale being placed in a couple of jobs that would permit him to attend the institution, so long as he also played baseball for his new college. Upon graduation from Hampden-Sydney in 1942, he was commissioned a radar officer in the Marine Corps. Beale served in the Pacific for two years, and then returned to the United States in time for the Armistice. He left the Marine Corps to pursue a civilian profession in his hometown of Blackstone, eventually deciding to attend law school at the University of Richmond.

The Korean War came and the Marines recalled Beale to active duty. He negotiated a delay in his activation orders by pointing out that if the Marine Corps permitted him to finish law school, the service would be getting not only a fully qualified radar officer, but also a lawyer. Not surprisingly, the Marine Corps assented. Beale graduated in 1951 and then went off to Korea. He alternated between legal and radar-communications assignments until his retirement in 1972. Later, as a more senior officer, Beale's sense of humor was as widely admired as his intellect. He, for example, would often defuse potential adversaries by telling them, "My home county, Westmoreland, produced military men like George Washington and Robert E. Lee, good company for a short, fat Marine, eh?" It would take a quick-witted and resolute potential adversary to overcome such humor.

Beale's service took an important turn in 1957 when, as a major, he was given a "special security clearance" and assigned to the NSG as the senior Marine for the Atlantic and European region, a posting that took him to London. There he worked for Captain John Lehman, a cryptologist for the U.S. Navy. While Lehman liked Marines generally, he was particularly fond of Beale and sent him to count-less conferences and meetings, thereby ensuring the Marine visited almost every cryptologic installation in Europe, the Mediterranean area and Africa. At these assorted conferences, events and facilities, Beale learned about the inner-workings of the SIGINT establishment, and he was exposed to the special communications networks used by U.S. forces to protect their own vital communication interests. Thus, in 1960, when Beale, the radar-officer-turned-lawyer-turned-special-intel-ligence-communicator returned to the United States for assignment, there were forces pulling him in two directions. Several influential officers sought to have him sent to Judge Advocate General training in Charlottesville, Virginia. Others wanted him at Headquarters. Finally General Masters, hearing of the conflict, told Beale to "park your seabag in the G-2's AO2F office, because that's where you will be working." It turned out that Masters, as usual, was right.

Working in SIGINT was not something that all officers aspired to; indeed, many tried hard not to even get "indoctrinated" into the Special Intelligence/Special Security system. One example was then Brigadier General Leonard F. Chapman. An artillery officer, Chapman had long resisted having access to special intelligence; he thought it would adversely affect his ability to command a major combat unit. But that ended when Charlie Beale, working at the behest of Generals Frederick Wieseman and James Masters arranged to ambush Chapman at Camp Lejeune.

General Chapman was the Commanding General of Force Troops, Atlantic, which was co-located on the base with the 2nd Marine Division. As the Commanding General, the 2nd Composite Radio Company fell under Chapman's authority. Beale had accompanied General Masters on his trip from the Headquarters to inspect various units at Camp Lejeune. When Masters indicated an interest in visiting the 2nd Radio, Beale quickly arranged the appointment, but he then made sure General Chapman knew General Masters would be dropping by to see Chapman's troops – the Radio Company. It would have been a grievous misstep in protocol had Chapman not been informed that another general was looking around his area. Needless to say, Chapman rushed to the Radio Company's location, only to be told that he could not be permitted to attend the briefing that would be given to General Masters unless he personally submitted to indoctrination into the Special Intelligence program. Under some duress, Chapman acceded to the requirement. As it turned out, that would be General Chapman's last assignment in the field; he would depart Camp Lejeune and move to HQMC and, in late 1963, as Lieutenant General, became Commandant Greene's very imposing Chief of Staff.

Charlie Beale was a talented lawyer and staff officer, and he personally knew several of the general officers then serving at HQMC including, of course, Masters. But Beale had learned of "special clearances" and "special communications" and "signals intelligence" only while serving in London in a staff position. He had no practical operational experience. Given his mission, to operate the special communications section of the G-2 and to build a SIGINT organization for the Marine Corps, Lieutenant Colonel Beale knew he needed an officer whose skills would complement his own, someone with the operational knowledge and practical experience that Beale lacked.

Captain John Lehman, USN, had previously served with the NSG in the Pacific. While he was there, he knew of a young Marine captain who was responsible for establishing the Marine Corps' complement to the Naval Security Group Activity, Kami Seya, Japan. That Captain of Marines was Alfred M. Gray, Jr. and he already had a wide reputation, especially among the young enlisted Marines and many senior naval officers who served in SIGINT. Gray eagerly sought every assignment possible for young officers, thereby gaining broad operational experience, while also building an outstanding reputation among the Navy's senior cryptologists. Lehman, knowing of Gray's capabilities, advised Charlie Beale that "if you ever get a chance to have Al Gray work for you, grab him."

Newly promoted Lieutenant Colonel Beale contacted Captain Gray, trying to talk him into accepting orders to work for Beale in AO2F section as the Officer-in-Charge, Naval Security Group Detachment, HQMC. Of course, Gray's reputation at NSA, at AO2F and throughout the Marine Corps had grown during his time in Hawaii, and Beale needed to capitalize on that experience. Gray, who was well beyond his directed communications tour by 1961, longed to return to duty with combat arms, either the artillery or infantry. Indeed, aggravating the possible assignment to HQMC was the fact that the only billet Beale had available was that for a major in MOS 2502, a communications officer. Gray would have to change his primary MOS.

The MOS issue was potentially a showstopper in convincing Gray to take the assignment. An officer's MOS designates his professional field and significantly influences assignments. Basically, Marine officers' MOSs are divided into two major groupings – ground and aviation. Roughly three times as many Marine officers serve in the ground component as in aviation specialties. Gray had been formally trained as an artillery officer but through his service in Korea he had acquired an additional qualification as an infantry officer. His assignment to communications had earned him a third MOS – Communication Officer. Gray wanted to return to a combat arms field and his goal remained to some day command an infantry battalion.

Although Captain Gray had no desire to become a professional communicator, Beale's description of his duties nevertheless attracted Gray to the offer. That he would be in on the ground floor, given the challenge of building a SIGINT capability for the Marine Corps, proved persuasive. Gray recalled the lessons of Korea, when the old-timers told him about the Marines learning of the Chinese presence before MacArthur did. And he knew from recent, in-depth experience in Japan and on Hawaii that SIGINT indeed could make a difference. Furthermore, Gray, because of his assignment in Hawaii, understood better than almost any other officer the need for strong support from HQMC if the radio companies were to grow into significant organizations.

Al Gray recalled the advice Colonel West had given him years before about assignments and the "Needs of the Service." Furthermore, he fervently believed that SIGINT/EW operations would save lives in combat and other situations. Consequently, after five years of sensitive overseas duty, principally operating in the Far East and Southeast Asia, Captain Gray entered the tumultuous environment at HQMC.

THE AO2F STAFF, 1961-1963

AO2F was the staff section within the G-2 responsible for SIGINT and special communications – highly classified systems designed to protect the secrecy of U.S. military communications. Captain Gray's specific billet was Officer-in-Charge, Naval Security Group Detachment, HQMC. But in practice, Gray's involvement and interests were much broader, and extended to all aspects of AO2F's functions; he was the G-2 Special Operations and Plans officer during his first assignment at Headquarters. He would prove to be as successful at the Headquarters building as he had been in the field.

Among the many factors in Gray's effectiveness over the four years of his first HQMC assignment were his relationships with his first boss there, Lieutenant Colonel Charles Beale, and with another officer with whom he served, Major Howard K. Alberts. Beale and Alberts were not ordinary Marines, but there were few of those in the early 1960s. That Beale trusted Alberts and Gray, and that they always rewarded that trust, permitted the three to become a very effective, though certainly not traditional, team of officers. Beale ensured that he personally took Gray around to meet the various staff officers, including the generals that they would be working for on daily basis. Beale also went out of his way to ensure that each officer knew of the special trust and confidence in which he held Gray. He also made certain that everyone knew of Gray's background and technical proficiency, thus paving the way for Gray to be accepted in the inner circle of the staff. Beale put forth the same effort for his other charge, Major Howard (Howie) Alberts, though Alberts already had a solid reputation around HQMC.

In addition to Gray and Alberts, Lieutenant Colonel Thomas McDonald was also part of AO2F; McDonald was an aviation EW specialist. Lieutenant Colonel (and later Colonel) Russell (Whitey) Andres, an experienced EW squadron commander, was Beale's deputy and eventually relieved Beale when that officer left HQMC in late 1963. Gunnery Sergeant Seavey was the Communications Chief for the special communications unit that supported HQMC; he also provided administrative support to Captain Gray. One of the air officers in AO2C, the adjacent office, was Major Lewis H. Abrams, an A-6 pilot with whom Gray worked closely during the period 1962-63. Sadly, Major Abrams was later killed while flying a mission over Vietnam.

One other important factor helped the cryptologic section to be successful. General Masters, the G-2 when Gray arrived in Washington, already knew Charlie Beale and respected him highly. Further, he knew of Captain Al Gray because of his interactions with NSA at the general officer level and from Gray's Hawaii assignment. Indeed, Masters's admonition to Gray that he redouble his efforts to build 1st Radio convinced Al Gray he had been on the right track. Masters realized that Gray, despite his relatively junior rank, had the respect and confidence of those at the NSA, and the General in turn supported Gray's efforts within HQMC. It was probably Masters who influenced General Shoup's decision to make Al Gray the Marine Corps' sole SIGINT Liaison Officer. It would be Gray who provided a single voice outside the Marine Corps on matters involving cryptology. Make no mistake about Gray's first boss at the G-2, General Jim Masters was a major force within the Marine Corps of the 1960s.

Howie Alberts, an enigmatic infantry-turned-communications officer with a degree in physics and physical chemistry from Rutgers University and a second degree in electrical engineering from the Massachusetts Institute of Technology, was an important member of the staff. Before landing in AO2F, Alberts's assignments at the Headquarters had moved back and forth between communications and logistics at HQMC, and his knowledge of the inner-workings of the Headquarters staff provided Beale and Gray many advantageous insights. Alberts was a particularly studious officer who had no time for trivial or foolish projects that occasionally arose within the Headquarters. Upon receipt of such items, Alberts would often slap a "confidential" security classification cover on the offensive routing slip and send it to the Women Marines for action. By the time the Women Marines decided the item did not affect them and sent it back to AO2F, the project would be most likely overcome by events, leaving Beale, Alberts, and Gray free to act upon more pressing projects. "Moon," as Beale and Gray called Alberts, was good for much more than diverting undeserving projects, however.

Moon was a large man who filled the doorway when entering an office – thus the nickname. More important than his large frame, however, was his extremely active mind. Alberts provided Beale and Gray with a highly technical engineering capability that was put to good use designing shelters and systems required for SIGINT, and the generators needed to power them. Alberts almost single handedly produced the first generator that provided the full range of power required by special communications and intelligence systems.[4] The generator that Alberts designed, developed, contracted for and fielded in nine months would take several years in the modern Marine Corps systems development process. Moon was a keeper and neither Beale nor Gray ever forgot his many technical contributions. But his knowledge in another area was perhaps even more critical.

Major Howard K. Alberts was also an expert on the budget and how to obtain the money necessary to pay for various programs. He had acquired that expertise by learning from the "little people" who worked anonymously in various cubicles at the Headquarters. Alberts delighted Beale and Gray with instructive charts and graphs that had titles such as "new year money," "old year money," "black money," and "no year money" – the very best kind! Following his tutelage, Beale and Gray aggressively sought funds for their programs, so much so that the duo was proclaimed the "gold dust twins" within HQMC. General officers and influential executive-service civilians, particularly those in the fiscal department, knew to put their hands in their pockets whenever Beale or Gray came calling. One remarked to Beale, upon seeing his approach, "I don't know how much this is going to cost me, Beale, but I know it will be something!"

Even before he had fully settled into the HQMC routine, however, Captain Al Gray knew there was an important item that needed his attention. The Operational Requirement that he had prepared for General Weller while still at the 3rd Marine Division awaited action at HQMC. Having staffed the requirement through three other headquarters, Gray was unwilling to now rest. Thus, one of the first actions undertaken by Gray was to establish that the Marine Corps required a special communications system Special Intelligence and Special Security Office activities at each headquarters. Charlie Beale ran interference for the new staff officer. Within a couple weeks, General Shoup signed the requirement.

Captain Gray provided the requirements analysis and Major Alberts designed an electronically shielded shelter. The shelter was small enough to meet Commandant Shoup's dictate that everything had to be helicopter transportable. It was also large enough to contain a KW-26 online encryption/decryption device, a 100-word-per-minute teletypewriter, a long-range single sideband radio for communications, and a flexible antenna that could be retracted. Delivered with it was the Alberts-designed portable generator needed for powering all the electronics. While Gray and Alberts were designing and developing the system, the Navy had accidently discovered that its communications were vulnerable to electromagnetic leaks that defeated subsequent message encryption and made U.S. communications susceptible to exploitation. That discovery led to the military establishing red-black criteria for all its communications installations, whether they were designed for shipboard usage or for work on the battlefield.[5]

As a consequence, the electronically isolated shelter that Alberts had previously designed was modified to include an acoustic isolation. That modification permitted the Marine equipment to pass tests necessary to certify it for Top Secret special communications. Designated the ODTT-4, it was the first product that came out of Marine Logistics Base, Albany; its successor equipment, the MSC-43 van saw service well into the 21st century. When Alberts and Gray designed and produced the state-of-the-art shelter, they had no idea that Gray would be employing them operationally less than three years later.

In 1962, 14 months after Captain Gray had requested that General Weller set the process into motion, the 3rd Marine Division and every other major Marine division, air wing and brigade headquarters, received the systems necessary to conduct special security operations in the field. Special Security Communications Teams became part of the Table of Organization, and their gear became part of each organization's Table of Equipment. Consequently, the Marines were the first service to have that capability at the tactical level; it would be years before the Army fielded such equipment. The achievement was one of Gray's finest moments, and he was still a captain.

Lieutenant Colonel Charlie Beale, Major Howard Alberts and Captain Al Gray had little in common in terms of their educations, their previous assignments in the Marine Corps, their appearances or their mannerisms. But they were very similar in terms of their professionalism, their belief in the special trust and confidence for Marine officers, their athletic backgrounds, and their sense of humor. They worked long hours, but usually had a very good time doing it. AO2F was located in a specially

Figure 3.1
Three Marines using the Alberts-Gray designed ODTT-4 in Vietnam in 1964.[6]

designated area of the Headquarters called "the tank." The tank was a specially constructed, concrete-reinforced vault used to house highly classified documents and special communications systems. Access to the tank was highly restricted. All visitors were required to have a special security clearance for entry, so most staff officers, indeed many general officers, were not permitted access. Moreover, generals, even the G-2, rarely came into the area where the AO2F section, along with several others, had their desks. After having won the battle to supply the special security communications equipment to General Weller and other major subordinate commands, Beale and Gray knew they had to address a requirement much closer to home.[7]

As late as 1960, when there were Special Intelligence messages addressed to HQMC, someone had to physically courier the materials from the Pentagon to the Naval Annex at Henderson Hall, where all HQMC was then located. When the requirements for the division and wing Special Security Communications Teams were approved, a Special Security Officer capability was established at HQMC. But more was needed. Lieutenant Colonel Beale directed Captain Gray to put together a briefing for the Commandant regarding the advantages that would accrue by having a separate command center for the Commandant, incorporating the Special Security Officer capabilities, located right at HQMC. Included in the discussion were the physical space requirements, the equipment needed, a budget, etc. On the day of the briefing, there was some sort of disturbance occurring in Goa – an obscure state in India. When General Shoup asked why such a command center was needed for HQMC, Beale replied that, for example, if the Commandant had his own command center then no one would have to interrupt him about any emergency developing in Goa, since all the relevant information would be available in the command center. Shoup then asked, "What idiot would disturb me with information about Goa?" and he strode purposefully from the conference room. "Not me," quietly answered Charlie Beale, though the Commandant was already gone.

The Chief of Staff, General Greene, who had sat through the briefing, told Beale and Captain Gray, "He likes it. Implement your plan and I will back you up." And with that, construction of a command center, with a full range of Special Security Officer capabilities, began at HQMC. Whether it was the enthusiasm of his briefings, or his mastery of the details, or his ability to relate to what kinds of information the command center might correlate and display that would be of use to the Commandant, Captain Gray's work was accepted, and senior officers often commented upon his professionalism. One thing is certain, neither Commandant Shoup nor his Chief of Staff tolerated incomplete, sloppy or unprofessional briefings.[8] The fact that Gray was able to pass muster with both meant the Captain was off to a good start at HQMC. Beale, Alberts and Gray had ushered the Marine Corps into the National Football League, at least with respect to special communications.

The workday routine required persistence and patience, and while challenging, it did not have the sense of urgency that satisfying an immediate operational requirement did. Usually one of the staff came in very early to collect and organize any special intelligence communications sent to the Headquarters. Such messages required that the general assigned to that section either sign or initial the routing slip, acknowledging they had read and understood the message. Each of the important staff officers had unique ways to initial the routing slip. These idiosyncrasies quickly came to the attention of the staff. General Greene, for example, whose handwriting was very meticulous, marked his acknowledgement of papers and messages with a "G" with a circle around it. Beale, Alberts and Gray consequently referred to him as "Circle G." Each day in the late afternoon, whenever all were in town, the G-2 section met in the tank to brief each other on the day's happenings, and to relay any follow-up actions needed to be completed the next working day. Beale might have to see "Green B" (Colonel Randolph Carter Berkeley of the Intelligence Section) again or perhaps Gray needed to provide more information to the "Red C" (Major General Robert Cushman) or the "Gray Y" Brigadier General Carl Youngdale. There also were nicknames used throughout the Headquarters; for example, "Tiger" was General Jim Masters and the "Razor" was General Ray Davis. "Brute" was the well-known moniker for then Major General Victor Krulak; initially, it was a sardonic reference to the General's diminutive size, but General Krulak enthusiastically embraced the nickname while still a midshipman at the Naval Academy.

While Al Gray made a point of never becoming entangled in senior officers politics, Charlie Beale was perhaps the master of them. Neither Beale nor Gray favored one side or the other, after all, what difference could a Lieutenant Colonel or a Captain make when the bull elephants in the Marine Corps leadership were rumbling? That is not to say that Beale and Gray were not aware of or attentive to such rumbling. As Charlie Beale reported, they "checked the weather each day before firing any shots." Beale primarily used Generals Freddie Wieseman and Jim Masters as his "sounding boards."[9]

One needed to spend only a few minutes with Charlie Beale to know that no matter what happened, work was going to be fun. Mixing the droll Howie Alberts and the inscrutable Al Gray with Beale was sure to produce a professional office environment, but it also made for levity during the day. In fact, whenever General Bud Masters was going on a trip with Commandant Shoup, he was sure to drop by the tank to ask if any of the staff, including Spook – as he called Captain Gray – had any "new jokes" that he could share with the Commandant.

Beale was not surprised at how effective his section was at getting things done. Not only did he have high expectations, but he also realized that he had assembled a capable staff. Alberts was an old hand at HQMC, having spent time in the supply department as a technical advisor to the contracting officer and in communications billets. Yet Alberts had never enjoyed the degree of success, or fun, that Beale and Gray brought with them. When asked about why Gray was so effective, Alberts remarked, using a baseball analogy, that Gray would set up the targeted officer, and then give him the "high, hard one" – a strikeout pitch in baseball parlance. While the work at AO2F was demanding, intense, and required great persistence, the section did have some built in advantages. For the most part, their projects were so highly classified that many other sections at the Headquarters and even generals never saw the subject, much less had the opportunity to protest whatever action Beale and company were advocating. For certain, the daily routine was seldom boring or even the slightest bit uninteresting.[10]

It was during the end-of-the-day staff briefings that various colonels and lieutenant colonels from other sections, primarily the G-2 and G-3, all appropriately cleared of course, would wander into the tank. Often they were simply trying to find out what happened, or perhaps their generals were still involved in meetings over at the Pentagon or the Joint Chiefs of Staff (JCS) meetings, and the HQMC staff could not go home until the generals returned and left work. Although classified information was passed on a strict need-to-know basis, rumors abounded throughout the Headquarters, and no group had more inside information than the guys in AO2F. Certainly no group was more naturally reticent – or bound by security constraints – than Beale and his officers, but they too engaged in the banter, chitchat that varied from lighthearted joking to fairly serious discussions, including speculation about which colonels might be selected as brigadier generals.

Given Beale's insider status and sense of humor, combined with Gray and Alberts's knowledge of all the important things that were happening, gatherings inside the tank were an essential aspect of staff interaction at the working level, and the source of many humorous stories. One crusty colonel, highly opinionated and very sure of his ability to pick future generals, asked lowly Captain Gray for his opinion regarding the colonels that might be selected for promotion. Gray cautiously put forth the name of Michael Ryan, an officer whose skills he knew and admired from when Gray served as a company commander in Ryan's infantry battalion in Korea. The colonel haughtily dismissed Gray's thoughts as so much balderdash. Of course, when later Ryan's name appeared on the selection list, Gray found his status as a soothsayer highly elevated, and his opinions even more actively sought. Perhaps it was Al Gray's knowledge of General Ryan's previous history with General Shoup that swayed his opinion.[11]

Although Beale, Alberts and Gray worked well together, that is not to say that everything went smoothly all the time. Strong-willed men often find sufficient reasons to disagree about staff tactics, priorities, and assignments, especially when there is no readily defined correct way to do things. And certainly issues arose within the triumvirate from time to time. Often, following a disagreement, Gray would go out for a walk. Finding himself at odds with Beale or Alberts, or simply needing time to reflect, Gray would leave the building and stride between wings of the Headquarters. As he paced to and fro, Gray would turn over in his mind the facts, the decision to be made, and the various courses of action. While Gray was pacing and chewing, often Beale, Alberts or perhaps Gunnery Sergeant Seavey, would be able to view him through a crack in the window of a nearby office (the tank had no windows). When Gray stopped, someone would announce, "he's on his way in!" Within a few minutes, Gray would return to the office, and predictably ask, "Now tell me again how we are going to do this?" Whatever disagreements arose, they never continued past the close of business. The section focused on getting things done, not worrying about who got the credit or who had the best idea.

Almost from the start of their relationship, Beale knew that he had gained a high achiever and a hard worker with his recruitment of Al Gray. First, his personal observation of Gray led to an assessment that his young staff assistant was a man to be reckoned with, and that he had a bright future. But Beale's evaluation was validated by a most unlikely source. Mr. White was an African-American security officer who often worked the midnight shift at the Headquarters. After a specified hour, anyone leaving or entering the building had to sign in or out on a logbook watched over by Mr. White. Often, Beale, who never met a person who was not a friend, learned from Mr. White that Gray had worked into the wee hours of the night. When Beale would arrive for duty, Mr. White would greet him with, "your man was here late again last night." Gray's seniors noted that he usually arrived at the office at 0530 and was typically the last officer to leave each evening. Beale was never quite sure of exactly what project Gray might have been working on, but after a few months he was very confident it was something important.

After General Jim Masters left the G-2 in early 1963, Brigadier General Carl Youngdale, a distinguished artillery officer, replaced him.[12] When General Youngdale left to join the staff at the Military Assistance Command (Vietnam) (MAC(V)), Major General Robert Cushman held both the G-2 and G-3 billets. Colonel Randolph Berkeley was assigned as G-2. Of course, none of the generals nor Colonel Berkeley had any background in SIGINT or EW, and each often permitted Beale and Gray to brief their programs to other general officers and the Commandant without them being present.

General Shoup was a man of outstanding personal reputation and integrity, he was not without personal foibles. The rumor at the Headquarters was that anyone who beat the Commandant at either golf or poker could expect immediate orders to Okinawa – an assignment that meant officers would be without their families for 13 long months! While the General was not a physically imposing man, few Marines could withstand his steely scowl.

Gray recalled working in the tank one Saturday morning. Answering a knock at the door, he was surprised to see one of the Headquarters' major generals. "What can I do for you, sir?" asked Captain Gray. "Well, Spook," answered the general, "do you have any footlockers?" Gray replied, "Sure, I've got a couple footlockers, sir." "Well, I have been ordered to Okinawa and need them this weekend, if you don't mind. I have to leave Monday," the general informed the startled younger officer. It turned out that the general had originally been slated to go to the 1st Marine Division at Camp Pendleton. However, when the Commandant learned that the general had been feathering his nest by orchestrating the assignment of many of the finest officers available to that famous unit, he immediately changed the slate and sent the transgressing officer to the 3rd Division on Okinawa. Such was General Shoup's manner.[13]

Not that the Commandant intimidated every officer. On one occasion Beale was carrying messages to the Commandant. General Shoup asked for his opinion of the quality and appearance of the Oriental rug in front of the Commandant's desk, a deep red carpet given Shoup by his Chinese nationalist counterpart. Beale replied that he liked the rug, since it "hid the blood that I sweat when standing at attention before the Commandant." General Greene later told Beale that Shoup had mentioned to Greene words to the effect "that fat little lawyer isn't afraid of me." While not exactly the truth of the matter, it demonstrated the character of relationship Beale enjoyed with senior officers, and the same characterization extended to Gray as well.[14]

One of Gray's fondest memories of that time at HQMC occurred one weekend in 1962. Gray had the duty as Assistant Officer of the Day, and thus it was his responsibility to deliver urgent messages to the Commandant at his quarters at the Marine Barracks, 8th & I Streets, Northeast, Washington.[15] On that particular Sunday, Shoup, after reading the messages, invited Captain Gray down into the cellar of the house, where the Commandant showed off his collection of fine saké (a Japanese rice wine) bottles and other souvenirs of his long service. General Shoup remembered Gray from his time at The Basic School, and also had remembered that Gray had long been assigned to Japan. Gray never forgot the courtesy and hospitality the Commandant had extended to him. Indeed, General Shoup was unfailingly courteous and pleasant to Captain Al Gray. It was something the younger officer tried to repay with interest when, more than two decades later, Gray was the occupant of the Commandant's house. The Commandant had come to know Al Gray a little more than most captains because Gray was the Commandant's Special Intelligence Officer and Special Security Officer; thus he had many more occasions to see General Shoup than other junior officers. Yes, General Shoup knew Captain Gray very, very well.

Figure 3.2
Gen David M. Shoup poses with his collection of saké bottles. He presented the picture
to Capt Gray after showing the younger officer around the Commandant's Quarters.[16]

A key task that Beale faced, and one for which he both required and relied on Gray's expertise, was the effort to put together the Marine Support Battalion and to make the Radio Companies into a Radio Battalions. The Marine Support Battalion (now called the Marine Cryptologic Support Battalion) would reinforce the Radio Battalions by providing a means for Marines with SIGINT specialties to work at various Naval Security Group Activities around the world when they were not serving with the Radio Battalions. Detachments such as Gray's 1ˢᵗ Special Communications Platoon did not belong to any higher cryptologic unit, but rather were assigned to Headquarters Company, HQMC. The envisioned Marine Support Battalion would become the parent organization for such units then working at both Naval Security Group Activities and at the NSA. Complementing that work was Gray's effort to identify and address the Marine Corps's foreign language requirements. Both projects led to noteworthy confrontations within HQMC.

WASHINGTON, LATE 1961

After one of his many assessment missions to Vietnam, General Maxwell Taylor, President Kennedy's military advisor, made several recommendations about how to provide increased assistance to the government of South Vietnam. Among them was one to provide an enhanced "communications intelligence" capability to the ARVN. The DoD and the NSA immediately set about responding to Taylor's ideas. An inquiry to all of the military services asking who could respond to the communications intelligence requirement brought a positive response only from the Marine Corps. The Commandant's reply was written and staffed through the Headquarters by Captain Al Gray, newly assigned.

In his most recent duty before HQMC, Gray had been the operations officer (S-3) for the 1ˢᵗ Composite Radio Company in Hawaii. There he had established a rigorous and innovative training program for the Company's officers and men that was built around flyaway detachments and supported heavily by NSA. While in the Pacific, Gray's Marines were frequent visitors to Army, Air Force and Navy operational sites located across the region. Though none of the SIGINT sites were in Vietnam, other Southeast Asia locations in Thailand and the Philippines provided excellent training areas. Thus, when NSA requested information about each service's communications intelligence units that would be available to send to Vietnam, Gray was able to quickly and effectively draft a favorable Marine Corps response. But, as it turned out, Gray's response caused a ruckus at HQMC.

NSA, instead of telling the Marines what it planned to do, had responded directly to the JCS, saying that only the Marine Corps could satisfy the Taylor requirement. Lieutenant General Charles H. Hayes was sitting in for General Shoup when the JCS were briefed; General Hayes knew nothing of the communications between Gray and NSA. He returned to HQMC with fire in his eyes!

Commandant Shoup was determined that his ground units would not be part of operations inside Vietnam. Official Marine Corps policy under General Shoup was that Marines should not be involved until and unless the United States undertook an effort to win a war in Southeast Asia. Piecemeal military commitments to Asia were anathema to Shoup; at every opportunity Shoup opposed expansion of the military effort in Vietnam short of the effort needed to win a war (the Commandant at that time was not a full-fledged member of the JCS, and voted only when discussing matters related to the Marine Corps). Thus, General Hayes, wholly aware of his Commandant's attitude toward Vietnam, was shocked to hear that someone at HQMC said Marines could meet the commitment.

Having prepared the Marine response to NSA, Gray was sitting in his office in the tank when the Deputy Assistant Chief of Staff, G-3, Brigadier General Norman Anderson came knocking at the door. He asked if anyone in the tank knew about sending Marines to Vietnam? Captain Gray acknowledged that, indeed, he knew about that. General Anderson told Gray to follow him. Gray thought they would be going to the G-3 offices, but Anderson continued down the passageway until he reached the offices of Lieutenant General "Fog" Hayes. General Hayes had an intimidating presence; he was a naval aviator who had served on Guadalcanal. When General Anderson told Hayes that Gray was responsible for alerting NSA to the Marine's capability, Hayes lit into Gray with the full force of his considerable authority. Did Captain Gray not know of the Commandant orders regarding Vietnam? Of course, Gray understood General Shoup's policy, but on this occasion, before answering he thought silence might be the best course. The young Captain was told to report to the Commandant's office at 0700 the next day to justify his actions. Gray, still new to HQMC, had no idea why he might be in trouble, though apparently he was.

Dutifully following his instructions, Gray approached the Commandant with a briefing about Marine Corps SIGINT capabilities. Six other generals, including the one who would become his main supporter, Lieutenant General Wallace M. Greene, were also in attendance. Shoup listened thoughtfully as Gray explained why and how the Marine Corps could provide elements of its 1st Composite Radio Company to successfully complete the proposed mission. Indeed, he pointed out that NSA had assisted the Marine Corps to develop the specific capabilities that were requested, and that he could not lie about such things. In the seven months between the time Gray had first arrived at the Headquarters (May, 1961) and the time the Marine response was given (early January, 1962) the AO2F had accomplished much, including, Shoup knew, the staffing requirement to support special communications systems for the Fleet Marine Forces. The briefing impressed Shoup, during which he was also assured that only the Marines could respond affirmatively to Taylor's recommendation. Since the commitment was to provide cryptologic support and did not involve Marine combat units, it did not constitute a level of involvement that Shoup opposed. Thus, the Commandant approved the message prepared for his consideration. Captain Gray exhaled, and then went back to work, planning the operation.

Al Gray developed a detailed plan to send the Marine SIGINT detachment to Vietnam. The mission was to teach the Vietnamese how to provide direct support for the ARVN operations. He briefed the plan and NSA and then went to Hawaii to explain the operation to the officers at 1st Composite Radio Company.

Gray wanted and expected to personally lead the detachment, but Lieutenant Colonel Beale successfully nixed that idea by telling all in the chain of command that Gray had a "plethora" of other duties that required his attention. Beale's choice of words became something of a standing joke between the two, and each could recall it vividly (and independently) more than 45 years later. As a result of his own non-availability, Gray recommended that Captain John Hyatt, whom he knew very well, lead the detachment.

Marine cryptologists were headed for action in Southeast Asia, though their number would not include Al Gray. But when one door is closed, often another opens. After all, Al Gray had become the master of accepting his assignment and then making the most of the opportunity.

FIRST BOOTS ON GROUND, REPUBLIC OF VIETNAM, JANUARY 1962

When Captain Al Gray relinquished his duties as S-3 (Operations) of 1st Composite Radio Company and went off to Washington, his successor as S-3 was his former assistant, Captain John K. Hyatt, Jr. A 1953 graduate of the United States Naval Academy, Hyatt was a third-generation Academy graduate. His father and grandfather were both accomplished naval officers, and Hyatt grew up in New England, thinking mostly about attending the Academy. As his goal neared, having successfully pursued an electrical engineering major, Midshipman First Class Hyatt entered his senior year without having given much thought to what he wanted to do after graduation.

Academy graduates chose their service based largely on class standing. Midshipmen were able to select among naval air, submarines, naval line, supply and the Marine Corps. In 1953, up to 16 ⅔% could choose to be commissioned in the U.S. Marine Corps. John Hyatt finally decided to choose the Marines, largely because he respected how the Marine officers stationed at the Academy went about their work, especially their interaction with the midshipmen. Marine officers, it seemed to Hyatt, were keenly interested in their students and treated them with dignity and respect while serving as company officers. After The Basic School, 2nd Lieutenant Hyatt was assigned to Communications Officer School; after all, few Marines had Bachelor of Science in Electrical Engineering degrees, and those who did were invariably assigned to technical MOSs. After his initial assignment in an Infantry Battalion, followed by a tour at the NSA involving COMSEC, newly promoted Captain Hyatt was given orders to the 1st Composite Radio Company at Kaneohe Bay, Hawaii.

John Hyatt initially was the Company's EW officer, responsible for training and briefing all FMFPAC, units with respect to Ground EW. To his surprise, Hyatt found that few of the officers in the Company, including himself, knew much if anything about cryptology. The Company's equipment was old and inadequate. Most of its personnel were new. Captain Al Gray, however, was a notable exception, and when given the chance to become Gray's assistant S-3, Hyatt jumped at the opportunity.[17]

In the few months the men worked together, Hyatt was impressed at how effective Gray was in getting things done. But Gray was often absent on Temporary Additional Duty with the flyaway detachments, and before too long, he was gone permanently, to Washington. That left the younger captain in his place, and John Hyatt was a quick study. When just after New Year's Day, 1962, 1st Radio Company received tasking from HQMC through FMFPAC, to send a detachment to Vietnam, it was he who carried the message to his commanding officer, announcing, "This one is for me." His enthusiasm for the opportunity met Gray's recommendation for his appointment. Hyatt had seen Gray take one important assignment after another, but with his cryptologic mentor gone to HQMC, Hyatt was determined to get personally involved in operational cryptology. With the commander's blessing, he set about forming a flyaway detachment of two officers and 40 enlisted men required to conduct operations at Pleiku, Vietnam, in support of the Army Security Agency field station in Saigon. Maxwell Taylor's recommendation that tactical cryptology be used to support the Army of Vietnam was now in actual motion.

Hyatt's detachment arrived in Vietnam in late January 1962. In Saigon, a U.S. Army Security Agency colonel briefed the Marines. Aside from some very general remarks about the country, the colonel did not have any technical information for the Marines, though he did admonish them, "Don't get involved in the black market for U.S. greenback dollars."[18]

The Marines were assigned to Pleiku, an outlying base in the Central Highlands near the Cambodian border that was headquarters to the Vietnamese Army's II Corps and its American advisors. Coincidently, the Army advisory unit also was a detachment of two officers and 40 enlisted. When an Air Force troposcatter (long range) communications detachment arrived, it coincidently also had two officers and 40 enlisted. Later in the war Pleiku was to become the scene of several significant military events, but in 1962 it was a sleepy place. Reporters wandered through from time to time, and all were interested to know, "What the Marines are doing here?" Hyatt was able to convince them that he and his men were doing nothing very exciting, while also asking that their presence be ignored. Happily, the reporters acquiesced to the request and nothing about the Marines was ever seen in the newspapers back in the United States. Hyatt's experience might have marked the zenith in military-press relations in South Vietnam!

Not much happened of interest during the four months Hyatt and his men were in the highlands. The in-country Army Security Agency officers, mostly located in Saigon, seemed unable to suggest how to exploit VC weaknesses because, apparently, little was known about enemy communications targets. Such targets, at least in the Central Highlands, were very few. Adding to the problem, the NSA representative was in Saigon, and the only secure way to communicate the highly classified information needed to conduct cryptologic operations from Saigon to the Pleiku base was a very slow and cumbersome link that required manual encryption and decryption. Thus, the Marines spent much of their time trying to sort through the entire radio spectrum trying to detect their targets. Though Captain Hyatt often went to Saigon to liaise, he never was able to find the people able to effectively assist the Marines' efforts. By the time John Hyatt returned home to Hawaii in the summer of 1962, he was frustrated that poor coordination with the MAC(V) and Army Security Agency units in Saigon caused the outcome of the mission to be less than he had projected. Unfortunately, as it was later determined, in 1962 Pleiku was not a target-rich environment.

The deployment had proven, however, the Marines could, on short notice, deploy thousands of miles to a forward operating area and conduct communications intercept operations. The concept that had been conceived and implemented by Captain Al Gray was confirmed to be operationally practical and logistically sustainable. As it turned out, in the not too distant future there were to be many opportunities for greater technical and operational SIGINT successes. In addition, much to the delight of the Chief of Staff, General Greene, the Marine Corps attracted positive attention from the NSA. Of course, the mission reflected positively at the DoD and even the Presidential level, while maintaining General Shoup's policy of avoiding combat operations in Vietnam. Everyone was pleased that the first Marine ground unit had gone to and most returned from Vietnam, and without incident.[19]

Some of the Marines from Captain Hyatt's remained in Vietnam, and were sent to Phu Bai, where they were in on the ground floor of organizing the 8th Radio Reconnaissance Unit (RRU). The 8th RRU would become one of the cogs in the American SIGINT effort in Vietnam.

GUANTANAMO BAY, CUBA, 1962

The Cuban revolution of 1959 did far more than overthrow a dictator; it brought a communist government to the New World. That Fidel Castro turned out to be an avowed communist surprised almost all Americans. When Castro embraced the Soviet Union for all kinds of financial and military support, most Americans were shocked, and the new Kennedy Administration in Washington was embarrassed. After all, the Democrats still lived with their soft-on-communism tag and now there was a full-fledged communist government within spitting distance of Key West.[20] President Kennedy could not have inherited a worse situation in the Western Hemisphere. Thus, much closer to home, Al Gray would become involved in using his cryptologic skills to lead Marines.

The CIA and Cuban refugees had come up with a half-baked plan to invade Cuba in 1961; the purpose, of course, was to throw out the communists and restore the property-owners who had fled and who had lost their possessions when the exiled former dictator, Fulgencio Batista, was swept from power. Unfortunately, neither Kennedy nor anyone else high in his administration paid much attention to the issue. The Joint Chiefs highly recommended against the operation as constituted, but no one took the initiative to stop it. Thus, when Kennedy made only minor changes to the initial invasion plans, both the exiles and the CIA were led to believe the young President would fully support the effort. Regrettably, Kennedy had not bothered to inform his Ambassador to the United Nations, Adlai Stevenson, about the invasion. Thus, on the morning of April 15, 1961, it was a highly upset, even mortified Stevenson who called the President's National Security Advisor, McGeorge Bundy, to find out exactly if the reports of U.S. planes bombing Cuba were true. Stevenson had been adamantly denying the U.S. would become involved in any invasion. When Stevenson's howls reached Kennedy, the President cancelled a second bombing attack against Cuban air force targets, despite having earlier approved the operation. The Cuban Air Force recovered sufficiently to deal with the small amphibious operation – having had plenty of advanced warning from spies, the loose lips of the exiles involved, and even Miami press reports. The would-be invasion turned instead into a fiasco labeled the "Bay of Pigs," a humiliation that left the Kennedy Administration red-faced, and put Cuban-American diplomatic relations into a deep freeze that would last decades.

But the Bay of Pigs was just the beginning of President Kennedy's problems with Cuba, and those to come were much more serious; so serious, in fact, they brought the world to the edge of nuclear conflict.

Castro had nearly completely wiped out opposition within Cuba, but the invasion attempt had shown how primitive his military systems, particularly aircraft and communications, were. He openly began operating as a socialist (i.e., communist) government. Also, he immediately turned to his newfound friend and mentor, Nikita Khrushchev, the Premier of the Soviet Union, for assistance in upgrading the island nation's defenses. By mid-1962 the Soviet Union was sending a steady stream of men and equipment – including lots of surface-to-air (defensive) missiles – to the island paradise located so near the U.S. Indeed, the Soviets thought of Cuba the same way the U.S. thought of Turkey and Norway, front row windows into their adversary. Moreover, the Cuban-Soviet-American relationship was exacerbated by personalities. The young, new American President faced a bully of the first order; and Nikita Khrushchev was confident that he could intimidate his inexperienced adversary. After all, an earlier war of words over a large Soviet nuclear test left Khrushchev thinking he held the upper hand in dealing with Kennedy.

The initial signs that a serious problem was developing occurred in early April 1962. Intercept of signals from a radar that was associated with Soviet missiles (designated by the North Atlantic Treaty Organiation as a "Barlock") indicated a new threat was present in Cuba. It was a charge the Kennedy Administration did not want to believe and which the Soviets steadfastly and aggressively denied. However, pictures from a U-2 reconnaissance aircraft left no doubt as to the actual goals of the Soviets and, on October 8, President Kennedy confronted Khrushchev with the evidence.

Captain Al Gray was tasked to lead the routine of HQMC, he was tasked to lead a special detachment to Cuba to support Kennedy's actions against the Soviet-Cuban threat. Gray had been requested by name by the NSA. Gray and his detachment's participation was so secret that his orders were signed personally by General Shoup, and no mention existed in Gray's service record. The threat was so great that Gray's "plethora" of duties had dissipated, at least temporarily.

While the U.S. had an extensive, expensive and pervasive cryptologic effort directed against the Soviet Union, the country was unprepared to deal with a military threat from Cuba, even if the primary focus of the threat was Soviet assets.

Thus, in response to the Pentagon and NSA's request, the Commandant personally directed that Captain Gray assemble a cadre of specialists and go immediately to Cuba using a Marine cargo aircraft. First, Gray proceeded to the NSA to get briefed on the mission and to receive additional special instructions from a senior operative of the CIA who was assigned to NSA. Reflecting the experience he had gained in the Pacific, Gray quickly assembled the unit. But secrecy ruled the day, and the assignment.

Indeed, to demonstrate how closely held activities such as Gray's assignment to Cuba was, one only has to consider this: the Commanding Officer of the 2nd Composite Radio Company at Camp Lejeune, North Carolina, the unit whose electronic intelligence detachment in Key West had detected the "Barlock" radar operating in Cuba during a training mission, never learned of Gray's detachment or its mission until many years after both he and Gray had retired from the service![21] That officer, then Captain (later Colonel) James Quisenberry, was a legend among cryptologists and took great pride in knowing what was going on. Yet in the early 1960s, the strictures against giving unnecessary people information on other than a strict need-to-know basis meant the Commanding Officer of the 2nd Composite Radio Company, a man with all the necessary clearances and whose unit would undoubtedly become involved in any large scale action against Cuba, was never informed that Marines had been sent to Guantanamo to conduct cryptologic operations. Of course, Quisenberry, as events would prove, was not the only Marine in the dark with regard to Gray's activities.[22]

Captain Gray's detachment included then 1st Lieutenant Donald J. (Jim) Hatch, who worked for Captain Quisenberry, and Marines quietly gathered from their duties at the NSA. One of Gray's initial tasks was to verify suspected locations of various radars and communications links located around the island. Among other vessels and locations, the Marines served aboard a tug specially outfitted with SIGINT equipment as seen in the photograph in Figure 3.3. As the tug worked along the Cuban coast in the dark of night, it was mistakenly detected and illuminated by spotlights from a Navy fixed wing, anti-submarine warfare aircraft. Gray feared the Navy plane might open fire, but finally the Americans were able to communicate and happily the episode ended without fanfare. Gray, Hatch and the tug were able to complete the circumnavigation of Cuba, locating or confirming Cuban communications and radar sites.[23]

Figure 3.3
Capt Al Gray, standing behind the technician, with the taller 1ˢᵗ Lt Hatch. [24]

Gray personally undertook other sensitive missions while in Cuba, missions that took advantage of his amphibious reconnaissance background. Those results are probably forever buried in the bowels of the intelligence community, known only to then Captain Donald Q. Layne and Al Gray. Layne had been a Communications Officers Course classmate of Gray's, and was in Guantanamo Temporary Additional Duty from 2ⁿᵈ Radio. The combination of Gray's orders and Layne's contacts resulted in a considerable intelligence haul. Colonel Layne's billets would intersect with Al Gray's several more times before Layne's retirement in the mid-1970s.

As the crisis wound down, Gray turned over to Lieutenant Hatch the responsibility to get the men home. Gray, with many sacks of classified material returned to Washington aboard the Navy/Marine version of the "Flying Boxcar," the R4Q. The aircraft supported HQMC and was often flown by Gray's close friend, Captain

Thomas Jackson. Tom Jackson always tried to arrange to be assigned to the mission if Gray was flying somewhere; early on, the aviator learned that Gray mostly went to unusual places off the beaten track. Over Homestead Air Force Base, Florida, however, the R4Q developed engine problems, stranding Gray, Jackson and the crew for several days while maintenance made the plane safe to fly again. Of course, the presence of the classified materials served to tie Gray to the plane. There was no liberty in Miami for the Captain now serving as a courier. After landing at Andrews Air Force Base, Gray loaded the bags into his Opel station wagon and attempted to deliver his "freight" to NSA. Regrettably, the CIA official that had assigned Gray the additional secretive mission had died of a heart attack, and no one knew anything about any special intelligence materials that a Marine Captain was tasked to get in Cuba. It took several days for Al Gray to sort out the proper procedure for dumping classified materials at NSA, but he finally succeeded. He was present in the Marine Corps' newly established command center (capable of handling special security communications) when the news was received that the Soviet convoy, believed carrying additional missiles to Cuba, had turned away from the island.

Captain Gray was also present when General Shoup was briefed that the crisis appeared over. Shoup had been more than a little concerned at the prospect of putting his Marines into harm's way, especially when the threat of tactical nuclear weapons was present. With the Soviets involved, that was not an empty prospect. The imposing Commandant, a hard but fair and very intelligent man, had tears in his eyes at the news. Obviously, Captain Gray realized, they were eyes of joy for not having to deal with exposing his men to a nuclear battlefield. It was a side of General Shoup not often on display, and one Al Gray never forgot.[25]

That both the Guantanamo and the Vietnam deployments were successfully executed by evolving Marine cryptologic units were vital in the support of Al Gray's future activities at HQMC. In addition to giving both Commandant Shoup and future Commandant Greene palpable measures of the success such units could achieve, the operations gave selective high-ranking officers insights that might not have otherwise been gleaned, adding to the reputation and respect for Marine cryptologic professionals.

But both Lieutenant Colonel Beale and Lucky II, Gray's beloved and very popular black Labrador Retriever, were happy to have the Captain back in town. There was much to do and never enough time to do it.

THE RADIO BATTALION CAMPAIGN PLAN, 1962-1963

General Hogaboom's recommendations had significant impact on how the Marine Corps was organized and equipped by the time General Shoup became Commandant. However, improving and expanding its communications and SIGINT capabilities, including ideas such as making Radio Companies into Radio Battalions, and forming a Marine Support Battalion (now known as the Marine Cryptologic Support Battalion) had not yet been implemented and remained high level, G-2 goals within HQMC. They were a large part of what Beale and Gray had been working on since 1961. Gray's Temporary Additional Duty assignment to Guantanamo had slowed progress, but when at HQMC, Al Gray was head down, knee deep, diligently doing the nuts and bolts required of good staff work.

By this time, Gray had discerned that his focus of main effort was to:
1. Create a totally new capability to provide SIGINT, special intelligence, ground-based EW and SIGSEC support directly to the Fleet Marine Forces; and
2. Complete the structure and capability to support the Naval Security Group Activities and Central Security Service requirements as well as other special requirements.

In order to complete such broad initiatives, Gray had to simultaneously advance on many fronts, all while maintaining and completing his normal, day-to-day staff work. He had worked hard to establish contacts with many staff sections that could assist him with his coordinatation among the many staff sections with whom he needed to interface. He faced a daunting challenge, but as his old platoon commander in recon, Bull Kraince, had observed years before, Al Gray had a knack for getting things done. Gray set his sights on completing a number of sub-tasks that would be vital should he achieve his overall objectives. Gray realized that perhaps the biggest obstacle in the entire effort would be the need to increase the personnel end strength of the Marine Corps. General Pate had already committed the 1,000 men to serve with the NSG world-wide, but if the Marines were to have radio battalions instead of radio companies, then they would have to increase the number of personnel authorized by some 300 – and achieving that goal was a significant, even daunting challenge.

Gray's work had evolved into a concept plan that envisioned a five-year effort, and he realized early on that he would need a lot of luck and much assistance. Furthermore, he had to avoid distractions in the way of naysayers and other obstacles to the maximum extent possible. A prerequisite to success was having a single office responsible for coordinating all the tentacles of the concept. His designation as the Marine Corps' SIGINT Liaison Officer was key. With that appointment, he was directed to represent the Commandant of the Marine Corps on all cryptologic and SIGINT matters related to the NSA, the DoD, the NSG, and all other service cryptologic agencies. To aid him, Gray was able to organize the informal task force needed to shepherd the work through HQMC; this task force included people from all the general and special staff sections, including civilians from the contracting and logistics communities. Gray arranged for people to be briefed into the program as appropriate, and he gave much thought to the art of getting things done.

The cornerstone of the plan was creation of a new Military Occupation Specialty for Marines: the 2600 field. This, by itself, was a massive undertaking. In addition to simply classifying the military skills required of the various personnel, also essential was MOS structure that provided promotion opportunities while identifying basic and advanced schools required. These issues were amplified by the fact that everyone in the new MOS would be eligable for promotion to Lance Corporal before they ever reached their first duty station – because all would receive at least six months to a year of basic training in their MOS. In addition, the military services had just expanded the number of enlisted ranks, which for the Marine Corps meant the new ranks of Master Sergeant and Master Gunnery Sergeant. Gray was fortunate to have men like Mr. Casey and Master Sergeant Keckler in the G-1 and Captain Don Koelper in the G-3. Their expertise was critical to the effort. Keckler, although assigned to Manpower, actually held an NSG detachment billet and reported to Al Gray.

A major goal was that both composite radio companies were turned into radio battalions, one for each Fleet Marine Force, Atlantic and Pacific. The Tables of Organization for radio battalions had to complement the MOS structure, and in that regard had to interface seamlessly with the Marine Support Battalion and the need to have a cryptologic Marine occasionally serve outside their MOS – such as drill instructors or in support of joint staffs. The Marine Support Battalion Table of Organization had to both meet the NSG and NSA requirements with respect to both numbers of Marines and their skill sets, but also they had to consider the fact that up to half of those Marines could be withdrawn to support the Fleet Marine Force – and thus augment the radio battalions. Similarly, the radio battalion Tables of Organization had to also consider the Marine Support Battalion augmentation when the requirements to provide direct support to the Force were determined.

The increase in personnel needed to make battalions was the crux of the matter, and for the Marine Corps, the G-3 had cognizance over force-structure issues. Thus,

Gray's relationships with the senior personnel in the G-3 and G-1 (Manpower) organizations was critical. Personnel levels for the Marine Corps, after gaining acceptance at HQMC, must go through the Department of the Navy (DoN), and then the DoD's fledgling Five-Year Forces Structure and Financial Plan before winning approval; it was not that simple for Al Gray's program, however. In addition to the HQMC-DoN-DoD approval path, Gray's work had to meet the then brand new requirements of the Consolidated Cryptologic Program (CPP). The CCP was a prototype plan, but it was fully integrated with Secretary of Defense Robert S. McNamara's new budgetary methodology. The CCP drill involved both the NSG and the NSA, both of whom had to approve the Marine Corps plan. It was (and remains) an excruciatingly difficult process that finally ends up at DoD, independent of the Five-Year Forces Structure and Financial Plan, and it had to be exceptional in order to win the approval of so many disparate parties.

While the budget and paperwork needed to justify an increase in the end strength was undertaken, even more important was trying to understand, and then satisfy, the underlying operational requirements. Gray undertook a comprehensive study and analysis of Navy and Marine general war and contingency plans in order to develop long-term cryptologic language program that met both Marine and NSG requirements. This was a difficult process. The plan had to ensure that methods were developed to ensure language fluency could be achieved by appropriate advanced and refresher training. Since many languages were quite obscure (for the Marine Corps of the 1960s), many Marines designated to receive training in languages such as Farsi, Arabic, Pashto and Kurdish had to cross-train in other cryptologic specialties so that there was flexibility in their assignments while also providing them promotional opportunities. This aspect of the plan required careful training quota management while all the time keeping an eye toward future requirements. And, of course, further complicating the effort, all the requirements for linguists had to be carefully integrated into the manpower tables of organizations to establish and justify each requirement. Accordingly, the process tied every language billet to a Table of Organization, which was a requirement of the Manpower Branch of HQMC.

It was the result of aggressively sending Marines off to language school that resulted in the second time Al Gray was summoned to meet with the Commandant. Make no mistake, Al Gray had cut no corners in building the 2600 field. He was properly schooled and well prepared by spending time with Captain Koelper and Mr. Casey, the personnel expert who explained in meticulous detail exactly how to build a Table of Organization. Casey was one of those highly competent, very professional civilians that General Greene had described in his welcoming lecture. Al Gray, ever the good listener, learned from the master. For example, each linguist was identified in a Table of Organization classified as "Secret." The classification was necessary because the Tables of Organization reflected current operational plans and each line in the Radio Battalion or Marine Support Battalion Table of Organization was fully justified. Also, the entire technical field reflected a pyramid shaped organization. As a consequence, the 2600s were the first to take advantage of the expansion of the enlisted ranks to include the new ranks of Master Sergeant and Master Gunnery Sergeant. Gray's work, prepared in close cooperation with Master Sergeant Keckler and in concert with Captain Koelper, all under the watchful eye of Mr. Casey, was painstakingly prepared and documented, designed to withstand the close scrutiny of his detractors, of whom there were many.

Nonetheless, questions about Gray's preparations abounded, in large part because the officers at HQMC did not have the background, expertise or even requisite security clearance needed to understand the importance of SIGINT and communications intelligence. In their minds it was heresy to assign Marines to learn such a breadth of exotic languages in numbers that were unheard of. But Al Gray had influential believers who wanted the capabilities of the Radio Battalions he envisioned. After his first round of briefings to the Commandant Shoup in 1962, the Chief of Staff, Lieutenant General Wallace M. Greene, Jr. requested a private 30-minute briefing about Gray's project. It was held in the classified work spaces. When, nearly four hours later, Greene prepared to leave, he told Gray, "Proceed to implement." Al Gray needed no further encouragement.

But determining the language aspects of the puzzle were particularly daunting and, at the end of the day, the method used by Al Gray was something of a SWAG.[26] Gray decided that the service needed 100 Russian linguists, 100 Chinese, 60 Spanish, 60 Vietnamese and 40 Arabic, and fewer numbers in other languages.

The further Gray's staff work progressed, the firmer the opposition became. And the debate was understandable. After all, few of the staff officers understood the issues presented by the Hogaboom study, and they had not read Commandant Pate's agreement with 31-Knot Burke. But the bottom line was that the dispute over people revolved around an age-old topic, if Gray persisted in making linguists, unless there was an increase in Marine Corps personnel end strength, those billets, if approved, would come out of some other program's hide. Since the infantry owned the most bodies in the Force, the infantry stood to lose the most. Though Gray was not yet prepared to present his study with respect to all cryptologic billets that would be needed, the language quotas alone were enough to boil the kettle. Major General August Larson, the Director of Personnel, had had enough of sending linguists hither and yon; he adversely reported Captain Gray's activities to Generals Shoup and Greene.

Captain Al Gray was summoned to the Commandant's office for another 0700 meeting, there to justify his actions and intentions. Besides General Larson, others at Headquarters were upset about Gray's efforts. The word in the passageways was that Al Gray had been beckoned to brief General Shoup regarding the Captain's aggressive fulfilling of language quotas that were not authorized.

By this time, Shoup was in his last year as Commandant (early 1963), and the G-2, General Youngdale, had no interest in attending a briefing when his officers might have their heads served on the Commandant's platter. Although a highly capable officer, Youngdale skillfully avoided the meeting, finding it convenient to be out of the office when it occurred. Dutifully prepared, Gray, the primary briefer, and Beale set off to encounter the officer they privately called the Poker Player, though everyone else called him the Commandant. Gray and Beale were apprehensive and very somber regarding the impending meeting. On the other hand, Gray had justified and re-justified each and every language requirement; and the lesser generals and staff gadflies, present to see the expected reprimand that most thought Gray would receive, intimidated neither him nor Beale.

General Shoup had already settled into the day, chewing on his first cigar, by the time Gray reached his office. "What have you done now, Gray?" asked the Commandant. Al Gray was a professional briefer. Al Gray, with no notes, got immediately to the point, explaining exactly who, what, when, where and why he had sent Marines, in bountiful numbers, to learn unheard of languages, and exactly how he intended to ensure they remained proficient in their craft.

Gray further explained to the Commandant that every linguistic requirement was tied directly to a current operational plan, and showed that each line in the proposed Radio Battalion and Marine Support Battalion Table of Organization was carefully and fully documented. He recapped how they had carefully reviewed all the general war plans for the northern and southern flanks of North Atlantic Treaty Organization as well as the Pacific, and they had studied all existing world-wide contingency plans. Gray covered how AO2F had coordinated with the intelligence community on both threat analysis and the determination of which languages were used for radio communications in various regions. For example, at that time, Flemish was the principal language of radio communications in a portion of Central Africa because of the Belgian influence. Finally, Gray told the Commandant that every Marine in the cryptologic and intelligence field – many who had two MOSs – had all voluntarily reenlisted for the opportunity to attend language school. The General was impressed, and his reaction to Gray's increase in linguists was positive and direct, "I am happy to hear that some officers in this Headquarters are not sitting around on their butts doing nothing." His actual language was more colorful, as it was often wont to be.[27]

Thus, Al Gray won another major skirmish on his way to having his concept turned into reality; but creating a new Military Occupational Field, building Tables of Organization, and identifying language requirements were hardly the only parts of the campaign plan that needed work. There were still a myriad other things to put into writing, that required ongoing coordination both within and outside HQMC, and which would necessitate travel to the far reaches of both the Atlantic and Pacific Commands. It was one thing to create a Radio Battalion, but quite another to get it accepted into the CCP. Such approval would also result in the need for SIGINT/EW/SIGSEC concepts of operation and doctrine. In addition, there were Tables of Equipment and appropriate logistics plans to be developed.

Along with the Table of Organization, each and every Marine battalion has a Table of Equipment. Gray had seen what needed to be built during his many deployments in Hawaii with 1st Radio Company. He knew that the equipment housed at land sites like Kami Seya were entirely inappropriate for shipboard or field use. With the assistance initially of Howie Alberts and others, Gray started designing, fabricating, building and shipping equipment and systems to the radio companies.

While the personnel aspects of creating a cryptologic involved controversy, endless travel and liaison, and careful planning and analysis, the Table of Equipment side of the equation benefitted from that old American standby – luck! Before Gray arrived HQMC, General Jim Masters, had learned that the Army Security Agency was going to declare a few boatloads of equipment excess and that Army Security Agency was preparing to get rid of it. The equipment was mostly housed in large vans or trucks but was still useful, though the Army had no need for it. It was a boon for AO2F, who declined to accept the vans or trucks but who grabbed all the internal components – the tape recorders, radio receivers, teletypewriters, antennae, and a hodgepodge of communications gear. All was sent to storage at the Marine Corps Supply Center, Albany, Georgia. There, Gray and Howard Alberts ensured that the equipment was stored in containers and marked "Confidential." The "Confidential" seal kept nosey intruders away from the gear and gave AO2F the time needed to build a program.

Since there was no Marine Systems Command, everything that was done required the cooperation of the Quartermaster General and other sections of HQMC, but the G-2, specifically AO2F, did all the acquisition planning. There were many things to consider, however. General Shoup had initiated a policy that a Marine would carry no equipment weighing more than 25 pounds; furthermore, all equipment and shelters had to be of a size that could be lifted by Marine helicopters of the day, H-34s. The H-34s were hardly heavy lifters.[28] But Shoup's policy served the Marine Corps very well during the Vietnam War years when new equipment was developed. Indeed, it was Shoup's guidance that led to Alberts's design for an air-conditioned shelter that Radio Battalions used long after the war ended.

Research, development and acquisition were experiences that served Al Gray in a good way in the years to come. In addition to the fine work done by Howard Alberts in the design and production of small vans and generators, SIGINT equipment moved ahead based on a work order that AO2F put in place at Albany, and a contract with Craig Corporation in Massachusetts. Lieutenant Colonel Gilbert Anthony Barrett, USMC (Ret) had been a warrant officer in Marine cryptology dating to World War II. A long time friend of Charlie Beale, after the war Barrett earned a commission and in the 1950s influenced the assignment of Beale to London. He preceded Beale in the AO2F billet, from which he retired and joined Craig Corporation. Beale credited Barrett with equipment achievements that lasted long after his retirement.

In addition to Craig Corporation, AO2F with Al Gray as the lead coordinator with the Office of Naval Research arranged with the Syracuse University Research Corporation to set up an active Science and Technology agreement. That contract provided the means for the Marine Corps to get research and development work undertaken. Syracuse had done a ton of radar related work during World War II and they had branched into Electronics Intelligence. They were heavily involved with Grumman Corporation to produce the Marines' EA-6A Electronic Warfare aircraft. With AO2F, Gray and Alberts, prodding them, Syracuse also started a Communications Intelligence arm. Dr. Gene Simmons and Mr. George Mader helped develop, for example, a version of the Zenith Transoceanic Radio that Marines could use to search for signals in the .5 to 200 megahertz band. They also developed gear that could be fielded without jumping through all the production hoops that most military equipment had to endure. Because the Radio Battalions would be buying only small numbers of units, it avoided the shake, rattle and roll testing and fully stocked spare parts inventories associated with normally developed radios or teletypewriter equipment. While initially AO2F's research and development efforts were the cause of great consternation among the Quartermaster General's hierarchy, eventually Gray was able to convince the powers to be that small-scale, limited quantity, purchases could be exempted from the normal production and replacement parts requirements. By tripling the number of spare components and spare parts estimated for maintenance and repair in the initial procurement, those low-density items would by-pass the normal 18 month Integrated Logistics Support provisioning requirement.

In the course of completing various aspects of the research and development work within AO2F, Al Gray often briefed Major General Wood B. Kyle, who headed all Marine Corps Research and Development activities. General Kyle was vitally interested in Gray's work and AO2F programs. Gray's meeting with General Kyle usually followed updates from Air Defense and assorted other programs whose briefing officer was Lieutenant Colonel E.E. Anderson, an officer who rose to be Assistant Commandant of the Marine Corps under General Cushman. Gray respected Anderson, though, in keeping with his modus operandi, the Captain never asked Anderson or anyone else at HQMC for any favors. In that way he maintained a strict professional relationship with all, and he was never beholden to anyone. General Kyle's awareness of Gray's work ethic and professional expertise would have implications for the younger man in future years, and not that distant. In performing his science and technology role, Gray also had to coordinate closely with the Office of Naval Research.

Any research and development products, or for that matter anything bought off-the-shelf, were eventually sent to 1st and 2nd Radio Companies. The Fabrication and Maintenance Department at the Supply Center, Albany, Georgia, was responsible for integrating all the components already stored at that facility with the new Craig receivers, the newly produced shelters and the generators. Albany was the focal point for the majority of the Table of Equipment for the SIGINT units. Getting things transported from the Supply Center involved another of Al Gray's civilian advisors, Mr. Meade, the transportation expert at HQMC.

Gray took special care to ensure all the required travel documentation was entirely correct, and Mr. Meade responded by ensuring there were no snarls or hiccups during shipment. Especially for gear going to 1st Radio, travel arrangements were fairly complex, first by trucks to the West Coast and then by air to Hawaii. It would not be the last time Al Gray would be the recipient of Mr. Meade's help.[29]

Within two years of Gray's arrival at HQMC, the Radio Companies were fully stocked with the gear needed for their enlarged Table of Equipment. Luck and hard work went a long way whenever the combination got together.

While building the radio battalion Table of Organization and Tables of Equipment, Al Gray greatly profited from the professional expertise of others within HQMC. Their advice was freely given and greatly appreciated as Captain Gray went about his duties. However, incorporating the direct support requirements of the radio battalions into the CCP was breaking new ground, both in terms of the unique ways that Gray envisioned the radio battalions would support the Fleet Marine Force, but also because the budgeting process itself was just recently introduced by Secretary McNamara and everyone at HQMC was learning about it along with Gray. He spent much time with General Frederick Karch and his staff in Plans and Programs, though it fell to Gray to understand how the nuances of the Marine Corps' future application SIGINT and EW would affect the CCP. It was Gray who had to implement those ideas in a way that would garner approval from both NSG and NSA. The big boss at Plans, Programs and Operations was Lieutenant General Henry Buse, an imposing figure of great intellect. It was General Buse who first started what would become commonplace at HQMC – calling Al Gray "spook."

It was a formidable task to develop appropriate concepts and doctrine that would guide the radio battalions' efforts in SIGINT/EW/SIGSEC. The EW aspects of the doctrine had to be coordinated with officers in the office of the Deputy Chief of Staff – Air. Gray established a close relationship with Lieutenant Colonel (and future Lieutenant General) Philip Shutler and Captain Stan Cox in Deputy Chief of Staff – Air, and their combined efforts produced outstanding results. But another group was more problematic; officers at Quantico had important roles to play in SIGINT/EW/SIGSEC and they had a different approach than the one advocated at HQMC.[30] The Quantico contingent was convinced that the Marines had to more resemble the U.S. Army, and more specifically had to emphasize the capabilities found in the Army's EW Battalions. That meant a prominent role for "jamming."[31] But jamming was a fundamentally different approach to the problem than was Gray's emphasis on SIGINT. Gray knew that the Marines could not afford two essentially different methods to providing direct support; Gray argued that the Marines would never have enough people to assign to both approaches and the service could not afford to equip two different organizations – Radio Battalions and EW Battalions – to do essential the same thing, i.e., exploit or disrupt enemy communications. His approach was to combine the efforts into one organization, which could choose to employ either method (SIGINT or jamming) when the situation dictated one or the other. As it turned out, Gray's idea was adopted and that was fortuitous, because his vision was the correct one. The Marine Corps never jammed the enemy's ground communications at any time during the Vietnam War – and neither did the Army. Nonetheless, fending off Quantico's proposals were time consuming.

The logistics concepts for some Radio Battalion equipment also required innovation, and convincing policy makers that innovation made sense always required missionary work. Early on, the Quartermaster General was Brigadier General John Hillary (Bud) Masters, the younger brother of General Jim Masters, and it was he who often came to the tank to get jokes from Colonel Beale or the "spook." Gray earlier had to convince the Quartermaster General's staff that the Marine Corps would actually deploy a small shelter with air-conditioning. Now he also had to convince that same staff that low density items unique to the radio battalion did not require the same logistics tail that much more common items required.[32] It was a battle, but the maneuver warfare techniques Gray employed eventually won the day.

Gray had many, many irons in the fire, and keeping them from overheating or even falling into the inferno demanded long hours and weekends at the office. When combined with his many trips to gather information or coordinate with other commands, Lucky II seldom saw his master, and Gray had little time for extraneous personal activities.

In the Pacific, Gray had embarked on a professional education program to teach Marines about SIGINT/EW and SIGSEC. He made countless briefings, both formal and impromptu, to a variety of groups. At HQMC, Gray and Lieutenant Colonel Beale continued their self-generated education program. Whenever invited, the duo, as well as Al Gray individually, made numerous presentations within HQMC and at Quantico. Classes at Communications Officers Course, the Amphibious Warfare School, the Command and Staff College, the National Defense University, the Industrial War College all heard the Marine Corps' leading practitioner of SIGINT/EW address the topic. Gray's enthusiasm for the subject matter was contagious, though Gray did not realize until years later that one of his presentations at the Communications Officer School so motivated at least one young officer that he volunteered for language school, which led to lifetime as a cryptologic professional.[33] Gray presentations were so good that he was usually invited back to wherever he spoke.

One cannot overstate the number of trips, visits, and inquiries Al Gray made while determining both the Tables of Organization and the Tables of Equipment for each proposed Radio Battalion and for the Marine Support Battalion. His papers reveal at least 33 sets of Temporary Additional Duty orders during his time at HQMC. Gray traveled to liaise with NSG locations around the globe; he made repeated trips to the Defense Intelligence Agency and the NSA, and while doing so he bolstered his already fine reputation at the Puzzle Palace, as many refer to NSA.

Though Gray had recently served in the Pacific and was familiar with most of the war plans in that region, nonetheless he reviewed them again. And while traveling to such locations as Edsall, Scotland and Karimasel, Turkey to meet with NSG representatives, Gray also took the time to review North Atlantic Treaty Organization plans. The purpose of all his visits was two-fold; first, he was trying to determine the number and types of linguists the Marine Corps needed in order to satisfy the diversity of language requirements where Marines might operate. Second, Gray was gathering information needed to create the various sub-specialties within cryptology and special communications.

One important sister service had offices much nearer to Gray. The Bureau of Naval Personnel shared the massive building called the "Navy Annex" with HQMC. One officer with whom Gray worked closely at the Bureau of Naval Personnel was then Lieutenant Commander Patrick March, USN, who as a Rear Admiral later commanded NSG. The information gathered at both the Bureau of Naval Personnel and elsewhere was essential to create a Table of Organization and create a MOS field, 2600. And while interfacing with organizations outside the Marine Corps took much of his time, Al Gray also devoted lots of energy to interfacing with the cryptologists assigned to 1st and 2nd Composite Radio Companies. None of those officers and Staff NCOs would be surprised at the results of Gray's work; they had been intimately involved every step of the way.

NSA was a frequent destination for Al Gray, and often it had nothing to do with increasing Marine Corps capabilities. Rather, it had to do with how NSA would provide direct support and direct service support to all the military services.[34] General Gordon Blake had tasked one of his civilian heavy hitters, Lee Sawyer, to come up with doctrine and procedures detailing how the secretive agency would support military units while they are deployed and engaged in operations aboard; such procedures would be used to develop NSA annexes to military operational plans. Sawyer, who had no background in such matters, was introduced to Al Gray. After all, the Marine Captain had come to the attention of many at Ft. Meade while leading his flyaway teams in the Pacific at 1st Radio; furthermore, Gray had written SIGINT annexes to various Marine contingency plans in the Pacific. Now, in 1962 and 1963, Gray was a frequent visitor to NSA. Sawyer was tasked to write how NSA would support important Pentagon war plans, and he used the Marine's experience to assist him.

Figure 3.4
The Inspector–General of the Marine Corps, Brig Gen T.F. Riley shakes
hands with Maj F.P. Wilson, Commanding Officer of Company "E," Marine
Support Battalion at Kami Seya, Japan. Capt Gray trails Wilson.[35]

Figure 3.5
A smiling Lt Col Charlie Beale reads the promotion order while
Maj Gen Robert Cushman, the G-2/3, and future 25th Commandant
of the Marine Corps, pins on gold leaf on Al Gray's shoulder.[36]

NSA functioned basically as a vacuum cleaner, all signals-related information the United States collected ended up at Ft. Meade, usually, it was joked, in some obscure cellar. Then, after the information had been sorted, processed, and evaluated, it was finally distributed to those who had a need to know. Passing processed information to SIGINT stations like the Navy's at Kami Seya was one thing. Each service's cryptologic stations were designed to exchange information directly with NSA. But supporting the military's operational commands was a much more convoluted affair; the MAC(V), for example, needed to receive critical intelligence in a timely manner while the intelligence was still actionable. NSA was required to develop plans to do just that.

Sawyer and Gray worked many afternoons, early evenings and weekends while developing the doctrine that General Blake finally signed in early 1965. It would be continuously refined and modified as technological innovations altered how NSA interfaced with its subordinate cryptologic agencies in each military service and how it got information to various operational commands, but Sawyer and Gray developed the initial plans and protocols; their efforts changed that dynamic. However, neither envisioned that their blueprint for the future would be applied almost immediately as the military situation in South Vietnam heated up. The cryptologic support team concept that Sawyer and Gray envisioned and that General Blake approved has remained in place through current (2012) conflicts. Equipment and procedures have changed with technology, but Sawyer and Gray's work remains the framework within which cryptologic support is provided to the operating forces.

In the midst of all his Temporary Additional Duty trips to gather information about cryptology, Gray was also chosen to be the G-2 representative on the Inspector-General trip to all three divisions and wings during the summer of 1962 as part of Brigadier General T.F. (Mugs) Riley's contingent. That trip took Gray to the East Coast, West Coast, Hawaii, and the Western Pacific. It gave Gray first-hand knowledge of what was happening throughout the intelligence field, who was training and who was skating, which units were aggressively operating and which needed a kick in the pants. Gray observed all the debriefs, not just those for intelligence, and he gained more knowledge of the operational and logistics posture of the Corps. For the intelligence representative, the trip was like another advanced professional development course. Importantly, he also learned more about EW as it is applied to air operations.

While conducting the Inspector-General inspection of the Marine Corps's Composite Reconnaissance Squadron (VMCJ), Captain Gray was introduced to Captain Moranville and Chief Warrant Officer Martin LaChow. In VMCJ squadrons, the pilots exist principally to serve as chauffeurs for the officers who sit in the backseat, or in the case of the EA-6B, the three other seats (it has a total crew of four). The "backseat drivers" are the officer-technicians who actually perform the mission. VMCJ aircraft are used to detect and locate enemy radars, or take pictures, or perhaps jam enemy radars. In the early 1960s, the backseat aviators were the real experts in EW. Gray was privileged to spend time with them and he learned much about the EW trade.

In the late spring of 1963, Al Gray lost his status as a company-grade officer. He became a Major of Marines, though, as he likes to joke, being a major at HQMC, especially such a junior major, makes one more like a "Lance Major." However,

Figure 3.6
Lt Gen James Masters greets Commandant Wallace M, Greene. Gray
considered himself privileged to have served with both those fine officers.[37]

the one perk that Gray thought came with his new status, a parking space closer
to the building, was denied him. As he received his new identification card and
the vestiges of his higher rank, he was informed that, due to a recent change, only
lieutenant colonels rated better parking. Other personnel changes soon occurred:
Howie Alberts was off to duty in Vietnam while Lieutenant Colonel Charlie Beale

left later in the year for duty as a lawyer at Camp Lejeune, North Carolina. His assignment at HQMC marked the last time Beale served in any cryptologic billet, though he remained a lifelong friend of Al Gray.

President Kennedy nominated Wallace M. Greene, Jr. to relieve General Shoup as Commandant, and the change occurred in September 1963. One of General Greene's priorities had an immediate effect on Major Gray. Wallace Greene was a futurist and considered long and mid-range studies to be key to ensuring the Marine Corps developed the concepts, doctrine and equipment required to stay relevant in the future. The new Commandant emphasized such studies and soon the Syracuse University was contracted to provide an inter-disciplinary study to determine what the world would look like in 1985. When the Syracuse Board of Regents balked at the undertaking, Captain Gray was sent to the University (he had already had several contracts with them) to explain exactly what the Marine Corps envisioned. The Board approved and one year later the University presented Greene with a five-volume study entitled, "*The World in 1985.*"

In addition to the perhaps predictable issues related to water or food shortages in Mexico, the study forecast a rise in global terrorism and suggested that the Marine Corps needed to tidy up relations with the Department of State. Taking the Syracuse product, Commandant Greene assigned Brigadier General Gordon D. Gayle the task of making the work specifically relevant to the Marine Corps. General Gayle's work ended with a study called "USMC 1985," the first long-range study produced by any military service. From it, supporting mid-range and short-range studies were created. Embedded in the studies were operational requirements, which were very broad and sweeping in the long-range study but more specific and detailed in the short and mid-range documents.

Al Gray was given responsibility to integrate SIGINT/EW capabilities into the plans, working closely with Colonel O'Donnell in the G-2 office and with the Research and Development staffs at HQMC and from Quantico. Colonel O'Donnell taught Gray to get a paragraph in the long Range Study in order to get a chapter in the mid-range plan. Their efforts resulted in the requirement for, among other things, the EA-6B, an all-weather EW aircraft. And, of course, Gray planted the seeds for future SIGINT capabilities and equipment in all the studies. General Greene's emphasis on long and mid-range studies, which General Chapman reinforced in the early 1970s, had significant impact on Al Gray's thought process as he advanced through his profession.

ALBERTS ARRIVES AT MILITARY ADVISORY COMMAND (VIETNAM), SAIGON, 1963

The AO2F staff section that had been so successful in a variety of endeavors at HQMC was broken up during 1963. Al Gray had been off on various Temporary Additional Duty assignments during much of 1962, including his visit to Guantanamo, Cuba. But the first of the trio to leave HQMC on Permanent Change of Station orders was Howie Alberts. Even Alberts, who had successfully fended off several possible transfers to Okinawa in order to stay at HQMC, could not turn down orders to join the staff of the Commanding General, MAC(V). Nor did he want to; after all, a war was a fitting place for a man of Alberts's skills.[38]

Newly promoted Lieutenant Colonel Howard K. Alberts, USMC, 2502/0302 arrived in Saigon in late January 1963. He made an ignominious entrance. During the 1960s, the summer uniform for Marine officers, Service Dress Khaki, was anything but comfortable when the weather was hot; and Saigon that January was very hot, and very humid. Throughout his professional life, Alberts took great pride in his uniforms, and had them tailor-made in Washington, D.C., by the same tailor who made uniforms for Generals Lewis B. Walt and Robert E. Cushman. Alas, despite the quality of his uniforms, and his pride in them, Alberts's body type would never permit him to win a starring role in any Hollywood movie.

Lieutenant Colonel Alberts's plane had stopped in Hawaii and again in the Philippines. Arriving with no air conditioning, the plane was forced to wait on the tarmac for over an hour at Tan Son Nhut airbase while Vietnamese customs officials checked passengers before permitting them to de-plane. To his astonishment, his new boss, the MAC(V) J-6, recently promoted Colonel Philip S. Pomeroy, United States Army, met Alberts at the airport. The new Lieutenant Colonel could tell that the Army bird colonel was disappointed by the looks of his new staff assistant. Alberts's uniform blouse (Marines refer to the uniform jacket as a "blouse") was thoroughly soaked in perspiration. Despite his best effort, Alberts chance to make a good first impression was lost. Seeing the disenchantment in Pomeroy's eyes, Alberts mustered all the conviction he could and said, "Colonel, if you were looking for somebody to pose for Marine Corps recruiting posters, you got the wrong person; but if you want someone who's going to go out and look for VCs, you've got the right one." Pomeroy was momentarily taken aback, but when Alberts reported for duty a few hours later, the Marine had a pleasant surprise awaiting him.

The J-6 was a self-described "straight arrow." He knew all about the world of special clearances, and possessed such clearances himself; thus, Pomeroy knew generally the missions associated with SIGINT and Communications Intelligence that he was responsible for directing. In fact, Pomeroy's first assignment in Vietnam had been to transition the American military to an online crypto-security system designed to thwart VC attempts to exploit communications.[39] However, his first words to Alberts at the office were to the effect that Pomeroy did not approve of listening to other people's communications, and he wanted nothing to do with such activity. Further, he did not even want to hear what Alberts or assistants were doing; he did adamantly insist, however, that Alberts keep Pomeroy out of trouble.

Colonel Pomeroy was the Commanding General's handpicked J-6; all the other "J's" on the staff were brigadier generals. General Paul D. Harkins was selected for the Saigon post based on his relationship with General Maxwell D. Taylor, the Chairman of the Joint Chiefs and the close confidant of President Kennedy. The Taylor-Harkins relationship dated back to World War II when both served on General George S. Patton's staff. At MAC(V), the J-6 (Colonel Pomeroy) was responsible for command, control, communications and special operations. The deputy was an Air Force colonel, and lieutenant colonels headed the various branches. Alberts's Plans Branch (it actually did "Special Operations") of the J-6 included an Army major as his #2 man, along with an Air Force captain and Navy lieutenant, and two Army sergeants who served as administrative assistants. After announcing his intention to never become personally involved with what he considered "ungentlemanly" activities, the J-6 surprisingly directed that Alberts attend all of General Harkins's staff meetings, making the Marine officer one of the very few deputies who attended all the Commanding General's staff conferences. Lieutenant Colonel Alberts was to sit directly behind his boss, ready to provide information in the event any questions about SIGINT or Communications Intelligence arose. Alberts happily agreed to follow orders, since they gave him a veritable *carte blanche*. Furthermore, in the staff meetings his seat gave him access to many interesting and exciting, frustrating and wearisome, surprising and unforeseen events, information and actions.

Howie Alberts's primary duties included coordinating with the representatives of the CIA and the NSA, as well as coordinating the efforts of military service cryptologic agencies. Both the CIA and NSA representatives and their organizations operated independently of MAC(V) and General Harkins, though during Alberts's time in Saigon, there was close coordination among the three. Generally speaking, anything going on that was highly classified or "spooky" fell under Alberts's purview. His task was to plan any ground SIGINT or Special Operations undertaken within South Vietnam. His plans would be coordinated among the other "J" sections, particularly the J-2 (Intelligence), J-3 (Operations), and J-5 (Plans), and

then passed to the staff of the Commander-in-Chief, Pacific, for possible implementation. While Alberts received generally favorable, even enthusiastic, support
for his plans, he never was involved with any resulting operation that might have
occurred. It was a strange way to operate, but one that provided more security since
the possibility for leaks in South Vietnam was reduced.

Alberts set about trying to get things organized in Special Operations. It was
anything but a simple assignment. The new Lieutenant Colonel of Marines faced
an uphill challenge in his billet, since the individual cloak and dagger organizations,
American as well as South Vietnamese, had been operating independently, without close staff coordination. Slowly but surely, however, Alberts began to grasp the
intricacies of the billet, including the personalities of various players. While the J-6
was one of Harkins's handpicked men, his avoidance of SIGINT events and activities left him an enigma to Alberts. But Howard Alberts, the man who exhibited an
outsized inability to suffer fools while serving with Charlie Beale and Al Gray at
HQMC, had learned a new skill in Saigon: he had learned to keep his opinions to
himself unless something really important was on the line. Thus, Alberts was able
to do his work without displaying the lack of respect he had for many on the staff,
including at times his boss. While Colonel Pomeroy was a fine professional and
knew more about theater and other high level communications than most professional communicators, his lack of interest in SIGINT was both a blessing and a
curse to Alberts's efforts.

Contrary to General Harkins actions to handpick his staff, the U.S. Army personnel policy in the early 1960s was to send to Vietnam Soldiers who were on their
twilight tours. That is, men who were near retirement and who had little chance for
promotion were shipped off to Saigon and MAC(V). There, Soldiers could fritter
away their last few years on active duty while serving in a place that few knew about
and even fewer cared about. Many Marines assigned to Vietnam remarked on the
Army personnel situation, including Lieutenant Colonel Alberts. While not every
Soldier was unmotivated awaiting retirement, too many were. Such officers and
Soldiers were neither a significant help to their South Vietnamese hosts nor their
American counterparts who were trying hard to do the best possible job under difficult circumstances. Further, such men were easy marks for the derisive comments of
reporters who interacted with them. The reporters, intent on breaking a story and
making news, were selective of whom they asked about what. They found it easy to
portray the military in less than favorable light, because in many cases their sources
of choice were not the first string military officers then serving in country.

Not just the reporters had issues with many of the American officers at the Headquarters. Alberts and the number of Army Command and Staff College graduates with whom he served were often frustrated, and had to work around their colleagues. The same held true when dealing with the South Vietnamese. When highly charged, aggressive and motivated American officers found the locals not able to meet their demanding expectations, the reporters could spin the story in an entirely different way, deriding the South Vietnamese as corrupt, poorly led, incompetent or, most likely, all the above. Of course, the crowning blow that led the reporters down the wrong path was provided by Pham Xuan An, the communist agent working for *TIME*, the American magazine. An was the reporters' most valuable source, and they depended on him greatly, yet all the while he fed them information intended to assist the communist cause.[40]

On the positive side, it did not take Alberts long to meet a very important player in Saigon affairs. That person, known publicly as the DoD Pacific Representative, was in reality the NSA representative, Colonel Richard Gales, United States Army. Gales operated with his own budget, one outside the MAC(V) purse strings. With it, he wielded enormous influence among the South Vietnamese, and he played the part while doing so, driving around the city in a huge, black, gangster-like Citroen limousine. But Gales was also an influential team player who reported directly to Harkins, but who also shared his information with the J-2 (Intelligence), J-3 (Operations) and J-5 (Plans). It was Alberts's J-6 Special Operations Branch that provided the primary MAC(V) liaison with Gales' far-flung organization. When it was decided to merge the efforts of CIA and NSA, a Special Operations Group was established. Gales and Alberts were guiding figures in the new Special Operations Group organization, ensuring closer coordination than ever before was achieved.

But just keeping track of who reported to whom, especially by November 1963 during the days before and after the coup against Diem, required a full-time secretary, so any effectiveness achieved by members of the intelligence community was mostly attributable to the personal relationships maintained by those involved. Unfortunately, the arrival of Ambassador Lodge in September led to the dismissal of one of the key players, the CIA Chief of Station, John Richardson. Gales and Alberts, however, had early on forged a close bond that continued into the future.

The CIA had established a program of dropping leaflets around the countryside and in North Vietnam. The leaflets were often developed in coordination with Ngo Dinh Nhu's security organization; sometimes they extolled the virtues of the Diem regime while other printings attacked the communists for their violence or land redistribution schemes. No matter what the message on the leaflets, they were dropped by pilots from third world countries working as contractors who were flying planes bought and maintained by the CIA, and otherwise known as "Air America." Alberts knew that the NSA contingent maintained direction finding as well as radar capabilities at bases throughout the entire region, and so he requested that those units track the CIA aircraft when they flew leaflet missions. Gales acceded to the request and redirected all his Southeast Asia assets in order to track the aircraft whenever they were airborne. In that manner, it was discovered that the contract pilots were simply flying out over the South China Sea and dropping their cargoes in the ocean, instead of risking getting shot down by VC or North Vietnamese gunners. Confronted with the NSA evidence, the CIA quickly put a stop to the "South China Sea operations." The pilots flew the routes prescribed and made the drops on the designated target, or they did not get paid.

CONCEIVING OPERATION TIGER TOOTH MOUNTAIN, 1963

One of the key issues addressed by Harkins's staff was the infiltration of North Vietnamese troops and supplies into South Vietnam along the infamous Ho Chi Minh Trail. Alberts was determined to prove the breadth and depth of North Vietnamese involvement. Though the Hyatt Detachment to Pleiku in 1962 found very few communist communications, Alberts was not ready to declare SIGINT a failure in that regard. Alberts knew that Hyatt had suffered from two major disadvantages. First, the Pleiku location was not optimal for intercepting the line of sight communications used by tactical units or those on the Trail; more importantly, Alberts had discovered from his NSA associates that the North Vietnamese were probably using an advanced multi-channel communications system provided by their Soviet allies. Hyatt's detachment, and indeed all of the U.S. cryptologic services, lacked the radio equipment necessary to exploit the transmissions from the Soviet system.

As a first step to any operation, Alberts carefully plotted the exact routes of the Ho Chi Minh Trail insofar as it was known to exist in late 1963. He also completed an in-depth map reconnaissance of the Vietnamese mountain ranges. With a timely tip from NSA, he was able to determine that if a communications intelligence unit was situated on Tiger Tooth Mountain (Dong Voi Mep, 1701), just south of the DMZ that separated North and South Vietnam, it would be able to "see" (actually "hear") any communist communications near Tchepone, Laos. Tchepone was considered a major base along the Trail. Since Tiger Tooth dominated the landscape,

Alberts concluded that even if Tchepone was not the communications focal point, a unit located on the mountain would have excellent coverage.

His first sounding board was Colonel Richard Gales; every morning, when Alberts was in Saigon, he joined Gales for breakfast and would discuss various activities. Afterwards, Gales' Vietnamese driver would drop Alberts at MAC(V) Headquarters, before speeding away from the comments and good-natured catcalls from the guards that announced Alberts's arrival. Gales liked Alberts's concept of establishing a Marine Corps signal intelligence unit on Tiger Tooth Mountain so much that he arranged for a CIA aircraft to take them to the Special Forces base at Khe Sanh, located not far from the DMZ and Tiger Tooth. From there, they conducted a helicopter reconnaissance of the area. Satisfied there were no apparent obstacles to the plan, they returned to Saigon where Gales arranged to brief the J-3, Brigadier General Richard Stilwell, United States Army, about Alberts's plan. Stilwell was a brilliant officer and had a very high reputation among the staff.

Alberts did his best song and dance routine at the briefing and Stilwell liked it. He immediately arranged for a briefing for General Harkins. Within 24 hours they were on Harkins's schedule; again, Lieutenant Colonel Alberts conducted the briefing. Colonel Pomeroy, true to his word, was nowhere to be seen; instead, Stilwell and Gales sat in to support Alberts. Harkins liked the concept but worried that there were too many VC in the area; when Alberts reported that intelligence estimates put only a single VC company in the area, Harkins responded, "If that is true, Alberts, get yourself up there on the mountain and conduct a personal reconnaissance."[41]

Colonel Gales obtained a CIA aircraft that flew the pair to Da Nang, where they met Lieutenant Colonel Tom Waite, United States Army, the deputy advisor to the ARVN's I Corps. From Da Nang, a Marine helicopter flew the three officers again to Khe Sanh, where inclement weather promised to undermine the mission. Low hanging clouds and lack of adequate flight aids made the Marine helicopter pilots very wary about approaching the area's highest peak while it was enmeshed by a very thick cloud cover. After what seemed an interminable delay, and following an emphatic harangue by Alberts, the aviators were convinced that they really needed to get onto Tiger Tooth. Once there, the three colonels, acting much like the three musketeers of old, tromped around the mountaintop. Gales used the time to test his sidearm, a fancy pistol of unknown caliber and origin. Waite, the only one with a carbine, watched patiently while Alberts, who carried only a .38 revolver, stomped around the top, imagining exactly how he would deploy a defending force. The visit convinced Alberts that a Marine rifle company could hold off attackers for a very long time. He and Gales returned to Saigon to finalize plans.

A second briefing to General Harkins won Alberts permission to proceed to the next level of planning. In his interactions with Harkins, and his observations at staff meetings, Alberts formed the opinion that the General was a highly competent man who knew what he wanted done, asked appropriate and penetrating questions, while displaying a high degree of professionalism.

Alberts's friends, Colonel Gales and John Richardson, the CIA Head of Station, agreed with his view of General Harkins; however, none of the three held then U.S. Ambassador Henry Cabot Lodge in high esteem. Lodge's replacement of Ambassador Frederick Nolting and the transfer of Richardson in order to permit the Diem coup to proceed were, in Alberts's opinion, two of the great mistakes of the war. Alberts had a close view of Nhu's secret agents, and while he had no illusions about the extent of Nhu's occasional excesses, he also was aware of the overall effectiveness of their measures. Further, Alberts was convinced that Diem was in the process of making peace with the North, a peace that would have permitted the Americans to leave Vietnam honorably, thus avoiding the war that cost America over 55,000 lives. While Alberts had no direct involvement with any aspect of peace talks that might have been underway, his relationship with Gales and various CIA types was such that he certainly picked up vibrations about such activity. But in late 1963 Lieutenant Colonel Alberts had no real time to think about what could have been with respect to Diem; he was conceiving *Operation Tiger Tooth Mountain* and getting his regular staff work done.

Alberts knew that a fundamental requirement necessary to get final approval for his concept was to make certain any unit sent on the mission would have the proper intercept equipment. He arranged to make another trip back to Washington; regrettably, his trip coincided with President Kennedy's assassination. At NSA, Alberts obtained the technical specifications of the Soviet system that he hoped to exploit. NSA had been able to take advantage of the targeted system, but only by using laboratory equipment to decipher signals captured on tape. The tapes were made using high-quality, high-speed studio grade tape recorders that were completely unusable in any combat environment, particularly one on a hot, wet, mountaintop setting with no air-conditioning! But Alberts's concept, one that he, Beale and Gray had discussed numerous times in their meetings in the tank at HQMC, was not to just make tapes. Rather, it was to have a tactical unit exploit the communications in real-time, something Gray had advocated in every discussion related to Marine cryptology. After meeting with Major Gray and giving him the details of the concept, it was the Marine at HQMC who took over responsibility for mission planning.

Major Gray thought he knew just the people he needed to accomplish the projected mission, the same company who held a Science and Technology Contract with AO2F. And AO2F's contracts with Syracuse resulted in almost immediate rewards in Vietnam.

The Syracuse University Research Corporation had the scientists and engineers well qualified to build what was needed. After all, Syracuse had been working on aviation equipment for the Marine Corps throughout the 1950s. They also had worked on only a verbal commitment, usually given by Captain and then Major Al Gray, to develop various radios and peripheral equipment for the mushrooming needs of the 1st and 2nd Composite Radio Companies. Contracts had always followed the Marines' verbal instructions. In this case, an entirely new piece of equipment was needed and there was not sufficient time to accomplish a full-scale development; rather a breadboard was needed.[42] Not just any breadboard, but one that could be operated and maintained by Marines in the field, with perhaps a little help from their technical friends. Gray was a strong proponent of what he called "fieldable breadboard models" to evaluate SIGINT equipment requirements.

The Syracuse engineers were eager to work with Gray; after all, he had proven reliable in contracting affairs and knowledgeable technically when they had worked with him before, and he seemed to only work on important projects! But the project he now described was very difficult, especially given the time constraints and the probable operational environment. Still, they could do it – if, and only if – a Syracuse engineer, Mr. George Mader, could accompany the Marines into the field. The engineer would bring along tools and supplies needed to keep the breadboard operational, and he would be there to teach the Marines how to operate their new contraption. Needless to say, that requirement further complicated Gray's plan. With NSA having provided the necessary specifications, and with Syracuse promising to provide the necessary equipment and technical expertise, Gray was ready to brief his plan within HQMC.

There had been an important change at the Headquarters in the months preceding Alberts's visit. General Wallace M. Greene, Jr. had replaced General Shoup as Commandant. General Greene was much more open to Marine Corps involvement in Vietnam, but he was particularly open to anything that related to Marine Corps interaction with other services and agencies, especially important, nationally significant ones like NSA. Commandant Shoup chaffed under the restrictions of his role on the JCS, being able to "vote" only when JCS discussed matters pertaining to the Marine Corps; General Greene was determined to expand Marine activities throughout the DoD, thus increasing the Commandant's role on the JCS. As a result, when an idea of using Marine Corps assets to support another NSA operation in Vietnam arose, General Greene was all for it. Major Al Gray had seen the transformation in thinking in the Commandants' corner office and, having honed the concept developed by Alberts, he was ready to act.

Although Major Gray had still not completed the staffing of the proposed concepts for the new organization of the Marine Support Battalion and the elevation of the Radio Companies to Radio Battalions, in large part because he had already experienced numerous periods of Temporary Additional Duty away from Headquarters, Gray knew he wanted to personally lead the operation Alberts envisioned. Thus, he set about lining up Marine Corps support for another Temporary Additional Duty trip, this time to Vietnam. Meanwhile, Alberts had returned to Saigon via Hawaii, where he discussed the proposed mission with the Director of NSA's Pacific Operations, Colonel John Morrison, United States Air Force. Morrison, who later served as a Major General in charge of NSA Operations, liked the idea but wondered who would protect the Marine cryptologists.[43] Alberts flew on to Saigon with yet another complication to ponder. Meanwhile, Al Gray continued working the issues from his HQMC office by liaising directly with Fleet Marine Forces, Pacific and already had a concept for security.

Once he arrived back on the ground at MAC(V) Headquarters, Alberts turned over to Gray the responsibility to conduct the staffing needed to get approval of the operation. Back channels communications (very highly classified communications between U.S. commands and often done on an informal basis between high ranking officers) indicated that both the Commandant as well as the relatively new Commanding General, FMFPAC, Lieutenant General Victor H. Krulak, had both informally approved the concept and promised to provide a Marine rifle company as security for the cryptologists.

In January 1964, MAC(V) formally requested that the Marine Corps provide a force that would be called Marine Detachment, Advisory Team 1, a designation that Alberts and Gray had contrived during their meeting in the tank. Three officers and 27 enlisted men from the 1st Composite Radio Company, and six Vietnamese and Thai linguists from NSA, would provide the cryptologic component of Gray's command. As cover for what was really happening, and as security for the operation, 76 Marines from an infantry unit (formed around the 2nd Platoon, Company G, 2nd Battalion, 3rd Marines) would conduct counter-insurgency training for South Vietnamese irregular forces located at Khe Sanh, the future site, in 1967, of a major Marine Corps battle of the war. Meanwhile, the cryptologic Marines and the rest of the security detachment, including an ARVN rifle company, would move onto the mountain and conduct communications surveillance operations.

Two civilians were attached to the Marines; the first was Gray's old engineer acquaintance from Syracuse, George Mader, and the second was an NSA representative and Vietnamese linguist, Harry T. Williams. The mission was important for several reasons. It marked the first commitment of American ground combat forces into South Vietnam, and it marked the first attempt to conduct tactical SIGINT operations against the North Vietnamese in their havens inside of, north and west of the DMZ and along the Ho Chi Minh Trail. It also was the first tactical operation against a Soviet multi-channel communications system.

Alas, Howie Alberts did not remain in country long enough to see the Tiger Tooth Mountain operation get started. Alberts's tour officially ended in February 1964. Despite the best efforts of several of his NSA contacts, including Colonel Richard Gales, Colonel John Morrison and others, Alberts, who had sought a follow-on assignment at the Vietnam desk at NSA, had his request denied. Consequently, after 22 years of service, Howard Alberts chose to retire and enter private industry. Within two years, however, Alberts was serving at NSA in the position he had wanted, but instead of being a Lieutenant Colonel of Marines, he was a scientist working for the Syracuse University Research Corporation.[44]

VIETNAM HISTORY, 1961-1963

WASHINGTON AND INTERNATIONAL POLITICS, 1961

The primary architect of the Vietnam War on the American side was no warrior, despite his service as an obscure Army Air Force staff officer during World War II following his graduation from Harvard. After the war he became a businessman whose abilities related to statistical analysis led to a meteoric rise through the executive ranks at the Ford Motor Company. His sound decision-making caused Henry T. Ford II to name him the first non-family member ever to be given the title of President and Chief Executive Officer of that venerable American car company. But Robert Strange McNamara had barely put his own furniture into the CEO's office when John Fitzgerald Kennedy summoned him to Washington to manage the DoD.

It is not clear how or why Kennedy decided on McNamara, but the President-elect pulled out all the stops in convincing Ford's young Chief Executive to take a giant pay cut and join the new Cabinet, which McNamara ultimately did. The new President simply could not appear to be reliant on the status quo at the DoD, a bureaucracy so large that it threatened daily chaos to even the most efficient managers. Kennedy had been elected in part because of a "missile-gap" that he claimed existed between the United States and its bitter Cold War rival, the Soviet Union. But McNamara soon reported that no gap existed; despite the news, and even if he disagreed with the assessment, Kennedy was hardly in a position to criticize the work of his new Secretary of Defense. In any event, the President could not afford to appear "weak on defense," an impression of Democrats that was largely responsible for twice leading American voters to elect Dwight D. Eisenhower to office during the 1950s.

A situation in Southeast Asia had soon become a blister to the Kennedy Administration's desire to convey the image of a strong, powerful foreign policy. It was not the situation in South Vietnam, however, but rather the unsettling civil war in the Kingdom of Laos.

Laos was threatened on many fronts, and the North Vietnamese in particular were quite active in disrupting the Kingdom. Essentially, Laos lacked a central government, and various factions vied for dominion over a country too weak to be a threat to its neighbors, but one centrally located in a region where communism was on the march. To be sure, there was no love lost between the Laotians and their Vietnamese neighbors, nor were there any political or cultural ties to other neighbors, the Cambodians to the south or the Thais to the west, or the Chinese to north. So while Ho Chi Minh had more than his hands full trying to unify Vietnam, he was also a dedicated communist intent on spreading his ideology throughout the region. American policy was based on challenging communism wherever it was found, and so the Laotian situation was one that provided a host of convoluted, complex, and unquestionably ambiguous realities that were more than enough to confuse even the best foreign policy experts. Nevertheless, it is questionable as to whether America had assigned its diplomatic first-string to the problems in Southeast Asia – though, perhaps in Kennedy's mind, he did.

Averill Harriman and John Kenneth Galbraith were two old Democrat warhorses who were very powerful within the party, and to whom the new President was beholden. Galbraith, the famous Harvard economist, who during World War II had kept a lid on inflation, was appointed Ambassador to India, by far the most important posting in Asia in 1961. It was Galbraith's understanding that he was to have broad influence over policy throughout Asia. Harriman, the former patrician Governor of New York (who preferred to be called "Governor,") was the Under-Secretary of State for Far Eastern Affairs. Appointed to the post largely as a reward for his years of service to the Democrat Party, his influence would probably do more harm to America than any other politician-turned-diplomat. In the early 1970s, it would be Harriman and Henry Kissinger who largely caved into North Vietnamese lies and threats at the Paris Peace Talks, but in early 1961-62 Averill Harriman joined with Galbraith to muddle American diplomacy in Laos.

One reason those well-regarded politicians, but diplomatic dilettantes, were left to negotiate for America in Laos was because the Secretary of State, Dean Rusk, was too busy dealing with what he considered the much more weighty issues related to the Cold War and the Soviet Union. Rusk opined that Laos was but a shadowy remote place when compared to the intensity associated with the Soviet diplomatic effort.[45] Besides, Rusk never met a decision that could not be postponed or avoided, while Galbraith and Harriman loved power, and power meant making decisions. No matter how commendable Galbraith's efforts were in India, and there is abundant evidence that he was extraordinarily successful there, his work in Laos was stunningly bad.

The fact of the matter was that the United States gave away the store in the Laotian Accords. In some circles, the Ho Chi Minh Trail was derisively called the Averill Harriman Memorial Highway. The factors leading to the Laotian diplomatic decision were poorly analyzed and researched, and it appeared that little thought was given to the consequences of their negotiations. Neither American diplomat seemed concerned or even interested, and President Kennedy jumped at the agreement, happy to have one less foreign policy decision in need of action. Indeed, American diplomatic incompetence during the Laotian negotiations of 1961-62 largely resulted in the Ho Chi Minh Trail being given sanctuary status for nearly six years, time vital to Uncle Ho's efforts to defeat the South.

Given the Administration's diplomats and their idiosyncrasies, and the downward spiral in the influence that General Maxwell Taylor was able to exert, it is not surprising, in retrospect, that the supremely self-confident Robert S. McNamara was thrust into a leading role in South Vietnam. That McNamara's power grew exponentially during the period 1961-1964 was a reflection of both his verve and confidence, and the lack, a near void, of status and influence held by the JCS. In the 21st century, it is almost impossible for people today to understand the lack of interaction among the President, the Secretary of Defense and the JCS in the early days of the Vietnam War. The situation was without parallel in recent American history, and is fully documented by then Major H.R. McMaster's book, *Dereliction of Duty*.[46] It turned out that there was not only no respect and no admiration between McNamara and his generals; there was not even basic communication.

SAIGON, 1963

Summer of 1963 was hot in Saigon, but that was hardly surprising. It was not only the weather that was scorching, but also politics and intrigue were approaching their boiling points. A series of American politicians, generals and journalists made pointed visits to Saigon during the period 1960 through 1963, all charged with reviewing the situation and assessing the leadership of the South Vietnamese. President John F. Kennedy had steadily expanded the military role of the United States, but he was not very confident in doing so, and he called for repeated appraisals by diplomats, military officers, family friends and close personal advisors. Reaction was mixed, creating a miasma that gave the young President lots to ponder. One of the more interesting, and controversial fact-finding trips to South Vietnam was made in September 1963 by then Major General Victor H. (Brute) Krulak, USMC, and Joseph Mendenhall, a senior foreign service officer. Krulak was to evaluate the military side of things, and Mendenhall the civilian. When they made their report to the President, Kennedy famously quipped, "You two did visit the same country, didn't you?" Such was the complexity surrounding the Republic of Vietnam's government and its affairs.[47]

For over seven years, the autocratic Ngo Dinh Diem and his powerful family had led the South Vietnamese government. Diem relied immensely on the advice of his younger brother, Ngo Dinh Nhu, who headed Diem's secret police, and Nhu's glamorous wife, Madame Nhu.[48] Because of Diem's increasing paranoia, fear of coups seemed to worry him more than the North Vietnamese or VC. Nhu's job was keeping the family in power, and he took it seriously. His secret police, funded primarily by the Americans, were ruthless and contributed significantly to contempt that groups like the Buddhists had for Nhu and his flashy, beautiful and highly opinionated wife. But, as is very common in Vietnam, family ties were the most important considerations. In addition to Nhu, other Diem brothers were prominent. The oldest living brother, and titular head of the family (the first-born had been killed by the Communists), Ngo Dinh Thuc, was the Catholic archbishop of Vietnam. A third brother served Diem as Ambassador to London, while yet another lived in Hué with their mother, where he ran the family businesses.

Key ambassadorships also were kept within the family. Besides the brother in London, Madame Nhu's father was Ambassador to the United States, while her mother served in New York as Vietnam's observer at the United Nations. Frustrating to the Americans, the family was extremely close knit and not especially inclined to the principles of democracy. Adding to the public relations problems, Nhu's glamorous wife was very controversial, openly extravagant, and quite outspoken. Worse, French was Madame Nhu's primary language, which served as a barrier to the mostly Vietnamese speaking population.[49] But many in Saigon, including many American officers, viewed her as the backbone of the government.[50] Thus, as South Vietnam faced off against Ho Chi Minh and his communist cohort, the ruling family lacked the charm and public support, to say nothing of the media support, enjoyed by their counterparts, the Kennedys, in Washington.

By late summer 1963, Diem and his government had significant troubles that extended well past any perceived lack of charisma, troubles that were associated with errors of both omission and commission. Much larger than any mistake caused by familial ties was Diem's intolerance of religions other than Catholicism. Diem, and especially his brother and sister-in-law, truly under-estimated the reaction that the Buddhists would have to his regime, which by this time was intense. Furthermore, he misunderstood, or more likely never knew, that some Buddhists were being funded and supported by the North Vietnamese and Ho Chi Minh. Such North Vietnamese support led to one of the most everlasting images of the war. On June 11, Buddhist monk Quang Duc was photographed as he was set ablaze by his fellow monks in a Saigon square.

An American reporter had been tipped in advance of the event, and his picture of the burning monk spotlighted the opposition to Diem. The Buddhists themselves characterized the event as a respectful protest of Diem's rule. The American press bought the story hook, line and sinker. In the days that followed, other monks killed themselves in similar ways. While there is no doubt that some Buddhists were fervently anti-Catholic, and that they had justifiable grievances related to religious prejudice, there is also no question that the North Vietnamese paid the monk's religious order in return for his sacrifice. The affair was much more than a simple protest, it was sedition combined with powerful anti-government propaganda, contrived by the communists, and it succeeded brilliantly. For the North Vietnamese perspective, one needs only visit the Thien Mu Pagoda (museum) on the west of the Citadel on the north side of the Perfume River in Hué. The communists proudly tell the entire story.[51] Washington, unaware of the communist connection, was aghast, and the pressure on Diem from the American government continued to escalate, so much so that on June 27, Kennedy announced that a new ambassador would arrive in Vietnam in September.

The Buddhist protests, combined with Diem's predisposition to appoint politically correct, as opposed to militarily sound, commanders began to cause significant problems. Indeed, the U.S. advisors had begun to report about the non-aggressive tactics of Diem's appointees, despite the overall tone of confidence emanating from General Harkins's MAC(V). And while the issue of not having fighting generals was problematic for Diem, it probably would not have been fatal but for the convergence of two factors: the new United States Ambassador and the American press.

The reporting of the Battle of Ap Bac, in January 1963, changed the war. The actions, comments and reports of the American advisor present on the scene, then Lieutenant Colonel John Paul Vann, became the source of controversy, frustration and even intrigue. It is interesting to compare the accounts of the contemporaneous reporters, David Halberstam, Malcolm Browne, Stanley Karnow and especially Neil Sheehan, to that of the later-day historian Mark Moyar.[52]

Whether Diem and his generals deserved criticism or not, Ap Bac represented a change in the American reporting of the war, and their attitude toward Diem. Those critical of Diem emphasize the lack of professionalism of his generals, his penchant for playing subordinates against each other, and even the malaise of his army commanders. Vann, whose service in Vietnam was largely praiseworthy and even heroic, may have had ulterior motives for the criticism he made of the ARVN actions at Ap Bac. But, who knows? Vann died in a helicopter crash supporting the South Vietnamese in 1973 while serving as the senior advisor to the ARVN commander of II Corps. There is no doubt that Diem's military appointments caused problems. And there is no doubt that Americans criticized those appointments. The question remains whether the alternative generals would have served Diem better? The problem of ARVN leadership arose just as the communists were, after two years of infiltration, gaining strength, confidence and again exercising their military might. *The Official History of the People's Army of Vietnam, 1954-1975*, edited by Senior General Hoang Van Thai and others, and translated by Merle L. Pribblenow, dispels any notion that the "rebellion" against Diem was a local one. Without communist supplies, and especially manpower, from North Vietnam, Diem and his government would have faced only unorganized and mostly unarmed opposition. Of course, the American reporters who both viewed events contemporaneously and then wrote their "histories" of the war did not have access to Pribblenow's translation, which was not published until 2005.[53]

As knotty as Diem's military appointments were, by early autumn 1963 his far more pressing issue was the U.S. Ambassador. Karnow's book provides a photograph, fittingly labeled "the Brahmin and the Mandarin," that pretty much reveals the relationship between Henry Cabot Lodge and Ngo Dinh Diem. Lodge, a relatively tall, thin Massachusetts aristocrat in a seersucker suit is seen looking down, perhaps even smirking, at the round and very short Diem, who, while smiling, is staring straight into Lodge's midsection. The photo might have represented the high water mark of their relationship.[54]

WASHINGTON, 1963

The mystique of the Kennedys and their "Camelot" era was at its height in the summer of 1963. The President and his lovely wife, Jacqueline "Jackie" Bouvier Kennedy, enjoyed immense public popularity. The American press corps was similarly smitten with the First Couple. Although the Kennedy Administration had stumbled shortly after taking office in early 1961 with its poorly conceived and even more badly executed Bay of Pigs fiasco, Kennedy was not subjected to intense press scrutiny and criticism was muted. When Kennedy rebounded and showed the toughness the nation expected during the Cuban Missile Crisis of October 1962, his star was in the ascent. Meanwhile, Jackie graced magazine covers and was the subject of countless magazine pieces that extolled her style, grace and sense of glamour. She was an icon to millions of women, and men, worldwide.

Domestically, Kennedy extolled and then pushed through a significant tax cut that resulted in a dramatic improvement to the nation's economy. Nonetheless, a wart was developing domestically; the civil rights movement was gearing up in the

South, where in 1955 Rosa Parks sparked a major domestic dispute that pricked the nation's conscience. The Kennedys had long tried to ignore the issues associated with civil rights. Race relations was a divisive subject among Democrats in the 1960s. When demonstrations and protests heated up across the South, the President and his brother, Attorney General Robert Kennedy, reluctantly came in on the side of Martin Luther King and his movement. Even though Kennedy's poll numbers had dipped, primarily because of his support for civil rights, he remained popular, though personally, like any good politician, he was very concerned about a second term. Indeed, aside from the civil rights situation, the only things that were causing Kennedy any real consternation were the rapidly developing circumstances in Southeast Asia, more specifically Vietnam.

The 1961-1962 situation in Laos, though murky, confused and ripe for North Vietnamese plucking, had been solved through a diplomatic solution that Kennedy found adequate, even agreeable. The President, anxious to show results without committing troops, had quickly signed off on the deal, not realizing its impact on future American involvement in Southeast Asia because of the sanctuary status it gave to the Ho Chi Minh Trail.

Despite the non-interventionist attitudes of Galbraith and Harriman, the people the Administration sent to Vietnam to assess the situation generally favored an active involvement. Among Kennedy's closest advisors, it was Maxwell Taylor who led the interventionist camp. A retired general, Taylor had impressed the Kennedy clan with his opposition to the normal military line of thinking during the Bay of Pigs debacle. Further, his advocacy of a *Flexible Response* was largely responsible for the Kennedy's change of military policy following his inauguration. Brought into the White House as the President's Special Military Advisor, Taylor made several forays into Vietnam, each time proposing an incrementally larger role for the U.S. In 1962, increasingly uncomfortable with his role as Special Military Advisor, Taylor was recalled to active duty and named Chairman of the JCS.

Chroniclers of the war are unsure of whether Kennedy actually wanted an expanded U.S. military role in Vietnam, but there is no doubt that Taylor did. At every turn Taylor supported an expanded role for the military, commensurate with a *Flexible Response*. His primary assistant was Major General Brute Krulak, whose official title was Special Assistant for Counter-insurgency Operations, but he worked very closely with Taylor and became a forceful advocate for military intervention. However, *Flexible Response* as a policy soon led to divisions among the advisors: what constituted "flexible" and exactly what should be the response? Applying the policy to the situation was anything but straightforward.

Reporters who were detractors of the Diem regime dominated Saigon in the summer of 1963, including Neil Sheehan, Peter Arnett, Keyes Beech, and the *New York Times*' Homer Bigart. These were mostly Americans who generally disliked the Diem Regime and who filed reports detailing every mistake, problem and indiscretion committed in Saigon. Bigart in particular had drawn the ire of Diem; his reporting was so virulently anti-Diem that the South Vietnamese President had him expelled in 1962. But Bigart had many like-minded friends and colleagues who remained. Not that Diem and his government were blameless; they were not. Facing a growing rebellion fueled almost exclusively from outside South Vietnam, the government showed surprising restraint, especially if compared to their North Vietnamese counterparts' treatment of their dissidents.[55] After significant internal debate, over which Ho seems to have largely played the role of referee, the communist invasion picked up steam at the very time Diem was under tremendous pressure from his allies.

Of course, there were no American reporters, or those of any other nationality, in the North observing the war and reporting on the actions of Ho Chi Minh's regime. Nevertheless, since Diem did not conform to American expectations of how a natural leader should perform, he was dismissed by most in the press as corrupt, incompetent and unpopular. Such were the charges that filled most of the history books written after the conclusion of the war. The reporters demanded a change in the government and they would soon get their wish, though the change would hardly represent improvement. In the end, the United States lost its best opportunity for future success.

WASHINGTON - SAIGON POLITICS, AUTUMN 1963

President Kennedy was increasingly concerned about events in Saigon. Charming, smart and very politically adroit, JFK (as most Americans of the time knew him) had to successfully maneuver through the minefield that was South Vietnam if he wanted to win a second term in the elections of 1964. In a single stroke, Kennedy thought he had solved both issues – how to win respect for his actions in Southeast Asia while also co-opting any Republican opposition to his policies there.

In the summer of 1963, perhaps the leading candidate for the Republican nomination for President was Henry Cabot Lodge, Jr. At that time Senator Barry Goldwater of Arizona had not yet become the major force in the opposition party. Lodge had been Eisenhower's Ambassador to the United Nations and then was Richard Nixon's Vice Presidential running mate in the 1960 election against JFK.

Further, he was a former United States Senator from Massachusetts, but lost his seat in 1952 when John F. Kennedy defeated him. Lodge was a patrician from a prominent New England family, one much better known (before 1960) than the Kennedys. President Kennedy approached him about the ambassadorship to Saigon. Lodge, perhaps thinking he could use the position to his political advantage, agreed. The appointment was announced June 27. The new Ambassador did have one important qualification: he spoke French. While the former Republican senator was politically ambitious and well known personally to JFK, he was not particularly astute. By going to Saigon, Lodge permitted Kennedy to stifle any Republican criticism of his foreign policy, at least with respect to Southeast Asia. Unfortunately, Kennedy's choice, based on political calculations and not what was best for the American-Vietnamese relationship, would end poorly for both men. Between the time that Lodge's appointment was announced, and the time he arrived in Saigon in September, the American President and his advisors had begun serious discussions of a possible coup against Ngo Dinh Diem.

Henry Cabot Lodge's actions in Vietnam represented, perhaps, the worst performance by an American ambassador at any critical time in history. He was a caricature for the Ugly American. Lodge neither was familiar with nor in any way understood the Vietnamese culture (although he did visit French Indochina in the 1930s), and he entered the country as though he were the proverbial bull in a china shop. He quickly, and without much consultation with American officials who had been in Saigon for any length of time, adopted the reporters' view of President Diem, considering him to be both corrupt and incompetent. Further, Lodge almost immediately put actions into motion that would in early November, culminate in the assassination of both Diem and his brother Nhu.

There is little doubt of the complicity of the Kennedy Administration in the coup that left the South Vietnamese government leaderless. Assistant Secretary of State Roger Hilsman, a Kennedy favorite, had as early as August written memos about how to handle Diem and Nhu after they were overthrown, and it was to Lodge that the Vietnamese generals involved in the coup requested American planes to whisk away the Ngo brothers after they were captured and subdued. The whole coup situation was the result of a "Ready, Fire, Aim" mentality. In a war effort filled with errors of both commission and omission, Diem's assassination was perhaps the most egregious.[56]

NOTES AND REFERENCES

1. Extensive interviews of Colonel Charles H. Beale, Sr., USMC (Ret) by the author during 2007 and 2008.
2. For the complete text of President Eisenhower's speech, see http://www.hnet.org/~hst306/documents/indust.html.
3. Millett and Shumlinson, *Commandants of the Marine Corps*, p. 370-71. The editors and their contributors provide valuable insights into all Commandants through General Robert Barrow. The chapters on Generals Shoup and Greene are particularly relevant to this chapter of Al Gray's story.
4. Alberts's design allowed a single generator to provide three kinds of power outputs: 12 volt dc, needed to raise and lower antennae; 60 cycle a/c, needed for most electrical equipment; and 400 cycle a/c, which the specialized equipment needed.
5. "Red-black" denotes an electrical separation between lines carrying special communications from those that convey regular communications.
6. Photo courtesy of Colonel Raymond Becker, USMC (Ret).
7. General Weller became a lifelong Al Gray supporter. Throughout his service, General Weller had been a major advocate for naval gunfire, and wrote many articles on that subject. He used to often visit Gray in the tank at HQMC, where the two would talk about the General's interest. After his retirement, General Weller presented Gray with his five large notebooks filled with materials about naval gunfire.
8. Millett, *Commandants of the Marine Corps*, p. 387.
9. Beale letter to the author dated 13 March 2007.
10. Extensive interviews of Lieutenant Colonel Howard K. Alberts, USMC (Ret) by the author during 2007 and 2008.
11. See Chapter 2. Ryan was awarded a Navy Cross for the same action at Tarawa when General Shoup earned a Medal of Honor.
12. Beale tells funny stories about almost everything related to his profession, but his descriptions of how general officers avoided interacting with General Shoup are among the most humorous. Youngdale, a fine officer who subsequently served as the G-2 to General Harkins in Vietnam in the early 1960s, was the junior Brigadier General at the Headquarters when he arrived there in 1963. As such, he had the responsibility for planning and organizing the Marine Corps Birthday Ball, a not insignificant task to any Marine at any location. Youngdale sweated bullets in the weeks leading to the Ball. Sometime afterward, General Shoup mentioned ever so casually to Youngdale that he thought the Birthday Ball went "very well;" that praise meant the world to the young Brigadier General.
13. The "Slate" is an annual plan that provides information regarding each general officer's future assignment. It is not official, however, until the officer receives orders; and as in this case, the "slate" can be easily changed.
14. Author interviews with Colonel Beale, 2008-2010.
15. The Commandant's house has been home to every Commandant since 1806.
16. From General Gray's private collection.
17. Colonel John Hyatt, USMC (Ret) served with Al Gray when both were captains in the 1st Radio Company at Kaneohe Bay, Hawaii. Hyatt was the "EW Officer" for the first couple years of his tour there, but then he was moved to the operations section as an assistant to Gray, who was the Operations Officer (S-3). He likened the experience to walking around picking up after someone who was tearing apart a house. He revealed that Gray, after writing a message to Commanding General FMFPAC requesting permission to do something, would hop into a vehicle and drive across the island to Camp Smith in order to "conveniently and coincidently" be there when the message was received. Often, Gray had a pre-written response that he simply handed to the appropriate staff officer along with an oral statement that, "Just send this and it takes

care of everything." While this might seem to imply that Gray was taking advantage of others, the opposite is more likely true. In the late 1950s few officers (certainly not even Hyatt, who was working with him) had the experience needed to fully comprehend the Marine Corps' Signal Intelligence program. Gray was simply helping things along, and providing his (unusual for the times) expertise. Hyatt believes that fully 90% of the training concepts, both at the NSA (Ft. Meade, MD) and at forward operational sites, together with the deployment methodology still used by the Marine Corps, can be directly attributable to Captain Gray's programs in Hawaii in the late 1950s, revised and expanded during his time at HQMC in the early 1960s. While Hyatt may have described his role as an Assistant S-3 as "picking up the pieces following after Gray," there is little doubt he thinks Gray to be the father of modern Marine cryptology. Hyatt interview with the author, 2007.

18. Hyatt interview with author 2008.
19. Several Marines from the detachment remained in Vietnam, assigned on Temporary Additional Duty to the 8th RRU, Phu Bai.
20. Attitudes toward Democrat politicians' foreign policy foibles dominated politics from the fall of China in the late 1940s through the election of Richard M. Nixon in 1972. Democrats running for President could not afford to be stuck with the tag soft-on-communism; it was a powerful factor that guided the foreign policy calculations of both Kennedy and Johnson.
21. The detection of the Barlock radar, by the way, shaped history, and it was done on a training mission by 2nd Radio. The Barlock is associated with Soviet missile systems, and their possible presence in Cuba dictated that more aerial reconnaissance missions be flown against the island. Those missions, in turn, provided the evidence that the Soviets had indeed deployed offensive missiles within a short range of the United States.
22. Interviews with the late Colonel James Quisenberry, USMC (Ret), then Commanding Officer of the 2nd Composite Radio Company. Also quite ironic was when the author mentioned this incident about Quisenberry to Colonel Beale, Colonel Beale admitted that he too probably did not know where Major Gray was or what he was doing! Beale said that "not knowing" was by far the best cover and deception story, because he could always answer, "I have no idea where he is" when asked about Gray's location or his activities. Gray was in fact traveling with his detachment under a request from the Secretary of Defense conveyed personally to the Commandant.
23. The late Colonel Donald J. Hatch, USMC, was the first to introduce the author to then Lieutenant General Al Gray in May, 1987, at the change of command of another mutual friend, Colonel John A. Bicknas. On that occasion, then Lieutenant Colonel Bicknas relinquished command of the 2nd Radio Battalion, the successor unit to the 2nd Radio Company. General Gray's personal involvement with what had been the 2nd Radio Company extended through his Commandancy. Bicknas had worked for both Hatch and General Gray, and he had served in Japan with then Captain Scott Laidig at Company E, Marine Support Battalion in Kami Seya and Misawa, Japan.
24. Photo from General Gray's private collection.
25. General Gray videotaped interview, 12 January 2010.
26. SWAG is a widely used term in the service and means Scientific Wild-*ss Guess. While Gray did lots of work to justify his results, in the end there was no definitive answer.
27. Author interviews with Colonel Beale, 2007-2008. Commandant Shoup used colorful language, and another word for "butt" was actually spoken.
28. During hot days in Vietnam, H-34s might be limited to carrying as few as four infantrymen and their equipment.
29. General Gray unfailingly refers to the old civilians at HQMC as "Mr. Meade, Mr. Casey, etc." He never just calls them by their last names.
30. By this time the Crossroads of the Marine Corps at Quantico was named the Marine Corps Development & Education Command.

31. Enemy communications can be attacked in two fundamental ways. First, the good guys can try to exploit enemy communications by listening to what is being said and breaking codes that might be employed, which is the role envisioned by SIGINT. Alternatively, the good guys can attempt to "jam" enemy communications by transmitting strong signals on the same frequencies the enemy is trying to use. Jamming sounds good, but it is very difficult to effectively achieve without also disrupting friendly communications or becoming a major target for enemy artillery, which can use direction finding to pinpoint the locations of jammers. Generally speaking, the only times during the Vietnam War when jamming was employed was when it was used against NVA anti-aircraft artillery and missile associated radars and anti-aircraft communications links. It was (probably) never employed against enemy ground communications.

32. Most civilians, and indeed many Marines, do not understand the complexity of military logistics. When an items such as rifles or trucks, radios or generators are placed into service, the spare parts, maintenance plan and training for the maintainers, storage of parts and procedures for moving them forward require an amazing amount of work – and money! If special purpose SIGINT/EW equipment, fielded in very low numbers, required the same approach as that used for rifles or general purpose radios, the logistics considerations would have made the SIGINT equipment too costly to ever employ.

33. Author correspondence with Robert Meck, Senior Executive, NSA, 2010-2011. In his papers, there are many other references to Gray's impressive presentation skills from appreciative recipients and audiences.

34. "Direct Support" means providing intelligence that is immediately useful and can be acted on; it might be a warning of an impending attack, or information that provides the location of an enemy unit. "Direct Service Support" is more general; it might include information about the frequencies used by various enemy units, or the procedures employed.

35. From General Gray's private collection. Captain Al Gray had earlier served at Kami Seya when the Marine contingent was designated 1st Communications Platoon.

36. From General Gray's private collection. Gray had a long relationship with General Cushman; Beale was a lifelong friend.

37. From General Gray's private collection. Both Generals were instrumental in building the SIGINT/EW capability of the Marine Corps.

38. All Marines used to cope with a "Overseas Rotation Tour Date." In the 1950s, 60s, 70s, and 80s, Marines were assigned to Okinawa individually, and their Overseas Rotation Tour Date was used to keep the highly unpopular, unaccompanied (by dependents), tours on Okinawa fair to all. But some, especially those who made themselves "indispensible" (especially at HQMC) could postpone the inevitable. Alberts would routinely argue that his skills and knowledge as a systems engineer were far more valuable serving at HQMC than they would be as a battalion or regimental communications officer. Thus, he stayed at HQMC for several years past when he should have been sent to Okinawa. However, the prospect of having an important billet on General Harkins staff made it easy for Alberts to pack his seabag and head to the Pacific.

39. http://25thaviation.org/history/id551.htm. Like many online websites associated with Vietnam-era units, this one has much interesting information. Link checked March 2011.

40. Perhaps the best account of the Vietnam War from the perspective of the reporters is A.J. Langguth's *Our Vietnam*. Langguth is a former *New York Times* reporter himself, and his account surely shows his cohort in the best possible light, written with the smugness of nearly 30 years of hindsight. Langguth is a fine writer but perhaps a lazy researcher. The book betrays early and often the author's biases, which can be summarized as follows: *The South Vietnamese were greedy, corrupt, dishonest, cowardly or all the above. The North Vietnamese were cunning, brave, patriotic, and misunderstood by the Americans, or all the above. American military officers (with few exceptions) were unrealistic, unimaginative, duplicitous in the South Vietnamese corruption, unknowing of Vietnamese customs and*

traditions, and generally uninformed. Most American bureaucrats were ill informed, worried about their own status and position, and worried more about internal politics than what was right or wrong. Liberal or left-leaning bureaucrats who opposed the war were exceptions; they were bright, able to predict future events, and very patriotic. Reporters, in general, were pure as the driven snow (though they might drink to excess and womanize), were military and foreign policy experts, were genuinely neutral with respect to their reportage, and were great patriots. Given the considerable expertise Langguth and his contemporaries claim to have had, it was too bad reporters could not conduct foreign policy or fight wars. And what is really too bad, given Langguth's communication skills, is that he was such an inadequate researcher. After all, the fact that Pham Xuan An was North Vietnamese spy while also being the source of much – if not most – of the reporters' (Sheehan, Karnow, and Halberstam among many others) knowledge of Vietnamese culture did not cause Langguth to reevaluate their insights and conclusions. And, of course, Langguth evidently missed the Buddhist-communist connection, even though it was well known long before 2000, when his book was published. Lacking knowledge of the connection, Langguth's analysis of the events misses the mark.

41. Interviews with the late Lieutenant Colonel Howard Alberts, USMC (Ret) and the author during 2007 and 2008.

42. A breadboard commonly describes a piece of equipment that is created in a laboratory and is not yet ready for production. It is something that actually works, but which might not represent the final design. Since it is largely handmade, the breadboard version of any product would not be as reliable or as rugged as the final production version, and therefore, the breadboard might need an engineer to keep it operational. Gray, Alberts and Syracuse Research Corporation produced several breadboards for SIGNIT operations over the years.

43. Interview with Major General John Morrison, United States Air Force (Ret) and the author, 2007.

44. When the ascension of General Wallace M. Greene, Jr. to Commandant, the new Chief of Staff at HQMC became none other than Lieutenant General Leonard F. Chapman, Jr., the long time protagonist of the "cryptologic" Marines. Alberts, returning to HQMC for retirement, learned from his friends that General Chapman, upon reviewing the request for Alberts to be assigned to NSA, responded, "Don't worry about this NSA thing; it is just Alberts working his bolt." And there ended the Marine Corps service of Howard Alberts.

45. Averill Harriman had been President Roosevelt's Special Envoy to Europe before the U.S. declaration of war in 1941, then Ambassador to Russia from 1943 to 1946 and finally Ambassador to Great Britain in 1946, so he hardly lacked diplomatic experience. Experience is one thing, effectiveness quite another.

46. As of 2012, H. R. McMaster is serving as a Brigadier General in the United States Army.

47. Halberstam, 277.

48. Vietnamese names are difficult to track for Americans. "Ho Chi Minh" is universally called "Ho" but "Ngo Dinh Diem" is always called "Diem." Diem's brother, "Ngo Dinh Nhu" is also always referred to as "Nhu." When looking for Vietnamese in indices, however, the problem is readily apparent. In some books "Vo Van Giai" is listed under "Giai," while in others he is found under "Vu." In this book we will only call "Ho" by his first name.

49. While trying to minimize her popularity and influence, some reporters alleged that Madame Nhu did not even write Vietnamese; the allegation stuck and was repeated often. See, for example, Langguth, p.90. It was not true, however.

50. Among those was Lieutenant Colonel Howard Alberts, and according to him, almost all the intelligence community. Author interview with Lieutenant Colonel Alberts, 2008.

51. There are many accounts of the event. See, for example Halberstam or Karnow, neither of whom mentions the communist connection. Indeed, there is even a Wikipedia.org page for Quang Duc, and it also does not mention any communist connection. This episode is perhaps the second most damning of those that clearly show Karnow's bias against Diem. The most damning would be Karnow's treatment of the communist-agent-turned-newsman, Phan Xuan An, whose story is told in An's biography, *Perfect Spy*.

52. Mark Moyar, *Triumph Forsaken*, etc. Moyar, of course, had the advantage of access to more resources than did the histories written by Karnow, Sheehan, and Halberstam. Langguth cannot rely on such an excuse to justify his work. Compare *Triumph Forsaken* with Karnow, previously cited, or Neil Sheehan, *A Bright Shining Lie: John Paul Vann and America in Vietnam*. Who actually knows what really happened? This author believes Moyar's account is more compelling.

53. *Victory in Vietnam: The Official History of the People's Army of Vietnam, 1954-1975*. Edited by Senior General Hoang Van Thai et al. University Press of Kansas, 2002, Lawrence. Translated by Merle L. Pribblenow.

54. Karnow, p. 270.

55. Pribblenow, pp.114-120.

56. Ellen J. Hammer, *A Death in November: America in Vietnam, 1963*. Ms. Hammer's work has received little attention in the United States, probably because she is critical of JFK, the American government and even the American press while relating the events associated with the Diem assassination. She is hardly a Diem apologist, and she sneers at the notion that Ho Chi Minh was nationalist. Consequently, her work was not prominently covered, if covered at all, by most American histories of the war.

CHAPTER 4

FIRST MARINE GROUND COMBAT UNIT ENTERS VIETNAM

SOUTHEAST ASIA HEATS UP

FIRST MARINE GROUND COMBAT UNIT ENTERS VIETNAM

Major Alfred M. Gray, Jr., USMC, was cold, wet and frustrated. He had been cold, wet and frustrated for five long days and five near endless nights. It was not the bitter, bone-chilling weather reminiscent of his time in Korea, where urine froze on the ground before it could puddle. Still, this cold was pervasive, it was depressing and it was unshakable. Gray's usual verve was still present, but his companions were largely unknown to him, and they surely were not his beloved Marines. Instead, he found himself stranded on a mountaintop with three South Vietnamese, two officers and a senior non-commissioned officer. The four had a handful of rice to eat but little more. The closest source of water was from a waterfall they had found some distance down the mountain. At night the men pooled their meager resources in an unfulfilled quest to stay warm. But simply put, there was no escape for the baleful dampness that saturated them, brought on by nearly constant rain and depressing fog. And even when there was no rain, and the fog lifted – if just for a little while – there was no sun. After nearly a week, Gray was hungry and knew his comrades were as well; but no one complained. The South Vietnamese, small, wiry, and tough, were used to such deprivations. Being famished in the field was nothing new to these dedicated anti-communists, who had been fighting Ho Chi Minh and his army for years.

One of Gray's associates was actually a Cambodian-born engineering officer who had joined the Army of the Republic of Vietnam specifically to fight Ho and his minions. The second was the company commander of the unit assigned to accompany Gray and his men on their mission. But it was the non-commissioned officer who was the most interesting to Gray. He had been a machine-gun company commander in the Viet Minh army that fought the French at Dien Bien Phu. Like many Vietnamese, he had believed Ho was a nationalist most interested in freeing Vietnam from its colonial masters. But when it became apparent to all Vietnam that Ho Chi Minh was in fact a committed communist, the former machine gun company commander and his entire company changed sides to the South Vietnamese. They went south in the mid-1950s with over a half million mostly Catholic peasants.[1] Not that communication among the small party was easy, because the Vietnamese spoke at best broken English; Gray, however, had a gift for languages and, more importantly, an eagerness to learn. And his proficiency for Asian languages was to prove a lifesaver in the not-too-distant future!

Gray wasn't exactly sure when the Marine H-34 helicopters that had taken him to Tiger Tooth would be able to return. His soon-to-be legendary penchant for planning had betrayed him. A near comedy of errors during the planning stages of the operation had conspired to misidentify the monsoon season. The monsoon in the southern part of what had been Indochina, which included Saigon, arrived earlier than the rains that blanket Tiger Tooth Mountain and North Vietnam, which are dominated by the Laotian Monsoon. Thus, when the Military Assistance Command (Vietnam) staff planned the operation, they anticipated that mid-May would be the beginning of the good weather that follows the monsoons.[2] Instead, Gray and his cohort undertook their reconnaissance during an unseasonable break in the precipitation; a break they thought represented the change of season. The helicopter that dropped them for an overnight reconnoiter was unable to return as planned; and five days later the weather was still bad and not getting better. The Vietnamese had packed their usual ball of rice and some vegetables, a ration that permitted them to live at least a week; thankfully, Gray had taken rations for two days, thinking that he had 100% reserve. Nothing was farther from the truth.

Gray's adventure would end only when he and the South Vietnamese walked off the mountain and fought through a North Vietnamese unit to reach safety. But that decision was not made hastily. While enduring the conditions, Gray had 22 more days to ponder the convergence of events that brought him to South Vietnam.

OPERATION TIGER TOOTH MOUNTAIN

The request for communications intelligence support that Lieutenant Colonel Howard Alberts had initiated in Saigon came to Washington via the SIGINT chain of command. The NSA was key; neither the NSG nor the Army Security Agency had the capability to do what Alberts's concept envisioned – exploiting tactical North Vietnamese communications. As a consequence of the inability of the plan to get traction at NSA, it had been rejected. Alberts's trip to Washington, when he met with Major Al Gray in the tank, had really been an attempt to revive the whole concept.

When Major Gray learned of the rejection he approached Commandant Greene about gaining his support. There was no greater advocate of Marine SIGINT than General Wallace M. Greene, Jr. On the day Gray approached him, General Greene had a budget meeting scheduled at the Pentagon with the Chief of Naval Operations and the Secretary of the Navy, Paul H. Nitze. "I want you to go with me to that meeting," the Commandant told the spook.[3] Gray, as might be expected, did what was ordered and took a place in the far corner of the room. He recalled that there was a knock down, drag out debate over the aircraft composition of Marine Air

Wings; Al Gray sat mute during that discussion intent on avoiding notice. As the meeting ended, General Greene asked Secretary Nitze to stay for a moment. Greene then motioned Gray forward and asked the younger officer to give the Secretary a summary of the proposed operation, including the organization of the forces that would be sent, the travel plan, the support requirements and the budget. The Secretary approved the plan and wished Gray well. As with all other aspects of Gray's work at HQMC, nothing would have been done had it not been for the active, resolute and absolute support of General Greene. The Commandant not only had given his approval to the operation, but also he won the support of the Secretary of the Navy. Indeed, wherever possible General Greene also greased the skids for Major Gray.

It took some time to get everyone headed in the same direction, but within a few weeks of Alberts's visit, wheels were turning and Major Al Gray was getting ready to deploy to Southeast Asia. Countless briefings were given and the detailed planning was finalized for deployment. Gray had initiated almost nonstop coordination with NSA, FMFPAC, the 3rd Marine Division and the 3rd Marine Regiment, and the Pentagon; and that was all before the Major even left HQMC. Greene's orders put into motion the movement of linguists from the NSA, and alerted appropriate commands to his expectations of support for the coming endeavor – it was April 1964 and the first Marine ground combat units were going to South Vietnam.

Taking his leave of Headquarters, Gray made a short stop in Hawaii to brief and solicit support from Lieutenant General Krulak and from then Colonel John Morrison, USAF, the Director of NSA's activities in the Pacific. General Krulak had been to Vietnam many times in the years leading up to the deployment, and he was keenly interested in Gray's plans. Krulak was so interested that he offered Major Gray his full support and promised to visit the Major and his men in the future. The whole operation was under intense scrutiny from both the DoD and the Department of State, and there were numerous naysayers who feared that the Marines might provoke and excite a reaction from the North Vietnamese that would draw the Americans into a land war. General Krulak knew Al Gray and respected his professional reputation; nonetheless, the Commanding General, Fleet Marine Forces, Pacific kept his keen eye on all aspects of the forthcoming operation.

Colonel Morrison had been one of the few officers in the USAF (then United States Army Air Force) officers to serve on Guadalcanal during that famous World War II battle. As a young officer, Morrison had run a radar site in those early days of the war. Experienced and savvy, Morrison had previously met Gray during the Marine's tour at 1st Radio Company; the Air Force officer was impressed by Major Gray's demeanor and his planned operation. Colonel Morrison knew that

SIGINT could make a difference helping the South Vietnamese and he was anxious to further involve NSA's capabilities.[4]

After the Hawaii briefings, Major Gray flew on to Okinawa to brief the operational staff there of his intentions to lead cryptologists into South Vietnam, supported by Marine infantry. Their concurrence was vital to getting the infantry needed for security for the mission. Among the officers who spoke with Gray was then Lieutenant Colonel Robert Barrow, the future Commandant. It would be the first of many future interactions between the 27th and 29th Commandants. Like General Krulak, Lieutenant Colonel Barrow found no fault with Gray's plan. Another officer then on Okinawa who Gray briefed was the new Assistant Commanding General of the 3rd Marine Division, Ray Davis. Of course Davis needed no introduction to Gray or Gray's methods.

One of Al Gray's first actions, while still back at HQMC, had been to arrange for a well-qualified second in command. 1st Lieutenant Robert Meck, USMC, had been led into cryptology following Captain Gray's lecture to the 1962 class of the Communications Officer Course. Lieutenant Meck was a Vietnamese linguist assigned to the Naval Security Group Activity, Philippines. Gray initiated orders for Meck to be prepared to join the Signal Engineering Survey Unit in Da Nang. The Signal Engineering Survey Unit was the cover story and name for the SIGINT portion of Marine Detachment, Advisory Team 1's activities. When Meck, sea bag in hand, met a C-130 that had landed to pick him at the Naval Air Station, Cubi Point, he was hardly surprised when a major in a flight suit – Al Gray – shook his hand, made a brief hello, and immediately launched into a briefing of the operation to come. The briefing lasted all the way to Da Nang. Meck, though, was familiar with Gray's professionalism. The Lieutenant recalled that Gray had informed him shortly before Meck's Communications School graduation that he would be assigned to the NSA and the Vietnamese language course, and that is exactly what happened. Lieutenant Meck was aware that Major Gray was not into small talk.

Bob Meck's first job was to be an interpreter for any Vietnamese with whom Major Gray needed to converse. He also became the de facto S-1, S-2, S-3 and S-4 for the entire operation. He lost his S-4 responsibilities when a future Marine Lieutenant General (and Commanding General FMFPAC) joined the unit in Da Nang. Then 1st Lieutenant H.C. (Hank) Stackpole arrived in time to take over the logistics support required to house and feed the infantry contingent that would arrive from Okinawa.[5]

Once in country, Gray had to make a call to Saigon, where he met then Brigadier General Richard H. Stilwell, United States Army, and others, including the officer who had replaced Lieutenant Colonel Alberts. As was his custom, however, Gray would not spend the night in Saigon; he quickly returned to Da Nang.[6] There, the G-3 of the U.S. Army's I Corps advisory team provided the Marines with a Toyota-built jeep. Both Bob Meck and David Gaddy, an old NSA acquaintance, recalled how Major Gray was able to shift gears without engaging the clutch, a trick that Gray never shared. The jeep was a welcomed asset to the newly arrived Marines.

Major Gray was anxious to get the operation underway. But there would be delays, aggravations and more than a little danger to overcome before the cryptologic Marines would make it onto Dong Voi Mep, otherwise known as Tiger Tooth Mountain. Aside from arranging the countless logistics requirements needed to implement the plan, the Major had a multitude of responsibilities to discharge. These ranged from a personal reconnaissance of both Khe Sanh and the mountain itself, establishing and testing the special communications from the mountain to Phu Bai and all the way back to Da Nang, the hub for major Marine air operations. Also important was liaison with the ARVN units that would support the mission. Of course, continuous coordination at MAC(V) Headquarters was, it goes without saying, essential – at least so far as the Headquarters was concerned.

As was his habit, Gray had developed a detailed operational deception plan even before arriving, given that he knew the enemy had countless agents and observers throughout South Vietnam. But in his plan he had failed to take into account the news reports by American journalists, and that would come back to haunt him.

Usually no detail of the military operation was too small to escape Gray's attention. For example, he was determined that his Marines enjoy the same culinary delights that he knew were available to the Marines serving with Air Wing. But when Gray's request for steaks twice a week reached the Marine aviator commanding at Da Nang, Lieutenant Colonel Robert A. Merchant questioned Gray's requisition in his communications to Fleet Marine Forces, Pacific (FMFPAC), which had over-all responsibility for the operation. FMFPAC's quick reply, straight from General Krulak, was, "Feed my highland Marines what they want!" Major Gray's requests were thereafter promptly filled, which should have reinforced to the Air Wing unit the understanding of the mission's importance. Of course, Lieutenant Colonel Merchant undoubtedly knew nothing of Gray's reputation at the Honolulu headquarters dating back to his time at 1st Composite Radio Company and his personal briefings for Lieutenant General Krulak, which had cemented the General's support

Figure 4.1
Maj Al Gray, Lt Col Waite (on right) and Col Warner, the senior U.S. Army advisor
in I Corps, 1964. Gray went throughout I Corps visiting with advisors, learning the lay
of the land, putting together an intelligence assessment and simply looking around.[7]

for Gray's mission. Besides, the Colonel also never knew the real goal of Gray's mission – he was not cleared.[8]

The first of Gray's contingent to arrive in Da Nang on April 18 were the cryptologic linguists from NSA, who would operate under the direction of an NSA civilian, Harry T. Williams. Williams was a former Army Security Agency Vietnamese linguist who went to work at the Agency following his military service. In the early 1960s, he had been a watch officer for Colonel Richard Gales' NSA operation in Saigon. Now, Williams was responsible for six Marine linguists. Their appearance was greeted by the Marine sergeant major from the Air Wing unit, and they were assigned quarters and shown where to eat and draw equipment. They were not, however, told where to go and what to do. As a result, the newcomers were unsure as to whether or not they should speak Vietnamese to the locals. Given the uncertainty, and the clandestine nature of the mission (in 1964, no one dared mention their association with NSA, or SIGINT or Communications Intelligence), the linguists decided that they should not display their language abilities pending Major Gray's arrival. The linguists included Staff Sergeant Dan Buckley and Sergeant Art Kidd (Vietnamese linguists), Corporals Connolly and Whitman (Vietnamese linguists-read and write capability only), and Staff Sergeant Richman with Sergeants V.C. Prater and Kreilich (Thai-Lao linguists), all from NSA.

The next day Gray, Meck and the Marines from 1st Composite Radio Company landed at Da Nang. Queried about their use of Vietnamese, Gray told his men to pretend they would be serving as advisors and to practice their language skills at every opportunity. That settled, the commanding officer had many more important questions to answer. While the contingent immediately set to work drawing equipment and establishing communications needed to support the mission, Gray, Meck, and the ARVN captain who would be assigned to his force took a helicopter out to the Special Forces base at Khe Sanh. There they met the Army captain in charge of the detachment, and the local Montagnard commander and his staff.[9]

While at the Montagnard training camp, Gray also met the local ARVN district chief and his assistant. Major Ngo Quang Truong and Captain Vu Vien Giai both impressed Major Gray. As it turned out, both would have much more contact with the American Marine in future years.

Khe Sanh was a major Montagnard training camp, and the locals provided the security for the Special Forces detachment and the Marines in and around the camp. Among the American officers that Gray met was a U.S. Army captain who was part of the ARVN advisory team in the vicinity. The captain was a Nisei, an American whose parents were of Japanese origin, and that coincidence that was soon to prove very fortuitous for the peripatetic Major Gray. After the initial combined planning and site recon session, Gray and his small contingent went back to Da Nang; the Marine infantry still was not in country.

Finally, on May 20, Major Gray returned from Da Nang accompanied by the infantry. For one of the linguists from NSA, it was all-home week. Sergeant Art Kidd had been a grunt before attending language school, and the very platoon in which he served in Hawaii, Second Platoon, Company G, 2nd Battalion, 3rd Marines, was the foundation for the infantry unit supporting Gray's cryptologists. 1st Lieutenant Raymond J. Otlowski commanded the infantrymen, who numbered 76 men; the rifle platoon was reinforced by a section of two 81mm mortars. Kidd was happy to see his former shipmates, but it was a little awkward explaining what his future role in the mission was going to be. Kidd had been one of the Marines who re-enlisted for an assignment to language school; Gray's aggressive use of language billets during his first years at HQMC was about to pay dividends. Everyone treated information about their own particular responsibility on a strict-need-know basis; thus, even when other Marines might have had an appropriate clearance, unless they also had a need to know the information, they never were told exactly what was happening. As a result, the Marine grunts were never told, and never knew, the precise nature of the overall mission.

Gray's detailed operational deception plan was aimed at defeating the NVA intelligence efforts. As it turned out, it was an American reporter who spread the word of the Marines arrival. No sooner had the Marines appeared than the renowned reporter, Keyes Beech, trumpeted their presence to the world. On May 21, 1964, in the *Chicago Daily News*, a piece by Beech, with the headline "U.S. Faces Military Involvement in Laos: Red Threat to Thailand Could Spark GI's Entry" contained this item:

> *U.S. Military intervention – if it comes – would not necessarily come through Thailand. It could just as easily – and perhaps more quickly – come from South Viet Nam [sic]. U.S. Marines from Okinawa could be landed in Da Nang, a modern city of 100,000 people on the east coast of South Viet Nam and the best port in central Viet Nam.*
>
> *In addition to a 500-man marine helicopter unit there has been a small but noticeable increase in marine strength at Da Nang in recent weeks. A marine security unit – ordered back to the States last December as part of a 1,000-man cut in U.S. forces here – has returned to Da Nang.*
>
> *Da Nang... has a marine helicopter unit now being used to support South Vietnamese troops.*
>
> *The same helicopters could just as easily be used to ferry American troops into Laos. The same forces could easily be supplied via Route 9, an all-weather road that crosses the narrow 50-mile waist of Viet Nam and enters Laos at the border village of Lao Bao just below the 17th Parallel...*

While not precisely on target, Beech's article even gave the proper area where the Marines would be operating, i.e., along Route 9, and he correctly forecast the use of the Marine helicopters to lift the troops. It would have been a very poor NVA intelligence officer who missed the threat that was announced, probably very unintentionally, by the American reporter.

It was not difficult for Beech to detect the arrival of newcomers, though perhaps he had been tipped by one of his many sources. No matter how he had learned of

Gray's unit, it would eventually cause considerable dissension among the Americans. Gray's men, designated Marine Detachment, Advisory Team 1, were ostensibly in the country to train the Montagnards at their base at Khe Sanh. Having visited the training base at Khe Sanh, Gray knew that his deception plan – that Marines were training the Montagnards – was perfect. After all the deception plan has to be believable and the unit conducting the deception has to be able to actually perform the mission.

While in Da Nang, Major Gray received a welcomed visitor. David Gaddy, head of the Vietnamese section at the NSA, had flown in accompanied by a Vietnamese linguist. The NSA manager was a very close friend of Gray's from his early trips to NSA in the late 1950s, when Captain Gray took several flyaway teams there for training. The linguist turned out to be a woman, Mrs. Gene Raymond, whom Gaddy had been able to sneak into South Vietnam because of how she spelled her given name. Gray quickly found a set of camouflaged utilities for Mrs. Raymond, though Gaddy was left to his civilian attire.

Two things struck Gaddy while riding around the airport with Gray. First, Gray wore a battered old revolver as his firearm. When questioned about it, he told Gaddy that it was a gift from an old 1st sergeant who had picked it up while serving in Nicaragua; Gray referred to it as his field weapon. Second, Gaddy was reminded how closed mouthed Gray was. While Gray drove them in the jeep through the airport, with Gene Raymond perched on the back and Gaddy in the suicide seat, they glimpsed an F-4 that had landed for some reason or other. The visit pre-dated the start of bombing missions and fighter-bomber activity in Da Nang was most unusual. Gaddy said to Major Gray, "Isn't that an F-4 over there?" Gray replied, "I don't see any F-4," and that was the end of the discussion. While Gene wanted to remain with the Signal Engineering Survey Unit, her gender made that impossible as a practical matter. Consequently, when Gaddy left after a few days, Mrs. Raymond left with him.[10]

Gaddy and Mrs. Raymond also visited the 8th RRU at Phu Bai. The 8th RRU had been the SIGINT site to which several Marines who were part of Captain John Hyatt's 1962 detachment were assigned upon completion of that mission. Manned mostly by Soldiers, but always including many Marines from the Naval Security Group, by 1964 Phu Bai was the hub of American SIGINT activity in I Corps. Besides visiting there to set up communications links, Gray and Lieutenant Meck also liaised with the 8th RRU about technical SIGINT matters. One Army Vietnamese linguist the pair met was Specialist Ralph Adams. The "Gray Ghost" made an impression on Adams and many others at Phu Bai. Adams recalled that whenever the Gray Ghost visited, personnel of all services expected things to happen. The Marine Major's enthusiasm, energy and determination had a positive effect on all the cryptologists, and Adams recalled that during his subsequent tours at Phu Bai he and everyone else were excited whenever Gray appeared.[11]

After the grunts arrived on the scene in Da Nang, Gray moved most of the unit, with the infantrymen, to Khe Sanh. Lieutenant Otlowski's Marines from 2/3 began training the Montagnards. The Marines settled into Khe Sanh while Gray awaited a chance to fly onto the mountain for a detailed reconnaissance. He got his first chance to glimpse Dong Voi Mep when General William Westmoreland flew into Khe Sanh to visit the Special Forces camp. The airstrip was away from Khe Sanh village, which is located to the west of what would later become the Marine base and the name of one of the most famous battles of the war. The Special Forces site of 1964 was an abandoned French fort close to the village of the same name. It was the first time that Al Gray ever met the General, who would soon command all U.S. forces in Vietnam, and the Marine was impressed. Westmoreland was on an indoctrination tour around the country in preparation for relieving General Harkins at MAC(V). After briefing the General about his operational plan, during which Westmoreland asked pointed, pertinent questions, events took an unexpectedly positive turn for the Marine.

Westmoreland's party had arrived in a pair of early UH-1E helicopters and the General offered to let Gray borrow one to go see Tiger Tooth personally. Major Gray quickly accepted the General's invitation. The helicopter crew flew the Marine to the top of the mountain and stayed with him while he did a quick 30-minute assessment. The flight back became something of an adventure when the UH-1E lost power while descending the backside of the mountain; fortunately, the pilots were able to restart the engine before the helicopter crashed into the DMZ. Thus, Gray got an initial first look at the mountain before the detailed reconnaissance with three ARVN officers from the unit that would provide additional protection for the Marines.[12] Westmoreland departed the area aboard the Carabou aircraft that had flown Gray into Khe Sanh. When the plane was subjected to small arms fire as it ascended, both pilots and the Vietnamese in the passenger compartment were seriously wounded, though Westmomeland was unhurt.[13]

During the wait before the recon contingent was to fly onto the mountain, Lieutenant Meck received word via courier from Saigon that the Foreign Broadcast Intelligence Service had intercepted a Chinese language report that announced the presence of U. S. Marines in Da Nang. Gray was furious at the receipt of the news, which he knew threatened to end the mission before he could even really start SIGINT operations. Gray quickly gathered the officers and Staff NCOs and emphasized the need for absolute attention to detail with respect to sound communications practices and operational security measures. Later, still before the operation actually kicked off, Meck got word from the Philippines that his wife was seriously ill. Gray told his lieutenant to immediately return home; Captain Charles McDonald, an old friend of Gray's from his days in Hawaii, replaced Meck as the #2 man of the contingent.

An ARVN infantry company commander, his leading Staff NCO, and an ARVN engineering officer were designated to accompany Gray on the recon trip to Tiger Tooth – Dong Voi Mep. Captain McDonald would remain at Khe Sanh with the rest of the detachment and from there provide communications to the higher ups in Saigon. The weather had been generally good in and around Da Nang and along the coastal plain, but the mountains had a largely dissimilar climate, one that would cause distress and anxiety in the coming weeks. The monsoon arrived in northern Vietnam and Laos about a month or so after it had blown through Saigon, but that weather detail was not generally known when the operation was conceived in Saigon. Thus, when there was a break in the clouds that hung over Tiger Tooth like a blanket, Gray and his group took advantage of the occasion, for they were quite anxious to get up on the mountain and look at it for themselves. Gray had failed to personally account for the local weather; instead, he had relied on Saigon's forecasts. The discrepancy between the timing of the monsoon in various regions of the country was not realized until some weeks later, but by that time, overlooking the important weather detail had bitten Al Gray, and hard.

STUCK ON TIGER TOOTH MOUNTAIN, 28 MAY-22 JUNE 1965

Major Al Gray and the three Vietnamese arrived on the mountain expecting an overnight stay. In order to confuse any North Vietnamese who might be observing the helicopters, the Marine pilots flew to a couple different locations in addition to Tiger Tooth. One mountain, Sa Mui, located a little northwest of Tiger Tooth was almost as high, though it was located on the North Vietnamese side of the DMZ. While Sa Mui was off limits to the Americans, in 1964 there was still not a clear modus operandi for American forces, and the North Vietnamese, if watching, could not be sure of where possible landings might occur. Furthermore, the South Vietnamese occasionally launched operations (usually unsuccessfully) into North Vietnam and Laos, using blackened aircraft flown by South Vietnamese pilots; helicopter operations were not limited to just areas south of the DMZ.

In late May 1964, Marine H-34 helicopters took the recon party to the mountain to drop them off. The landing occurred without incident, and Gray immediately started his recon over the same ground that he had visited less than a week before. Gray had to establish a detailed operational plan, and he was doing so with allies who also were experienced combat leaders. A harbinger of future events occurred when, a couple hours after the small group landed, the weather turned bad. Gray could only hope that with the next morning would come a weather interval needed for the helicopters to return from Da Nang and pick up his small contingent.

An extra night on the mountain would be inconvenient for the group, but by no means significant. The chance that North Vietnamese would be roaming around on top of the mountain was quite remote; Gray and his friends had their canteens, packs and a normal complement of food and accoutrements, small arms and ammunition. However, given the expected circumstances for the recon, they did not have tents, extra ponchos, changes of clothing or other items that they might have carried had they anticipated an extended, or even a two-night, stay. Happily though, each of the Vietnamese carried a large roll of rice that was typical of the ARVN.

Since evaluating communications to and from the mountain were part of this initial reconnaissance mission, the four men had both a field radio and a longer-range AN/GRC-9 HF radio. The AN/GRC-9, as it turned out, was a lifesaver, since it did not depend on batteries. One man would talk on the radio while another cranked a mechanism that supplied power. But as their evacuation was delayed, then delayed again, and again, and again, concern about the safety of the quartet rose, particularly in Saigon.

There, Lieutenant Colonel John LaSpada, USMC, had replaced Lieutenant Colonel Alberts in the J-6 Plans (Special Projects) Branch. LaSpada had served with Alberts and Al Gray at HQMC and thus was very familiar with Gray's professionalism, tenacity and perseverance. Furthermore, Captain Charlie McDonald, Gray's second in command, was also very knowledgeable about his boss's methods and resourcefulness. McDonald was able to speak convincingly with his old acquaintance, Colonel LaSpada. As a day stretched into a week, and then two weeks, LaSpada was able to assure his superiors, including Gray's old boss, General Carl Youngdale, now the J-2 in Saigon, that Gray and his fellows were fine. Chiefly he did so because that was precisely what Gray was reporting from the mountaintop.

Gray and his small band stuck there were not discouraged or particularly worried, though Gray was very anxious to get the mission started. The company commander was an ARVN lieutenant who had been a graduate of the French Academy in

Saigon; he was a fine officer. His senior NCO, a master sergeant, had been fighting for years, most of time for the North Vietnamese. As previously noted, the master sergeant had served in the Viet Minh and had fought the French at Dien Bien Phu. There, he had commanded a machine gun company, so his combat experience was quite extensive. The fact that Gray had previously fought the communists in Korea created an instant bond between him and the veteran Catholic sergeant. The third Vietnamese officer was along to assist in sighting defensive positions and establishing helicopter resupply points. More than getting to know his new friends, however, the time on the mountain gave Al Gray time to indulge in one of his favorite pastimes, learning another Asian language. It was not easy and for the most part the fact that everyone in the party knew a smattering of Chinese helped immensely.

The fact that he was stranded on a mountaintop was worrisome, but the far bigger concern for the Marine Major was what the reaction might be in Saigon, or in Honolulu, or most especially in Washington. Gray was under tremendous pressure

Figure 4.2
Gray and Friends at Khe Sanh before they were stranded on Tiger Tooth Mountain. The picture was taken while the four awaited transportation to the top of the mountain.[14]

not to escalate the war. Countless decision-makers, and even more people behind the scenes, fretted that the Marines might do something to provoke an expansion of the war. Gray well knew, and understood, that he had to not give even the appearance of any problem that would permit the naysayers to end the mission. That consideration not only weighed heavily on Gray, but it greatly influenced each and every decision he made.

The Vietnamese spoke very little English, but Gray's interest in and proficiency with languages eased the communications issues among the group. Gray had not had time to learn much of the language before deploying, but he previously had taught himself a little Korean, lots of Japanese, a token amount of Mandarin Chinese, and even a little Tagalog and Thai. Naturally inquisitive, and having an obvious aptitude for languages, Gray found himself in a veritable immersion course.[15] The fact that Al Gray was interested in learning their language gained him high respect from the Vietnamese, which undoubtedly helped make the situation more tolerable to all involved. Japanese and Chinese Kanji characters are very similar, and using the dirt, Gray would draw the Japanese character for river, for example; the Vietnamese all knew some Chinese and they would respond with the appropriate Chinese symbol and the Vietnamese word, and so the conversations went, painstakingly slowly. But none of the group was particularly upset or the slightest bit impatient; and all got along just fine.

Each of the Vietnamese, as was their custom, had a carried a bundle of rice, and that rice became the group's primary food source, shared equally among the group. Early rationing had prolonged the meager supply, but a daily handful of rice did not go far in quelling hunger pains, not that any of the men complained. All were military professionals, and each had previously endured difficult situations before this situation arose.

The issue with the weather was exacerbated by the air wing's policy that all the helicopters had to return to Da Nang each night. There was usually a short period in the morning when safe flight operations could have occurred, had the helicopters been sitting at the strip near the Khe Sanh Special Forces site. The location was almost perfectly safe. But the fear of losing an aircraft trumped rescuing a Marine major and his cohort. By the time the call went out to Da Nang that the planes could safely fly to Tiger Tooth, the weather would change in the length of time needed to fly to the area, thus foreclosing the possibility of landing at the top of the mountain. This set of events repeated several times, and caused growing frustration among those stuck on the mountain. It would not be the only time that the aviator's commitment to saving their aircraft overrode operational requirements involving

Al Gray. In fact, the "planes first mentality" that Gray encountered on this first major operation in Vietnam in 1964 would be repeated 11 years later.[16]

As the second week extended into the third, Gray and his cohort began to reach the limits of their survival skills. In the course of their daily patrolling regimen, they had found a couple different water sources, small streams that sprung out of the mountain. They even located a beautiful waterfall on the mountain, though its beauty provided nothing in the way of sustenance. The major problem with the water was that after the first few days they had no more Halazone tablets – pills that were widely used during the war to purify contaminated water. So thirsty they were not; but cold, wet and miserable they were. The biting dampness that permeated the mountain also went right through them. Their clothing was never really dry, and while they shared their meager resources for warmth whenever one tried to rest, sleep was neither deep nor satisfying. Gray normally slept only three or at most four hours a day, but in this situation he got away with even less. Active throughout the day scouting and patrolling, his nights were also full pondering his situation. He was well familiar with the excellent North Vietnamese SIGINT capability.

As a consequence, he was loath to spend much time on the radio, lest the NVA do to him exactly what he planned to do to them, exploit communications. When communications did occur, often Esperanto was the language of choice between the Marines. Esperanto is a language the Marines use to practice SIGINT during Fleet exercises; on Tiger Tooth, it was used to confuse any would-be listeners.

The Marines at Khe Sanh were in daily contact with those stranded 11 miles (as the birds fly) to the north, and together they quickly worked out a scheme for changing frequencies and transmission times in order not to be predictable. The Khe Sanh contingent would then relay Gray's daily situation reports to Saigon through the communications relay link that had established at Phu Bai. That relay permitted good contact with Air Wing in Da Nang and with Saigon. Unfortunately, the MAC(V) weather forecasters were not helpful for men stranded on a mountaintop in the DMZ. Further, even the Marines at Khe Sanh had little idea what was going to happen, weather-wise, on Tiger Tooth before Gray and the others experienced it. Thus, without a helicopter positioned at Khe Sanh with the mission of extracting the recon party, there was no ability to react instantaneously to the weather. When a brief period of sunshine might occur, it had passed by the time the helicopter flying from Da Nang got into a position to land. Through such a combination of factors, but due principally to the weather, Gray's stranding extended from three weeks into four.

By the time the first 20 days had passed, Gray knew that he and his party were quickly coming to the limit of their ability to continue without food and proper rest.

They were nearing the end of their already meager daily ration of rice; the water also had begun to affect the group's health. Gray was losing his voice, and the conditions were tapping his strength. Always a powerful man in great physical condition, Gray found that climbing down, up and around the mountaintop was becoming increasingly difficult. Thus, development of an alternative plan for evacuation became the point of emphasis for the small assemblage. All agreed that they needed to walk off, since it appeared that helicopters could not land to evacuate them.

Gray remained very concerned about COMSEC, and given their prolonged stay, he was apprehensive that their communication links had been discovered. To thwart the possibility of NVA Communications Intelligence analysis, Gray struck a plan of speaking Japanese with an American Nisei Army advisor located with a 155mm howitzer section in the Lang Miet Xa area. The pair of 155mm guns was the ARVN's most northern and western position, and the Nisei captain was in a very isolated area. If Esperanto confused the enemy, Japanese should surely provide an even higher degree of communications safety. Fortunately, the captain spoke enough Japanese to communicate with Gray, who was quite conversant in the language following his service in Japan in the 1950s. Gray told the captain about the date and time his party could be expected to reach the artillery outpost. They also came up with a challenge and password that the party would use in the event they encountered friendly forces, and discussed the route from Tiger Tooth to Khe Sanh that would most likely be quickest and safest. They also planned some artillery fires in case the enemy was encountered. Of course, the best of intentions, and tactics, often go awry. The enemy has an uncanny way of injecting themselves in a manner that disrupts even the best of plans.

At first light, about 0500 on a cold June morning, after awakening yet again to a heavy fog, Gray led his small group down the west side of the mountain along the ridgelines. Straight line the distance west was about five miles, but the route was hardly straight. Finally, as they approached a stream named Kha Ta Bong, they had to plunge into the savannah grasses, there being no trails to use. The grasses made for tough going, cutting arms and ripping uniforms, and the small party had to frequently stop to pick leeches from each others' bodies. When they finally reached the stream they turned south.

The normal order of march was Gray, the master sergeant, the engineering officer and finally the company commander, who provided rear security. All went well until the party neared the area north of the abandoned village of Lang Soot, which was located along the small stream that the party was following. Rounding a bend in the trail, Gray found himself looking into what turned out to be a small company

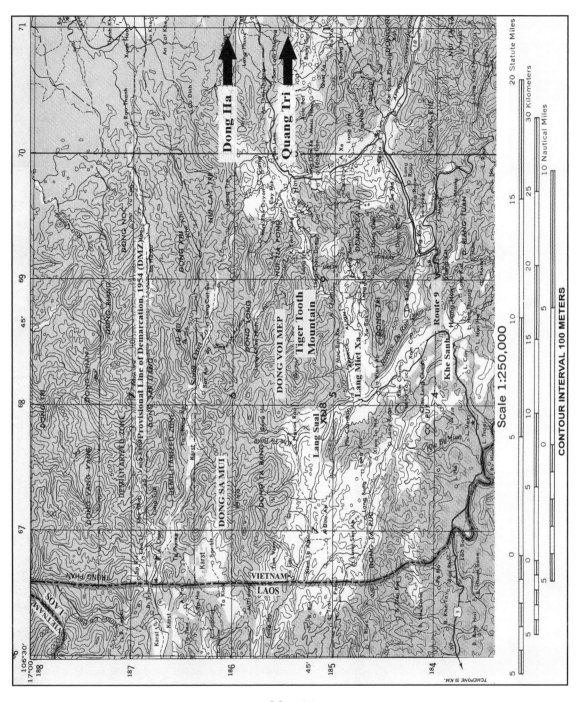

Map 4.1
Dong Voi Mep and the area north of Khe Sanh.
Adapted from Army Map Service, Corps of Engineers.

headquarters area. Eye to eye with a VC who had been taking a bath, Gray was able to beat his enemy in getting off a shot. Tired, weakened and knowing he was probably outnumbered, Gray decided that surprise and daring were more likely to be successful than trying to run and evade. Throughout his career, Gray told subordinates that a good plan violently executed was far better than the perfect plan delayed. Firing his carbine with well-aimed shots and yelling to his cohort to follow him, Gray's completely unexpected attack wreaked havoc in the NVA camp. The ARVN master sergeant rushed to the aid of his American companion and displayed the kind of marksmanship that should be expected of such a combat veteran. But things did not go perfectly; in his haste to get into a good firing position at the beginning of the fight, Gray did not notice a punji pit booby trap, something designed to protect the VC campsite. His punishment for momentary inattention was a painful, though not life-threatening stab in his left leg. But he had help coming, and soon.

While in the midst of a very active firefight, Gray was able to call for artillery support from the 155mm guns at Miet Xa. Their field radio had been saved for just such an occasion, and Gray put it to immediate use. Long Soot was one of the places that Gray and the American Nisei captain had arranged for pre-planned fires. Long-range fire from South Vietnamese artillery, located just within range, scattered the VC who were mostly across the creek from the small Allied group. The incoming barrage proved ruinous to the VC Company, and it killed their company commander. Pre-planned artillery is always a good thing; in this case, it was a real game changer.

The NVA left alive had scrambled into the bush and were trying to escape as fast as possible. Gray directed that the ARVN commander and sergeant conduct a hasty search for documents or anything of intelligence value. While the search was carried out, Gray scouted the trails leading from the camp for any sign of activity. The Marine was anxious to get whatever intelligence data might be found, but he also did not want to give the NVA time to regroup and return. He hobbled back to the location of his cohort and quickly cleaned the wound as best he could.

The initial rush of adrenalin that carried the group through the VC camp was tempered by the fact that not only was Gray injured, but also the ARVN engineer had a serious bullet wound in his leg, and now could not walk. He lamented to the group that he would have to remain behind, certainly to become a prisoner of the enemy. Gray dressed his own injury while the Vietnamese anxiously evaluated their officer's wound. In the end, the American determined that he would be able to carry the smaller Vietnamese and ordered the sergeant to load the injured engineer on his back. Gray would carry the ARVN officer the 10 remaining kilometers to safety.[17]

But the recon-group-turned-attack-force now faced another dilemma. Gray could not be sure where the enemy had gone, in what number or with what weapons. And Gray and his friends' strength were now significantly diminished; besides their wounds, the allies were more exhausted and Gray was grappling with at least an extra 130 pounds. The Marine decided that he had to move with speed rather than stealth, and that meant sticking to trails as opposed to trying to muscle their way through the dense undergrowth that characterized the area. Moving off the trails would have been far safer, but Gray doubted his companions had the physical strength required, even if he did. And truth be known, he probably did not. But sometimes luck is better than great planning, and Gray's small faction reached a small ARVN outpost at about 2030 (8:30 P.M.) local time, having covered a distance of about 15 miles and fought a firefight en route.

The good news was that documents collected from the NVA proved to be a treasure trove for Marine and especially ARVN intelligence professionals. For Gray's Marines, they represented the first real documents collected on their mission. For the ARVN and MAC(V) J-2 (Intelligence) sections, the documents provided additional proof of what was already known, that the NVA were operating in strength in South Vietnam; interestingly though, the extent of VC operations on the Northwest Frontier were largely unknown in Saigon. It turned out that the Special Forces and the ARVN never actually patrolled north of Route 9 and never really looked under the double and triple layers of jungle canopy that covered the area.

The captured papers also revealed additional data about unit identification, unit strength and other operational and logistical concerns. Most importantly, they identified the VC infiltrators in all the villages in northwest South Vietnam; it also gave specific examples of how the VC had organized each village to provide them with supplies. For example, one village might be tasked to provide 200 punji stakes each month, while another ferried supplies to hidden communist stashes. Needless to say, the ARVN were able to very quietly, but effectively, remove the VC sympathizers and eradicate the internal threat for many months after the document seizure. For men like Sergeant Art Kidd, the documents represented the final stage in his professional training as a linguist, and the first opportunity he had ever had to exploit the enemy's own documents.[18]

The bad news was that Major Al Gray required some rest. Moreover, he was probably suffering from some sort of throat infection. Though the Vietnamese outpost where he and his cohort had walked treated them to a feast, Gray could not eat – even though quite hungry! The next morning the ARVN loaded Gray and the others into a truck and delivered them to Khe Sanh and a reunion with Captain

McDonald and the rest of the Marines. After a quick debrief, Major Gray then took a helicopter to Da Nang and reported to the air wing's medical staff. His throat was really hurting. The corpsman gave him a bottle of hydrogen peroxide with orders to gargle every hour. He would follow those orders, but only after getting some much needed sleep, about 24 hours worth.

Gray permitted himself two days rest and recovery time before again pronouncing himself ready to conduct the main portion of the mission. After flying to Saigon to report what had happened, he emphasized the intelligence haul that had already been made. But Al Gray contemplated little trouble in Saigon. Major General Richard Weede, whom Gray knew from HQMC, was the Chief of Staff to General Paul Harkins. The J-2, Intelligence, was his former boss at HQMC, Brigadier General Carl Youngdale. Though they listened intently to what he had to say, two Marine generals treated the occasion more as a welcome home ceremony than anything else. Trouble there was, however.

When Major Gray briefed the MAC(V) J-3, Brigadier General Stilwell became worried about the Marines being credited with training the locals, a mission he felt was solely the purview of the U.S. Army's Special Forces. Consequently, he disapproved that aspect of Gray's deception planning. While the Major had been stuck atop the mountain, Keyes Beech had continued to hound Saigon about what the Marines were doing in Da Nang. Now, with Stilwell prohibiting the ready answer from being disseminated, Beech's reporting raised questions but gave no answers.[19] But were the NVA paying attention?

The Stillwell debacle really aggravated Major Gray. By the time the Army general in Saigon, far away from the scene denied the plan, the Marines had already successfully implemented it! There never was complete trust and respect between the Montagnards and the South Vietnamese, but in a month Major Gray, Captain McDonald, Lieutenant Otlowski and especially their Marines had earned the admiration of both groups. The District Chief, Captain Truong (who later became the Commanding General of the ARVN 1st Division) and Captain Giai, who later commanded the ARVN 2nd Regiment and who was as good a fighter as Al Gray ever saw, both became long-time friends of Al Gray. A couple years later, the relationship between the Allied officers would later pay big dividends for both sides.

No one in Saigon, however, brought up the possibility of cancelling the mission, so Al Gray flew back to Da Nang immediately.

Gray never stayed in the South Vietnamese capital, it was one of his inviolate rules. Besides, he was in a hurry to get started. He reasoned that his whole mission was in jeopardy if he did not get his cryptologists up and operational on Tiger Tooth

Mountain. The Beech article had been published over a month before; the Chinese Foreign Broadcast Intelligence Service intercept had been noted before Gray's reconnaissance, and Marine helicopter activity around Khe Sanh and even Tiger Tooth might have attracted unwanted attention. On a positive note, the monsoon was over or nearly over and the weather improving daily. Thus, three days after walking off Tiger Tooth, Gray and his first element of Marines and ARVN were flown back to the site picked for the primary position. Before landing on Tiger Tooth, however, Gray insisted that another aspect of the operational deception plan be fully implemented, which meant the helicopters flew to and appeared to touch down on Sa Mua Mountain and other mountain heights in addition the actual objective.

He had another administrative duty to attend to before he could actually begin operations on Tiger Tooth, however. The intelligence haul from the captured VC documents had come to the attention of the U.S. Army Senior Advisor for I Corps, Colonel Warner, and his deputy, a Lieutenant Colonel Waite. Both officers were insistent on nominating Major Gray for a Silver Star medal.[20] What a great story, the Soldiers thought: a Marine officer spends almost four weeks stranded atop a mountain with three ARVN, then walks 15 miles to safety, fights his way through a VC company, calls artillery to destroy the enemy, captures the most important intelligence collection ever seen in northern I Corps, and then carries a wounded ARVN officer 10 clicks to safety. Gray deserved to get a medal, or so thought the Soldiers. But Al Gray was not seeking personal rewards, he had a mission to fulfill; if the folks in Saigon got wind of all the shooting and fighting already involved, they – after being sufficiently worried before learning of any firefights – might decide to cancel Gray's whole operation. No, Gray assured the colonels, he was most happy to remain anonymous and thereby permit the venture to go forward. After careful consideration and prolonged debate on the merits, the American Soldiers relented.

However, years later more details of the events of the walk off the mountain came to light. While investigating General Gray's papers, a citation of a Vietnamese Cross of Gallantry was discovered. The elaborate certificate, dated 28 September 1966 and signed by Lieutenant General Hoang Xuan Lam, the ARVN Commanding General in I Corps, is written – as one might expect – in Vietnamese. However, there is an accompanying translation, reproduced here:

> *"For heroism and exceptionally meritorious conduct. Major GRAY provided the courageous leadership and drive to overcome hazardous terrain, adverse weather and for [sic] separated ambushes and returned with the Unit intact."*

Obviously, the Vietnamese knew more than we do; we have only learned of a single ambush. By this time, Gray's old friend Lieutenant Colonel Ngo Quang Truong was the G-3 of the 1ˢᵗ ARVN Division. Our guess is that Colonel Truong or perhaps Major Giai, whom Gray also met at Khe Sanh, were responsible for nominating him for the award.

OPERATIONS ON TIGER TOOTH MOUNTAIN

Gray had pushed hard to get the operation underway, knowing that his delay atop the mountain had set back his schedule. Finally, the weather permitted the helicopters to carry the contingent to the top of the mountain, most of the cryptologists accompanied Gray, though several, led by Harry Williams and including Sergeant Kidd, stayed at Khe Sanh. Williams's profession as an NSA analyst prevented him from conducting operations at the front, and even his presence in Khe Sanh was questionable, though the Montagnards provided a large measure of security and their base had not been disturbed by VC or NVA activity to date. The infantrymen were split between a group that remained at Khe Sanh providing security for the Detachment Team #1 base camp while also satisfying the "training" deception, and those who

Figure 4.3
View of camp at Khe Sanh, 1964[21]

went to the mountain to augment the ARVN Company providing direct security for the cryptologic element. The men, both infantry and cryptologic, would periodically rotate between the two locales – the top of the mountain and the Khe Sanh base, though Gray remained on the mountain throughout. In addition, Gray had positioned communicators at Phu Bai and Da Nang so that they could relay information about the mission to both the authorities in Saigon and those back at NSA.

As was his habit, Gray immersed himself in every detail of the operation, without interfering or micro-managing unless such action was needed. He often went on patrol with the ARVN or infantry Marines, but he did that more as an observer than as a patrol leader. He would not hesitate to pass along "suggestions" as to how certain missions could be done better or more efficiently, but he rarely directed subordinate leaders while they went about their missions. Rather, subordinates would receive instruction about how to improve operations in private conversations away from the men. Gray expected professionalism from those under his command, and so long as officers and Staff NCOs exhibited it, he did not meddle. He handled the cryptologists in a similar manner. While he had the background and experience needed to perform most assignments, Major Gray normally led through discussion, interviewing and suggesting; he anticipated that his men would conduct themselves in a proficient manner, and they usually did. However, when something needed to be done immediately, the men had no doubts that Gray's orders were to be explicitly followed!

Harry Williams, the NSA civilian accompanying the mission, recalled that Gray never told him exactly what to do, though he often had suggestions. Williams clearly had the idea that the Major expected him to get on with it though he never gave detailed orders. Williams learned that Gray's suggestions were, in effect, mission-type orders. However, in the eyes of his Marines, Williams recalled that anything Major Gray said quickly became gospel to his men.[22]

Gray never had to ask what was going on, because he was always out and about determining for himself what the men were doing. Whether it was an infantryman in a foxhole, or a linguist listening to the radio, or a technician tuning the breadboard intercept equipment, Gray would contact him sooner or later. He might appear at high noon on a weekday, or during the mid-watch on a starless night. Whenever it was when the men least expected Gray to appear, he did. They, like others before them, soon adopted the moniker the Gray Ghost for him, given his wandering ways.[23] Not only did the Gray Ghost come calling, but soon he also knew the men's names and had learned more than a little about them. Years later, after having not seen or served with him for a long time, men who were junior enlisted Marines in 1964 were surprised to have then Lieutenant Colonel, or Colonel or even General Gray call them by name, and recount stories of their times together. Gray had much more than a passing interest in the lives of his men, and he used his fine memory and capacity for names and dates to inspire his troops. It was a style of leadership that ingratiated him to all who served with him. Each man thought his commander considered him to be the most important part of the mission, whether he was an analyst or a rifleman, a linguist or a fire team leader, or just an ammunition humper for the machine guns. And to Gray, each was. But Major Gray was doing much more than learning about his men. He was anxious for technical success on the mission, and it was slow in coming. The breadboard electronics worked well enough that the Marines were able to determine the presence of the Soviet communications system, proving that the North Vietnamese were indeed using it. However, real-time exploitation remained outside the grasp of the small contingent.

During his time on Tiger Tooth Mountain, Gray had a chance to mull over the entire plan for the operation and the mistakes that had been made. Of the latter, there were at least two that were noteworthy: first, Gray convinced himself that he would never again rely on others for detailed weather information; he would always personally check with the meteorologists. Second, he remained troubled that his deception plan had not been followed; going forward he had to ensure that such

Figure 4.4
Gy Sgt Dan Buckley, Sgt Art Kidd, National Security Agency
Representative Harry Williams, and S Sgt Rich Richmond.[24]

Figure 4.5
Maj Gray with unidentified Captain from the Security Force discussing some matter. Gy Sgt Joe Satterthwait seated on left, M Sgt Murray Sklar seated on right. Lt Robert Meck standing in foreground. Satterthwait was one of the Corps' best Vietnamese linguists; Sklar was a crypto-analyst.[25]

Figure 4.6
Maj Gray in camouflage utilities at Khe Sanh. S Sgt. Rich Richmond is kneeling in the left front; Lt Bob Meck is shirtless, and other members of the cryptologic detachment.[26]

plans were coordinated throughout the chain of command, lest others object for what Gray considered administrative, not operational, reasons. The latter mistake became decisive.

While Gray fretted over the lack of progress in technical signals exploitation, another, more ominous, problem arose. North Vietnamese or VC infantry started probing the Marine and ARVN position. At first the contacts were very minor; indeed, the fire from friendly forces might have been attributed to inexperienced infantrymen shooting at shadows. Finally the enemy unleashed a heavy attack against Gray's men; all were in their first real firefight. Gray led from the front, constantly exposed to enemy fire while moving from position to position, hurling grenades down the hill and encouraging his men. Indeed, Sergeant Virgil C. Prater was so inspired by his commander's performance that he nominated Gray for a Bronze Star.

Following the attack, Al Gray knew that he would have to abandon the position after a significant firefight that left no doubt that his location had been compromised. Even though there had been no friendly casualties, given the extremely sensitive nature of the mission, its commander realized that he could not remain on the mountain. More worrying to Gray, the Allied unit saw a North Vietnamese flag flying above a distant, far-away position. Even though the American-Vietnamese patrols could not find the NVA unit, Gray knew the enemy was out there somewhere. Gray's leadership during the firefights, coupled with his performance during the nine days of continuous rain earlier in June, when Gray and many of his men – American and Vietnamese – suffered debilitating illnesses, was also mentioned in Prater's proposed Bronze Star citation. It was the second time during the operation that Gray encountered such efforts in his behalf, but on this occasion he handled it much more quietly. Although he appreciated Sergeant Prater's efforts, Gray simply filed away the Sergeant's letter somewhere in his personal papers and it never saw the light of day.[27]

Nearly simultaneous with the probing, the cryptologists had picked up another Chinese Foreign Broadcast Intelligence Service broadcast that said the Marines were operating in the mountains in the north of South Vietnam. Who might have told them? Keyes Beech had finally received an answer from Saigon about why the Marines were in the country. The answer was not that they were there for training; instead, the military command gave Beech the real reason for Gray's visit. Of course, Al Gray did not learn of that aspect of the fiasco until nearly the end of the mission. But if the Chinese knew, then so did the North Vietnamese. The NVA's SIGINT capabilities were well advanced even without help from American reporters and loose-lipped military officers in Saigon.

Not only were the people in Saigon's MAC(V) very nervous by now, but also they ordered Gray to terminate the mission on Tiger Tooth Mountain. Gray knew that the risks to the Marines and their ARVN protectors possibly outweighed the success they had been achieving. Therefore, he set about continuing the mission, but in a different location.

In mid-July the Marines and their ARVN escort were heli-lifted off Tiger Tooth Mountain, evacuated from Khe Sanh, and returned to Da Nang. But the mission was not yet finished. Both Bob Meck, who tracked the mission from his location in the Philippines, and Al Gray wondered if it was the report of Keyes Beech that led to the probes on Tiger Tooth? Al Gray never underestimated his enemy, and in Vietnam he learned that such respect was highly justified.

OPERATIONS ON DONG BACH MA

Major Gray convinced the powers to be that the mission could be continued, and he had found an excellent location to do just that. Dong Bach Ma was an abandoned resort area located northwest of Da Nang in the high mountains. It was a place where the French and later the Vietnamese used to escape the summer heat that permeated the lowlands along the coastal plain. The key feature at Dong Mach Ma was a former French schoolhouse that would serve as the operations center for Gray's small unit. But first, Gray had to safely move his men from Da Nang to the mountain resort area.

Well before 1964, it was clear that the North Vietnamese and VC had an excellent and elaborate spy network set up throughout South Vietnam. Indeed, there were few secrets once information was shared with South Vietnamese authorities. Again Gray's penchant for operational deception came to the fore. Soon after Gray and his men had arrived back in Da Nang, Lieutenant General Brute Krulak landed at the airfield. He had promised to visit Gray and this was fulfilling that vow; but there were also other considerations in play. In almost every operation that Gray ever participated, the "Higher Headquarters" always wanted to reduce the size of the combat contingent. Gray had requested a company but had received what amounted to single, though heavily reinforced, platoon. Krulak did not doubt Major Gray's plan, but there was inordinate pressure being brought to bear in both Saigon and Washington to reduce the size of the Marine detachment. Everybody thought fewer men could accomplish the mission, though those of that opinion were never located near the site of the operation nor were they going to put themselves in harm's way. But such is the way of the world, and thank goodness General Krulak was more than willing to run interference for his Marines. After reviewing

Gray's plan and flying round Dong Bac Ma several times, satisfying himself that Gray's preparations were sound, the General called the Major into his quarters at the airfield.

The Air Force very agreeably had parked the Marine General in one of their air-conditioned trailers. Major Gray was quite familiar with the Air Force installation, since he often used it to send and receive special intelligence messages. Thus he knew many of the officers and senior NCOs who worked there. Krulak, dressed in some sort of Asian kimono and holding a drink, greeted Gray. He told Gray he approved the Major's plan for a reinforced infantry company to provide security; the General then asked Gray to prepare a message reflecting his endorsement of the plan. Though Gray had never drafted a message for General Krulak, he could draw on his experience at HQMC and previously at FMFPAC to know what Krulak might have expected to see. When Gray presented the General with his draft message, Krulak fiddled with minor changes and said, "This is pretty good, Major." Al Gray replied, "Well, sir, I have never prepared a General Krulak-gram before." The General then insisted that Major Gray join him in having a beer. And so it happened that the first time Al Gray ever drank alcohol when outside the United States he did so at the prodding of Lieutenant General Brute Krulak. If one is going to drink, General Krulak was certainly an exceptional, fascinating and even daunting companion with whom to indulge.

Instead of using helicopters, Gray had found enough trucks to transport his men in one convoy from Da Nang to Dong Bach Ma. However, the route was anything but direct, and it included traversing the infamous (to Marines) Hai Van Pass, one of many locations along the route that was very susceptible to ambush. Gray devised a simple deception plan for the movement, one that would, hopefully, foil his adversaries. He let it be known that the unit would rehearse the movement on Sunday; the rehearsal would only go as far as the Hai Van Pass, where the unit would turn around and return to its base at the Da Nang airfield. The full trip to Dong Bach Ma would be made on the following Tuesday in early August. Then Gray ensured that the barbers, laundries and concessionaires serving the Marines got the details of the movement.

As was standard operating procedure for any Gray-led unit, the detachment was saddled up and ready to roll early on Sunday morning. The men were looking forward to getting the rehearsal over with so they could enjoy a peaceful afternoon in Da Nang. Only a very few knew that when the trucks rolled out onto National Route 1 on their way to Hai Van, there would be no return. Instead, the trucks rolled on and on, up and over the treacherous Hai Van Pass, not stopping until they reached the mountains and the old French schoolhouse. The trip could not have been more

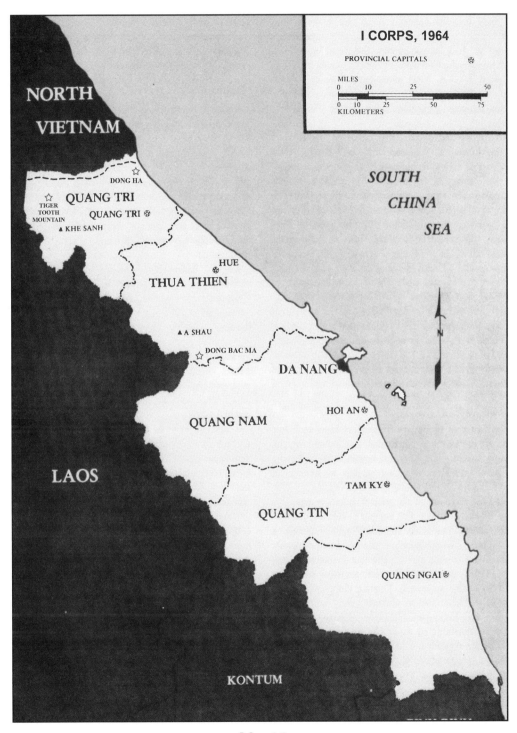

Map 4.2
Northern Provinces of The Republic of Vietnam. Map adapted from History and Museums
Division, Headquarters, Marine Corps series, U.S. Marines in Vietnam, 1964.

Figure 4.7
Through the efforts of Harry Williams, Ray Becker, Art Kidd and Bob Merle, the following
Marines have been identified (tentatively!): Front Row, (left to right); Sgt John D. Gott,
2575(?), Cpl Robert P. Merle, 2574, unidentified, Capt Ray Becker. Second Row, (left to
right): Cpl Dion A. Kirk, 2571; Cpl (?) Green; Cpl Paul L. Purnell, 2571; five unidentified.[28]

uneventful, or more beautiful. The rice paddies that dominate the coastal plain gave way first to small foothills and then the rugged mountains that run along the western boundary of South Vietnam. During the trip, the only hint of war was the live ammunition carried in each man's weapon. There was some excitement, nonetheless.

There was one aspect of the movement to Dong Bach Ma that had escaped Gray's normally laser-like focus. The mountaintop resort was protected by Regional Forces. These irregular forces were one step below the regular army troops, and one step above the Popular Forces; Popular Forces typically operated in very small groups near their homes and villages, and often were observed as a single man guarding a bridge, with a World War II era carbine as his only weapon. But Regional Forces operated in slightly larger units and possessed automatic weapons, and they had more military training. Certainly the fine, but abandoned, homes in the area, owned by the Vietnamese elite, warranted protection. As guards, the Regional Forces did very little outside their defensive position, though they were very capable of defending themselves and their property.

The Marines rolled up to the entrance to the area only to encounter about a platoon of Regional Forces with their weapons locked and loaded. No one had mentioned to them to expect the Marines; or perhaps they had, but the anticipated arrival date was the following Tuesday, not Sunday afternoon. Gray dismounted from his vehicle, and stood on the middle of the road asking permission to enter. The Vietnamese interpreter and Marine linguist interpretor, Seargent Slater, who accompanied Gray translated from behind a nearby tree for protection; Gray was not confident enough in his nascent Vietnamese language skills to get through the budding confrontation. After a few minutes, which to Gray seemed an hour, the Regional Force commander permitted the Marines to enter. The excitement was over and the Marines got to work. Gray surmized the Regional Forces were never told of the plan.

After arriving in the new base, Gray directed the deployment of security forces while the cryptologists set about erecting antennae, installing generators and setting up other support equipment needed for operations. Within a couple hours the Marines had resumed cryptologic operations against the NVA and VC.

Gray was the master at discharging all aspects of his job. But while he communicated with his Marines extensively, and everyone knew everything appropriate for them to know, Gray never revealed his sources, his familiarity with many prominent senior Marines, and he never was in the least braggadocios about himself or his past accomplishments. Thus, while the cohort of Marine Detachment, Advisory Team #1 grew to respect and admire him, they had little if any insights into his career other than that created by the impression he generated. They thought he knew his trade better than any other. Sergeant Art Kidd, one of the Vietnamese linguists, feared that Major Gray might not get promoted because he was so far outside the mainstream of assignments that led to an officer's career advancement. As it turned out, Sergeant (later Captain) Kidd need not have worried about the man he called the most professional officer he ever met.[29] But while the men had little insight into Gray's standing as a Marine officer, Lieutenant Meck was certain that his detachment commander was destined for big things. Meck had observed Gray in several different situations and environments, and he marveled at the Major's ability to get things done, and he considered Gray the finest officer he had ever met.

The Signals Engineering Survey Unit's mission was a clear success. Analysts at NSA and within the intelligence community were quite happy with the information gathered on both Tiger Tooth Mountain and at Dong Bach Ma. The detachment also provided a good start upon which Marine cryptologists could build in the coming years. By mid-1967, elements of the Radio Battalion were very successful,

Figure 4.8
The French Schoolhouse at Dong Bach Ma served as the Marines Operations Center[30]

very nearly decisive, exploiting NVA communications. And when that finally happened, Al Gray would be present, playing an important role.

A request that Major Gray be extended in Vietnam to set up additional SIGINT operations against the North Vietnamese was denied, because according to Headquarters, Gray again had a "plethora" of duties to be completed at the Headquarters. Thus, in late August 1964, having turned the unit over to Captain Ray Becker, Major Gray returned to Washington. In one of the many coincidences that proves it is a small Marine Corps, Becker again relieved Gray less than two years later in Vietnam.

Gray and his men had proven that Marine cryptologic efforts could deploy rapidly, conduct intense operations against a largely unknown foe, and be successful. It was the very mission he and his men had trained for since he joined the 1st Composite Radio Company in 1958. Their efforts and their professionalism impressed the Director of the NSA, whose personal note to the Commandant about Major Gray and the detachment's work contributed to the growing reputation within NSA and the intelligence community for Marine SIGINT capabilities. More importantly, it

Figure 4.9
The main road into Dong Bach Ma was "paved" by cans.[31]

rewarded the special trust that the Commandant, Wallace M. Greene, Jr. had previously displayed toward the SIGINT/EW personnel at HQMC.

But it was also fitting that no good deed go unpunished. For Al Gray, ordered back to Washington, it was a case of jumping from the frying pan back into the fire; the fire of controversy at HQMC and his coming encounter with Lieutenant General Leonard F. Chapman, Jr., the new and very imposing Chief of Staff.

BACK INTO THE FRYING PAN, SEPTEMBER 1964-NOVEMBER 1965

While Gray was in Vietnam, and even before, changes occurred at the HQMC. Lieutenant Colonel Charlie Beale left HQMC to become the legal officer at the Marine Corps Base, Camp Lejeune, North Carolina. No one remained from AO2F who had an in-depth understanding of the cryptologic plans that Gray had devised. Moreover, Secretary McNamara's Pentagon had formal procedures for enacting new plans and programs; these remained a daunting hurdle for the CCP Change Proposal that Gray had been diligently working to pass through the system prior to leaving for Vietnam.

Figure 4.10
Maj Gray (in tiger stripe cammies) briefing the infantry unit[32]

There also remained considerable opposition to the possibility of having to take out of hide 300 additional Marines to do cryptology. Among the deeply concerned was the newly appointed Chief of Staff, the very imposing (and future Commandant) Leonard F. Chapman, Jr. Chapman dominated the Headquarters, projecting a forceful image that could easily overawe the staff.

After being gone nearly six months, Major Gray returned to the Headquarters in late 1964, where he found his cryptologic project in a shambles. While Gray was in Washington, he had smoothed the waters at HQMC, at the NSA at Fort Meade, and at all levels of the Pentagon. But with the peripatetic Major off on assignment in Vietnam, and with Beale transferred, new men were running the AO2F section; first Lieutenant Colonel Andres and then Lieutenant Colonel Koehnlein, both superb officers, headed the cryptologic section. Neither had the detailed knowledge that Gray possessed about the CCP; thus, the momentum needed to push the new Marine concepts through the highest levels of the Pentagon floundered. The proposal to increase Marine end strength and create Radio Battalions was not justified properly and, as a result, it was disapproved by the Office of the Secretary of Defense.

Fortunately, Gray's foray into Vietnam had received very favorable comments from Lieutenant General Gordon Blake, the Director of the NSA. In a letter to the Commandant dated 28 September 1964, General Blake spoke highly of the Marines efforts, and particularly lauded Major Al Gray. His letter said in part, "I am particularly impressed by the performance of Major Gray, who directed the operation successfully despite formidable logistic, terrain and weather problems. His report covering the Signal Engineering Survey Unit activities was excellent." More importantly, the Marine Corps' embryonic SIGINT efforts had been noticed and had received glowing acclaim. If General Greene needed any reassurance of his long-time support of Al Gray's efforts, the letter from General Blake certainly provided it.[33] It gave Gray's immediate efforts a real boost.

The Pentagon denial of the proposed cryptologic change left the Marine Corps embarrassed. Gray had poured his heart and soul into the proposed program change proposal for nearly three years before leaving for the temporary duty in Vietnam. Now, upon his return, he was stunned to find that it had little support even within HQMC. Further, Gray was irked to discover that the influential staff at the Pentagon simply did not understand how or why the Marine Corps had requested additions to the Radio Companies that would make them Radio Battalions, nor did they understand how an expansion of the role would help the national security efforts at NSA.

With no alternatives available, and his project stymied, Gray did what he was told to do back in 1962 by General Greene – he sought a briefing with the Commandant. In his previous show down meeting with Commandant Shoup, Gray had been summoned to the meeting as a result of other staff sections objecting to his methods and means of sending linguists to far-flung schools in great numbers. This time was different; Gray would be doing what he was ordered to do by then Chief of Staff Greene. In late 1961 General Greene had said, "I'm 400% behind you and if you ever need help, come see me." Major Al Gray felt compelled to bring the current state of affairs to the Commandant's personal attention.

All proposed meetings with the Commandant went through the Chief of Staff, so General Chapman immediately learned of the purpose for the meeting. He also aggressively sought to prevent it. It must be noted that General Chapman was not in any way part of the previous meetings between General Greene and Major Gray. But Gray was nothing if not persistent and he got on the Commandant's calendar, fully knowing that the Chief of Staff stoutly opposed his briefing. True to his word, Commandant Greene quickly approved Gray's suggestion to resurrect the cryptologic elements within the Marine Corps. With his Commandant's blessing, Gray completed an 800-page reclama to the Pentagon's rejection and then successfully staffed the Program Change through the process. The Radio Battalions were born. But their creation was not without additional difficulty, and it took more guile on the part of the Marines and Major Gray.

As important as gaining General Greene's approval was, however, Gray also had survived the dust-up with Lieutenant General Chapman. In the process, the younger officer earned the respect of that future Commandant. Even so, it would be a few more years before Gray realized Chapman's newly found respect for the younger officer.

Once the Commandant had approved going forward with the reclama, it had to be successfully staffed through HQMC. Then it went to the Pentagon. There, other very formidable people like Dr. Eugene G. Fubini, the Assistant Secretary of Defense for Research and Engineering, had to be convinced. The head of Defense for Research and Engineering held a powerful position in 1965. Even before reaching Dr. Fubini's organization, the Marines also had to win the approval of the NSA. They accomplished the latter goal, in part, by agreeing that three Marine intercept positions in both the Atlantic and the Pacific Regions, with their requisite analytic and reporting requirements, would support the national intelligence requirements of NSA. General Gordon Blake, who had previously written the Commandant after the Signal Engineering Survey Unit deployment in 1964, decisively supported the Marines in large part because their approach was decidedly different from the three cryptologic services at that time. Although the Marines would be under the aegis of the NSG, the Radio Battalions would be authorized to report directly to NSA; however, the Marines would not become a fourth cryptologic service. The three service cryptologic agencies tried very hard not to be subservient to NSA. By giving NSA six dedicated positions, the Marines earned the vital support of that agency. It was a small price for the Marines to pay, and it yielded tremendous dividends for the nascent SIGINT operation. For example, any time NSA developed a new tool or application program, the Marines got it first. And with the NSA approval and support, the Marines reclama was pushed through the Pentagon and the original CCP Change Proposal was approved. The Radio Battalions came to fruition.

Major Gray realized that Tables of Organization and Tables of Equipment do not create operational units, especially when the Marines assigned might not have any practical experience in their assigned duties. When working out the details for the Tables of Organization, Tables of Equipment and linguists, Gray and his principal assistant, Master Sergeant Barney Prosser, knew they also needed to develop and establish guidelines for how the units were to operate. Thus, the pair wrote a draft Fleet Marine Force Manual (FMFM) for SIGINT/EW operations and initiated the the approval process at Quantico and HQMC.

Major Edward Resnick, a gifted communicator and experienced cryptologist, replaced Gray in AO2F when Gray was transferred to Vietnam in the late summer of 1965. Major Resnick was a graduate of Japanese Language School at Monterey, California, and had served in a cryptologic billet in Japan. He was also a close friend of Al Gray, and the turnover of duties was effortless. Resnick completed the staffing process and the classified manual was published as the first SIGINT/EW/SIGSEC operational doctrine. The guidance set forth remained in place for many years and was just another aspect of the "behind the scenes" work accomplished by Major Gray before his departure from HQMC.

Adding to the myriad of details that Major Gray had to master was the fact that the CCP, which provided the funding for all SIGINT units, including the new Radio Battalions, received extra close scrutiny at the Pentagon. Part of McNamara's effort to modernize, streamline and make the Pentagon more efficient, the CCP was the first major program subjected to the rules of McNamara's Program Change Proposal procedures. In October 1964, when Brigadier General Frederick Karch transferred away from HQMC, where he had been the Deputy Chief of Staff for Programs, he penned a memorandum to the G-2 lauding Major Gray's "organizational ability, persistence, accuracy and patient attention to detail" as being significant factors in the Marine Corps doing so well in Program Change Proposal cycle that year.[34]

Gray also had his critics, one of whom wrote: "Gray continues to make progress in learning to ask for help when he has too many details to handle and to delegate and guide, rather than try to do everything himself." Left unsaid, however, was exactly how Major Gray, the junior officer in the section and only a captain for most the tour, was to delegate and guide the senior officers – the lieutenant colonels and colonels – in getting his work done! That remains a mystery to this day.

Both Commandant Shoup in 1963 and Commandant Greene in 1965 quickly, and very strongly, affirmed Gray's work. The former New Jersey athlete, the former mathematics student who left college without a degree, the former reconnaissance-communications sergeant, and the former artillery-infantry officer had become the Marine Corps' leading practitioner of cryptology. The officer whose constant companion was his black Labrador Retriever had overcome all obstacles to establish the SIGINT and special intelligence capability that was envisioned by General Hogaboom years earlier.

In many ways the genius of Al Gray was not reflected by what he achieved as a grizzled Commandant at the end of a 41-year career, but rather what he achieved as a young captain in Japan and Hawaii and then as a new major at HQMC in the early 1960s.

LEAVING HEADQUARTERS, 1965

Gray's time at Headquarters was gratifying. He made friendships that extended well past the retirement dates of all involved, and he accomplished several noteworthy actions, the most prominent of which was resurrecting and significantly expanding the Marine Corps' cryptologic capabilities. As he had demonstrated in Vietnam in 1964, the potential contribution of Radio Battalions and the evergrowing long-term capability of the Marine Support Battalion would have far-reaching effects, and soon.

The SIGINT/EW efforts of Marines throughout the Vietnam War not only had considerable negative effects on the enemy, but they also undoubtedly saved American lives. Far from being a technologically backwards adversary, the North Vietnamese had their own, very well-developed and effective, cryptologic capability. But the assets that Beale, Alberts, Gray, and their allies had conceived, designed, procured, defended and shepherded through the labyrinth of HQMC policies and procedures would prove essential in Southeast Asia. Further, these capabilities have grown and been refined over time. They have proven their value to the Marine

Corps and to the Nation in every conflict since Vietnam and continue to provide vital support today.

While in Washington, Gray also had earned the respect of those with whom he came into contact, and that included almost everyone at the Headquarters and many in the Fleet Marine Forces. He was called the best practitioner of SIGINT in the Marine Corps, an officer often requested by name by other services and NSA. High praise for a junior major who had already earned three MOSs. Because of his billet and the access it provided, Major Gray knew and was known to most of the senior leadership of the Marine Corps. His relationship with generals such as David M. Shoup, Wallace M. Greene, Leonard F. Chapman, Louis Wilson, Robert Barrow, Robert E. Cushman, Jr., Victor H. Krulak, Raymond G. Davis, Frederick Wieseman, Herman Nickerson, Donald Weller, James Masters, Carson Roberts, Michael P. Ryan, Henry Buse, Wood B. Kyle and Bruno Hochmuth would be helpful in accomplishing future missions and tasks. Those and other senior officers knew of Gray's clandestine assignments to Cuba and Vietnam, and they had come to value also his insights into and understanding of intelligence activities.

The HQMC tour had shaped Gray's life as a Marine in several exceptional ways. Besides providing insights into how senior officers conducted their business, his daily routine provided Gray with knowledge of just about everything happening in the Marine Corps. A voracious reader with a near photographic memory, little had escaped Gray's notice. Blessed with an insatiable curiosity and desire to improve through self-study, any topic with which Gray was not already knowledgeable became a target for after-hours reading. When asked informally of his opinions about subjects, queries that often occurred when Gray was carrying the special communications message board, Gray was usually able to make a meaningful contribution regardless of the issue presented. Thus, it was hardly surprising that Major Gray exerted more influence than his rank or experience might suggest. And given all the staff working-level knowledge he received from serving with men like Charlie Beale and Howie Alberts, it is also not unexpected that when he returned to serve in HQMC for his final tour of duty in 1987, as Commandant, he was able to capitalize meaningfully on what he had learned in the early 1960s.

But more than learning how the powerful generals and high-ranking officers did business, Beale, Gray and Alberts had built a solid reputation among the junior officers and enlisted men that they encountered. No request for assistance went unanswered. Whether the inquiry came from an officer unsure as to how to proceed or a staff sergeant looking for some obscure office in some remote wing, each of the triumvirate took the time to personally escort the Marine to where the request could be answered. Gray especially has had countless Marines remind him of when he took time to help them accomplish some undertaking when his personal assistance made their jobs easier. Gray had received such kindness and respect from men like Beale, Alberts, Keckler, Koelpner, Meade, Seavey, Prosser, Casey and innumerable others, kindnesses he repaid with considerable interest.

Although Al Gray had met and interacted with a multitude of important Marines of all ranks, he steadfastly abided by a cardinal rule: all his relationships were professional. That meant he never requested or sought private gain as a result of his access or his acquaintances. He took whatever assignments and tasks he received, and he went about completing them to the best of his ability. His daily routine, which started early and ended late in the evening, could have, perhaps, been modified had he enrolled in more college courses in order to finish his degree, for example. But Gray felt the work he was doing was far too important to be put aside for individual goals. He never asked for personal favors, and he never put himself in a position where he owed anyone anything. That he would be successful maintaining that style was evident in a note he received from the president of a future promotion board, but that is getting ahead of the story.

Still, though he did not seek help from others, there were officers and Staff NCOs, like Lieutenant Colonel Charlie Beale or Master Sergeant Prosser, who would do anything in their power to assist the Major. Among more senior officers, now Brigadier General Ray Davis had returned to HQMC after a short tour in intelligence in Europe. Davis had known Gray dating back to his trip to Japan in 1957. He well knew the tremendous work ethic and accomplishments that typified Gray's time at HQMC, and he was determined to support the younger officer however he could. Knowing that Gray would leave HQMC for Vietnam, a move delayed from the spring of 1965 until nearly the end of summer, Davis on several occasions asked Gray about his choice of future duty. Gray, true to form, always responded with a simple request – he wanted to return to combat arms. When Gray finally left in late August, Davis quietly told him that he had sent a note to his best friend in the service, then Major General Lewis Walt, the Commanding General of III MAF in Vietnam, asking Walt to ensure Gray was assigned back into combat arms. Davis also gave Gray a picture of himself as a general officer, with the inscription, "You have contributed to the intelligence mission far more than anyone will ever know!" That picture remains one of General Gray's most cherished mementoes from his long service. And the leadership example provided by General Davis was never forgotten by the younger officer.

Figure 4.11
Maj Al Gray receives a Letter of Commendation for outstanding efforts while assigned to HQMC. Ironically, Lt Col Robert Merchant presents the letter. Perhaps the expressions on each officer's face reflects their time together the previous year in Vietnam, when it was Lt Col Merchant who questioned Maj Gray's need of "steaks" only to be overruled by Gen Krulak.[35]

Major Al Gray had completed his duty well at HQMC. He took Lucky II to a special place in Missouri. *Baier's Den* was internationally known for fine bird dogs and "Old Fashioned Missouri Quail Hunting." It not only had a high quality kennel appropriate for the king that Lucky II had become, but also it was a shooting preserve. Gray arranged that his big Lab would receive lots of field training while he was in Southeast Asia; moreover, the owner promised to send Gray a monthly report card on how well Lucky was doing. During summers the camp attracted kids learning to shoot and hunt, and Bud Baier ensured Lucky was in the middle of all the activities. Al Gray thought that perhaps Lucky would miss him, but the dog was surely going to have lots of new adventures!

With everything settled, Gray repeated the journey traveled by so many Marines in late 1965, the trip through Okinawa into the widening warzone in Southeast Asia.

SOUTHEAST ASIA HEATS UP

WASHINGTON, 1964-1965

General Wallace M. Greene, Jr., had changed the Marine Corps policy about involvement in Vietnam since ascending in 1964 to the Commandancy, following General David M. Shoup's retirement. Shoup's position was strongly against land wars in Asia unless the United States fought to win, a characteristic missing from American involvement in Korea. Greene, however, was an adroit reader of Washington's tea leaves, and by early 1965 it was obvious that the new President, Lyndon Baines Johnson of Texas, was committed to saving South Vietnam from communist expansion in Southeast Asia.

China became a communist state during the Presidency of Harry S. Truman, the Democratic President who preceded Republican Dwight David Eisenhower in that office. Consequently, Truman and his fellow Democrats of that era were branded as being soft on communism, albeit the label was not entirely properly applied. Then Truman saw the error of his foreign policy and when Greece nearly fell to communist rule, Truman enacted a policy of containment, fighting communist expansion wherever and whenever it was found. While such commitment did not stop the election of Dwight D. Eisenhower in 1952 and again in 1956, it remained a hallmark of Democrat politics. Throughout the era that spanned 1950 into 1960, Democrat politicians were determined to escape the *soft-on-communism* tag.[36] It had affected Democrat John Fitzgerald Kennedy during his brief presidency, and now it dominated the thinking, and political computations, of Lyndon Baines Johnson, or LBJ as he was known.

Johnson had grown from a relatively unknown back-country Texas politician to the powerful Majority Leader of the United States Senate. Johnson was a large man, standing 6'4", weighing over 200 pounds. He was also vain and profane – but lacking in self-confidence. Johnson had been defeated by Kennedy in the Democratic primaries leading to the 1960 Presidential nomination to oppose Richard Milhous Nixon, the sitting Republican Vice-President. But Kennedy had unexpectedly, almost shockingly, chosen Johnson as his running mate. Then, only two and a half short years after being elected, Kennedy was assassinated, and Johnson became the 36th President of the United States of America.

Concern for Vietnam did not control Johnson's foreign policy toward Southeast Asia; political calculations about his reelection in 1964 did. Having achieved that goal, and routing Senator Barry M. Goldwater of Arizona in the process, the insecure President of the United States began worrying about his next election in 1968; success that year would mean he would serve as Chief Executive longer than any man since Franklin Delano Roosevelt.

Johnson would go against the majority of his own party to sign the Civil Rights Act of 1964. He would bully through the Congress his broad, comprehensive welfare entitlements collectively called *The Great Society*. He proved a far more effective leader in enacting his legislative programs than Kennedy had been during his short administration, yet Johnson remained insecure, self-doubting, and given to delusions that those around him, the leftovers from Kennedy's administration, were working against his best interests. After all, how could a country boy from Texas, a graduate of Southwest Texas State Teacher's College compare favorably to the central character of the media-inspired Camelot, John F. Kennedy, the wealthy, urbane, socialite, Harvard graduate? But through all his insecurities, Johnson, in fact, did have one small, but growing, consideration that could potentially derail his reelection, and it was the war in Vietnam. In that regard, it must be noted that Johnson inherited the Kennedy policy and Kennedy's senior advisors on Vietnam lock, stock and barrel! Surely, at least for the first years of Johnson's tenure, the U.S. policy toward Vietnam was the Kennedy policy.

Kennedy had all but excluded Johnson from his Administration's deliberations about Vietnam. Indeed, it seems likely that all Johnson knew about Vietnam dated back to his unexpected, and hardly informed, recommendation that President Eisenhower avoid a land war in Asia. More so than ever, Robert Strange McNamara, the Secretary of Defense, was largely responsible for shaping the new Administration's actions in Southeast Asia. In 1963, McNamara's colleagues at the State Department and the hapless Ambassador to South Vietnam, Henry Cabot Lodge, had permitted, if not organized, the assassination of the South Vietnamese President, Ngo Dinh Diem, thinking him to be corrupt and incompetent, even though the Americans making the decision hardly understood the situation in South Vietnam. Johnson would, ex post facto of course, denounce American complicity in the Diem assassination. Though Lodge had been quickly replaced, Johnson continued to rely on the "best and brightest," and especially McNamara for advice about the budding war.[37]

But more than Kennedy ever did, Johnson assumed a personal involvement in the military affairs in Southeast Asia. In the coming years, he would crow far, wide and loudly about how he personally kept the military under foot, deciding, for example, such mundane matters as what size bombs could be used against specific North Vietnamese targets – targets as small as wooden bridges.

Throughout the American war effort, Johnson never sought and certainly never heeded the advice of the JCS. The President demanded that the JCS rubber-stamp his policies; and to their eternal discredit, they did. Their advice reached him only after being sharply modulated, and usually muted, by Secretary of Defense McNamara.

So while General Greene was adept at seeing what direction the Johnson Administration was headed, he became unable to influence it. Greene (as reflected in various Marine Corps estimates) believed that the American efforts in Vietnam would require far more men and equipment than McNamara and the Administration projected. Furthermore, Greene, and his top generals, Krulak in Hawaii and Walt in Vietnam, saw the war as a battle against an insurgency, with the United States establishing and holding the populated areas along the coast, defending them against VC and NVA incursions. However, Johnson's selection to head the war effort, General William C. Westmoreland, favored a war of attrition, not pacification, thereby frustrating the Marine Corps position. And since Greene was not yet a full-fledged member of the JCS, he had even less weight on the dysfunctional – under Johnson and McNamara – JCS.[38]

The Marines had landed battalions first at Da Nang and then two more in March 1965, at Chu Lai, a small airfield complex south of Da Nang. The initial mission of the Marine infantry was simply to protect and defend the airfields and other American assets. Gradually the mission was expanded to patrolling and expanding the perimeter. In the late fall 1965, the Marines conducted their first full scale offensive, *Operation Starlite*, in northern Quang Tri province. Throughout the fall, the number and complexity of the Marine Corps force in South Vietnam grew. Greene continued to press for a pacification mission; indeed, throughout the war Marine Corps actions and hopes were tied to pacification as opposed to the search and destroy (attrition warfare) tactics dictated by Westmoreland. The Marine commander in South Vietnam, Major (then Lieutenant) General Lewis B. Walt, pressed for pacification to the point he was almost relieved by General Westmoreland. In late 1965, the command elements of the 12th Marines artillery regiment began to arrive, going ashore in Da Nang and establishing their Headquarters near the 3rd Marine Division Command Post.

SAIGON, 1964-1965

There is an old adage about being careful about what you wish for. Ambassador Lodge, the whole battalion of American and international reporters, and everyone else calling for Diem's removal should have heeded that adage before permitting the coup against Diem, the coup that resulted in the South Vietnamese President's assassination. There were two (at least) major blunders associated with overthrowing the regime, an event that beyond a reasonable doubt Ambassador Lodge and Assistant Secretary of State Hilsman envisioned and sanctioned. The first was that ARVN generals who planned the coup d'état were not capable of executing a competently executed coup. It was so badly carried out that President Kennedy, only two weeks from his own assassination, was said to have gotten sick when he heard the gory details. The second and far bigger mistake was that despite the protests about Diem no one had identified a capable candidate to replace him. Consequently, with Diem gone, the entire years of 1964 and 1965 were wasted on coups, counter-coups, imaginary coups, and prolonged political infighting among ARVN generals.

There was simply no leader capable of stepping forward into the leadership vacuum at the top of the South Vietnamese government. Air Marshal Nguyen Cao Ky was highly popular, extremely capable and very willing, but Ky was far too junior to be accepted by the army generals. The loss of Diem's leadership was a grievous blow to the goal of South Vietnamese independence from North Vietnamese communism in many ways, but particularly in the military realm. All the top generals were Diem's handpicked leaders; in I Corps, General Tri was not only effective but also highly popular. Until a new leader could become established in Saigon, the friction among the military leadership was so pervasive that effective resistance to the VC and North Vietnamese was haphazardly applied at best. As a result of the void, all programs to fight VC and NVA re-infiltration back into the South either were significantly curtailed or simply ended. In the countryside, no one knew, and only a few cared, who was in charge in Saigon. The people wanted security and for too long during those critical years they received none from the South Vietnamese government.

In the meantime, American advisors tried to keep the ARVN engaged, though with mixed results. The situation in Saigon became an open sore for Washington. Ngo Dinh Diem had been by far the best Vietnamese to stand up to Ho Chi Minh, and now his friends had eliminated him without Ho lifting an arm. President Johnson recalled Lodge when circumstances surrounding Diem's death became known, but Hilsman and his ilk were never replaced. And Johnson, again bowing to political calculations, even returned Lodge to Saigon briefly in 1965. Unfortunately, for two very important years, neither the object of NVA aggression, nor the government providing by far the most aid to it, had informed, committed leadership. Meanwhile, in Hanoi, Uncle Ho marched inexorably forward.[39]

NOTES AND REFERENCES

1. John Guilmartin class notes, *The History of the Vietnam War*, Fall, 2010, The Ohio State University. In the aftermath of the 1954 Geneva Accords, about 860,000 people fled from North Vietnam into South Vietnam. Of that number about 600,000 were Catholic, including at least 10 bishops and ⅔ of the priests. More refugees came south throughout the war; see Chapter 7, for example. The exodus of the Catholics made over a half million acres of rich farmland available for redistribution, though the communists also blamed the U.S. for their food shortage in the mid-1950s, saying the loss of the Catholic peasants hampered production. Left unsaid, however, is how many peasants were killed by the communists; some estimate as many as 1.5 million.

2. The monsoon for most of Indochina is essentially reversed for the coastal strip east of the Annamite Mountains from a point just north of Vinh to south of Nha Trang. The southwest monsoon runs from mid-May to mid-October with several weeks of transitional weather in between. It brings wet weather to everywhere except the coastal strip. The northeast monsoon runs mid-September to mid-to-late December. It brings dry weather and clear skies to Indochina west of the Annamites. A practical example of the weather patterns was *Operation Starlite*. The Marines conducted the first major offensive action after the introduction of major U.S. combat units in 1965 because the Marines were operating in the only dry area of Vietnam.

3. Videotape interview with General Gray, May 4, 2009.

4. Interview with Major General John Morrison, USAF (Ret) in 2007.

5. Al Gray seemed to attract high quality officers and men. Consider the Marine Detachment, Advisory Group 1 contingent: Bob Meck left the Marine Corps for a career at NSA, where he retired after serving as, among several important assignments, NSA Representative to Japan; Lieutenant General H.C. Stackpole served as Commanding General, FMFPAC when General Gray was Commandant; Harry Williams retired from NSA while serving as Deputy Director, Pacific Operations. Sergeant Art Kidd was later commissioned and retired as a Captain. Captain Ray Becker retired as a Colonel.

6. Unlike many officers who looked forward to the allure of spending a night in Saigon, Gray never remained there overnight.

7. From General Gray's private collection.

8. The incident was hardly even a distraction for Lieutenant Colonel Merchant; he was awarded a Legion of Merit for his performance in Da Nang in 1964.

9. The Montagnards were given their name by the French, and they are a people indigenous to the mountainous region along the border between Vietnam and Laos. There were six or eight major tribes of Montagnards in the sparsely populated highlands; fiercely independent, they first fought as French-led guerrillas against the communists. Their struggle continued until long after the fall of South Vietnam in 1975.

10. Author interview with David W. Gaddy, May 2009.

11. Author telephone interview with Ralph W. Adams, August 2011.

12. The day was further complicated when General Westmoreland decided to take the C-130 (that had brought Gray's men to Khe Sanh) to visit the A Shau Valley. While taking off the plane attracted VC/NVA small arms fire and Westmoreland was slightly wounded. Author videotaped interview with General Gray, 4 May 2009.

13. Lewis Sorley, *Westmoreland: The General Who Lost Vietnam*. (Advanced reading copy). Lewis Sorley was the faculty advisor for General Gray's study group at the Army War College, and the two have remained good friends ever since. Sorley provided General Gray with an advanced copy of his book in the fall, 2011.

14. From General Gray's private collection.

15. Al Gray's maternal grandfather lived with the Gray family during the 1930s and he was an accomplished linguist. He had grown up in Switzerland, and spoke German, including a couple different dialects, and French. Young Al got up at 4 AM each day to see his grandfather off to work; together, early each morning, the two would discuss a variety of things, including the differences in languages that the grandfather spoke. Gray's father may have been his best friend and mentor, but it was from his grandfather he learned to love foreign languages. Esperanto, the Armed Forces language used to practice SIGINT, was based roughly on Latin and Gray was fluent in it.

16. On purely anecdotal grounds, it seemed to many Marine grunts that the Marine Air Wing went to great lengths to protect its helicopters, while the Army seemed to have countless helicopters and was not concerned at all at the possibility of losing them. The Marine Corps in Korea had introduced the concept of using helicopters in vertical envelopments, but the U.S. Army in Vietnam greatly expanded the idea. Furthermore, the Army had aviation resources that the Marines could only dream of having.

17. A "click" is 1,000 yards. The author first learned of General Gray carrying the ARVN officer off the mountain from then Corporal Robert C. Merle, who was a French linguist in the detachment. The story was confirmed by Lieutenant Colonel Alberts.

18. *My Life as a Marine*, (1988) privately published by Captain Arthur Kidd, USMC (Ret) and made available to the author.

19. Video interview with General Gray 4 May 2009. General Gray and General Stilwell later became very good friends, when as a Lieutenant General Stilwell was Deputy Commander, III Marine Amphibious Corps and worked with then Major General Ray Davis, who of course was a great supporter of Al Gray. But it was a most unhappy Major Al Gray when he learned that General Stilwell had denied a major aspect of his Deception Plan.

20. The author first learned of General Gray carrying the ARVN officer off the mountain from the Corporal Robert C. Merle, who was a French linguist in the detachment. The story was confirmed by Lieutenant Colonel Alberts. Author interview with Lt. Col. Alberts, who had learned of Colonel Waite's recommendation while tracking Gray's progress.

21. From General Gray's private collection.

22. Correspondence between former Deputy Director, NSA Pacific, Harry T. Williams, and author, 2007-2011.

23. In every job he was ever given, Gray made a habit of practicing the "walking around leadership style" that Larry Bangs first noted in Japan. Whether as a captain of a cryptologic unit, or as a major in the artillery, or as the Commandant, Gray could be expected to show up in unusual places at surprising times, looking for information that would help him better execute his duties or improve conditions for those serving in his command.

24. Photo courtesy of Captain Art Kidd, USMC (Ret).

25. Photo courtesy of Robert Meck's private collection.

26. From General Gray's private collection.

27. Sergeant Prater's recommendation never saw the light of day until discovered by the author among General Gray's personal files.

28. Photo courtesy of Harry T. Williams' private collection.

29. Interviews with Captain Art Kidd, USMC (Ret) and the author during 2008-2010.

30. From General Gray's private collection.

31. From General Gray's private collection.

32. From General Gray's private collection.

33. From General Gray's private collection. General Gray's papers include the response to General Blake from General Greene dated 2 October 1964. The papers also include two short, hand-written but undated notes to the G-2 from the Commandant questioning why it was taking so long to get "Major Gray" an award for his good work in Vietnam, both signed with the "Circle G" that was the moniker Charlie Beale and Al Gray assigned the Commandant.

34. From General Gray's private collection.

35. From General Gray's private collection.

36. When President Truman permitted Mao-Tse Tung to defeat Chiang Kai-shek and take over China, and ceded all of Eastern Europe to the Soviet Union, the Republicans were able to paint the Democrats as "soft-on-communism." Truman's actions in Greece in 1948 assuaged the image somewhat, but the tag stuck throughout the Eisenhower's two winning elections in 1952 and 1956. President John F. Kennedy and later President Lyndon B. Johnson, both Democrats, were intent on overcoming that public perception of the party. Thus, Kennedy and especially Johnson's actions in Vietnam were more than a little influenced by their desire to not be seen as being "soft on communism." What might Harry Truman have done in Vietnam? Perhaps Truman may have inserted an American Expeditionary Force? In 1945, it was Truman's aggressive support of the Nationalist Chinese, using the United States Army Air Force, which prevented a quick communist victory.

37. Halberstam, 305.

38. See McMaster for the best insights into the situation.

39. *The Official History of the People's Army of Vietnam, 1954-1975*, (2005) translated by Merle L. Pribblenow, dispels any notion that the "rebellion" against Diem was a local one. Without communist supplies, and especially manpower, from North Vietnam, Diem and his government would have faced only unorganized and poorly armed opposition. Of course, the American reporters who both viewed events contemporaneously, and then wrote their "histories" of the war did not have access to Pribblenow's translation, which was not published until 2005.

CHAPTER 5

BACK TO COMBAT ARMS
MAJOR AMERICAN COMBAT UNITS ARRIVE IN SOUTH VIETNAM

BACK TO COMBAT ARMS

It was only a matter of time before the North Vietnamese decided to strike hard at the Marine artillery that had been so effectively battering them for months. The Marine Corps was in the process of assembling its largest, and by far most potent, artillery unit ever, bigger even than those that covered American infantry during Korea, and larger than the artillery groupings of World War II. The guns of the 12th Marines were the decisive weapons on the I Corps battlefield, raining down with unfailing accuracy and dispensing death and mayhem on suspected Viet Cong or North Vietnamese Army positions; those enemies found in the open were subjected to deadly barrages. The North Vietnamese command was determined to strike back, but because they lacked artillery of their own inside South Vietnam, they had to rely on sappers, highly trained, highly effective, and well-motivated combat engineers who would attack using stealth and surprise. The first major sapper attack against the Marines happened on the night of April 17-18, 1966, in Quang Nam Province, about 15 kilometers northwest of Da Nang.

Alpha Battery, 1st Battalion, 11th Marines (A/1/11) was located well forward of the 3rd Marine Regimental Command Post and several hundred yards northwest of Kilo Battery, 4th Battalion, 12th Marines (K/4/12). An hour and 40 minutes past midnight, mortar fire showered both batteries. It would be A/1/11 who absorbed most of the attack. At least one company of North Vietnamese sappers, using Bangalore torpedoes, quickly and efficiently penetrated the battery's defenses from the North, East and West. A listening post outside the lines had been overrun. The attack was well planned, skillfully executed and extremely violent. In a matter of minutes the Marines had suffered five killed in action and more than a dozen wounded who needed evacuation.

The North Vietnamese Army sapper attack had severed the landline communications between A/1/11 and the 4th Battalion's Fire Direction Center, although radio communications remained intact. Radios are never trustworthy, nor do they provide the confidence and sense of well being that a simple telephone line does. The unknown always generates a myriad of questions, and the fog of combat is at its most dense when units are under attack and other units try to determine how best to assist.

The Regimental Communications Officer, Major Alfred M. Gray, Jr., was standing watch in the 12th Marines Fire Direction Center at the time of the attack. Gray was a notorious night bird, given to being present when least expected. Further, he quietly lent his multifaceted qualifications to help out whenever needed and was well recognized as a team player. As more people streamed into the Fire Direction Center, including the

Regimental S-3 and many senior officers from the nearby artillery battalion that had responsibility for A/1/11, the noise and confusion increased as news of the attack spread. Everyone was excited, trying to learn what was happening; the tension was palpable. However, Gray's firm hand and calm demeanor was evident as he busily coordinated medical evacuation requests, kept the Division Combat Operation Center informed, and issued orders for a relief force to be organized.

One of those who had entered the Fire Direction Center was more than a casual observer. Colonel James M. Callender was the Commanding Officer of the 12th Marines; he had the responsibility for combat effectiveness of the regiment. The colonel, an artilleryman since World War II and a legend within the Marine Corps, watched silently for several minutes and then announced, "Quiet everybody, Major Gray is now the S-3 of this Regiment; everyone not on duty clear the FDC." With those words, Gray assumed a much broader task within the regiment – and the immediate task of assisting the beleaguered Marines of A/1/11.

The attack had begun at 0140, but an aerial observer was able to call for fires and within an hour, the Viet Cong had been repulsed with heavy losses. By 0310, A/1/11 had requested medical evacuation (medevac) helicopters to evacuate its 16 seriously wounded Marines. By 0320 the medevac had been completed and the Viet Cong soldiers who had been within the lines were either dead or had withdrawn. By 0430, Major Gray's relief force arrived at the position and completed the stabilization of the situation. At first light, Lieutenant General Walt arrived; Gray briefed him and explained what had happened, and how well the Marines had fought back.

The first attack against the Marine artillery had been repulsed. The Marine Corps had lost five good men, one gun had been destroyed and another badly damaged, but the Marines had inflicted a heavy price on the attackers, and the coordinated, measured and deliberate response had proven to the North Vietnamese Army that the Americans were not to be taken lightly.[1] Colonel Callender had found a new Regimental S-3, Major Al Gray. Gray would remain in the job for the next year, a post that was a lieutenant colonel's billet.

III MARINE AMPHIBIOUS FORCE HEADQUARTERS, DA NANG, OCTOBER 1965

With orders in hand, Major Gray went through the incoming processing procedures on Okinawa and reported to III MAF Headquarters in Da Nang. It may be considered a miracle that Al Gray ever reached Vietnam since he should have been stopped at Okinawa. When Marines, or any member of any service, have worked in special intelligence for a lengthy period, they are usually precluded from combat assignments for at least a year. The theory was that such people should not be exposed to situations were they might be captured and interrogated. But in the summer of 1965 there was a big buildup going on in Southeast Asia and most likely an overworked administrative officer failed to note the "Hazardous Area Restriction" in Gray's Officer Qualification Record, the document that shows an officer's prior history and provides his records for any new command. Years later when asked about this, Gray just smiled and noted that his security sponsorship was under the cognizance of the NSA at the time, and as he often does, went on to another topic. For whatever reasons, Al Gray landed back in the war zone. However, a new obstacle to his quest for returning to combat arms suddenly appeared.

Colonel Leo J. Dulacki was the formidable G-2 on Major General Lewis Walt's staff – of course, General Walt had three staffs! General Walt was serving simultaneously as Commanding General, III MAF; Commanding General, 3rd Marine Division; and Commander, Naval Component 116. Naval Component 116 included the naval base, the Seabees and other naval units in and around the port of Da Nang. Yes, the General was busy. Colonel Dulacki carried considerable influence because of his broad knowledge and professionalism. He had, for example, recently been the Naval Attaché in Moscow, a unique assignment for a Marine colonel. Besides being influential, Dulacki had other motivations. He knew that one of the superb members of his staff, newly promoted Lieutenant Colonel P.X. Kelley, a future Marine Commandant, would soon be leaving for an infantry assignment. Dulacki, who would later rise to Lieutenant General, sought a routine change to Gray's orders, and asked General Walt that Gray be assigned to the G-2, since he knew that the incoming Major had excellent intelligence credentials. The General had a quick and unequivocal reply, "No." Nor did General Walt provide any explanation for his curt response. Dulacki was stunned by this reaction, but knew better than to argue his case. Dulacki, of course, never knew of any communiqués between Generals Walt and Davis on the subject of Al Gray's future assignment.[2]

When Gray reached the III MAF personnel officer, he was told that he was being assigned to the division, and that transportation would take him over to Hill 327 (where the division command post was located) in the morning. Gray, letting no grass grow under his feet in his quest to avoid duty at headquarters, quickly bummed a ride over to the division, foregoing normal transportation the next day.

3rd MARINE DIVISION HEADQUARTERS, DA NANG, OCTOBER 1965

Colonel James M. Callender, USMC, the revered commander of the 12th Marines was in need of a communications officer. The 12th Marine Regiment was the artillery arm of the 3rd Marine Division. An artillery regiment is a large and diverse organization charged with providing support to infantry and reconnaissance units and attacking by fire suspected enemy locations and formations throughout the Division's Tactical Area of Responsibility. But in this case, the 3rd Marine Division had raided Callender's staff and selected Major H.L. Fogarty, a superb Marine officer and gifted communicator, to command the Division's Communication Company. It was an important assignment, Callender well knew, but in his view not nearly as important as the one left vacated. The 12th Marines were ashore and expanding their footprint every day.

Marine artillery battalions and batteries were spread across the entire of I Corps, the northernmost military region in South Vietnam. Despite Fogarty's best efforts, communications among the regiment's far-flung subordinate units and the units it was supporting, both Marine Corps and ARVN infantry formations, were not yet well established. Now, his primary communications expert was gone and Callender required assistance – better sooner than later!

One of Callender's good friends on the Division staff was Colonel Robert W. Port, USMCR, the G-1 (Personnel) officer. Colonel Port, looking out for Colonel Callender's best interests, asked Major Fogarty if he knew of any communicators that would be arriving in the near future. Fogarty was a good man to ask because he had recently been the communications officer monitor at HQMC – he was the officer who made all the personnel assignments related to communications officers. Fogarty knew Al Gray very well. The two had recently served together at HQMC, and Fogarty was also well aware of Gray's professional reputation. As a result, he assured both Colonels, "Gray is due any day and he can do anything." With that recommendation, Callender accepted his new communications officer, a Marine he had not previously met. Nonetheless, Colonel Callender and Major Al Gray were to form an important, and mutually supporting, relationship over the next six months. Having successfully maneuvered past both the Force and the Division Headquarters, Al Gray was finally going to get to do what he did best – be a field Marine.

A billet as an artillery regiment's communications officer was not the duty Gray sought, but he knew to take what he got and make what he wanted.

The 12th Marines of 1965 and early 1966 was hardly a typical Marine artillery regiment, which is by itself a very, very large organization full of guns, trucks, jeeps, radios, tents, mess halls, and all sorts of sundry equipment. An artillery regiment is far more complex than an infantry regiment; while both are commanded by a colonel, the artillery organization has more lieutenant colonels and majors, and more master sergeants and master gunnery sergeants, than its infantry sister, and it has almost as many men. When Al Gray was welcomed aboard the 12th Marines, the Regiment also included three firing batteries from the 1st Marine Division's

Figure 5.1
Col James Callender and Maj Al Gray after they received the Vietnamese Cross of
Gallantry in the late fall 1965. Gray's award was for his actions on Tiger Tooth Mountain
in 1964. The citation for that award is the only source we have that Gray was involved
in multiple firefights during his walk down the mountain with the three Vietnamese.[3]

artillery, the 11ᵗʰ Marines – whose headquarters had not yet arrived in Vietnam. The Regiment had a wide swath of I Corps to cover with an organization that, besides the three batteries from the 11th Marines, included the force-level 8" howitzer and self-propelled 155mm gun batteries. Colonel Callender and his staff were sufficiently busy, that is certain.

While Al Gray focused on the technical and operational aspects of his assignment, early on, in October 1965, he came face to face with the brutality of the war. While visiting one of the forward Marine units north of Da Nang, early in the morning a young Vietnamese girl came running toward the lines, desperately seeking help. Communists, who disapproved of his leadership and politics, had assassinated her father the night before. The wanton killing of village leaders got precious little attention from the American and international reporters covering the war – and such events were practically never mentioned on American television, even though, in 1966 alone, over 1,000 village and district chiefs loyal to the South Vietnamese were assassinated. After all, it would have been "bad" television, and thus it was ignored. Gray understood very well the situation, and not just because of his stay in Vietnam in 1964, when the struggle to control the local civilian populations was pretty much left to the ARVN.

Al Gray had plainly seen the reporters' biases against the South Vietnamese government, whose every wart became the fodder for daily dispatches back to America. But this particular incident involving the young girl was even more horrific: not only had the communists killed the girl's father, but also they chopped off both her arms at the elbow. It was an act beyond cruelty and barbarism; this was the essence of pure evil and reminder to Al Gray and the Marines of the lengths the communists would go in order to control the population while eliminating the political opposition.[4]

While reflecting on the horror of war, Gray's immediate task was to continue Major Fogarty's efforts and establish reliable, secure communications within the regiment. It was a complicated undertaking. The very hot and humid weather affected equipment adversely. Furthermore, the regiment was fielding a new family of tactical radios. Gray started the process in his now familiar manner, traveling to each and every location and listening attentively to the requirements, learning the problems and issues, getting to know the personalities and quirks of the various Marines with whom he would be working, and generally familiarizing himself with the area and the unit. Early on, Gray focused on squeaky wheel leadership, concentrating on making sure fundamental requirements were met. While his efforts were indeed made difficult by the arrival of the new family of VHF communications equipment, in the long run that equipment was to prove much more reliable than its predecessors.[5]

Most Marine Corps tactical communications used frequency modulated (FM) radios that have a line-of-sight range of several miles. However, because of the vagaries of radios, the Marine doctrine was to place landline communications between important headquarters locations. When working properly, landlines provided reliable, telephone-like connections between the distant parties. Of course, purposeful cutting of telephone and telegraph wires has been a favorite sport of combatants since the American Civil War, when Samuel Morse's invention was first used on the battlefield. And wires were subjected to other daily hazards. Stray artillery or mortar rounds, tracked vehicle movements, and ravenous troops (friend or foe) searching for wire to hang personal items or build *hooches* – the name given haphazardly constructed living quarters when in the field – were all the enemy of the wireman and those reliant on telephone (or during the Civil War, telegraph) communications on the battlefield.

Often too, the physical distance between two locations, or the dangers posed by travel linking them, was too great to actually lay wires. Instead, early in the Vietnam War the Marine Corps initiated widespread use of the multi-channel radios. Some of these operated on normal military FM frequencies, but others used higher micro-wave frequencies. In either event, the links required tedious attention to detail and often demanding skills to be activated, and once established, were hard to move in a timely fashion. All this characterized the battlefield that became Al Gray's communications domain, ranging from five miles north of Phu Bai to eight miles south and west of Chu Lai, roughly 2,000 square miles. Gray saw most of it – from the seat of a jeep or perhaps a Mighty Mite, from low altitude passes in L-19/O-1 spotter aircraft, or from helicopters.[6]

Throughout their history, Marines have been nothing if not flexible. In December 1965, important communications links still relied on AN/PRC-8 (Armor), AN/PRC-9 (Artillery) and AN/PRC-10 (Infantry) family of FM radios (with vacuum tubes) that dated back to Korea. By linking them with larger antennae and changing batteries *every hour*, the 12th Marines were able to achieve reliable connections for up to 18 miles. However, the battery replacement became a logistical nightmare for Marines, and thankfully, the AN/PRC-25 back pack and the AN/VRC-12 vehicular mounted, *transistorized* FM radios started to replace the older equipment.[7] However, the transition was a painfully slow process because there

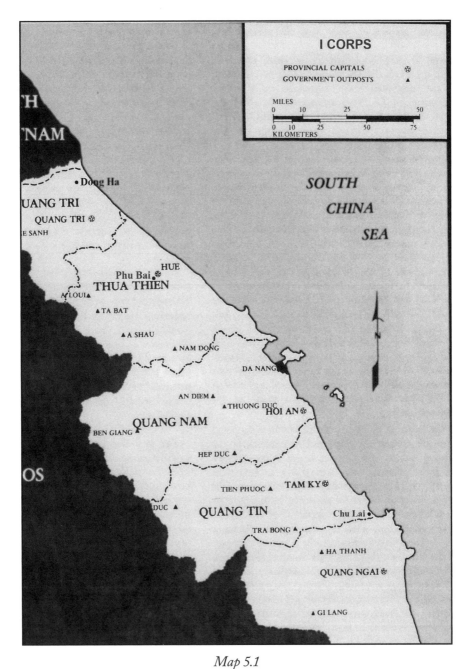

Map 5.1

The Marine Corps was assigned responsibility for the five northernmost prov-
inces of the Republic of Vietnam. The heaviest fighting for the Marines took
place just south of the De–Militarized Zone, and in the area around An Hoa,
southwest of Da Nang. Map adapted from History and Museums Division,
Headquarters, Marine Corps series, U.S. Marines in Vietnam.

were not sufficient numbers of new radios to go around. Consequently, for several months the new radios were only issued to units directly involved with operations. It would be a year before the 12th Marines successfully disposed of their PRC-9s. The PRC-25s were important not only because they provided excellent long-range (but still line-of-sight) communications, but also because they had a battery life of more than 24 hours. Almost every time the regiment fired one of the 45,247 rounds during December 1965, radio communications were involved. With the artillery averaging over one round fired every minute, there was a lot for the Marines to talk about.

During January 1966, an emergency program to provide additional PRC-25s gave Major Gray and his superb, veteran Communications Chief, Master Sergeant Harry Sieple, the opportunity to distribute 25 of the radios throughout the regiment. This significantly improved the reliability and range of the artillery's infrastructure. Each of the firing battalions as well as the two headquarters units (12th Marines and Headquarters Battery, 1st Battalion, 11th Marines) took possession of four of the new radios. While the 25 sets made a difference, there were still far too many requirements not yet satisfied; hence, the assets had to be pooled for allocation based on operational needs.

The number of communication links within the artillery regiment is staggering, especially for a regiment the size of the 1966 version of the 12th Marines, which was reinforced by units from the 11th Marines and the U.S. Army. Consider that each battalion had three or more firing batteries and a headquarters battery. Additionally, the infantry 4.2 Mortar Companies were transferred to the artillery regiments in the late 1950s; those units functioned as separate firing batteries. Each battery had at least four forward observer teams. That meant that each battalion had a minimum of 16 radios (3 x 4 + 4) to as many as 28 (6 x 4 + 4) sets on its primary tactical network. Oft times battalions requirements were far greater; during January 1966, 1st Battalion, 12th Marines had six firing batteries under its control. Such calculations did not include provisions for resupply convoys, which are critical to the artillery's success, coordination with infantry or supported units, communications within the regiment, or equipment failures. Twenty-five PRC-25s undoubtedly helped Gray and the 12th Marines, but at least four times that number were needed.

Still, there were also many other tasks to be accomplished, including cabling all the wires and putting them overhead or burying them to avoid most of the hazards brought about when wire remained on the ground. In addition to his communications duties, Gray held engineer equipment responsibilities that were demanding; his section provided all-important power and mobile generator support for the regiment. Still, Gray found other outlets for his boundless energy.

Figure 5.2
Lt Col P.X. Kelley (left) and Maj Ernie DeFazio, Commanding Officer and Executive
Officer of 2nd Battalion, 4th Marines, February 1966. Maj Gray visited 2/4 several times
to see his friend and mentor, Ernie DeFazio. During a Gray visit to 2/4 in April, 1966,
south of Marble Mountain, the two future Commandants discussed the situation with
Maj Ernie DeFazio. Gray knew P.X. Kelley well throughout his career, and had great
admiration for the charismatic leader. As proof it's a small Marine Corps, this picture,
taken by the author over 45 years before this book was written and 25 years before the
author first met Gen Gray, shows P.X. Kelley, who preceded Gen Gray as Commandant
of the Marine Corps, with one of Gen Gray's best friends and early mentors.[8]

As soon as he joined the regiment, he voluntarily began standing late night watches in the FDC. While his constant travel to meet and coordinate with subordinate units gave him a keen awareness of the tactical situation throughout the 12th Marines region, standing watch provided a perspective not otherwise attainable, and it gave Gray ample opportunity to renew his artillery skills, though it is unlikely they ever diminished very far.

The events of 18-19 April 1966 had dramatically changed his assignment. Before that day had finished, Gray had the wheels turning while pondering the NVA sapper attack on A/1/11 described in the introduction to this chapter. What were the implications for the artillery going forward? After leading the relief column to the site of the attack, and speaking with the Marines involved, Gray had many thoughts. First and foremost, he was very proud of how the Marines, though surprised by a skilled enemy, had fought so well and routed the 40-50 sappers who had infiltrated the lines. The Marine toll in dead and wounded was substantial, but it could have very easily been much higher but for the bravery demonstrated at every level of the battery, from those in the gun pits to the Staff NCOs and officers.

Indeed, it was in discussing the guts and heroism of the officers and men that Al Gray was able to subdue General Walt's anger towards those in the charge of the battery. When the Commanding General arrived on the scene soon after sunrise, the wash of the incoming helicopter's propellers blew askew the poncho liners that had been covering the Marine dead. The General was aghast at the scene of bodies lying uncovered, and not until Major Gray quietly explained the circumstances surrounding the events of the night did the General return to his normal self.

This was no local VC unit using hit and run tactics; this attack had been well coordinated. A 50-60 round mortar barrage on K/3/12, the battery closest to A/1/11, had kept Kilo busy the very moment the sappers struck with their Bangalore torpedoes. Further, the road connecting the two units had been mined in order to slow any relief column intent on assisting those under attack. Finally, Gray's discussion with those who had observed the enemy's actions raised more questions about the enemy's motives. Why had the sappers been obsessed with seizing the gunpits instead of simply destroying the guns? If their objective was to destroy the guns, they could have done that much more quickly and much easier than their actions demonstrated. Upon reflection Al Gray decided that perhaps destroying the unit was not the real objective; the real objective had been to seize the guns, turn and aim them toward the Da Nang airfield, and then fire rounds in that direction. Gray broached the idea with the Division Headquarters, but received no support for his theory. There would be time to resurrect Gray's thoughts, and vindicate them, but not until special intelligence led to another operation more than a year later.

Soon after assuming the S-3 (Operations, Plans and Training) billet, Major Al Gray made two quick changes. First, he expanded the role of the FDC. By doctrine, the artillery regiment's FDC is supposed to be an effective Alternate Command Post for the 3rd Marine Division; Gray ensured it was. Less noticeable but certainly as important, Gray also reinstituted survey and meteorology operations throughout the I Corps area. Such action was vital since it resulted in vastly improved accuracy for the artillery. Survey and meteorology activities had been suspended; they were dormant because of the limited security resources, the vast distances separating the 12th Marines and the heightened VC activity. However, by drawing on the experience of his superb Survey Officer, Warrant Officer Lou Hosek and his resourceful Staff NCO In Charge, Staff Sergeant Seabury, Gray planned this year-long effort utilizing only artillery resources.

Gray quietly began to mold the exceptional talent serving in the FDC/Combat Operations Center (COC) complex into a well-oiled team. In what became a trademark of his leadership, he integrated intelligence with operations and made Major Wayne Ditman, the S-2 and senior aerial observer, a vital part of the planning team. Informal classes and sharing of knowledge was emphasized with the goal of professional growth for all. Gray took officers like Captain Al Barry (later a distinguished Colonel) under his wing and the two became lifelong friends.[9] These activities soon paid off when the 12th Marines were assigned responsibility for coordinating all rear area security operations for the many disparate military units functioning throughout the Da Nang complex. That effort required extensive coordination with various combat support and combat service support organizations in the area. An important aspect of the coordination, for example, was the planning for supporting fires for various nightly patrols and other actions. As was his custom, Gray never went to bed until all patrols checked in, ensuring that fire support would not be needed.

That Colonel Callender held his Operations Officer in high regard there can be little doubt. Callender's comments about the performance of Al Gray were exceptional. The Commanding Officer, whose reputation as an artilleryman was without peer, greatly valued the Major who had been posted to a lieutenant colonel's billet. Years after the war had ended, Gray received a personal letter from a former sergeant from Headquarters Battery, 12th Marines. Patrick Nicolosi, in a 2-page handwritten letter, recalled his admiration for Major Gray, and told of an exchange with Colonel Callender. While pointing towards Gray, the Colonel said to Nicolosi, "Do you see that man? One day he will be wearing stars." Nicolosi could only say, "Aye, aye, sir," because he knew that the Colonel was right.[10] Gray's personal files are filled with letters from his men, all thankful for his leadership and extolling his exemplary character.

DAILY 3ʳᵈ MARINE DIVISION COMMANDING GENERAL'S BRIEFING, DA NANG, VIETNAM, 1966

By 1966, Major Al Gray's reputation as a "spook" was well known within selected intelligence and operational circles of both the naval services and the NSA. Further, his assignments throughout the Pacific in the 1950s, his work at HQMC in the early 1960s, his efforts before and during the Cuban Missile Crisis, and particularly his mission to Vietnam in 1964 were well known to many Marine general officers, including those in command in Vietnam. Major Gray was the indisputable Marine expert on matters related to SIGINT, but also he was widely respected by the Marine intelligence and operational communities as a whole because of the quiet assistance he gave other professionals through the years. Hence, it was perfectly natural that senior leaders would seek to utilize Gray's expertise given his convenient nearby location. After all, the Headquarters of the 12ᵗʰ Marines was just down the hill from the Headquarters, 3ʳᵈ Marine Division. Further, Major General Wood B. Kyle now commanded the Division and he was personally well aware of Major Gray. When Al Gray was serving in AO2F at HQMC, he regularly briefed General Kyle, who then headed Research and Development.

The S-3 of the 12ᵗʰ Marines was a likely candidate to give the artillery briefings at the Commanding General's briefing, and that Gray did. But he routinely arrived in the Headquarters ahead of the scheduled briefing time and stopped by both the Intelligence Section (G-2) and the G-3 (Operations) to get the latest information. The SIGINT section was a separate, limited-access area within the G-2, but Gray maintained his special clearances, of course. He also knew many of the Marines working in the special intelligence section; indeed, in practically no time he would know all of them. By visiting daily, he was able to keep up-to-date and detect trends early on, and respond in an informed manner when or if he was asked his opinion about various items. Besides, Gray had lots of personal knowledge and information about the state of the war throughout I Corps. In his role as the artillery S-3, he made almost daily visits to outlying artillery and infantry positions throughout the 12ᵗʰ Marines Tactical Area of Responsibility, which stretched from Chu Lai in the south to the DMZ in the north. As a result of all that, Gray's presence at the Commanding General's briefings soon became anything but optional; he was expected to be there. And he was called upon to speak up when intelligence items were discussed.

Even when Major Gray and the 12ᵗʰ Marines moved north to Dong Ha, III MAF sought out his opinions as various intelligence data were developed. Yet all the interaction between Gray and various III MAF commanders and staff was done informally. Gray neither sought the spotlight of attention nor did he seek to benefit personally from his relationship with any of the generals. After all, his primary duties were those as the Operations Officer of the 12th Marines, a billet more than demanding enough for any officer. Although he never discussed his activities with anyone, a few senior officers within the III MAF knew the contributions that Gray was making, albeit informally, and behind the scenes.

After several months of having multiple assignments, for example he had remained the Communications Officer in addition to having the S-3 responsibilities, Gray was relieved of his communications tasks when Captain Ray Becker was assigned to the artillery regiment. Becker knew Al Gray well, having previously relieved him near the end of the 1964 SIGINT operation in Vietnam. Becker was hardly content in his new assignment; after all, Al Gray knew a lot about the communications requirements of the 12th Marines and rising to Gray's professional standards was challenging to say the least. Happily, Gray not only aided the younger officer whenever it was appropriate, but he also served as friend to Becker. The pair shared affection for chewing tobacco, and spent some time discussing the war while enjoying a chew. Becker also provided a sounding board for Major Gray; he was someone to whom Gray could express his frustrations and even anger about events or incidents. Whenever Gray's anger did flash, Becker noted that it passed very quickly without further retribution or any lingering resentment toward others. Becker thought that in Gray's eyes everyone started with a clean slate with each new dawn.

Becker recalled an incident when the survey team had been manning an observation post west of Dong Ha, but found themselves in difficulty, thinking perhaps they had been subjected to a gas attack. Chief Warrant Officer Hosek and his men were positioned high in observation tower and could smell the unmistakable odor associated with tear gas. Their call to the regimental COC set into action a well-rehearsed procedure. When Gray, who invariably spent the nights near or in the COC, left the bunker and starting walking toward the truck park, the regiment's quick reaction squad would rush to their assigned ¾ ton truck. As Gray calmly walked the 100 yards or so to his jeep, he would formulate a plan. Before climbing into the vehicle, Gray would brief the reaction force as to their mission, situation and plan of action. In very little time the force was off to the observation post, where Hosek and his men were retrieved. It turned out that some ARVN soldiers had popped a tear gas canister, unbeknownst to the Americans. Gray made sure there would not be a future repetition of that event, and the survey team returned to Dong Ha with the quick reaction force. Colonel Ben Read was furious that Gray would unnecessarily expose himself to the possible danger of a nighttime ambush.

Gray accepted the Colonel's critique, but wondered what other course of action was appropriate given that the survey unit belonged to the S-3. It would not be the last time that Gray would take personal action to protect his men in Vietnam.[11]

Even though Major Gray wanted to stay with the combat arms for assignments, his reputation among the General Officers inexorably drew him back into intelligence-related tasks. He had worked diligently to become the Marine Corps' most experienced SIGINT officer, and he could not avoid reaping the fruits of his labor. Even though he made no attempt to second-guess the assessments or analyses done by others, the general officers sought Gray's evaluation of critical items. All the intelligence work Gray did was an aside to his regular duties; nonetheless, such efforts would dramatically influence his future assignments. But he would not learn that, to his chagrin, until July 1967.

ASSISTANT COMMANDING GENERAL'S OFFICE, 3ʳᵈ MARINE DIVISION, DONG HA, OCTOBER 1966

The NVA was not slow to react to the increased presence of the Marines in I Corps. As Marine operations in and around Da Nang, Chu Lai and the Hué/Phu Bai area made the insurgency efforts of the local VC much more difficult, the NVA stepped up intrusions into the northernmost parts of I Corps, just below the DMZ that separated North and South Vietnam. Whether the NVA was trying to divert the Americans or whether their actions were part of a coordinated offensive will probably never be known; one thing is certain, the appearance of NVA units in the DMZ and the areas west of Dong Ha got the attention of the Marines and their boss in Saigon, General William C. Westmoreland.

The III MAF Headquarters ordered Major General Kyle to move his Command Post to Phu Bai in October 1966. The transition occurred simultaneously with the movement of the 1ˢᵗ Marine Division, under Major General Herman Nickerson, into the former Command Post of the 3ʳᵈ Division on Hill 327 west of Da Nang. Earlier, as a prelude to the 3ʳᵈ Division's move north, General Kyle had established a forward command post under Brigadier General Lowell E. English in the Dong Ha area. General English was placed there to take charge of the defense of the northern I Corps Tactical Zone.

Brigadier General English, the 3ʳᵈ Division's Assistant Commanding General, had a straightforward mission: defeat the NVA in the north. In early July, he had moved several infantry battalions and a large portion of the 3ʳᵈ Battalion, 12ᵗʰ Marines to the area west of Dong Ha as part of *Operation Hastings*. English's combat units, designated Task Force Delta, initially had set up the artillery at Cam Lo and moved two battalions of the 4th Marines, the 2nd and 3rd, into the DMZ west and north of the new artillery firebase. The infantry units quickly found the NVA divisions they sought, and English began planning to expand the operation.[12]

Part of his plan was to move significant artillery resources to the area around Dong Ha, nine miles south of the DMZ. Dong Ha was a small town, but once the Americans expanded the old French airfield, it became the most important Marine logistics base north of Da Nang. Dong Ha also possessed a water route to the ocean; by using the Cua Viet River and various tributaries, the Navy was able to bring boats as large as Landing Craft Utility to a landing area very near the airfield. Thus, the Navy could deliver tanks, trucks, bulldozers and even the largest artillery equipment on Landing Craft Utilities. Consequently, the Hai Van Pass, the natural obstruction to ground traffic north from Da Nang along National Highway 1, could be circumvented.

All source intelligence placed two NVA divisions in the areas west of Dong Ha and throughout the DMZ. Marine infantry and reconnaissance units quickly confirmed the presence of those divisions. As *Operations Hastings* ended in August and *Operation Prairie* began, General English continued to push more units into the area. More and more artillery was essential for fire support. While air strikes during the Vietnam War were often devastatingly effective, the weather and night attacks by the NVA often neutralized American air power. (In 1966, smart bombs and the technology used to attack Iraq in 2003 were but far-in-the-future dreams of American Airmen.) That left artillery, complemented by naval gunfire along the coast, to provide the firepower Marines would need to face the NVA.

Major Al Gray, based on his habits of visiting subordinate and supported units, and having traveled extensively throughout the region as early as 1964, was well familiar with English's mission and the area it covered. Already, the Marines were operating west along National Route 9, his earlier stomping grounds during his 1964 Tiger Tooth Mountain operation. The old Montagnard training base and airfield were still there, though the native peoples who used to live there were all but gone.

As luck would have it, Colonel Benjamin Read, the new Commanding Officer of the 12th Marines, was assigned to a court-martial on Okinawa when the decision was made to move the 12th Marines north to better support General English's mission. The regimental Executive Officer was temporarily indisposed and so it was Major Al Gray who answered General English's summons on October 9, 1966. English laid out the plan to the artilleryman, and asked how many flights of C-130s, the Marines' stalwart cargo plane, would be required to move the regiment. Surprising the General, Major Gray replied that the artillery would move as it was intended to move, using its own rolling stock. Furthermore, the Regiment would be ready to pick up and move in accordance with the General's timetable, i.e., immediately. Major Gray returned to the 12th Marines Command Post and briefed the subordinate commanders and their staffs on the concept for deploying the rest of the Regiment north to the vicinity of Dong Ha.

Moving an artillery regiment out of its many entrenched positions to new locations 50 miles north was anything but an ordinary planning evolution. Many challenges faced Gray and his Operations staff. First, only a single line of communications, National Route 1 – *the Street Without Joy* – could be used, and that meant the regimental convoys would have to traverse the Hai Van Pass, where ambushes were a common occurrence.[13] After that, the convoys would have to pass through miles of country not fully controlled by the ARVN or U.S. forces. Adding to the possible confusion, there were multiple starting positions of the regiment's battalions and firing batteries, and the movement order had to be planned and scheduled in detail so that logjams did not develop along the route of march. In addition, since there would not always be fire support provided by artillery firing from fixed positions, units had to be ready to deploy and fire quickly if adjacent units were ambushed or attacked along the way. But firing batteries were able to stop and fire – in support of themselves or others – in a matter of a few minutes. Artillery support would never be long in arriving no matter where along the route trouble might occur. As a young Lieutenant during his first night in Korea, Gray had planned and executed a Close Station March Order; this one was a bit more complicated – by several orders of magnitude!

Gray, working with the division staff and other commanders, had helped develop innovative *Rough Rider* support tactics. Using checkpoints, pre-planned fires, aerial observers and communication relays, Marine truck convoys had excellent support and were able to safely operate throughout northern I Corps. Thus, when it was the artillery regiment itself that moved, many of the tactics and techniques to be used were already well understood.

Rough Rider Convoys were groups of vehicles organized to travel from one safe haven to another within I Corps. For example, if food and ammunition needed to be quickly moved from Phu Bai to Dong Ha, a Rough Rider would be sent. It mostly consisted of 6x6, 2½-ton trucks, and often included communication jeeps, Ontos (a tracked vehicle mounting six 106mm recoilless rifles) and sometimes tanks or amphibious tractors. The VC and NVA units would sometimes try to ambush these convoys, especially if a pattern had developed. In reaction, the 12th Marines developed tactics that provided artillery support all along the route of advance. Air cover provided by observers flying overhead was a key aspect of convoy support.

One of the biggest challenges Gray faced was the need for continuing support for those Marine and ARVN units remaining in the areas around Da Nang and Chu Lai. As a result of their move north, the 12th Marines would be transferring that responsibility to the artillery arm of the 1st Marine Division – the 11th Marines. It was very important to Gray that the 11th Marines become familiar with the ongoing interaction between the Marines and the ARVN. Gray had long been very proactive about cooperating with ARVN units, and he made a point of giving them equal time and attention. His willingness to try to speak Vietnamese (despite his lack of formal training) and his reputation among the AVRN – a reputation dating to his withdrawal from Tiger Tooth Mountain in 1964 – permitted him to be a very effective liaison between the two allies. That his old friend from that 1964 operation, now Lieutenant Colonel Truong, was G-3 of the 1st ARVN Division helped Gray immeasurably. The ARVN artillery was used primarily to support its infantry, but Gray was able to draw on ARVN resources when he needed to and Gray's good relationship with the ARVN was maintained throughout his time in country. Truong and Gray met often in the course of their duties. Not surprisingly, when the South Koreans committed troops to assist the South Vietnamese, Gray also provided liaison to them. After all, he was familiar with their language. The 11th Marines would also assume primary liaison responsibility for the Korean Marines Brigade, which operated south of Chu Lai.

When the batteries moving north arrived in and around Dong Ha, they had to be ready to fire immediately. During Gray's time as S-3, the interlocking firebases that would become known as Leatherneck Square were established. Only Cam Lo had been occupied prior to the arrival of the 12th Marines Headquarters. Deciding where to position the firing batteries, and determining the proper composition for each location, was one of the 12th Marines' biggest decisions. Everything in and around Dong Ha was going to be new for many of the Regiment's firing batteries, though not for Gray; after all, he had been coming and going from in and around Dong Ha dating back to 1964.

The 12th Marines began their passage north bright and early on the morning of October 10, 1966. Major Gray would lead the command north as Colonel Read was still on Okinawa serving on the aforementioned General Court Martial, and the regimental executive officer was to remain in Da Nang.

The long columns marked the day; the artillery had more than 120 trucks, 80 jeeps of various types, and its guns, both towed behind trucks and self-propelled. Some officers and men, particularly those charged with use and custody of classified

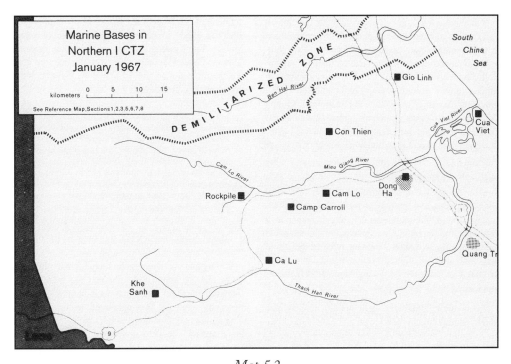

Map 5.2
Leatherneck Square was the name given the interlocking artillery firing positions just south of the De-Militarized Zone; it consisted of Gio Linh, Con Tien, Cam Lo and Dong Ha. Camp J.J. Carroll also held significant artillery. Map adapted from History and Museums Division, Headquarters, Marine Corps series, U.S. Marines in Vietnam, 1967.

materials, would fly into Dong Ha on the ubiquitous Marine C-130 transport planes. They were a definite minority, however; nearly everyone and everything went by ground. The arrival was pretty much on time and on schedule, but Gray had overlooked a single – and important – detail.

Normally, infantry units provide local security for artillery positions, because artillery units do not have sufficient numbers of men to both fire their guns and also repel a ground assault. So when the details of moving north were planned, the 12th Marines assumed that for the first night they would be able to "circle the wagons" wild west style inside the infantry's lines, then at first light move to establish new positions to the west of the infantry. The senior infantry unit in place at Dong Ha was the celebrated 4th Marine Regiment. When the artillery finally arrived after nightfall, in the midst of a pouring, bone-chilling monsoon rainstorm after a long arduous day on muddy roads, they were refused permission to situate the guns inside the infantry perimeter.

This frosty reception and uncooperative attitude angered Al Gray, who decided on the spot to move about a mile west of the infantry and establish what would become the Artillery Plateau. Gray's units did circle the wagons and assumed a defensive posture for the night, with the artillerymen providing their own security. Tents were erected and a barbed wire perimeter was established. Sandbags were filled and the artillery unit created a bare-necessities position. The 12th Marines would remain at that location until the unit left Vietnam in 1969. The reception the regiment received that cold and rainy night near Dong Ha was a negative leadership lesson that Al Gray never forgot; cooperation and assistance were the trademarks of his efforts in every billet he ever had; in war-time, such traits were critical.

The evening of the arrival provided for a typical Al Gray motivational happening, however. Although he never drank while serving abroad, Gray often carried a bottle of scotch in his pack. Making the rounds that night, he offered the young Marines who were awake on guard duty, or who were putting in sand bags, or who were pitching tents, the opportunity to take a pull. Most happily agreed to the unexpected present. Having ridden all the way from Da Nang to Dong Ha, in a torrential rainstorm, in far from even minimally comfortable conditions, then working through the night to establish a new position, without complaint and with all due diligence, the troops reflected the pride in their unit, their mission and the Marine Corps. They were good, and they knew it. Al Gray knew all he had to do was point them in the right direction and mostly stay out of the way.

The swiftness and smoothness that characterized the move from Da Nang to Dong Ha was a reflection of Al Gray's walking-around leadership style. Because Gray personally knew all the subordinate commanders within the 12th Marine Regiment, down to the battery commanders, and knew most of the senior Staff NCOs, he also knew who could be trusted to use their initiative and resourcefulness, and who needed detailed orders or perhaps had to be cajoled into action. He identified which units had good morale and which had even higher morale and could be entrusted with important assignments without rigorous planning. Because he was so familiar with the regiment, he was able to respond positively to General English's requirements, and he was able to meet them in a timely fashion, with or without the cooperation of the 4th Marines. Indeed, the arrival incident would prove to be the exception for Gray. Cooperation with higher, subordinate, supported and allied units was the cornerstone of Gray's leadership style. He always believed anything was possible if it did not matter who got the credit.

12th MARINES HEADQUARTERS, DONG HA, OCTOBER 1966

The 12th Marines quickly moved to establish firing positions throughout the northern portion of I Corps. Marine infantry and reconnaissance units were operating from the coastline of the South China Sea westward as far as the Laotian border, and from the DMZ southward to Hue and Phu Bai (and indeed throughout

I Corps). Artillery needed to be responsive and effective throughout the whole area. Planning the operations and building the necessary firebases was sufficient to keep any major of Marines active.

However, Colonel Ben Read faced additional challenges not of his own making. Around Dong Ha and the area south of the DMZ, the North Vietnamese outgunned the Marines. The workhorse of Marine artillery, the 105mm howitzer, had a range of about seven miles. The larger artillery pieces, the 8-inch howitzers and 155mm guns, had a longer range, but those pieces were far fewer in number and had limited supplies of ammunition. The NVA had significant large caliber artillery and, by 1966, rockets located just north of the DMZ. The primary NVA artillery piece was the 130 mm howitzer, which the People's Army had in great numbers. The Soviet-built weapon could match up with the longest-range Marine gun, the 155mm howitzer, but the NVA enjoyed a huge advantage in the number of firing batteries they could place on the battlefield. From their position north of the DMZ, the communists could reach well into South Vietnam and attack the Marines by fire. Given the

Figure 5.3
Lt Col J.J. Snyder, Commanding Officer of 2/12, Maj Al Gray; and
Lt Col Edwin Rudzis, Commanding Officer of 4/12.[14]

vagaries of the weather, and the fact that all-weather precision air attacks remained something missing until well into the future, the situation was daunting. By the fall, it was clear the Marines needed additional support.

Major Gray prepared a requirement for long-range artillery that Colonel Read forwarded to General Walt. The Commanding General wasted no time asking General Westmoreland for the necessary resources. They were soon forthcoming in the form of Task Force Bravo, a battery of the Army's 175mm self-propelled guns. The 2nd Battalion, 94th Artillery, which had three more firing batteries of 175mm guns soon followed.

The first to arrive, Task Force Bravo, assumed their new firing position west of Dong Ha, soon to be renamed Camp J.J. Carroll, one of the newly constructed pillars of "Leatherneck Square." Two Marine 105mm howitzer batteries and Headquarters, 1st Battalion, 12th Marines were already at Camp Carroll. In October 1966, Task Force Bravo was ready to fire. But much to the surprise of the battery commander, Captain Vanderslice, Army artillery doctrine would soon be put on its head.[15]

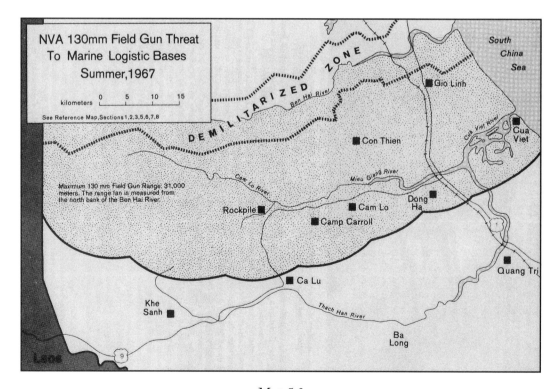

Map 5.3
Map reprinted from History and Museums Division, Headquarters,
Marine Corps series, U.S. Marines in Vietnam, 1967.

The U.S. Army's doctrine for employment of artillery called for the 175mm guns with their 34 kilometer (21 miles) range to be located the furthest from enemy lines. Doctrine also called for the guns to be moved quickly after firing so that the enemy could not locate the American heavy artillery and subject it to counter-battery fire. The requirement for movement was an important reason that the 175mm guns were self-propelled. They were mounted on a tracked vehicle frame, so that when the 25 foot long barrel was added, the vehicle was transformed into something akin to a prehistoric predator. To civilians, the 175mm self-propelled guns appeared to be a giant, menacing tank. To the Marines in I Corps, they looked beautiful.

Far from being placed to the rear of all other artillery, Task Force Bravo would assume firing positions adjacent to the Marine 105 batteries. Indeed, for the next two years and more, Task Force Bravo and the 175mm guns of 2nd Battalion, 94th Artillery (2/94), which arrived October 27, would often be among the American guns closest to North Vietnam. And, far from having to move each time they fired, these same guns would be placed in fixed firing positions, unable to shift sites except by moving the sandbags that surrounded them in order to provide some protection against incoming rockets, mortars and artillery.

The primary reason for moving the 175mm guns to Camp Carroll was to support the Marines operating far to the west in the mountains around the old Special Forces airstrip at Khe Sanh. An additional mission, dubbed *Operation Highrise*, was to augment efforts to fire into North Vietnam. The 175mm guns could effectively shoot a large projectile more than 21 miles. Their capability provided depth and power to the operation, and kept the artillerymen of the U.S. Army very busy. Major Gray, the S-3 of the 12th Marines, worked closely with the Commanding Officer of 2/94 to ensure the unit deployed the Army's big guns effectively throughout the area.

Lieutenant Colonel Richard G. Trefry, United States Army, had organized and trained 2/94 when the battalion was reconstituted at Fort Sill, Oklahoma in 1965, and then he brought the unit into Vietnam in 1966. The battalion's arrival near the DMZ prompted visits from General Westmoreland, and of course, Lieutenant General Lewis Walt, the Marine Commanding General. The NVA did not formally visit, but presence of the largest artillery pieces in the world did not go unnoticed. By late fall 1966, the artillery ante in Vietnam had been raised significantly.

After the Army's long guns arrived, the Marines had a better answer to the NVA long-range artillery. The base at Khe Sanh would become an important position blocking infiltration routes through the western mountains, while the logistics base at Dong Ha grew exponentially in importance. The 3rd Marine Division moved there, concentrating its firepower and its nine maneuver battalions, augmented by two reconnaissance battalions, amphibious tractor and tank battalions, and other combat service support units. In addition to Marine units, the 3rd Division included several other Army units. One Marine favorite was the Army's Dusters. Dusters mounted a pair of 40mm guns on a track vehicle frame, and their firepower was awesome. They were highly sought by units in fixed positions as a means to discourage ground assaults, and Dusters were used widely to protect convoys.

The arrival of the 175mm guns also enhanced the 12th Marines aerial observer capabilities. But the improvement did not come without some moments of worry for Lieutenant Colonel Trefry. When Trefry first arrived, he responded to Marine inquiries about his unit's capabilities by saying that they had a complete complement of men and equipment, in accordance with the Army Tables of Organization and Equipment, except that he was missing his aerial observers and their aircraft. The range of the 175mm guns made aerial observation of targets a necessity. But the Marines were also short of aerial observer capabilities, and so Colonel Benjamin Read, the Commanding Officer of the 12th Marines, and just about every other officer in the Marine chain of command up through Lieutenant General Walt, encouraged Lieutenant Colonel Trefry to aggressively seek his missing aerial observer assets. Indeed, General Westmoreland would be visiting in early November, and the Marines hoped Trefry might raise the issue with the Commanding General, MAC(V). Trefry thought he might try.

General Westmoreland actually arrived at the end of October, eager to see for himself (after all, he was an old World War II artilleryman) how the Marines had employed their newly arrived heavy artillery. In particular, Westmoreland wanted to learn more about Khe Sanh, and how the Marines planned to defend the distant, very isolated base. Trefry knew that firing west to support the base was one of his top priorities, but the elements had conspired to deny him the opportunity to lay his guns properly.[16] Fog, rain, and constant drizzle, the very same kind of weather that Major Gray had experienced during his earlier operations in the vicinity of Tiger Tooth Mountain, again prevented the best plans of the artillerymen to be implemented. Despite his finest efforts, Trefry had made little progress. No ranging rounds had been fired, and the guns not measured, because no one could see exactly where the rounds landed. No one wanted a misdirected round to cause injury to friendly troops.

Westmoreland was beside himself when told of the lack of progress in aiming the guns. Indeed, Lieutenant Colonel Trefry saw his career flash before his eyes. His battalion had been on the ground for three days, and yet they were still not prepared to fire their primary mission in support of the defense of the I Corps Tactical Zone. Swift intervention by Lieutenant General Walt and others took the pressure off Trefry, but the 175mm gun battalion commander did not have the confidence to raise the issue of his aerial observer assets – indeed, he was happy to still be in command of his battalion![17] Not only did Trefry remain in command, his career flourished and led him to the White House where, as a Lieutenant General, he served as Senior Military Officer during the same time that General Gray was the Commandant of the Marine Corps. But their relationship started in 1966 just south of the DMZ.

When the Army battalion eventually received its detachment of L-1 Observation Planes, Gray obtained permission to organize the Regiment's Aerial Observer activities as a means to enhance operations. Since the start of their deployment, the 3rd Marine Division's aerial observer efforts utilized OV-10 aircraft and those crews flew valiantly throughout the Marine Tactical Area of Responsibility. But as often is the case, the requirements for aerial observation far exceeded the allocation of assets; thus, the timely arrival of Army L-1 spotter planes provided a significant increase in capability for the 12th Marines, and units operating in northern I Corps. All the regimental AOs, both Army and Marine Corps, flew from the airfield at Dong Ha. All their efforts were under the direct supervision of the peripatetic, hyper-energetic S-3 of the 12th Marines, Major Al Gray. He had organized the aerial observer efforts, recruited and helped train officers to perform aerial observer duties, and ensured the program supported all the disparate activities going on within the III MAF Tactical Area of Responsibility, from watching over Rough Rider convoys to supporting infantry units operating in the field. In addition, aerial observers also provided an excellent means for gathering information about both friendly and enemy movements, including identifying potential firing positions for the elusive NVA artillery.

Though he started flying aerial observer missions while in Da Nang, flying became a bigger part of Gray's days in and around Dong Ha. He flew mornings or afternoons, since most NVA activity took place at night, when he typically spent the majority of his time in the COC/FDC. The Major also flew many missions over southern North Vietnam, and to the west as far as Laos. Few, if any, knew the countryside and the disposition of units as well as Al Gray. The expansion of the aerial observer program was crucial to supporting operations in the northern I Corps area from late 1966 until the Marines left in 1970.

Gray was also very proud of splendid Marines such as Captains Pat Pate, Steve Gimber, Glen Golden, Gerry Garvick and 1st Lieutenants Ed Brown and John

Fanning.[18] These officers, most with no formal training, conducted almost daily missions over some of the most hostile territory in Vietnam.

One day at the S-1 office, Gray was stunned to learn that his nomination to receive an Air Medal was about to be approved. He quickly took steps to squash such an award. First, he feared that if he were awarded the medal it might attract unwanted attention from the powers to be; after all, given the special intelligence security clearances he maintained, flying should have been prohibited, unless specifically authorized. Secondly, he was spending time aloft to learn about his adversary and to find new ways, and new places, that he could bring the decisive weapon of the war – artillery – to bear on his enemies. Gray did not seek and did not want any Air Medals.[19]

1st Lieutenant Douglas Beard, U.S. Army Reserve, remembered the first time he met Major Gray. Gray had tasked 2/94 with providing aerial observers and he wanted men who were not short-timers, would be dedicated to the mission for an extended period, and would not be called back to the battalion for other duties.[20] Beard was impressed by the professionalism shown by the Marine Major and he was not deterred by Gray's requirements for professionalism. That Gray demanded that every aerial observer know all the unit call signs, each unit's area of operations and daily situation in the Tactical Area of Responsibility seemed reasonable to Beard. Soon the young Army Lieutenant actively sought assignments with the older Marine.

On one aerial observer flight, Beard and his pilot watched as a Marine position came under fire from inside North Vietnam. Beard could see the muzzle flashes and wanted to direct counter-battery fire against the NVA position. However, there was also helicopter activity above and to the east of the Marine position, and consequently Beard could not get permission to fire pending resolution of Save-A-Plane calculations. Whenever helicopters are flying, the artillery must ensure the safety of the aircraft. But Beard was highly agitated; seldom could he pinpoint the NVA firing position during an actual attack. His requests for fire went unheeded until a voice using the call sign for the 12th Marines S-3 came on the air and authorized Beard's request be granted.

It was not unusual for Al Gray to be hanging around the Alternate Division Command Post listening to the radio. When he was not out and about performing his walking around leadership tasks, he routinely was monitoring the radio, especially if there was action occurring. Many of his troops thought he was omnipresent, and his access to the radios monitoring every unit in the Tactical Area of Responsibility would reinforce that opinion. Continuing the habits formed as early as Korea, when Gray slept, it was only for a couple hours and it was usually near the radios.

The S-3 of the 12th Marines got involved with many things, not always directly related to combat. On night in late December 1966, as *Operation Prairie* was winding down, Gray heard an angry senior Marine advisor to one the Vietnamese Marine Battalions operating around Con Thien yelling into the radio. Using intemperate language, the advisor claimed that "some artillery battery was operating on his tactical *push* and interfering with our control." Push was the American slang term used for frequency during the Vietnam War. Gray quickly arranged for the Vietnamese Marines to use an alternative spare frequency and then established communications with the intruder. The offending Marine operator turned out to be someone desperately trying to establish communications with his parent unit because a snake had bitten his buddy. Noting that the Marine used the call sign "Tinge Hotel," which was used for telephone communications in Vietnam by Hotel Battery, and knowing that Hotel Battery had recently redeployed to Okinawa as part of the Special Landing Force, Gray asked the Marine his location. The radioman came back that he was at a crossroads leading into the Northern Training Area – on Okinawa! Gray then realized what was happening: *ducting*.

His first clue was that it was standard operating procedure for units to reverse their radio and telephone call signs when redeployed to Okinawa. So what had been his telephone call sign in Vietnam, became a radio call sign on Okinawa. Secondly, because of earlier duty in Japan reinforced by his observations during operations atop Tiger Tooth Mountain in 1964, Gray was keenly aware that *ducting* was an atmospheric phenomenon associated with Frequency Modulated (FM) radio signals in that area of the world. A radio signal, trapped between two layers of the atmosphere, would bounce along becoming all the stronger while travelling thousands of miles – even though FM signals are usually limited to line-of-sight ranges. On Tiger Tooth Mountain, Gray's Marines routinely heard Japanese fishing boats; now the frequency used by Vietnamese Marines at Con Thien was being subjected to interference from radio signals emanating from Okinawa.

Having heard the young operator's desperation, Gray told him to hold on. Meanwhile, he made a connection with the Division switchboard and had himself patched through to III MAF, from which he was patched to Okinawa. From there, he contacted Battalion 2/4 to tell them of the problem with a snakebite victim in the Northern Training Area. Instead of simply quelling the advisor's anger, Gray got to the root of the problem and by doing so helped a Marine in need thousands of miles away. A later message confirmed that there was a happy ending to the story.[21]

Though Gray did a superb job as S-3, he had great support from many professional artillerists then serving in important billets throughout the 12th Marines. Lieutenant Colonels J.J. Snyder, Edwin M. Rudzis, Willis L. Gore, Leslie L. Page,

Figure 5.4
Maj Gray returning from an aerial observer mission in 1966.[22]

Warren E. McCain, Marshall E. Campbell, James R. Gallman, and David G. Jones as well as Majors Samuel M. Morrow and Paul E. Wilson were all very professional and dedicated officers who worked with Gray to improve operations through the regiment. They taught him well, and they all worked harmoniously to achieve very dramatic, and highly effective, results. Indeed, J.J. Snyder was among the most intelligent artillery officers Gray ever had the pleasure to serve with, while Major Bill Spiesel, the regimental S-4, provided outstanding staff support.

Gray also got to watch General William C. Westmoreland up close and personally during his time with the 12th Marines, especially after the move to Dong Ha. Al Gray was first introduced to General Westmoreland at Khe Sanh in 1964, when the General visited the Marine Advisory Unit #1 during the Tiger Tooth Mountain operation. Now, the Commanding General was highly interested in the possible invasion plans of the NVA across the DMZ. Traveling with two young United States Air Force majors in tow, Westmoreland on several occasions visited General English's Task Force Delta during the late fall of 1966 into the early winter of 1967. He enjoyed peering into North Vietnam, all the while taking notes on his omnipresent 5X7 cards. Gray was able to see the officer that *TIME* magazine had named Man

Figure 5.5
The International Observer Outpost located by the bridge across the Ben Hai River north of Gio Linh and Dong Ha. "Monitoring" by the international forces was completely ineffectual. [23]

Figure 5.6
Lt Jack Perry and Maj Al Gray shortly after their arrival in Dong Ha.
Note the mess hall under construction in the background.[24]

of the Year, and he made a lasting impact on junior officers. He asked the right questions, showed concern for the men, and he was by no means haughty or aloof, but rather he seemed to value everyone's opinion of the situation. Gray was impressed.

At the other end of the spectrum, Major Gray also took time to cheer up and encourage young staff officers who toiled in relative anonymity doing the often ignored but essential administrative and logistics assignments. One such officer was 1st Lieutenant Jack Perry, a tall, athletic artilleryman from Wisconsin who was plucked from a firing battery to be the Regimental S-1, the Personnel Officer. It was a job that provided little chance for glory, but ample opportunity for administrative blunders sure to bring on criticism or derision. Gray liked the young Lieutenant and often included him in quick trips away from the regimental area. After moving to Dong Ha, a frequent salve for Gray's restlessness was an excursion to the DMZ and the International Observer Outpost along the Ben Hai River. Besides trips to

Figure 5.7
Maj Al Gray at Dong Ha, 1966. Note the field jacket he is wearing.
Yes, it could get chilly, even cold, in Vietnam.[25]

the DMZ outpost, Perry recalled that after he and another lieutenant had baseball gloves sent to them from home, they would have impromptu ball games in some dried out rice paddy. The younger officers were amazed at the skills Major Gray exhibited when he joined in the games.

Al Gray played a role in bringing the Army's big guns to northern I Corps; that action was highly publicized and came to the attention of most Americans. But other Al Gray actions hardly were known to anyone. Ever since his first contact with them in 1964, Al Gray had remained in contact with the Montagnards who lived at the western end of Route 9 and beyond. Gray had "adopted" four children at an orphanage near Khe Sanh while serving in that area in 1964; during his time with the 12th Marines he was able to keep in touch with the orphanage and the children. The financial aid Gray provided gave the orphans a modicum of joy and a few extra trinkets.

Figure 5.8
Four orphans adopted by Al Gray. He lost track of the children after 1969, when Americans
left the base at Khe Sanh and only returned to that area during combat operations.[26]

ALTERNATE DIVISION COMMAND POST, DONG HA, 1966

With the movement of the 3rd Marine Division to Phu Bai and the forward
Command Post at Dong Ha, communications within and around the Division's
Tactical Area of Responsibility changed significantly. Instead of being near the III
MAF Command Post and very close to the Da Nang airfield, the Division was
now separated from both those by the Hai Van Pass, and it subordinate units were
mostly north of Phu Bai, closer to the DMZ.[27]

It was after the move to the Dong Ha area that Al Gray's work as Regimental
S-3 really accelerated. There were many tasks to be accomplished, and most required
simultaneous execution. Among the first was setting up the Alternative Division
Command Post. Gray had emphasized this task soon after becoming the S-3, while
still in Da Nang. Now, with the Division's Main Command Post located in the
Phu Bai area, and the 12th Marines west of Dong Ha, there were more than a few
technical and administrative issues to be resolved. But Al Gray was also a student
of communications, and he put primary emphasis, regardless of his assignment, on
ensuring all signal requirements were satisfied as soon as possible. And when basic
requirements were met, then Gray demanded alternative measures be implemented.
That usually meant having wire links to back up radios and microwave circuits

whenever possible. Communications officers who worked for Al Gray were rarely bored by having nothing to do. NVA artillery was more than sufficiently capable of destroying antennae, knocking out microwave equipment, and generally disrupting Marine communications. Unlike areas in southern I Corps, were communications links might be solidly in place for years, there was always work to be done in and around Dong Ha.

From the time that Major Gray and the 12th Marines reached Dong Ha until well after he left, a principal activity along the DMZ was the construction of the McNamara Line. Before construction began, however, the pros and cons of such an effort were widely discussed. Al Gray was never a significant voice during the debate, he being only the S-3 of the Artillery Regiment. However, that is not to say that he did not have an opinion and that the senior officers of the Marine Corps did not seek his thoughts.

Over the objections of the entire Marine hierarchy, the Secretary of Defense and General Westmoreland ordered III MAF to construct a trace from the banks of the South China Sea toward the mountains near the Laotian border. Gray, like his senior commanders, believed the construction was foolhardy at best, and operational malfeasance at worst. It cost the Marines 200 dead and over a 1,000 wounded, and that was just while it was being built. Then, following construction, the Marines were tied to fixed positions in order to cover the trace. Of course, the patches of bare ground hardly stopped infiltrators, though perhaps it did limit such activity to fast and slightly brazen runners. When the NVA wanted to move major units south, they simply went around the plowed ground to the west, through the mountains and jungles there. Al Gray was familiar with all aspects of the man-made feature; many a day saw him flying as an aerial observer over the entire trace into North Vietnam, and other days he visited the artillery units located on it. But orders were orders, and Gray was mission-oriented. His regiment had five battalions of artillery, two separate batteries and all provided inter-locking protective fires for each other. The trace did nothing that enhanced their situation.

Towards the end of 1966, complaining about the McNamara Line was so widespread that the Marine Corps put out the word that discussing it with reporters was forbidden. The *Associated Press* ran a story in late 1966 entitled "Wall of Silence." The unnamed *Associated Press* reporter wrote of how the Marines disparaged the "Wall," and how they wished the troops tied up watching over it could have been put to use in operations against the enemy. Though Major Gray was knee deep in decisions related to protecting the line, little did he realize that in a few more months he would be up to his neck in the very middle of the McNamara Wall.

Figure 5.9
Major Al Gray, circa 1966. Picture was probably taken in the vicinity of the Gio Linh Outpost.[28]

Colonel Ben Read, Commanding Officer of the 12th Marines, had earned a Navy Cross in Korea when the 105mm howitzer battery he commanded provided critical support as the 1st Marine Division withdrew from the Chosin Reservoir. Colonel Read lauded Gray as having a "tremendous professional background which combines the highest level of proficiency in communications, artillery, infantry and intelligence." Further, he pointed to a series of actions competed by Major Gray. Read cited the fact that while Gray was the S-3 the Regiment had fired a half-million rounds, while controlling up to seven firing battalions as well as two separate batteries. But Read went out of his way to discuss Gray's actions related to the Regiment's move to Dong Ha.

The Commanding Officer pointed out that Major Gray, while coordinating support for *Operation Hastings*, formed three batteries using supplementary weapons that did not have a Table of Organization structure to support them. Three firing batteries created out of hide, thereby ensuring that each artillery position was supported by at least three others.[29] Colonel Read also wrote of Gray's continuous involvement – at great risk to himself – in personal liaison with and reconnaissance for those forward batteries. According to Read, it was the result of Al Gray's efforts that the fires of five massed battalions could be brought to bear on any point along the Forward Edge of the Battle Area – by which he meant the McNamara Line. Further, all that was done while also permitting convoys to and from Dong Ha and all along the Cua Viet River to have artillery protection. Read, as Colonel Callender had before him, also mentioned Gray's resolve to see the war through to a successful conclusion, something consistently noted while Gray was in Vietnam.

Gray's third Regimental Commander, Colonel William R. Morrison relieved Colonel Read, who became the G-3 of the 3rd Division. By the January 1967 Change of Command, things were really heating up in northernmost I Corps. As a result, *Al Gray's duties were about to change.*

MAJOR AMERICAN COMBAT UNITS ARRIVE IN SOUTH VIETNAM

WASHINGTON, 1966

The Vietnam War escalated to a much higher level of combat during 1966. Robert Strange McNamara, the iconoclastic Secretary of Defense, had been the principal architect of the war, but he spent more time with an obscure Army Lieutenant General, Alfred D. Starbird, than he did with the Joint Chiefs. Moreover, Starbird was able to get on McNamara's calendar almost instantaneously; something denied even the Chairman of the JCS.[30] As American troops poured into South Vietnam, as the air war against Ho Chi Minh escalated, and as diplomatic efforts to stop the fighting stopped and started with the frequency of rush hour traffic, McNamara's influence started to wane. President Johnson was slowly but surely concentrating decision making into the White House, or more precisely, into the Oval Office.

The Secretary of Defense had assumed the role of the primary architect of the Vietnam War since at least November 1963, when Lyndon Baines Johnson assumed the Presidency following the assassination of John Fitzgerald Kennedy. While Kennedy was alive, responsibility for the growing war had been spread among several of the President's principal advisors; but when Johnson made the transition into power, he concentrated accountability for Vietnam in the hands of his horn-rimmed, fast-talking Pentagon chief. It was power and responsibility that McNamara sought; the Secretary had, during his five years in office, demonstrated disdain (at best) for the JCS, though his relationship with them was complex. McNamara was nothing if not self-confident; but his self-confidence was largely misplaced. From the advantage of hindsight, *arrogant* is not too strong a word to describe the former Ford chief executive and his systems analyst minions who ran the largest department of the Government.[31]

By late 1965 and going into 1966, McNamara had become uneasy about the effectiveness of the American air campaign against North Vietnam. Various Air Force officers, including the redoubtable General Curtis E. LeMay, promised to bomb Ho Chi Minh's country back into the Stone Age, evidently failing to notice that North Vietnam was not highly industrialized. Indeed, North Vietnam already resembled a Stone Age country much more than one that depended on manufacturing, production and technology. And given the very significant limitations placed on air attacks against high priority targets by the President, that the American planners thought a bombing campaign could be effective in bringing the North to the negotiating table was a noteworthy mistake in the American war effort. The Air Force and Naval Air advocates had much too much influence about how to assist South Vietnam to defend against an insurgency that was initiated and supported by a foreign country (North Vietnam), which was in turn massively supported by two world powers, the Soviet Union and the People's Republic of China. As long as the Americans found it politically impossible to bomb (or mine) either the port of Haiphong or the rail lines from China, air power could not be decisive in ending the aggression. By early 1966, the top brass of the Air Force and Navy should have realized that; sadly, they did not.

As the war turned in directions he did not like, McNamara was looking for alternative strategies. Plus, he had remained close to Jacqueline Kennedy; and she, among others, was fervently telling him to stop the killing. By 1966, McNamara was struggling to see a clear path for American success in the war. The Secretary viewed war through the prism of statistics and technology, and he was highly curious when a group of scientists piqued his interest in using technology to stop the North Vietnamese invasion of South Vietnam.

McNamara knew that United States needed a different strategy to slow down the North Vietnamese invasion. When a Massachusetts Institute of Technology scientist proposed that something akin to an electronic fence could be constructed as a barrier to the North Vietnamese, the idea appealed as much more than an intellectual novelty to the brainy Secretary of Defense. He quickly established a working group to investigate the possible efficacy of the idea. Acting quickly, a super-secret organization blandly named the Defense Communications Planning Group was created to implement what would soon be called the *McNamara Line*.[32]

The 1960s were a different time for American military strategists, especially with respect to the military secrecy and types of projects done outside the view of Congressional oversight. Those were the days before the lurid publicity caused by the unprecedented – and unlawful – release of the Pentagon Papers. Moreover, in 1966 the American press had not yet turned against the war. Stories from and about Vietnam generally supported the American military and its efforts, and the anti-war movement – particularly among members of Congress – remained little more than nascent aggravation. When McNamara set up an organization with a very large and a top-secret budget, it was done quietly and without opposition. Indeed, it was not until after 1970 that more than a very few members of Congress – or any of the press – even found out about the existence of the Defense Communications Planning Group, and that was after the organization had already spent more than $3.1B – a enormous sum in 1970 dollars.

To run the biggest, and most secret, effort since the Manhattan Project, McNamara selected Lieutenant General Alfred Dodd Starbird, United States Army. General Starbird had been part of the nuclear testing program and was highly respected as a technical manager. Furthermore, he had the chutzpah to lead what was a largely unaudited, unaccountable scientific engineering effort that pushed technology in many areas, but primarily in the areas of bombs, sensors and computer processing of copious amounts of data.

Defense Communications Planning Group was an engineer's paradise. Budgets were (almost) unlimited; ideas were kingmakers. No expense was too great and no investigation too remote to be undertaken. Defense Communications Planning Group engineers and scientists routinely flew anywhere and everywhere – often first class – to advance their projects; finally, the checks and balances that characterize most research and development efforts certainly did not inhibit them. And these were the cream of the American engineering crop; those from places like MITRE (the commercial arm of the Massachusetts Institute of Technology) and the leading industrial companies augmented the best government scientists and technical managers. Their efforts were multi-faceted and included large-scale integrated computer systems. Starbird and his engineers and scientists had concocted a system that appealed to McNamara as a way to save lives, be more effective than boots on the ground, and use technology to replace Soldiers.[33]

It was in theory a relatively straightforward system. Sensors would be placed along a line south of the DMZ. The line would be a trace plowed free of vegetation that would extend from the South China Sea in the east to the Laotian border in the west. Sensors would also be airdropped all along the length of the Ho Chi Minh trail that extended from North Vietnam along the entire western border of South Vietnam, through Cambodia and Laos all the way to the area southwest of Saigon. The sensors would be tied to transmitters that broadcast the data that could be gathered by a specially configured aircraft; from the aircraft, the data would be relayed to the computer located in northern Thailand. There, operators would interpret, analyze and react to the information, usually by sending bombers against the targets generated by the sensors. It was a novel approach to warfare, and one that in 1960s was fraught with technological challenges.

Except for the airframes, everything else had to be developed pretty much from scratch. The sensors, be they noise, seismic, electromagnetic, had to be developed; software designed to collect and integrate the data into forms absorbable by humans required design and development, and on 1960 era computers, when memory was small and hugely expensive, and software design was an art form. Even radio data links were new and had to be made reliable; and, of course, precision-guided munitions were in their infancy.

Though General Starbird confronted many technological challenges, McNamara was enthusiastic in assisting any way he could. Perhaps in McNamara's view, developing new technology was much more entertaining and interesting than trying to sort out how to defeat the enemy on the battlefield. It is not clear that McNamara ever fully understood the Joint Chiefs plans for Vietnam, in particular Commandant Greene and the Marines' counter-insurgency strategy. Since the Joint Chiefs increasingly were isolated and out of touch, and given that General Westmoreland, who after all was a McNamara appointment, favored an emphasis on "search and destroy" operations, it is doubtful the Secretary had the time or the inclination to investigate alternative strategies. It was also during 1966, in his quest to develop metrics that could be used to determine if the war was being won, that McNamara emphasized the use of a "body count" as a scorecard to evaluate enemy losses. There was no more useless, senseless or irrational metric to resolve combat effectiveness and efficiency than the body count.[34] In the end, the only people fooled by it were in the Pentagon and White House.[35]

As the personnel buildup gathered speed during 1965 and into 1966, there still was no clear consensus about: (a) how many troops were needed; (b) how the troops should be employed; (c) what the division of effort between the Americans and the South Vietnamese Army should be, an effort made impossible by the lack of a stable South Vietnamese government. And as the military expansion occurred, the President's decision not to activate the reserves, but instead add more active duty Soldiers and Marines, caused additional tumult and confusion. All the top military strategists had a vague idea that South Vietnam needed to be saved; no one could gain a consensus for his own personal view of the means to do it. General Westmoreland, Ambassador Taylor, General Greene, Secretary McNamara and just about every other important player advanced an opinion; in the end, President Johnson adopted the one of two approaches that was not based on professional military expertise – his own (McNamara's was the other).

Other than McNamara, the leading architect of the war during the period 1961 through 1965 was General Maxwell Taylor. Taylor had caught the attention of the

Kennedy Administration by advocating a policy of *flexible response* to enemy aggression. By 1966, it was clear that no one could articulate clearly exactly how flexible response was supposed to work.[36] As military concept, it sounded much better to politicians than the Eisenhower strategy of *massive retaliation*. As with many other revolutionary concepts, however, the devil was in the details. *Flexible response*, as a military strategy, would be thrown into the scrap heap of bad ideas as soon as the war ended. *Flexible response* became, in reality, incrementalism; it did not work on the ground in South Vietnam, in the air over North Vietnam, or at the negotiating table in Paris.

THE AIR WAR, 1965-1966

While President Johnson, Secretary McNamara, Ambassador Maxwell Taylor, General Westmoreland, and – to a much lesser degree – the JCS dithered over how to conduct the ground war in South Vietnam, the air war against Ho Chi Minh was even more disjointed and unorganized. The air war advocates, led by the bombastic General LeMay, thought that aggressive bombing would dissuade the North Vietnamese from their path of aggression. Early on, however, the results of wargaming, where LeMay was a principal participant, showed that no amount of air power would bring the communists in North Vietnam to their knees, unless it was applied against key targets like posts, rail lines and power plants. All those were off limits in 1966, and remained so until President Nixon took office.[37]

Throughout 1965 and 1966 the American administration tried to use air power alternatively as a carrot and a stick for the communists. After attacks against American airbases in the South, Johnson would order retaliation against the North. And when the Gulf of Tonkin affair happened, Johnson's first impulse was to bomb the communists.[38] But the Administration never developed a strategy and stuck to it. Rather, targets seemed to be developed haphazardly by people who knew nothing of air warfare. Johnson often bragged that the military did nothing without his express approval, and that included selecting which aircraft would drop which bombs on which targets from exactly which approaches. It was madness at best and malfeasance at worst.

Targeting was a tortuous, slow, convoluted process dominated by Lyndon Johnson and his Tuesday Lunch Group. As a result, the communists could gradually adjust their defenses to meet the challenges caused by the bombing. Americans will never know how many casualties were the result of Johnson's egotism. The diagram below shows how difficult the targeting process was.

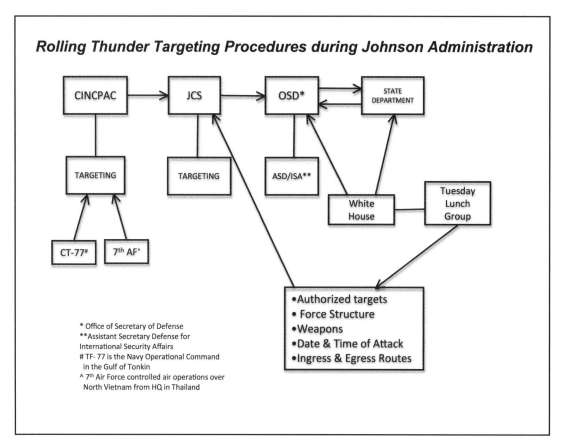

Figure 5.10
Rolling Thunder Targeting Procedures during Johnson Administration.
Diagram by W. Hayes Parks, used with permission.[39]

Never before had a Commander-in-Chief injected himself so forcefully and, as it turned out, so ineffectively into military tactics. When the White House, and especially a lunch group, decided the ingress and egress routes for tactical bombers, while also choosing the type of aircraft, its bomb loads, and the exact date and time of the attack, then a whole regiment of officers in the chain of command should have been protesting or perhaps resigning. Who exactly were the members of the bi-weekly Tuesday Lunch Group? The group consisted of Lyndon Johnson, Secretary of Defense Robert McNamara, Secretary of State Dean Rusk, Press Chief George Reedy, and occasionally Chairman of the Joint Chiefs, Army General Earle Wheeler. Wheeler was a lifelong military professional, though as an infantry officer he went through World War II and Korea without much combat experience. No one else in the group was qualified to comment on any aspect of the air war, much less select targets and determine approaches and altitudes appropriate for bombing the objectives. Joseph A. Califano, Johnson's Special Domestic Advisor and former McNamara Whiz Kid, and Harold Brown, the esoteric Secretary of the Air Force, though not members of the Lunch Group, were influential Johnson military advisors. Despite their obvious intelligence, neither had the slightest qualification to comment upon or influence military tactical and strategic matters.

The Vietnam air war was different from previous air campaigns. Unlike World War II or even Korea, it was not the swashbuckling fighter pilots who engaged in air-to-air combat that were the real heroes of the effort. There were some air-to-air engagements over North Vietnam, but they were minor events, if not wholly extraneous, except, of course, to the pilots involved. In 1965 through 1972, the real heroes of the air war, the guys with the biggest cojones, were the pilots asked to fly their fighter-bombers against a variety of objects that were extremely well defended by a host of anti-aircraft weaponry ranging from 12.7mm machine guns to surface-to-air missiles. Moreover, after a while, the North Vietnamese could figure out which routes of ingress and egress the attackers were likely to use. Since the Air Force launched their planes from Thailand, and had to refuel in-flight, they approached their targets at high altitude, in full view of North Vietnamese radar. The Air Force pilots had no chance of using the element of surprise to reach their objectives. Navy pilots, taking off from carriers located in the Gulf of Tonkin, started much closer to North Vietnam and could sometimes achieve surprise. But the Naval aircraft were restricted in their bomb loads and flew at the mercy of the weather. Not until the Gulf War in 1991 would United States Air Force and Navy pilots attack such heavily defended targets as they did in North Vietnam. That such men had to strictly follow guidance issued by the White House was morally wrong.[40]

During 1965 and 1966, the air war was conducted under various code names, though *Rolling Thunder* and *Linebacker* are the two monikers most associated with the bombing over North Vietnam. The bombing never yielded the results that Johnson and the air war advocates intended, perhaps because no one seemed to know exactly the objective of the bombing. The attacks seldom were made against good military targets, and the timing of the attacks never fooled anyone. It was as though Johnson, McNamara and the others never considered the concept of surprise in planning American bombing missions.[41]

Sometimes Johnson used the attacks as an incentive for the South Vietnamese government to become more efficient. Other times it was intended to be retribution for North Vietnamese attacks against American air bases or naval units. And, almost as an aside, Johnson and his advisers also thought the air attacks might force the North Vietnamese into negotiations. But the attacks started and stopped almost willy-nilly. Seldom did the decisions to stop bombing appear based on anything more than the President's gut feeling. Pilots and aircrews were sent into combat largely on whims and received respites not based on results, but rather on the mood of the occupant of the Oval Office. If there ever was a coherent policy for the conduct of the air war against North Vietnam, it was never apparent. Never in history had the United States conducted war in such a manner.

Certainly there was never any way to know what the effects of the attacks were inside North Vietnam. During this time frame, American intelligence efforts were not particularly effective at any level – tactically or strategically. The Administration remained almost paralyzed at the prospect of China entering the war. As a consequence, President Johnson refused to permit an attack on any targets that were even tangentially associated with the Chinese. But the Red Chinese Army remembered well its bruising fight against the Americans in Korea little more than a decade before, and many observers, including Al Gray, thought there was little likelihood of the Chinese seeking another confrontation with American firepower in Vietnam. Further, the Chinese and Vietnamese, while joined under the banner of international communism, were also old and bitter enemies at the national level. Indeed, during 1979 the little known Sino-Vietnamese War was fought between the two countries *after* the Americans left Vietnam; the war was short, but violent. Sadly Johnson and his national security apparatus dramatically over-estimated the Chinese risk. That, perhaps, is not surprising since Southeast Asia was never high on Secretary of State Dean Rusk's agenda. Even with over 500,000 Americans fighting in the region Secretary Rusk kept his eye on the Soviets, almost to the exclusion of other areas. Moreover, despite his tight control over the information about the war and his personal, close supervision, at the end of 1966 Johnson lost a nationally known and highly regarded potential ally for his position.

New York Times reporter Harrison Salisbury, the first regular *Times* reporter in the Soviet Union following World War II, was invited to North Vietnam in 1966. No doubt his connections with various communist officials help lay the groundwork for the invitation. In late 1966, Salisbury reported in the *Times* that the Americans were deliberately bombing civilian targets in the North. While Johnson, and right wing supporters of the war, protested loudly at Salisbury's accusation, nonetheless it was another nail in the rapidly constructing media coffin of the President of the United States. And it was surely a nail that no American President deserved. Salisbury not only had communist friends, there are suspicions that he had communist leanings himself. Some substantiation of this did not come out until his papers were researched following his death in 1993. It would have been disconcerting enough that a respected columnist from one of the country's self-proclaimed leading newspapers had hidden communist leanings, but to have it later determined that the columnist had, in fact, himself been a communist and part of that discredited cause should have been known. Salisbury's opinion would have been viewed much more critically. Even today in 2012, Americans are not ready to get their news analysis from self-proclaimed communists; they were much less likely to accept such a person in the mid-1960s.[42]

No matter how hard he tried, Johnson could not keep the left-wing followers of his vast domestic initiative – *The Great Society* – behind his war effort. And make no mistake; Johnson was devoted to his *Great Society* programs while hating every dollar he had to spend on the war. Despite LBJ's attempt to provide both guns and butter, the nation and the nation's economy suffered.[43]

MARINES IN VIETNAM, 1966

For the Marines in Vietnam, 1966 was a year that saw the tempo of operations become ever faster. Individual VC and small cells became less and less a target, while VC mainline units and the NVA become more problematic. It was still difficult to be a village elder in the countryside, especially one loyal to Saigon, because communist nighttime assassination squads remained active. In areas close to Marine enclaves, however, increased American patrolling reduced the ability of insurgents to move around during periods of darkness.

By June 1966, Generals Westmoreland and Walt could not ignore the threat posed by a full-scale NVA invasion of the northern part of I Corps, in and around the DMZ. The famed 1st Marine Division, the unit that won Guadalcanal, arrived in March, its appearance slowed by a lack of military sealift. But with more maneuver battalions available to him, General Walt moved the 3rd Marine Division north of the Hai Van Pass, with Task Force Delta and the 12th Marine Regiment (artillery) locating in and around Dong Ha, just south of the DMZ. The 1st Division was headquartered at Da Nang and was also responsible to Chu Lai. The divisions were fighting different wars. In the south, the 1st was involved in counter-insurgency and security operations, an effort that had come to almost a complete stop in the spring when the South Vietnamese Commanding General of I Corps, Lieutenant General Nguyen Chang Thi was removed. That event almost led to another coup against the Saigon government, a coup that was averted because Air Marshall Ky, serving as Prime Minister, did not blink when Thi did. Meanwhile, north of the Hai

Vann Pass, the 3rd Marine Division was doing exactly what General Westmoreland desired, seeking out and fighting with major VC and NVA units.

By the end of the year, there were more than 40,000 Marines in South Vietnam. The 26th Marine Regiment had been reactivated and all three of its infantry battalions arrived in-country during 1966. Because the Marine Corps had decided upon an individual replacement policy, i.e., instead of rotating units there would be individual replacements to satisfy personnel losses, the first (and most experienced) Marines to have landed in 1965 were rotating back to the United States beginning in March. By June, in many infantry and artillery, recon, tank and amphibious tractor battalions, and in the air wing and support units, almost all the men were new to Vietnam – including officers and Staff NCOs. Of course, a distinct minority of Marines, whose number included Major Al Gray, extended their tours of duty voluntarily, but their overall number was small. The result was, of course, that tactical lessons had to be relearned, and instead of III MAF units having two years of combat experience at the end of 1966, they had one year of experience two times.

Simultaneously with the expansion of the war was the almost 50% increase in the size of the Marine Corps. The Marine end strength went from 212,000 in 1965 to nearly 400,000 by 1969. President Johnson was dedicated to not using the military's reserve forces, so expansion of the active component was the only way to get the numbers needed to prosecute the war effort. This rapid mobilization had a profound effect on small units; instead of infantry platoons being led by a 2nd Lieutenant aided by a Staff Sergeant with about 12-14 years of experience, the platoon sergeant might be a sergeant with fewer than eight years experience. Squad leaders were no longer sergeants with more than six years in service; they were typically corporals or even lance corporals with less than four years of active duty.[44] To expedite the mobilization, boot camp was reduced by nearly 50% in duration and Infantry Training Regiments were turned into drafts for Vietnam. Inside Vietnam, rifle company commanders found that an important training goal was to ensure their Marines could shoot straight. By 1967, many of those rifle company commanders were captains with only two years of service, as opposed to the company commanders who arrived in Vietnam in 1965 with generally six years of service. President Johnson's choice to not call up the reserves had far-reaching implications for small units, and none were advantageous or in any way desirable.

By the end of 1966, many errors had been made by American and South Vietnamese decision-makers. President Johnson had put his personal imprimatur on the war. General Westmoreland had made the decision to fight big battles and get into a war of attrition without fully recognizing the extent to which Ho Chi Minh was willing to expend Vietnamese lives. The South Vietnamese could not unify behind a single leader, though by the end of 1966 President Thieu was firmly in place and many dissident generals were in exile; too often the effective and experienced military leaders who were dissenters, like General Thi in I Corps, were also removed.

But through it all, the American fighting man continued to do his duty in a faraway land under increasingly thorny conditions. Despite the personnel rotation problems, morale among Marines in Vietnam, and the Soldiers and Sailors who served with them in I Corps, was high and a can-do spirit was flourishing.

NOTES AND REFERENCES

1. Smith, Charles R. *A Brief History of the 12ᵗʰ Marines*, p 49-50.
2. Lieutenant General Leo J. Dulacki retired in 1974. A Russian linguist, he had been one of the few, if not only, Marine colonels to ever serve as the Naval Attaché in Moscow. In the early 1960s, when General Gray was building the Radio Battalions at HQMC, then Colonel Dulacki was serving in intelligence billets on the Joint Staff and then at the Defense Intelligence Agency. Dulacki well knew about Al Gray. Later, following his retirement, Dulacki and Gray would share a laugh about General Walt's reaction to having Gray assigned to the G-2. As a footnote to this footnote, in January 1966, Dulacki was assigned to be Chief of Staff of the 3ʳᵈ Marine Division. Major General Wood B. Kyle had taken command; Dulacki again thought he could bring Gray back into intelligence; Gray, of course, was then serving as the Communications Officers of the 12ᵗʰ Marines. When he approached General Kyle, Dulacki got the exact same response that General Walt had given him! General Gray had great admiration for General Dulacki, knowing that he had commanded the 1ˢᵗ Battalion, 7ᵗʰ Marines in Korea and that he served two tours at Defense Intelligence Agency. As the III MAF G-2, Dulacki had played a significant role in the planning for *Operation Starlite*, the first successful major operation against mainline VC units, which resulted in over 600 enemy killed. General Gray, in keeping with his reluctance to never mention conversations he had ever had with general officers, never told Dulacki of his discussion with General Ray Davis – the man who had called General Walt on his behalf in hopes of ensuring Gray reached a combat arms billet when Gray left HQMC in 1965. Generals Walt and Gray also had a close association after Walt's retirement. General Walt visited each of General Gray's commands after the younger man became a flag officer, and Commandant Gray visited General Walt's retirement home in Mississippi.
3. From General Gray's private collection. For the full account of Tiger Tooth Mountain, see Chapter 4.
4. General Gray videotaped interview, 12 January 2010.
5. VHF stands for Very High Frequency (30 to 300 megahertz) communications, the same as low-dial over the air television signals. VHF, Frequency Modulated (just like the FM portion of home radios) is the normal means for tactical, plain voice, military communications.
6. The Mighty Mite was smaller than a normal jeep and had only two real seats; it was designed to be helicopter-transportable by the early Marine helicopters – which had poor lift capabilities. Passengers in the rear sat on the top of the fenders supported by an aluminum "back rest" that folded up into place. It did not make for a comfortable ride. The introduction of the CH-46 and CH-53 helicopters, with their much heavier lift capabilities, mercifully killed the Mighty Mite by the late 1960s.

7. According to as reliable a source as General Creighton Abrams, the AN/PRC-25 radio was "the single most important tactical item in Vietnam."

8. From Scott Laidig's private collection.

9. In one of the many coincidences found in this book, Captain Barry was assigned to command a battery that supported 2/4 when Lieutenant Colonel Kelley was the Commanding Officer and the author was a young Lieutenant. The author met Barry on several occasions, but knew him only as "skipper." He passed away soon after this project was started, and we never got a chance to interview him for the book. At Colonel Barry's funeral, General Gray, as he normally does, got down on one knee and extended his condolences to Mrs. Liz Berry.

10. From General Gray's private collection. Letter dated August 28, 1984, from Patrick Nicolosi to Major General Alfred M. Gray, Jr.

11. Author telephone interview with Colonel Ray Becker, 2009.

12. Before and during *Operation Hastings,* the author was a platoon leader in G/2/4. Lieutenant Colonel A.E. (Gene) Bench led 2/4 north, having recently relieved Lieutenant Colonel P.X. Kelley as the Battalion Commander.

13. National Route 1, which runs from Hanoi to Saigon, was memorialized in the classic Bernard Fall book, *Street Without Joy (1961).* Fall's book should be required reading for any serious student of the Vietnam War. General Gray read the book shortly after its publication.

14. From General Gray's private collection.

15. The 2nd Battalion, 94th Artillery maintains an informative website that is full of personal accounts about 2/94, their adopted orphan, Task Force Bravo, and their service with the Marines in I Corps. http://www.2ndbattalion94thartillery.com/

16. "Laying the guns" refers to ensuring that the artillery is properly and specifically sighted and aimed. This is particularly important for 175mm guns, whose long range would easily cause casualties to friendly forces if the guns were only a little off their intended locations.

17. Interview with Lieutenant General Richard G. Trefry, U.S. Army (Ret) by the author, April 2008.

18. After his retirement, General Gray worked to award John Fanning a Distinguished Flying Cross; successful, General Gray then participated in the awards ceremony at Marine Barracks, Washington.

19. Air Medals are awarded based on the number of combat missions flown. Quick trips in helicopters do not count for anyone other than the aircrews. aerial observer missions flown over North Vietnam counted double. From October 1966 through July 1967, Gray flew innumerable aerial observer missions, and most were over North Vietnam. Lieutenant Perry, the S-1, badgered Gray to account for his air missions in order to qualify for Air Medals; Gray simply ignored the younger officer. When push came to shove, and he was about to get the air medal, Gray relied on his close friend, the Division Legal Officer, to squash the medal. That friend: Colonel Charles Beale. Author interviews with Colonel Beale, 2007-2010.

20. A "short-timer" was a person with only a little time remaining in country, after which he would rotate back to the "Land of the Big PX" – the United States. There was little reason to train short-timers in new projects or missions, because they would depart for home soon.

21. The poisonous Habu is a well known and highly respected inhabitant of Okinawa.

22. From General Gray's private collection.

23. Picture compliments of Lieutenant Colonel Jack Perry, United States Marine Corps (Ret), private collection.

24. Picture compliments of Lieutenant Colonel Jack Perry's private collection.

25. Picture compliments of Lieutenant Colonel Jack Perry's private collection.

26. From General Gray's private collection. There were a number of Americans who provided financial help to Vietnamese. Those who were able to re-establish contact

after the end of the war found that they had to send any monies to the local village (communist) chief, not directly to the people. It is one of the many signs that the people of Vietnam, while prospering as of 2012, are not free.

27. When the 3rd Marine Division moved to Phu Bai, the 1st Division moved to into the 3rd Division's former Command Post near III MAF Headquarters and the airfield at Da Nang.

28. From General Gray's private collection.

29. "Out of hide" means creating something using only one's existing assets. It is a favorite Marine expression, and typifies how the Corps gets things done.

30. Halberstam, p. 216.

31. There are many sources for information regarding McNamara. Though Halberstam, Langguth, and Karnow are generally critical toward the Secretary, Moyar has a decidedly harsher view. In the end, it is fair to say that no one admired McNamara other than a few of his closest friends. He had completely alienated the military; President Johnson had shunned him (after giving him a Medal and naming him President of the World Bank;) and the anti-war crowd viewed him as one of the principal architects of a war they hated. McNamara's memoir of the war, *In Retrospect: The Tragedy and Lessons of Vietnam* is viewed in many ways. Arthur Schlesinger, Jr., in a jacket comment, asks if anyone can recall a public figure admitting his errors and finds the account "brave, honorable, honest and altogether compelling." This author finds the book to be altogether dishonest, self-serving, and written too long after the events to represent "the truth." Furthermore, the humble, error-prone McNamara of 1995, when his book was written, is but a caricature of the bold, arrogant, all-knowing McNamara of the early 1960s. Also see McMaster.

32. Paul Dickson penned the best, near contemporary account of the "McNamara Line" and the organization that developed it. *The Electronic Battlefield*, 1976, Indiana University Press, Bloomington.

33. Dickson, Paul. *The Electronic Battlefield,* Indiana University Press, Bloomington and London, 1976. Dickson offers a very good, concise portrait of the short history of the Defense Communications Planning Group and the electronic battlefield. Established to support the McNamara Line, that the Defense Communications Planning Group was important is reflected by their budget – from 1966 to 1972 they spent over $3.1B and one year they gave the military services $678M that they could NOT spend – all in 1970 dollars! Included in the book are stories about how the Marines got the first acoustic sensors, how sensors played an important role in the battle for Khe Sanh, and how a Marine Recon team employed a "sensor ambush" to wipe out about 80 NVA. Of course, General Gray (then known far and wide by his nickname the "Gray Ghost") never appears in the book, or few other books for that matter, and so his very significant role in getting the sensors from the Defense Communications Planning Group, a super-secret organization that was disbanded about 1972, is not told. Indeed, it was the Director of the Defense Communications Planning Group, General John D. Lavelle, USAF, who personally arranged the transfer of the sensor program to the Marines, using then Lieutenant Colonel Gray as the conduit. More about that in Chapter 9, Volume 2.

34. The term body count was used in Vietnam as a means to measure success long before the arrival of the major combat units in 1965. However, as one of McNamara's primary measures, the "body count" became the source of countless reports and evaluations. As a young lieutenant in August 1966, the author was the acting company commander of G/2/4 on *Operation Prairie*. Our company was assigned the mission to provide machine gun fire to suppress enemy fire and cover the withdrawal of another company. We quickly set up on high ground overlooking the enemy position and began pouring M-60 machine gun fire towards it. On that occasion, no one in our company observed a single enemy soldier. However, the enemy activity ceased and the other company was able to move out. Our Battalion Commander determined that we should be given

credit for 13 enemies Killed in Action (KIA) (probable), though there was no way of knowing if we wounded any, or killed many more.

35. McMaster points out that President Johnson repeatedly would ask the Joint Chiefs how to "kill more Viet Cong?" For example, see p. 265-8.

36. McMaster, p.10.

37. Karnow, p. 399-400.

38. The "Gulf of Tonkin" episode, an attack by North Vietnamese torpedo boats against U.S. Navy ships operating in international waters, is generally regarded as the provocation that started the full-out war against North Vietnam. Exactly what happened is still the subject of many questions; conspiracy theorists think the event was a ruse created by the Navy to draw the United States into war. The U.S. Navy stoutly defends its analysis and reporting of the circumstances surrounding the unprovoked attack. The two primary ships involved were the destroyers USS *Maddox* and USS *Turner Joy*. The author served briefly under the Commanding Officer of the *Turner Joy*, Commander Robert Chauncey Barnhart, Jr., when he was the Captain of the USS *Jouett*, Commanding General 29, in 1970. Captain Barnhart seemed a fine and honorable gentleman, someone devoid of self-aggrandizement; it is doubtful he would have been party to a cover up or assist in generating false information.

39. W. Hayes Parks, "Rolling Thunder and the Laws of War," *Air University Review*, Vol. XXXIII, No. 2 (January-February 1982), 14. Parks was a Reserve Marine Lieutenant Colonel and Air War College expert in the Laws of War and the Air War over Vietnam. Among many teaching positions at professional military schools, he taught at the Naval War College where he became acquainted with Dr. John F. Guilmartin during the period 1984-1985. It was from Parks that Guilmartin first learned of how widely admired then Lieutenant General Alfred M. Gray was throughout the Marine Corps.

40. Dr. Guilmartin might quarrel about which pilots had the biggest cojones. As a Jolly Green Giant air rescue pilot, Guilmartin earned two Silver Stars for picking up pilots, some Air Force, some Navy, shot down over North Vietnam.

41. Larry Engelman, "The End of the Golden Chain," interviews with Brigadier General Richard Baughn (September 2009), Pushing On, http://lde421.blogspot.com/2009/09/and-edsel-genius.html. Then Colonel Baughn commanded a squadron of F-105s that flew over North Vietnam from their base in Thailand. Baughn and his contemporaries referred to President Johnson and Secretary McNamara as the "grade school teacher and the Edsel genius," references to Johnson's days teaching school and McNamara's role in the design of the Edsel. The entire series of General Baughn interviews with Dr. Engelmann makes for very interesting reading.

42. The case of Harrison Salisbury and his political motivations is disturbing. Even Stanley Karnow, no friend of the American war effort, refutes Salisbury's claims and shows they were based entirely on communist sources (Karnow, p. 489-91). Salisbury clearly demonstrated his desire to support a communist perspective in his reportage from Hanoi. That his sponsor there, the confirmed Australian communist, Wilfred Burchett, sought to undermine the American war effort there can be no doubt. And, of course, the *New York Times* gave credibility to Salisbury's reporting even if the papers' editors were unaware of his ideological motivations. Yet the "traditional" historians of the war from the Karnow, Langguth line decry government-inspired attempts to belittle Salisbury by accusing him of communist ties. Indeed, Langguth practically ridicules the accusations of Salisbury's communist connections and, instead, applauds Salisbury's reporting. Langguth, whose book was written in 2000, should have known of Salisbury's communism and that his writing represented largely, if not all, communist propaganda. Perhaps Langguth chose to ignore it, just as he ignored the role of Pham Xuan An, or perhaps Langguth has other motives (Langguth, p. 433-7). For Salisbury's relationship with Wilfred Burchett and the latter's role in influencing Salisbury's copy from Hanoi – if Burchett did not write it himself – see Robert Manne, *Agent of Influence: The Life and Times of Wilfred Burchett*, No.13, 1989 The Mackenzie Institute, Toronto, 1989.

Similarly, the effect that Pham Xuan An had on various American reporters during the war has largely been ignored by academics.

43. Irving Bernstein, *Guns or Butter: the Presidency of Lyndon Johnson*. New York: Oxford University Press, 1996. Even when the author is sympathetic to LBJ, the tragedy of his role as Commander-in-Chief comes through.

44. When the author arrived in Vietnam in February 1966, he relieved a 1st Lieutenant, Christopher C. Cooney, who became Executive Officer of Hotel Company, 2nd Battalion, 4th Marines. The next day, Lieutenant Colonel P.X. Kelley took command of 2/4. All the other platoon leaders were also 1st Lieutenants. The author was the only grunt 2nd Lieutenant in the Chu Lai complex. All the members of the platoon were combat veterans of *Operation Starlite*, where the unit had landed on top of a VC regimental headquarters. Three months later, the author was among the most experienced infantry company-grade officers in the battalion, and none of the enlisted Marines had previous combat experience except for that gained following their arrival. By *Operation Hastings* (July) all the Staff NCOs were new to Vietnam, and the author was the senior lieutenant in the battalion. There were no 1st lieutenant platoon leaders. One Captain, J.J.W. Hilgers, the author's first company commander, had extended and was the Battalion Operations Officer. However, the Battalion Commander (Lieutenant Colonel A.E. Bench), Executive Officer and other staff officers were new to Vietnam. Such was the personnel rotation cycle common to most Marine units.

CHAPTER 6

GRAY COMMANDS AT GIO LINH OUTPOST

GRAY COMMANDS AT GIO LINH OUTPOST

JUNE 1967

Major Al Gray sat in a folding chair on the roof of his command bunker; the crew-cut Major quietly listened and observed the night scene. Across a deep trench line in a large, combined Combat Operations Center/Fire Direction Center, monitoring a bank of tactical radios was a solitary radio operator, and perhaps a few as-yet-uncaught vermin. No other Marines occupied the normally crowded and often lively nerve center of the Composite Artillery Battalion, Gio Linh, Vietnam. Gray's command was located just south of the De-militarized Zone that separated North from South Vietnam. It was one of the cornerstones of Leatherneck Square, a series of four combat outposts north and west of Dong Ha that supported United States and Army of the Republic of Vietnam infantry and reconnaissance operations in northern I Corps.

Gio Linh was unique for several reasons; perhaps the most important was its location. Originally constructed by the French, and later used by the South Vietnamese, it was being considerably modified by the Seabees and Marine Corps engineers to serve as a foundation stone of the ill-conceived McNamara Line. It was the northernmost fixed American position in South Vietnam. But Gio Linh was also particularly significant to the North Vietnamese. The communists had promised in their propaganda broadcasts to destroy the American position and drive the Marines from the outpost. The North Vietnamese Army spared no effort to accomplish their goal.

During March and April 1967, Gray's unit endured over 160 casualties, including more than 60 on a single day, all the result of incoming artillery and rocket barrages. The North Vietnamese Army had great skill as artillerymen, and they had the advantages of range and mobility over the Marine artillery, even after Gio Linh was augmented by the United States Army's 175mm Guns. Airstrikes designed to silence the North Vietnamese Army batteries were rarely completely successful, and great persistence characterized the enemy operations. Gray had grappled to come up with tactics, or new defensive measures, that would blunt the relentless nightly onslaught. Finally, this night he had implemented his gambit, one whose daring he hoped would be rewarded both by improved morale and fewer losses among his men.

His chain of command, particularly those in Saigon, had objected to the measures that Gray was now undertaking. In fact, he had been specifically forbidden to attempt what his men were currently doing. But the chain of command was not present at Gio Linh, absorbing the mind-numbing, ear-shattering, morale-busting explosions that rocked the bunkers each night, inflicting casualties on both men and equipment. Gray had noted over the previous weeks that the North Vietnamese Army were not directly observing his outpost, since they already knew with unerring precision the location of each gun emplacement and bunker, and there was nothing the Free World Forces could do to alter them. Plus, good intelligence and counter-intelligence information confirmed his ideas about North Vietnamese Army tactics. Therefore, he was fairly certain, though not 100% positive, that under the cover of darkness, his men could leave their position without being detected.

While the men and equipment at Gio Linh left the outpost and carried out its mission from positions two to four miles away, Gray and his single radioman implemented their deception plan. Gray seldom conducted any operation without a well-conceived deception plan. And deception was important, given the North Vietnamese Army proficiency in signals intelligence. The Marines had to ensure that they gave no hint that they were doing anything out of the ordinary. Should the North Vietnamese Army detect that the entire garrison was outside the confines of their entrenched, well-protected positions, the possibility for even greater casualties was present. Gray, alert atop the bunker while his operator was transmitting on several radio circuits, had no active communications with his men, for they were operating under radio silence. Although the commander spent the entire night apprehensive of the possible outcome of his actions, Gray also had many reasons to believe the new tactics would be successful.

The anticipated North Vietnamese Army barrage arrived at 2200, right on schedule. That hour permitted the North Vietnamese Army units to displace in darkness to new positions while arriving in time to conduct their barrage. They then could make good their escape to new hiding places before daylight betrayed them to American spotter aircraft. The North Vietnamese pumped several hundred rounds into the Gio Linh outpost, creating a cacophony of sound but inflicting no significant damage. One gun emplacement was hit, but since neither the artillery piece nor those serving it were present, the only thing disturbed was the dirt. Thousands of sandbags present likely suffered additional holes, and many would require replacement since they were blown to smithereens.

Early in the twilight, just before the sun rose over the South China Sea, Soldiers, Sailors and Marines maneuvered back into Gio Linh, met by Major Al Gray's enthusiastic welcome, which usually meant that any unwary troops were in danger of Gray's now infamous left jabs to the shoulder or upper arm of the unsuspecting victim of his greeting! The Red Man would be in full chomp and anyone wanting a portion of chew could be sure that his Commanding Officer would provide one. The success of the new tactics represented perhaps Gray's highest personal achievement to date.

The garrison had passed their first quiet night in the many weeks, despite pumping over a thousand rounds of their own into North Vietnam. The events of the evening would be repeated regularly, although never predictably. For the next month, the Composite Artillery Battalion's total casualties – including all the other units present at the outpost – had been reduced to two. There was only one thing more important to Gray than taking care of his men and that was accomplishing his mission. That he could do both was priceless.

12ᵗʰ MARINES HEADQUARTERS, ARTILLERY PLATEAU, APRIL 1967

Al Gray had been the S-3 (Operations Officer) of the 12ᵗʰ Marine Regiment for 12 months. He also previously served as the Regimental Communications and unofficial jack-of-all trades officer following his arrival in the fall of 1965. He had been responsible, in part, for a series of innovations and refinements that added to making Marine artillery the most feared and deadly force on the battlefield. Having patiently served his time on the regimental staff, Gray had been told he was slated for duty with an infantry battalion in the summer of 1967.

His last field command had been three years earlier when he led the Marine Advisory Team 1 to Tiger Tooth Mountain and conducted special operations north of Khe Sanh, and later at the Dong Bac Ma region northwest of the Hai Van Pass. Although he had served in a lieutenant colonel's billet as S-3 of the largest artillery unit formed since World War II, Gray was still a major, and he hoped to be assigned as executive officer of an infantry battalion.

But in the northernmost I Corps, the Marines had established four fixed combat outposts that also served as artillery firebases; together these combat outposts were called Leatherneck Square. These outposts were located north and west of the key logistics base at Dong Ha, which was the southeast corner and which also served as the command post of the 12ᵗʰ Marines. Gio Linh was almost directly north of Dong Ha and was the northern and eastern most artillery anchor. Con Tien was six miles west-south-west of Gio Linh and connected to Gio Linh by the "trace," which was also was known as the McNamara Line or McNamara Wall, a strip of land 600 meters wide that had been cleared by bulldozers to remove all vegetation. The fourth outpost, Cam Lo, was located almost directly south of Con Tien and nearly due west of Dong Ha (see Map 6.1). It is important to note that the Gio Linh combat outpost is often confused with Gio Linh village complex, home to the 6ᵗʰ RVN District Headquarters, located about 4 miles to the southeast.

In addition to Leatherneck Square, Camp J.J. Carroll was established as another large, multi-force combat base; it was located about 10 kilometers southwest of Cam Lo. These bases provided interlocking fire to support each other, and they

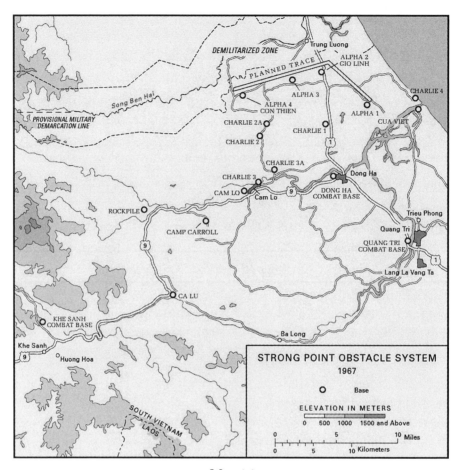

Map 6.1
Map reprinted from History and Museums Division, Headquarters,
Marine Corps series, U.S. Marines in Vietnam, 1967.

supported both American and ARVN infantry and reconnaissance operations as far west as Khe Sanh and north into the DMZ and North Vietnam. In April 1967, majors commanded the units protecting the corners of Leatherneck Square. With the exception of Gio Linh, each of the outposts was commanded by an infantry battalion organization augmented by a variety of artillery units and supporting arms: engineers, tanks, amphibian vehicles, Dusters, and Ontos units. Each outpost was loaded for bear; and rightfully so, because the bears soon came hunting.

Besides Gray, the other commanders in Leatherneck Square were Majors Donald J. Fulham, James Woodring and Ted Willis. Gray was good friends with all three and had greatest respect for their leadership and professional knowledge. Fulham, for example, had distinguished himself as Brigadier General Lowell English's G-3 with Task Force Hotel. Further, he had extended his tour to take an infantry command, 1ˢᵗ Battalion, 4ᵗʰ Marines. Gray considered Woodring to be a superb tactician. Woodring also was cool, calm and an expert marksman; when the NVA attacked his Command Post, Major Woodring actively assisted his defenders by killing several enemy with well-aimed shots from his 1911 Model Colt .45 caliber pistol. Major Ted Willis was also exceptionally competent and all three would serve together in future years.

Another important mission of the artillery was to provide support against the rapidly growing threat of North Vietnamese artillery and rockets. Since the Marines had arrived in the area around Dong Ha the previous summer, the NVA used increasingly effective mortar fire to welcome the newcomers. During the period January through early March 1967, the mortars were much more than a distraction; they were a real threat. However, a more deadly menace loomed large. In March at Gio Linh, Gray investigated a crater that he and others thought had been made by a large caliber artillery piece, or perhaps even a Soviet-made large caliber rocket. The chain of command in Saigon, however, discounted their analysis.

Al Gray had actually been in and around Gio Linh from the time the 12ᵗʰ Marines arrived at Dong Ha during the previous year. As the enemy mortar attacks gained steam, and as Gray (and many others) observed while flying Aerial Observer missions over the DMZ and southern parts of North Vietnam, the threat of artillery was increasingly obvious. The aerial observers had observed that the NVA had developed a large number of sites in depth that could be used by their artillery units across the southern reaches of North Vietnam, in that part of Quang Tri Province controlled by them. Although vacant, these positions could be occupied very easily at any time; the NVA artillery was coming and the Marines knew it. When the Commanding Officer at Gio Linh requested reassignment in mid-March, 1967, Major Gray requested and was given command of the Composite Artillery Battalion and all the U.S. forces at the Gio Linh Outpost. While he was the S-3, he had encouraged the units everywhere, and especially at Gio Linh, to prepare well-bunkered positions that would provide more protection against artillery, even though that threat had not yet materialized. In the period January through March, the NVA mortars were quite effective, but still the Marines, Soldiers and Sailors in northernmost I Corps had not experienced the far more deadly artillery or rocket attacks.[1]

When Gray took over in mid-March, his first command was very clear: "Dig!"

The Major demanded that each position go down one foot each day. Improving the defense would become a never-ending proposition for the Soldiers, Sailors and Marines of Gio Linh. Digging, filling endless stacks of sandbags, laying wire for communications between positions, reinforcing the tops of bunkers, repairing and reinforcing the tower that served as an observation post, these were the back break-ing and detail demanding tasks that filled every man's days. Of course, the gun crews continued to provide fire support throughout the area.

Gray's new operational command was extensive and complicated. In addition to always having a 175mm Gun Battery from the Army, Gray's artillery included a battery of towed Marine 105 howitzers, a battery of self-propelled Marine 8" howitzers, and a battery of Army self-propelled 105 howitzers. Augmenting the artillery was a reinforced platoon of Marine tanks, a company of Army M42 self-propelled anti-aircraft guns called "Dusters," and at least a platoon of Marine Ontos vehicles – each of which carried six 106 recoilless rifles. At least one reinforced Marine rifle company was deployed around the perimeter. In addition, because of Gio Linh's position along the "McNamara Line" or trace, the outpost was usually home to major elements of two Marine engineer battalions and Seabees, whose equipment greatly assisted when Gray gave his order to "dig." The tanks, which had plenty of ammunition, were also employed to assist in *Operation Highrise*. Ramps were built and the tanks elevated their guns to their highest point and fired along with the artillery. Although these disparate units were under Gray's operational control, he did not have administrative authority.

Since his was a "Composite Battalion," Gray had no regular staff officers. Men like Marine Captains Pat Pate, Glen Golden, Steve Gimber, and E.L. Cody, as well as Army Lieutenant Doug Beard were assigned to the Composite Battalion from other units, and they rotated every month or so. Consequently, Al Gray worked with a succession of staff during his nearly four-month stay at Gio Linh. Given the lack of water and the fact that supplies had to run the gamut of NVA artillery to reach the outpost, combined with the mission to fire 1,000 rounds into North Vietnam, Gray was up to his neck in logistics as well as operations.

Yet there was another aspect to Gray's assignment as Commander, Composite Artillery Battalion and Free World Forces, Gio Linh. The "Free World Forces" were the 2nd Infantry Regiment of the 1st ARVN Division that was located just east of Gio Linh, responsible for the area all the way to the coast. Fortunately, Al Gray's old friend from the Khe Sanh District in 1964, Vu Vien Giai, who was now a Lieutenant Colonel, commanded the ARVN unit. Another acquaintance from the Tiger Tooth Mountain expedition, Colonel Ngo Quang Truong, the G-3 of the 1st ARVN Division, remained in close personal contact with Gray, making coordination with the Vietnamese nearly seamless. Neither Vietnamese officer had the slightest difficulty of the ARVN regiment being under the operational control of the Marine Major. In fact, their respect for and trust in Al Gray was demonstrated when Giai disclosed that he had an agent buried in a local VC cell. By sharing that information with Gray, the allies were able to capitalize on the agent's intelligence. The communists may have had informers among the ARVN units, but at Gio Linh in early 1967, Gray knew the ARVN intelligence apparatus was also functioning well.

Giai's openness gave Gray confidence to make important decisions involving the local ARVN. Besides Giai being a close friend, the U.S. Army advisor, also a major, assigned to the 6th District Headquarters at Gio Linh village, was a fine officer who worked well with the Commanding Officer of Free World Forces, Gio Linh Outpost. Their relationship was solid despite the obtuse chains of command that could have easily thwarted cooperation and mutual support. The ARVN reported up their chain; and the U.S. Army advisors operated independently of the local American tactical units and had their own chain of command. It was a confusing situation and made command and control far too difficult. Nonetheless, the trio established a very active and very effective counter-intelligence operation in and around Gio Linh and throughout the area. All that gave Gray a high level of confidence that he knew what was happening outside the wire at night. In return, the Army advisor and the officers and men at the 6th District Headquarters knew Gray's people would support them as needed.

By the late spring of 1967 the menace of NVA artillery was more than just an intelligence item; it was a verified hazard that had inflicted real casualties on the Marines. On April 18, 1967, the spectacular craters created during an attack against Camp Carroll drew gasps, and more, from no less a combat veteran than Lieutenant General Lewis A. Walt, the Commanding General, III Marine Amphibious Force (III MAF). When Lieutenant Colonel Richard Trefry, the commander of the 2/94, reported that crater analysis indicated that his unit had been attacked by a very large caliber weapon, and an unexploded portion of a shell casing seemed to be part of a new Soviet rocket system, Walt had jumped aboard his helicopter and headed for Camp Carroll. When shown the crater, the General's reaction was the same as any average Soldier or Leatherneck, "Holy shit!"[2]

That same night the outpost at Gio Linh had been hit very hard by North Vietnamese artillery. The attacks represented the first large-scale use of artillery and rockets against American forces during the war and would pre-date the siege against the Marine strongpoint at Khe Sanh. The first battle at Khe Sanh began in the spring and continued through the summer of 1967. Threats heightened again in the late fall. In December, Khe Sanh would become the site of one of the most famous battles of the war. The NVA attacks of April 18, 1967, were every bit as savage.

The North Vietnamese were clearly capable of outgunning the Marines prior to the arrival of the Army's big guns. And even with 2/94's effectiveness, the artillery exchanges were never lopsided affairs. Yes, the North Vietnamese were very able artillerymen. For example, they often fired late in the afternoon when the sun's reflection would mask their muzzle flashes, making it nearly impossible for the Marines to detect their positions. And, as Gray was to learn personally, their night firing – which seemed to always involve changing positions – was very effective.

The Marine casualties at Gio Linh had shocked Colonel William R. Morrison, the new Commanding Officer of the 12th Marines, but he knew that if his former S-3 had not begun the preparations in expectation of artillery, not mortar, attacks, the personnel losses would have been even greater. The position was the northernmost, fixed American location in South Vietnam, and yet the Marines there were not yet well entrenched. Identified as the northeast underpinning for the McNamara Line, Gio Linh enjoyed spectacular views in every direction, especially north across the Ben Hai River into North Vietnam. Further, although the Marines could not operate inside North Vietnam, they could attack by fire any targets they found there. The artillery could reach almost 14 miles into the North, attacking troop concentrations and supply lines leading south. Plus, daily (usually nightly) harassment and interdiction fires were designed keep the enemy from massing north of the DMZ. In Morrison's mind, however, not enough had been done earlier to protect the artillerymen at Gio Linh.[3]

Earlier in the year, MAC(V) had passed on to III MAF another mission for the 12th Marines designated *Operation Highrise.* Gio Linh and especially the long-range 175mm guns of the Army's 2/94, often augmented by naval gunfire from U.S. Navy ships offshore were primarily responsible for *Highrise.* The mission was to fire 1,000 rounds each day into North Vietnam and the DMZ.

Highrise was the brainchild of the MAC(V) Commander, General Westmoreland. Westmoreland was a World War II artilleryman, and he was intent in striking the NVA any way he could. The primary reason that the chain of command was not receptive to Gray's tactical innovations was their fear that the result might detract from the *Highrise* mission.

Among the keys to *Highrise* were the Army's longest firing artillery weapons that had arrived in I Corps in the late fall of 1966; these guns could shoot a 174-pound projectile up to 34 kilometers, thus reaching far into North Vietnam. They also provided the range needed to support the Marine outpost at Khe Sanh from the 2/94's headquarters at Camp Carroll. But as the Marine artillery in northern I Corps was being beefed up, the enemy was not waiting idly. And after their initial attacks in mid-April, the incoming fire from the NVA was regular and seemingly incessant.

There was little time for being bored or scared, though the incoming barrages created unsettled nerves among the defenders. The combination of personnel casualties and equipment losses created a situation that was so severe that units assigned to Gio Linh usually spent no more than 30 days there. Even arriving at the outpost was a surreal experience. Often Marines or Soldiers who had been in other parts of Vietnam, or even other areas of I Corps, simply were stunned when they first got to Gio Linh, where NVA artillery usually took time to give the new arrivals a cruel welcome. This account, from Army Lieutenant Greg Smith, portrays the raw emotion that met newcomers:

*Account by Lieutenant Greg Smith, C Battery FDO,
regarding the displacement to Gio Linh*

"*Since C Battery followed B and D Batteries, by the time it was our turn, the NVA artillery, rocket, and mortar batteries had precise firing data to every target up there. Captain Mc Cord, CO, lead the convoy in his jeep. I do not remember his jeep driver's name, but he was probably the biggest guy in the Battery* [height and bulk]. *I had a good view of everything with my head out of the hatch of the FDC APC. We were hit right as we started to turn into the Gio Linh outpost off Highway 1.*

However, the aforementioned driver of the CO's jeep jumped out and dove in a ditch when the rounds started coming in. The problem was that he left the jeep right in the middle of the road going in and effectively prevented the entire convoy from moving, and we were strung out along the road.

After a minute or two, Captain McCord had to get back in the jeep and drive it out of the way himself so that we could get the guns and FDC into the outpost.

Once in, Lieutenant Andy Tenis was busy trying to get the guns into position and laid and I was trying to get the FDC track in and the FDC set up. Obviously there's a potential for a certain amount of chaos and confusion anytime a firing battery moves into a new position, but doing so while receiving artillery incoming was particularly stressful.

I remember standing outside the FDC bunker, watching shrapnel from the incoming rounds kick up dirt around me and heard it ping off the metal of the used powder canisters that were used to shore up the bunkers, when Captain Hiser [Captain Hiser had been the Officer Candidate School Artillery instructor at Fort Sill] *came up on the side of me. He must have noticed the stunned look on my face as I stood there, almost overwhelmed by the sheer terror of the Gio Linh environment, when he came up right next to me and shouted "Candidate Smith!"; just like back in OCS. That quickly snapped me back to reality (I think I even instinctively came to attention). Then he offered a few words of encouragement, smiled, shook hands, and said, "It's All Yours, I'm Leaving." I believe that was the last time I saw Captain John Hiser."*[4]

Indeed, the enemy considered their artillery attacks so successful that they are mentioned in the *Victory in Vietnam: Official History of the People's Army of Vietnam, 1954-1975*. Seldom can the reader associate events in American histories of the war with those in the translation of the NVA's accounts; the artillery and mortar attacks of March and early April are an exception. Ho Chi Minh was so excited that he personally commended the artillery units involved. Ho's words in describing his artillery forces, "legs of bronze and shoulders of iron, fight well and fire accurately" became the slogan of the artillery branch of the NVA. Nonetheless, reading *Victory in Vietnam* and comparing it to the known – and well-reported – events on the ground, cause any reader to realize that the NVA document is much more propaganda tool than it is an accurate accounting of the war.[5] That is not to say, however, that the NVA artillery in particular was not as effective as the book claimed – it was!

Those involved with firing 1,000 rounds each day into North Vietnam needed little additional tasking in order to keep busy. Thus, the men in the firing batteries and the tankers had no problem burning their calories; they were always extremely active. The infantrymen, however, lived a rather melancholy existence most days. Other than digging, filling sandbags, improving their bunkers, and hurling verbal jousts at the artillerymen, there was not much for the infantry to do during daylight hours. When not digging or filling, they tried to relax by improving their suntans, reading and re-reading letters from home. At night, the infantry was responsible for manning listening posts outside the perimeter.[6] Manning a listening post with the enemy near about was tense enough, but manning a listening post while also on the receiving end of nightly artillery or rocket barrages was particularly stressful for the grunts. Indeed, even getting to the listening post was an adventure at Gio Linh, since

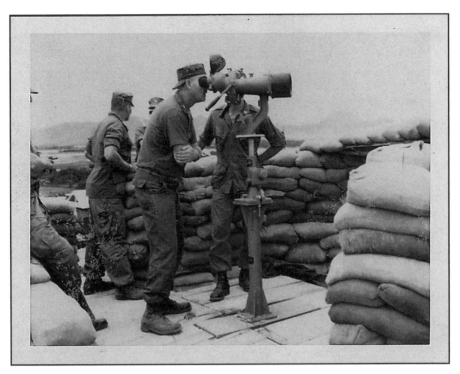

Figure 6.1
Col Benjamin Read, Commanding Officer of the 12th Marines,
peers into North Vietnam during a visit to Gio Linh.[7]

poorly mapped minefields ringed the outpost. Some of the mines dated to French days, the South Vietnamese had placed others, and finally the Marines added their own. Gio Linh was a prominent position and clearly a good one for artillery, and mines were an important defensive measure for any military's fixed positions.

Night passage of a minefield, even one laid by friendly forces, is a cheek-puckering experience to even the most hardened veteran, but given that tours of duty in Vietnam seldom extended past 13 months (and then only on a voluntary basis) few grunts were combat-hardened in 1967. And since the grunts regularly rotated in and out of Gio Linh every 30 days or so, no one became intimately familiar with the minefields. Adding to the complexity, incoming artillery often blew to bits the markers used to designate routes for safe passage, making activity in and around, but definitely through the minefields, even more perilous.

Major Gray was busy keeping the nearly 900 Marines, Soldiers and Sailors focused on improving their defenses while also honing their artillery skills to increase effectiveness. In addition, the need for secure, reliable communications with the 12th Marines at Dong Ha required his constant attention. Surprisingly, given all the work ongoing at Gio Linh, Gray still maintained the astonishing pace he had set for himself as the Regimental Operations Officer. He still flew Aerial Observer missions several times a week; and often special couriers from the III MAF staff visited him, asking for his interpretation of various intelligence reports, particularly that from the Special Intelligence sources that he had become so associated with during previous assignments. The fact that Gray was no longer located near the Division Headquarters meant his presence at the Commanding General's daily briefings was no longer possible. But his counsel was still sought no matter where he was located; that aspect of his assignment never changed.

The new Commanding General of III MAF, Robert E. Cushman, had replaced General Walt in June. Cushman, Gray's old boss from the G-2 section at HQMC, retained the habit of running intelligence information and activities by Al Gray in order to get the younger officer's assessment. Once General Cushman sent up a working paper that addressed the possibility to jamming NVA ground communications, and asked Major Gray to analyze the situation. Gray knew very well that American ground units "could not jam their thumb," and wrote that on the report. Further, Gray knew that it was more important to listen and learn than it was to try to disrupt enemy communications – an attempt he felt doomed to failure at the outset. General Cushman took his advice, and the issue of jamming went away, much to NSA's delight and the Army's regrets. It had been an ill-advised U.S. Army plan to do active EW in I Corps.

As for still flying aerial observer missions while in command at Gio Linh, there was considerable method to Gray's apparent madness. By analyzing the attacks on Gio Linh that were the result of rockets or large caliber artillery, Gray was able to fly over the likely firing positions and thereby try to discern what the NVA used to select such positions. Then, carefully plotting the known firing positions along with those he discovered might be used in the future, the resulting picture gave the Marines an excellent basis for targets for Gio Linh's outgoing Harassment and Interdiction Fires. Since his orders – perhaps ill-conceived – were to fire 1,000 rounds a day into North Vietnam, Gray's men had plenty of ammunition to shoot at the suspected targets. The NVA revealed after the war that artillery was the American weapons system that they most feared. Surely the professional, continuing efforts of all the American aerial observers added to their discomfort.

Gray recalled flying over Khe Sanh during the early battle there. This was before the siege that grabbed national and international attention, when the NVA sought to duplicate their success against the French at Dien Bien Phu. While the first battle for Khe Sanh was less well known, to participants it was just as lively. One day as Gray circled overhead he received a radio call from one of the battalion commanders in the fight. Sure enough Gray recognized the voice as that of his good friend, "Billy Mpool". Billy realized it was Al Gray and soon the callsigns were dropped in favor of first names as Bill and Al conducted their deadly business. The Air Force had seven layers of attack aircraft stacked high above, ready to deliver their lethal cargo atop the attacking NVA regulars. Soon, the aerial observer, Al Gray, helped deliver several sticks of bombs in support of Lieutenant Colonel William Masterpool's 3rd Battalion, 4th Marines. At the height of the battle, Gray flew twice a day over Khe Sanh.

Speaking of ammunition and 1,000 rounds a day ordered fired into North Vietnam, the effort needed to sustain Gio Linh was a logistics challenge of the first order. Almost everything had to be trucked from Dong Ha to Gio Linh, a relatively short, 7-mile drive up Route 1. But it took numerous truck loads just to supply the artillery ammunition, and that did not count the transportation needed for regular supplies – food, water, building materiel, medical supplies and the like. And there was a major issue that greatly exacerbated the entire issue – the NVA were fond of firing artillery or mortars at the resupply trucks just as they got to Gio Linh. On one occasion they scored a direct hit on one of 2/94's trucks that was filled with 175mm ammunition. The resulting explosion was quite memorable, though the Soldiers involved escaped serious injury by jumping from the truck and running toward the direction of the firing.[8] Adding to the complexity of the resupply effort, sometimes the VC would try to ambush any resupply convoy operating at night between Dong Ha and Gio Linh. The 2/94 chroniclers reported several such attacks.

Something that non-artillery people seldom consider was the firing life of the gun barrels. For 175mm guns, their barrel life was quite short when they fired ranges that required a maximum charge (Charge 3). Given the frequency that the artillerymen fired their guns, which is to say very, very often, the 27-foot barrels required replacement after every 300 rounds. Needless to say, Gio Linh soon had spent 175mm barrels to use for reinforcing for bunkers and storage areas. Each barrel had to be brought into Dong Ha via the river, then transported to Gio Linh (or the other outposts in Leatherneck Square) by the 2/94 Service Battery. Soon after the Army units arrived, the sight of several gun barrels rolling down Route 1 or out Route 9 was commonplace. It became just another of the myriad of logistics considerations that were lost on most men who served in Vietnam. But there was no doubt that without the hard work of the truck drivers, supply people and logisticians, the war could never have been prosecuted as well as it was.

But if anyone wondered about having to worry only about enemy activity, consider this. One of the 2/94 lieutenants responsible for resupply to the outpost made this entry on the unit's official website:

Account by Lieutenant Martin McKnight of Service Battery

"Here is one for the record books. I got a speeding ticket at Dong Ha. One afternoon, I got a call that 175 ammo was needed at Gio Linh. I did some quick calculations and knew we were going to get back close to dark. I told everyone it would be a hurry up job. We rushed to the ammo dump, loaded up, and headed north. Before we got off base, I was pulled over and given a speeding ticket by a Marine. What a way to run a war! We did make it back slightly before dark."[9]

But make no mistake; while getting speeding tickets trying to delivery ammo might have been funny, the support provided by the large range Army artillery was certainly no laughing matter. Indeed, it was crucial not only in saving many recon patrols or others who found themselves in harm's way far from any other form of fire support, but also the 175mm gun batteries were decisive against NVA batteries and rockets that may well have overpowered Marine artillery had the Army units not been in northern I Corps. Yes, much as the Soldiers admired the courage and resourcefulness of the Marines, the Marines in the know realized that they had a large debt owed to 2/94 and Task Force Bravo. General Lew Walt personally commended those units on many occasions.

GIO LINH OUTPOST, REPUBLIC OF VIETNAM, 27 APRIL 1967

In the weeks since Major Gray had arrived, the defensive positions in and around Gio Linh were several feet deeper, the bunkers more protected and the trench lines offered more shielding for the men. But the fruits of their labors were severely tested on the night of April 27, when a prolonged North Vietnamese artillery attack hit the outpost.

It had not taken the North Vietnamese artillery long to adapt to the presence of the U.S. Army's huge 175mm guns. Indeed, as they had displayed throughout the war, the NVA was nothing if not adaptable. They had learned that if they unleashed their attacks from within 5,000 meters of the 175mm batteries, those batteries could not be used to shoot counter-battery fires, because of a danger close situation.[10] Left to defend the base at close ranges was Charlie Battery, 1st Battalion, 12th Marines (C/1/12).

As the Soldiers of D/2/94 looked on, unable to fire their weapons, the Marines of C/1/12 gave back as good as they were receiving, and they were being hit extremely hard by at least two batteries of NVA artillery, who knew the Marine positions with precise detail.[11] After some time was spent locating the enemy, the Marines counter-battery fire was effective in ending the barrage, but not before C/1/12 had suffered nearly 80 casualties and the loss of all but one of their 105mm howitzers – though that sturdy weapon was still firing only because the Marines had placed lumber under the barrel so that it was supported and still able to be used. The Soldiers marveled at the Marines dedication to their duty, a fresh man filling in immediately when someone became a casualty. Some guns had been repaired more than once as gun crews struggled to keep their battery in action.

Marine artillery, indeed all artillery, is fond of describing itself as *"The Queen of Battle, adding dignity to what would otherwise be a vulgar brawl."* Nothing is further from the truth. Anyone on the receiving end of a well aimed, purposeful, and deliberate artillery barrage would never use the word "dignity" as part of his description of the incident. In fact, just the opposite is true. Courage has many descriptions, and many manifestations, but at least as impressive as any is the conduct demonstrated by artillerymen while they themselves are under fire. During any infantry action, except for an assault or during moments of sheer panic when the combat occurs at close quarters and resembles a free-for-all rather than a planned attack, the individual grunt is usually low to the ground and perched behind any cover he can find, be it a rock, a tree, a gravesite, or a ditch. Sometimes even rice stalks hide the combatants from the aimed-fire of their enemy. But normally artillerymen work in gun pits, with no overhead cover of any kind.

Sure, there are usually (always in fixed sites) sandbags or other protection around the periphery of the gun pit, but there is nothing overhead to protect the men and their guns; and, after all, incoming fire comes from overhead. So the men toil as explosions occur all around them. They can never be sure that the next round will not land directly on top of them; they are also uncertain as to the well being of their friends and compatriots in nearby pits, though the sounds of outgoing rounds can hardly be missed. One thing makes the experience tolerable – they have their own job to do. They have no time to ponder *what if* or worry about being killed, or perhaps worse, maimed. They do their duty and work like banshees. Their adrenaline rush augments their already well-conditioned bodies and they can maintain an aggressive pace all day long if needed. And artillerymen know – at least they hope – that their efforts are causing their enemies at least as much pain and suffering as is being inflicted on them.

During the attack of April 27, Gio Linh suffered more than 80 personnel casualties – almost one man in every ten was wounded and several were killed. Nonetheless, the units there accomplished their mission and they were ready for action the next day. The combined efforts of the various interlocking outposts of Leatherneck Square defeated the NVA attack on Gio Linh, just like it defeated every other major attack in I Corps, thanks to the effort demonstrated by every Soldier, Sailor and Marine. Yet few were awarded medals for their valorous conduct. Indeed, perhaps the bravest acts went unnoticed and perhaps those who performed the most courageous of acts died in anonymity, which is why most medals for valor awarded to individuals really reflect the heroism of all who participated.

One Soldier who was not anonymous and whose heroic conduct did not go unnoticed was Staff Sergeant Hubert Cornett of 2/94. During an incoming barrage, one of the 175mm gun pits suffered a direct hit. Cornett was the motor sergeant for "C" Battery and had just completed an overhaul of the hydraulic system of one of the guns when a second gun took a direct hit. The artillery piece was afire and there were explosions going off all around. The powder charges of the 175mm guns are nearly six feet long and weigh 150 pounds, and when pieced by hot, burning metal they can turn into an improvised explosive device, which in turn could cause the 175mm shell canisters to explode. Cornett jumped on the burning gun and put out the fire, even while more incoming continued to explode nearby. His efforts prevented a much larger disaster. Al Gray pushed hard to have the Soldier decorated appropriately. It was something the officers and men of 2/94 long remembered about the Marine Major under whose command all were happy to serve, despite the circumstances at Gio Linh.[12] Al Gray took care of all his men, it made no difference which uniform they wore or even what country they called their own.[13] Gray was able to assist in the recognition Staff Sergeant Cornet received because he had personally observed the action. In many other cases, the fact that Gray had operational control, but not administrative control, of the units made following through on well-earned awards much more difficult, even impossible.

However, there were other distractions besides being shot at nearly 24-hours a day.

One day in early May, Gray got a call that "thousands of refugees are coming down Route 1 from North Vietnam." The order from higher headquarters was to stop these civilians at any cost. Major Gray, located at the northernmost fixed site along Route 1, was charged with that responsibility. On this occasion, as well as several others, Gray's close ties with the ARVN came in handy. Gray's friend, the Commanding Officer of the 2nd ARVN Regiment, Lieutenant Colonel Giai, thought that there was a good chance that the civilians were, in fact, refugees, though neither he nor Gray doubted the possibility of some communist or NVA agents in the crowd. Gray went to the bridge on the Ben Hai River that marked the boundary between North and South Vietnam and met Giai there. An adequate security force, including several machine guns, took up positions nearby. But it seemed apparent that these really were civilian refugees. Their clothing was pitiful, they were wailing in a manner most Americans observed sooner or later in the tour in South Vietnam, and they had children with them, lots of children.

Al Gray decided on the spot that there was no way he could simply shoot such people, and so he and the ARVN developed and implemented a plan to search every fourth or fifth person. They found nothing, of course, and the refugees were eventually herded into camps south of Dong Ha. It was a hard decision for a major, acting against orders, to make. But Gray well remembered seeing refugees in Korea, and he recalled his time on Tiger Tooth Mountain with the old Master Sergeant who had led his company south in the early 1960s. As far as Al Gray ever knew, there were no repercussions because of his refusal to follow orders. The American and ARVN forces did everything to help these mostly Catholic refugees who had been driven out of the North by the oppressive communist regime. The newcomers were settled into refugee camps located in rear areas.

GIO LINH OUTPOST, REPUBLIC OF VIETNAM, 8 MAY 1967

The North Vietnamese had mounted a formidable assault on Con Tien (Hill of Angels) during the night of 6-7 May. The defenders were hard pressed. A key aspect of the defensive plan of the 3rd Marine Division was the interlocking, mutually supporting artillery outpost locations just south of the DMZ, implemented while Al Gray was the S-3 of the Artillery Regiment. As a result, Gio Linh was a vital part of both providing close artillery support around Con Tien, but also for firing counter-battery fires against NVA artillery that could be located. On that fateful day, the Composite Artillery Battalion, Gio Linh, would fire more than 4,000 rounds, while simultaneously being on the receiving end of nearly 3,000 rounds of incoming fire. Imagine: outgoing fire averaged more than 167 rounds per hour for 24 hours, though actually the fire was more concentrated and not spread uniformly across the entire day. And while 167 rounds were sent down range every hour, the Marines, Soldiers and Sailors at Gio Linh were on the receiving end of 125 rounds per hour. Nothing like it had been seen since the artillery duels during the Battle of Okinawa in World War II.

The NVA attack against the outpost's Marine 105mm howitzer battery resulted in more than 60 wounded; all the wounded occurred in the firing pits as the Marines were firing their guns. Most the guns of the battery were heavily damaged and needed replacing. The attacks of late April and early May proved that the Americans were not the only combatants skilled at planning artillery assaults; the NVA knew equally well how to fire suppressing fires in support of their ground attacks.

The artillery duels of April 27 and May 8 compelled Major Al Gray to renew his thinking about how to best counter the nightly barrages his men experienced, while still carrying out his mission to fire 1,000 rounds a day into North Vietnam. His eventual course of action reflected another form of the courage different from that his artillerymen displayed when engaged in an artillery duel with their foes. Although his men had performed magnificently while under daily incoming barrages, Gray fretted about the large number of casualties that Gio Linh had suffered. Like all commanders, he hated casualties. He was concerned about the future success of the mission unless he could find a way to reduce the injuries to his men while still accomplishing his mission.

Al Gray discerned that the only way to really escape the incoming fires would be to change the position of his firing batteries, but moving Gio Linh outpost was not possible. Not only was it a lynchpin of the McNamara Line, but also it was the best artillery firing position in its immediate vicinity. But what about maneuvering out of Gio Linh, firing, and then returning before the enemy realized what was happening? Gray took time to carefully draft a plan that would do what he envisioned and passed it up the chain of command for endorsement. Although the higher Marine commands liked the plan, approval was denied in Saigon.

The plan had been relatively simple. Gray had proposed that all the units in Gio Linh would be formed into a task force. After sunset, and before the nightly NVA barrage arrived, the task force would move out of the outpost and take up preplanned positions east or west, usually two to four miles away. The proposed firing position, as well as the route of march, had been carefully studied and calculated. The task force would set up in a defensive perimeter, with the infantry screening the artillery and tanks. Once everyone was in their assigned position, they would proceed to fulfill a portion of the evening's planned fires and then move again to new firing positions. An hour or so before dawn, when the NVA were typically inactive, the task force would return to Gio Linh. Of course, if caught in the open away from their trench lines, sandbags and bunkers, the Americans might take some casualties, but that was already happening. But Gray's risk assessment concluded that discovery by the NVA was not likely. The NVA had no need to observe Gio Linh and direct fires onto targets there. Gio Linh was on every map of South Vietnam dating back to before World War II. Without observers, so long as the Americans maintained radio silence, the NVA would have little ability to detect the movement, at least as Al Gray figured. Those far to the rear had made a different calculation. And Gray's knowledge of the local VC/NVA capabilities from his work with Major Giai further supported his impending decision. As a result of those factors, Gray was certain that the commander on-site was better qualified to make a local, tactical decision, and he did.

When the nightly incoming barrages continued, Gray decided that he had to act, whether he received permission or not. Captain Pat Pate was a young artilleryman who served as Gray's S-3 for the Composite Artillery Battalion. He had worked closely with Gray to develop the plan sent earlier to the chain of command. Now Gray turned to him to finalize the details of the plan, but with a twist. Gray knew that a critical part of the preparation was the deception plan. It was a key for many reasons, but not the least being the effectiveness of the North Vietnamese SIGINT efforts against Free World Forces. Gio Linh had long been a one of the most important targets not only of North Vietnamese artillery and rockets, but also Ho Chi Minh's propaganda efforts pinpointed Gio Linh as a focal point. And while Gray was supremely confident that officers like Captain Pate could perform the artillery operations effectively, he knew that few American officers anywhere had conducted deception actions.

The deception would have to be carried out from Gio Linh. Normal radio chatter on normal radio frequencies, all emanating from Gio Linh, would have to continue throughout the night, otherwise Gray realized that enemy direction finding could quickly discover that the occupants of the outpost had moved. So while Task Force Pate operated under strict radio silence, Gray and his lone radio operator enthusiastically chattered away all night, just as they would have if everyone had been there with him. He also coordinated his operations with the 2nd ARVN Regiment activities as well as Gio Linh District Headquarters, another ARVN organization, which was located about three miles south of the Gio Linh Outpost. These combined efforts greatly enhanced the probability of success.

The operation could not have gone more smoothly. The Marines, Soldiers, and Sailors had a morale boosting adventure that took them away from the nightly onslaught. Most importantly, for the first time in several months, the men of Gio Linh had worked and then slept under the stars, uninterrupted by incoming artillery. The mission had been accomplished when all planned fires were sent into North Vietnam on time and on schedule, in accordance with a plan developed by Captain Pate and approved by Major Gray. When Pate ordered his men to form into a column to return to Gio Linh before sunrise, there to be met by a jubilant Al Gray, all knew something special had taken place. The men knew exactly why Gray had taken such a significant risk to leave the fortifications of their semi-permanent home. After all, the higher commands had already determined that 30 nights at Gio Linh was about all normal men could withstand. But nights like this past one, while it kept the men busy and on edge, was in fact restful, and went far to boost morale.

Meeting Al Gray when he was more exuberant than normal could be injurious to one's health. Major Gray had always been physical and loved to jab, some would say punch, troops in the arm or shoulder while extolling their accomplishments. But no one complained of any abuse; indeed, Gray's methods created close relationships between him and his men. That he usually would also provide a chew for those needing a refill was just icing on the cake. Gray was consistently positive and inspiring to his men, though that was not always the case with his respect to his officers. While he was quick to praise, he also usually did it in such a way as to leave no doubt that things could have been done better and more professionally.

In early May, Major Gray also received welcomed help for his FDC when 1st Lieutenant Douglas Beard, United States Army, arrived at Gio Linh. Lieutenant Beard had flown as an Aerial Observer with Gray, working out of the artillery headquarters at Dong Ha. The young Army artilleryman was in awe of the Marine Major, thinking Gray to be the most outstanding leader that he had ever served with. When Colonel William Morrison, Commanding Officer of the 12th Marines, approached Beard about trading flying and leaving his relatively safe – grunts would even say posh – cot in Dong Ha to go to Gio Linh and live in an insect-infested bunker, subjected to endless hours of incoming fire, the Lieutenant jumped at the opportunity. Despite the promised deprivations, he looked forward to being reunited with Major Gray. Beard enjoyed flying and thought himself to be a very capable aerial observer, but his admiration for Major Gray knew no bounds. He packed and left immediately for Gio Linh.[14]

Al Gray quickly gave the Army lieutenant a hurried indoctrination course on FDC operations and procedures, and within days of his arrival Lieutenant Beard was directing actions on a nightly basis. Of course, he remained closely observed by his mentor, since Gray seldom was far from the Fire Direction bunker when anything of significance was happening. But Gray was the penultimate teacher, more than filling the role first identified as important for Marine officers by Commandant John A. Lejeune more than 40 years before, a role Al Gray and other officers took very, very seriously.[15] Predictably, Gray gave his subordinates lots of room to grow and expand their professional capabilities. Mistakes were tolerated so long as they did not involve loss of life or equipment, but also each error would be carefully and tactfully corrected, so that the officer (or NCO) was not likely to repeat it in the future. Among the important lessons to be learned at Gio Linh, being alert in one's surroundings was arguably the most important.

It was a brave, and usually new, man to Gio Linh who did not keep at least one ear cocked for the distinctive, distant sound that would alert the base to incoming mortar, artillery or rocket fire. When such a sound was heard, men rushed into covered positions. Here is one account of this experience:

Account by Lieutenant Greg Smith, USA, 2/94 C Battery FDO at Gio Linh:

> *"I think everyone has a ton of memories about Gio Linh. That was the most unbelievable month of the whole tour. I remember the line of guys outside Captain McCord's tent at Dong Ha the day before we went, pleading not to go.*
>
> *I remember the officer calls that Marine Major Al Gray held outside, with Major Gray sitting relaxed in his lawn chair smoking a cigar and the rest of us sitting on the front 3 inches of our chairs with one ear cocked for that 'sound' from the north that told you there was 2 or 3 seconds to get down before the round came in. One time we were attacked during an officers call and Gray just got up and walked (not ran) to his bunker puffing on his cigar, while the rest of us dove for cover and looked up at him from a ditch…"*[16]

Unfortunately, the sound of the incoming rounds was not always heard. One reporter found himself nearly a casualty, when he, Major Gray and many others were caught outside as an NVA barrage struck Gio Linh. The American artillery was in the process of firing their daily 1,000 rounds into North Vietnam, and the noise generated by the outgoing fire masked the distinctive "pops" that signaled the fact that enemy artillery or mortars were firing. As Lieutenant Smith described above, hearing that noise meant running for cover for most the Gio Linh community. Of course, that did not include the artillerymen who were manning their guns, they continued firing unabated, though perhaps their target changed.

Gray was still patched up from a wound received earlier on May 12, when he was wounded by shell fragments throughout his back and head, and was concussed by an incoming round. However, on May 14, during the late morning hours, while Gray was speaking with a reporter, one of many NVA rounds slammed into the command bunker, penetrating several feet of sandbags before exploding. The sandbags absorbed most the shell fragments, but the blast of the round knocked over the reporter and threw Al Gray across a trench several feet from where he had been standing. The reporter, Jim G. Lucas of the *Washington Daily News*, observed Gray as the Marine arose and tried to speak. Although Gray's lips were moving, no sound was heard. Either Lucas's hearing was momentarily deafened by the concussion from the blast, or Al Gray was temporarily discombobulated.[17] Far more seriously, however, the barrage killed several Marines and several others were seriously wounded. Lucas described how the men at the guns later increased their volume of outgoing fire, in part to cover the arrival of helicopters that had come to carry the wounded to field hospitals or perhaps to the USS *Comfort* Hospital Ship located offshore. The wounded would be quickly loaded and the aircraft would depart as soon as possible, hoping their presence was not used as motivation for the NVA to send more rounds down range.

No one could know when the NVA might decide to send another barrage toward the Americans. Left unreported was any finding of the accuracy or effectiveness of the outgoing fire; the NVA, on the other hand, had used their knowledge of Gio Linh location combined with their hidden firing position to strike the Allies at a vulnerable time. But one thing was consistent; the NVA always seemed to attack whenever a new unit arrived – a new artillery battery or a new infantry company – and their artillery or rocket barrages often arrived simultaneously with American resupply convoys. Lucas used a quote attributed to Marine Captain Pat Pate that compared the NVA artillery tactics to those of the Japanese: "both were formidable." Lucas stayed at Gio Linh several days, and gave Al Gray one of his books with this inscription, "To the men at Gio Linh who know more about war than anyone." Lucas wrote several articles about the Marines at Gio Linh and intended to publish more in a book, though, sadly, he never was able to finish that project before his untimely death.[18]

Evacuating the casualties did not end the excitement on May 14, however. Early in the evening, Gray was outside the COC/FDC with Lieutenant Beard serving as the watch officer. They were alerted to an unexpected emergency outside the bunker. Less than 10 hours after being knocked senseless, Al Gray had serious business to attend to, and it required intense concentration.

MINEFIELD OUTSIDE GIO LINH OUTPOST, REPUBLIC OF VIETNAM, 2100, 14 MAY 1967

A three-man infantry detachment left their defensive positions at Gio Linh to proceed to a listening post northeast of the outpost; the route required that they travel in safety lanes through or around the friendly minefields that had been placed around the outpost by French, ARVN and Marine engineers. This was a nightly occurrence, and the duty was hazardous in several respects. Often there was incoming artillery fire and men in the open were particularly vulnerable. Adding to the challenge, the older mines had been sensitized by the exploding, incoming artillery. Further aggravating the situation was that safety lane markers and safety stakes were often destroyed by enemy fire, which was the case that day. Finally, the not-so-simple act of walking through a minefield provided enough of a pucker factor that other hazards might seem less important.

But at night, in positions that were brand new to them, and when there is little light to see by or any way to guide them, Marines easily could become disoriented, and this patrol did. Their intended path through the field that consisted of M-2 and M-16 anti-personnel mines was a circuitous one. One man tripped an M-16 that instantly killed him and left his two companions wounded and unable to move. Their calls for help however, were quickly answered. Alerted by the explosion at about 2100 (9 PM), everyone inside the perimeter knew something was amiss.

First to arrive at the site was Major Gray. He had been having a chew and sitting quietly atop the command bunker. Hearing the disturbance and realizing the explosion was nearby, but without the noises associated with incoming mortars or artillery, Gray moved quickly to the perimeter where he was joined by Captain E.L. Cody, Jr., the S-4 of the 2nd Battalion, 12th Marines, whose Delta Battery was then serving at Gio Linh. Gray assessed the situation and knew that there was no map of the minefield locally. While radio operators in the command bunker tried unsuccessfully to reach the engineers in Dong Ha, Major Gray decided how to approach the wounded. The distance the victims had penetrated into the minefield, about 40 meters, and its physical layout meant that Gray had to use a bayonet to probe along the outside layer of mines, some of which were attached to trip wires, and then continue straight through another layer of mines before finally reaching the wounded. This was done while crawling on his hands and knees. Staff Sergeant Daniel Magalie, a combat engineer, followed Major Gray into the field, marking their route with new safety stakes and safe lane wires. The whole effort had to be illuminated by aircraft flares in order to provide a modicum of light. When at about 2200 the nightly incoming NVA barrage started exploding all around, a surreal atmosphere cloaked the scene. Which was the bigger hazard to Gray and Magalie, the remaining M-16 mines or the NVA barrage?

When he reached the first wounded Marine, Gray directed Magalie to return and lead stretcher-bearers to his position. Meanwhile, the Major administered first aid and tried to lift the spirits of the injured and extremely frightened Marines.

Entering a minefield and probing one's way through it, at night, is extremely hazardous. Doing it while also subjected to artillery shells bursting all around is well beyond dangerous.

After several hours of tedious and dangerous work to save the Marines, Gray and his group extracted the wounded from the minefield and had them evacuated to the aid station at Dong Ha. Gray returned to the body of the third man to ensure there was nothing that could be done for him. Gray then went back into the minefield and remove the body after first light the next morning. Captain Cody reported that Gray's calm demeanor and steadfast resoluteness while under heavy fire made the whole rescue possible.[19]

While Major Gray was busy trying to save lives in the minefield, Lieutenant Beard was extremely active in the FDC. A newly arrived Marine captain was serving as an observer, getting on-the-job training while Beard concurrently directed pre-planned, outgoing fires; called for and then adjusted a C-47 flare ship mission to provide illumination throughout the area; alerted and coordinated the base defenses; and called for more medevac helicopters. Later in the evening, as things calmed, the new captain congratulated Beard on how smoothly he had operated throughout the night's hectic events. Beard was pleased to accept the Marine's compliments, but replied, "In about two minutes we were going to get our butts chewed by the boss." Beard understood the captain's surprise at his reply, realizing that the captain had not yet had the pleasure of working for Al Gray.

Sure enough, Al Gray stormed into the command bunker at about 0500 (5 AM) and immediately ordered an officers' call in five minutes. The officers quickly gathered and heard Gray's animated lecture for the next 45 minutes. Three Marines had become casualties for no good reason. Gray hated casualties and demanded that immediate steps be taken to improve the base's emergency plan; changes were implemented on the spot. Not only did the plan improve, but also a few junior officers had learned a lot more about leadership.

While Beard was able to report many of the events that night, he was not privy to one important aspect of the episode. While crawling around in the minefield, Major Gray was hit by shrapnel from incoming shells or from sensitized mines exploding nearby. Gray realized that the wounds were not life threatening, and he was loath to acknowledge what had happened. Policy was that if any Soldier, Sailor, airman or Marine received three Purple Hearts as a result of wounds received in action, that individual would be removed from the warzone. He had been wounded on May 12 and again on May 14, but Gray had no intention of being sent home. Consequently, Major Gray made his way to the corpsman, had his wounds cleaned up and wrapped, and then returned to the FDC. The corpsman was happy to accommodate his Commanding Officer and not mention the incident in his daily medical report.[20]

Needless to say, the sight of their Commanding Officer entering a sensitized minefield to try to save three of their comrades was inspirational to the Marines, Soldiers, and Sailors of Gio Linh. That he succeeded in saving two provided additional motivation to his men. Gray had always had an uncanny ability to extract the very best effort from those with whom he served, and his action on 14 May 1967, provided a palpable reason for his men to follow the active, upbeat and highly professional officer of Marines.

When Lieutenant Beard's 30 days at Gio Linh ended in early June, he returned to Dong Ha to resume his duties as an aerial observer. Beard sought out Colonel Morrison and told the Colonel that he wanted to submit an award nomination for Major Gray. The Colonel scoffed at the young Soldier and said, "Major Gray is not trying to accumulate medals; he is just dedicated to winning the war."[21]

The sight of Gray sitting on the roof of the bunker was common to all who served at Gio Linh. His tattered chair provided one of the few creature comforts he allowed himself, but from that perch he had good fields of observation northward and he could hear the distinctive pop associated with of incoming rounds. That was very important, especially when the NVA used mortars to attack by fire. The Marines had counter-mortar radar with the artillery, but, in 1967, the technology was only effective (time-wise) if it was aimed at the same quadrant from which the fire came. From the time of the characteristic "pop-pop" until the time the shells landed on the target was typically 30-41 seconds, depending on the range. If Gray (or anyone) yelled the quadrant where the sound was detected, then the counter-mortar radar could quickly be changed to face the challenge.

Though the outpost had high observation towers (see Figures 6.2 and 6.3), Gray had the most experience of anyone and he could often detect the flash or bang and alert the radar operator faster than the word would be passed down from the towers. Thus, Gray usually positioned himself on the roof at times when he anticipated an attack, as seen in Figure 6.6. There was not much Al Gray did that was not purposeful; even sitting atop his bunker had a rationale!

MINEFIELD OUTSIDE OUTPOST GIO LINH, REPUBLIC OF VIETNAM, 2130, 27 JUNE 1967

In early June, Alpha Battery, 1st Battalion, 40th Artillery (A/1/40) of the United States Army joined the firing contingent at Gio Linh. Nicknamed "Automatic Alpha" by the Marines, the self-propelled 105mm howitzers (M108) could fire very quickly, but even more importantly they could quickly traverse 360 degrees to respond to a threat in any direction.[22] The Soldiers thus provided a capability the Marine artillery did not have. Although the bigger, heavier artillery of the 2nd Battalion, 94th Artillery provided a much larger explosive (174 pounds) that could be hurled more than 32,000 meters by its 175mm guns, the Soldiers and weaponry of the A/1/40 provided a rapid fire, highly accurate capability against NVA gunners who tried hard to stay within the minimum effective range of the 175mm guns (5,000 meters).

Six weeks had passed since Major Gray had entered the minefield to save three Marines. It had been an electrifying, terrifying and action-filled six weeks. Gray's Composite Artillery Battalion had fired more than 42,000 rounds into North Vietnam or in support of infantry and reconnaissance operations in or below the DMZ. Gio Linh had also absorbed at least 15,000 incoming rounds. While Gray's new tactics had minimized his casualties, the ever-present threat of NVA artillery was enough to make the men edgy. On this night, the entire Gio Linh contingent had remained inside the perimeter. Gray tried very hard not to develop patterns that could be predictable in any aspect of his military life and, for the most part, he was successful; creating a pattern involving troop movements out of Gio Linh would never be permitted.

On June 27, a new infantry company arrived, in keeping with the monthly unit rotation at Gio Linh. Echo Company, 2nd Battalion, 9th Marines (E/2/9) assumed the duty as the infantry guardians of the outpost. The Commanding Officer of E/2/9 was Captain (and future Lieutenant General) Robert Johnston, USMC.[23] While Echo Company's Marines were battle-tested, they were brand new to Gio Linh, and therefore the NVA sent their normal welcoming present – a heavy artillery barrage. Captain Johnston had been alerted to the NVA tactics, so he and his men were quick to find their assigned positions and be ready for the incoming volleys. What they received was the full measure of the NVA capabilities; it was no half-baked attempt to unnerve the newly arrived infantrymen, it was the real deal.

Johnston had not known Gray before his arrival, and he noted that perhaps the reason Gray walked, never appearing to rush, into a covered position when incoming was expected, was simply to provide leadership for the troops. Gray seemed, at least to Johnston, fearless. But that was the image Gray wanted, and knew he needed, to project, especially to units newly arrived at America's northernmost outpost. What Captain Johnston observed was almost exactly what Army Lieutenant Smith had seen earlier.

The artillerymen shared the danger equally with those supporting them, but the artillery had the advantage of fulfilling their mission, which meant they had to shoot early, late and often during the day and night. The infantry, hunkered in their foxholes and bunkers, had little to do during incoming barrages except watch over the minefields, pray their silent entreaties, and take the periodic listening post duty that required leaving the perimeter.

For Echo Company 2/9, their welcoming barrage was just one aspect of what would be a long night. Paths through the minefield, which were re-marked after every barrage, were again destroyed, but not before the Marines on the way to the listening post were well into danger.

The explosion in the minefield was not heard at the command bunker. But Soldiers of the Army's self-propelled 105mm howitzer battery, A/1/40, heard the noise and cries for help. Major Gray received notification and hurried to the perimeter, where he met Specialist 5th Class John P. West, an Army medic who had no previous combat experience. West would accompany Gray as they figured out how to approach the injured Marines. Again, as happened during the previous minefield incident, Al Gray expected the nightly barrage from north of the DMZ would soon arrive. Going into the minefield, never a picnic, would be hazardous in the extreme, and Gray would be doing far more than pushing his luck. After all, he had already done that as recently as the prior month.

It was bad enough that the mines had been sensitized by months of incoming artillery landing throughout the minefield. But from recent experience Gray knew that slowly probing while crawling forward was the only way to safely navigate the dangers. But on this occasion he did not have an aircraft on-station providing flares to light the area. The only illumination came from 81mm mortars, and that is hardly sufficient for someone probing for mines and looking for booby traps. In addition, the wounded Marines were about 100 meters inside the minefield. This action was to be far more daunting than Gray's May 14th foray into the extremely hazardous area that surrounded the Gio Linh outpost.

He was only halfway to the victims when fate began falling from the skies – the NVA attack had started. Gray had to present a calm demeanor and give his men confidence. After all, incoming shells did not discriminate between good Marines and those less worthy, between Soldiers and Corpsmen, or between officers and men.

Gray knew, though, that all those present would be watching his actions and manner, and while his stomach was churning and he privately wondered why fate was tempting him yet again, he knew that acting agitated or nervous, worried or afraid would not have an effect on the aim of the NVA artillery. It would hit him or not, and so showing a calm, measured demeanor is what he expected of himself, and he well knew it was what the men expected of him. Captain Johnston was aghast at the sight of his commanding officer serving as a mine-clearing device, though he never knew that this was Gray's second time to perform such heroics.[24] Gray reached one wounded Marine, but the other was only inches away from a booby-trapped mine; Gray told him to freeze and not move a muscle, and that he would be back for him, though it might take 30 minutes or more. Major Gray carried the wounded infantryman to safety before returning to the one frozen in place. Following his orders exactly, the Marine had not moved, and he was very happy when Gray came back to disarm the booby trap and lead him to safety. As before, Al Gray went back into the minefield after dawn to retrieve the body of the dead Marine.

Specialist West said of Gray's actions, "Even though it was my first time having to react under such hazardous conditions, I can only say that I would feel completely secure doing it again under the supervision of Major Gray. His leadership (I repeat) was so superb, and safety precautions so thorough that it is really to much to explain on paper." He continued, "As an Army man, I close my statement by saying, 'I salute the Marines for such outstanding leadership and officers.'"[25]

Captain Robert Johnston's description of Gray's actions are equally revealing about the man who commanded all the forces at Gio Linh, "For the next hour and a half, Major Gray directed the evacuation with such composure, despite incoming enemy rounds that were landing in and near the minefield claiming one casualty among the evacuation team, that every Marine immediately gained self confidence and quickly responded unhesitatingly to his orders. The uncommon courage and outstanding leadership displayed by Major Gray was an inspiration to every Marine involved that night…Without his leadership, there is little doubt that the effort to remove the Marines from the minefield would have resulted in more injuries."[26]

Though the second trip into the minefield was even more harrowing in every respect than his first, few Marines, Sailors or Soldiers at Gio Linh realized it, because most were new to the outpost and had no knowledge of Gray's previous foray into man-made danger. What really mattered was that Gray's efforts resulted in saving Marines. That was reward enough for Al Gray.

General Lewis Walt made it a habit to visit wounded Marines on the hospital ship USS *Comfort* each day, and he spoke with the African-American Marine whom Gray had led to safety. *Comfort* was often positioned offshore of the northern I Corps Tactical Zone. The General was a great troop leader and had a real connection with his men. On the morning of 28 June, he visited Gio Linh Outpost to review the situation. The III MAF Commander took Gray aside and said, "That was a brave thing you did last night." Personal recognition from General Walt was special, and

Gray observed another example of good leadership. A few weeks later, when Gray encountered his very good friend and former boss, Colonel Charlie Beale, Beale told him, "You better lay low! I heard you've been wounded at least five times!"[27]

GIO LINH, REPUBLIC OF VIETNAM, IN THE NEWS, 1967

There were other reporters who visited Gio Linh besides Jim G. Lucas, and while they may have been on the receiving end of some NVA artillery, none had the close brush with death that Lucas and Al Gray endured on May 14. The outpost was the focal point for several news articles.

A *New York Times* article by Tom Buckley is reproduced here in its entirety. Note the different spelling convention used by the *New York Times* as opposed to the *Stars and Stripes* article that follows below; Gio Linh becomes Giolinh, Dong Ha is written Dongha, etc. While Americans did a good job of butchering Vietnamese place names, the spellings used by the *Stars and Stripes* more closely resemble those used by the Vietnamese themselves, though to the Vietnamese "Hanoi" will always be "Ha Noi."

Isolated American Unit near Buffer Zone Awaits Attack as North Vietnamese Close In (Buckley, T. New York Times 15 May 1967, reprinted with permission.)

> GIOLINH, South Vietnam, May 15 – Maj. Al Gray sat on a folding aluminum and plastic chair on the roof of his bunker, chewing tobacco and gazing north into the darkness.
>
> Three-quarters of a mile away lay the unmarked border of the demilitarized zone. Beyond curled the Benhai River, the boundary between the two Vietnams, and a line of low, ragged hills silhouetted by the light of a crescent moon and thousands of stars.
>
> To the west, a strip 200 yards wide, cleared by bulldozers last month, stretched like a black stripe seven miles to Conthien.
>
> "You know," said Major Gray, "there are 440,000 Americans in South Vietnam, and they're all behind us."
>
> This place is called Camp Hill. It is the northernmost American position in Vietnam, an artillery stronghold 800 yards long and 300 yards wide dug into the red clay of Hill 41, on Highway 1, five miles inland from the South China Sea.
>
> Six hundred Army and Marine artillerymen, tankmen, and infantrymen are stationed here. Major Gray, of Point Pleasant Beach, N.J., a husky, red-haired Marine gunner, is their commander.

Since the beginning of March, when the guns were moved into position from Dongha, seven miles down the road, they have fired more than 85,000 rounds into North Vietnam and the demilitarized zone, seeking to damage or destroy roads and bridges, supply dumps, troops and artillery and missile emplacements.

The men of Camp Hill have had to take in return 5,000 rounds, the heaviest sustained enemy barrage of the war. It is a dangerous, comfortless place, and in the last two weeks, two of the camp's defenders have been killed and 40 have been wounded.

Now the North Vietnamese quickening the tempo of their attacks in the northern provinces of South Vietnam, are moving their guns, rockets and mortars ever closer to the camp.

Intelligence agents have reported that two enemy regiments are sifting through the thickets on the south side of the Benhai River. The men of Camp Hill have no doubt that after the North Vietnamese attacks on Khesanh, far to the west, and on Contien, at the other end of the cleared strip, their turn is next.

"We'd been told to expect an attack by 5,000 troops," said Major Gray. "It could come within the next couple weeks, maybe the next couple nights, maybe tonight."

"The youngsters at the guns have found out that Friday is Ho Chi Minh's birthday. That's when the attack will come, they say, but they don't seem disturbed about it."

It was 10 P.M. The men stood by their guns, but the camp was dark and quiet. The doorways of the bunkers were masked to keep in the light. The few men required to pick their way among the trenches had red lenses on their flashlights.

The ringing telephone called Major Gray into his bunker. When he returned he said, "We have a report from the border. Two thousand North Vietnamese are supposed to be massing in six positions. The nearest one is only 1,500 meters from here. I've asked for immediate air strikes. As soon as we get the grids plotted, we'll fire, too."

Minutes passed, then the jets from Danang roared past without lights. Jagged flashes appeared to the northwest. Seconds later the roar of the bombs rolled across the empty fields to the camp.

The sky was alight. Four intensely bright lights, a few seconds apart, flashed at an altitude of about 1,000 feet. They were strobe flares, dropped by a reconnaissance plane that was taking pictures. Over Contien, which was being shelled by mortars, flares rose, first jade green, then a succession of yellows.

On the barbed wire that ringed the camp, a trip flare went off. The men on the command bunker threw themselves flat.

"That one was on the wire," Major Gray told one of his sergeants. "Get someone down there to check right away."

The jets continued to scream by. From the east came the distant thump of the eight-inch guns of the heavy cruiser St. Paul, five miles offshore.

The guns of Camp Hill, which had been firing sporadically during the evening, joined the cannonade. The four 175-mm. guns spoke with a vivid flash of powder and a brutal, crushing roar. Their 200-pound shells left a trail of shivering sound, rising and falling and fading away like a choir of spirits.

The bark of the camp's six 105-mm. howitzers was shorter and sharper. The 90-mm. howitzers mounted on the camp's nine tanks had, from 100 yards away, a mellow boom like that of a kettle drum.

Against this chaos of sound the 40-mm. rapid-fire guns chattered almost amiably of all the camp's armament.

In 30 minutes the first mission had been completed. The guns were firing only a round or two, minutes apart.

The youngsters at Camp Hill's guns were still awake. When the guns are silent men dig their bunkers deeper, fill sandbags and stack their ammunition that, along with food, comes by truck along the hazardous road from Dongha.

"They're great kids," one of the officers said, "It takes guts to stay at those guns. They do it and they go back to sleep, but after 30 days of it, they begin to get shaky. We try not to keep them here longer than that. We rotate them back to their outfits and bring up other batteries."

Major Gray and his officers said they were not worried by the prospect of attack. They said Camp Hill could stop anything the North Vietnamese could send against them.

Further back, some staff officers were not so sure. "If the North Vietnamese are willing to spend 1,000, maybe 1,500 men," one of them said, "they might just be able to overrun Giolinh with a night attack. They couldn't hold it, but they might just overrun it."

At midnight, the firing and the bombing had stopped.

"I would say," Major Gray observed, "that the silence is ominous." Then he laughed and went down into his bunker to try to sleep.

At 1 A.M., the stars were beginning to fade. S.Sgt. Dick Reid, a big man with a gentle manner who has spent 31 months in Vietnam, sat on the roof of the bunker drinking a can of warm beer.

"There's the Southern Cross," he said. "When it's peaceful like this, you could almost forget there's a war on."

Radiophoto of The New York Times (by Tom Buckley)

Marines on the observation tower at Golinh, northernmost marine base in South Vietnam. Cpl. William Alpert of Manhattan mans 20-power binoculars, while Pfc. Andrew G. Darby checks his machine gun. The tower is a frequent target for enemy artillery.

Figure 6.2
May 14, 1967, radiophoto of the observation tower at Gio Linh, manned by Cpl William Alpert and PFC An** G. Darby, by the New York Times (by Tom Buckley).[28]

Buckley's remarks at the start of his article about Al Gray sitting on the roof of the bunker gazing north could probably have been attributed to almost anyone who observed Gray during his days, and nights, at Gio Linh. Though the *Times* reporter implied Al Gray was relaxing, he was staying alert to provide early warning against mortar attacks.

A second article, written by Ray Bedford, appeared in the *Stars and Stripes*, the daily newspaper serving the troops in Vietnam. The piece is reproduced here:[29]

Gio Linh is one of the dirtiest places in Vietnam and it commands one of the most beautiful views in the world.

The high ground around he artillery plateau has been stripped for safety, leaving hard, red earth that turns to thick, red mud when it rains.

The plateau looks like something out of a World War I movie, with trenches spider-webbing through the perimeter, linking the deep underground bunkers where men eat, sleep and fight.

It commands a panoramic view. Below, to the north, is the demilitarized zone with gentle rolling hills and blue-green Ben Hai River lacing its way through the center.

The men at Gio Linh can hardly remember the last time they were not shelled by the North Vietnamese. Some say it was April 25 and others claim it was April 26. But all agree that there has been only one day of peace at Gio Linh in some time.

No other unit in Vietnam has had as much continuing contact with the enemy as these men who support and man the 175mm and other guns and tanks that cover the DMZ and southern reaches of North Vietnam.

Almost every day, they take casualties. Most of the casualties occur because the men continue to man their guns during attack so they can return fire and aid other units in the need for artillery fire.

Recently, when Con Thien, 7 miles to the west, was under heavy ground and artillery attack, the men at Gio Linh fired more than 2,000 rounds at the enemy while under an artillery attack themselves.

The paper also carried several pictures of the outpost. Figure 6.3 shows the observation tower that dominated the Gio Linh skyline. While the tower provided an excellent view into North Vietnam, it also provided the North Vietnamese with a clear, easily identifiable aiming point into Gio Linh. Photos in the article give a good idea of the trenches and firing holes that were described in the *Stars and Stripes* article.

The Soldiers, Sailors and Marines who shared the "Gio Linh" experience faced some of the most concentrated NVA artillery attacks of the war. Leatherneck Square was clearly in the cross hairs of the North Vietnamese gunners. The fact that the communist propaganda machine made special mention of Gio Linh added to its notoriety. Not that Camp Carroll, Con Thien, and Cam Lo did not also receive tremendous amounts of incoming artillery fire; they did. But Gio Linh's location as the northernmost allied artillery position, and the fact that it was a former French position (and thus well marked on every communist map) added to its allure to the NVA forces.

SPOTTERS IN TOWER CAN SEE INTO NORTH VIETNAM AS THEY DIRECT GUN FIRE INTO ENEMY POSITIONS.

Figure 6.3
Circa May 20, 1967. Since the tower doubled as an aiming point for North Vietnamese Army
artillery, it took a special breed of Marines or soldiers to man the structure. Note that the
spotters also took their positions during the nights, when incoming barrages were expected.
Often, they could see the muzzle flashes of the North Vietnamese Army guns, and thereby
adjust return fire against those positions. Reprinted here with permission, Stars and Stripes.

Many Vietnam veterans were not subjected to continuous artillery and rocket
attacks, and thus, they cannot imagine the violence associated with the NVA artillery
and rocket and mortar attacks. These attacks were easily the most severe since the
Korean War, and arguably more effective against the American positions than those
in Korea over 15 years earlier. After all, the McNamara/Westmoreland tactics of a
static defense along the "McNamara Line" – where Gio Linh was the easternmost
anchor – made the Americans sitting ducks. On the other hand, the communist

gunners could move around, and they quickly adopted the tactic of splitting their guns into single units or sections of two. Such tactics made the NVA positions even harder to find, making counter-battery fire from the Americans much less effective. Given that the *mission at Gio Linh was to fire 1,000 rounds into North Vietnam each day*, the place was seldom quiet. Most days, and particularly most nights, the NVA returned the favor with interest.

The Soldiers of 2/94 had come to know some of Gray's habits, displayed repeatedly over the years in other locations. The men of the long-range guns, whose fire often provided cover or even deliverance for Marine infantry and especially reconnaissance units, became favorites of such grunts. It was not an unusual happenstance for Major Gray to personally accompany some Marine in search of the gunners who had saved their hides. Gray would deliver the thankful Marines to 2/94's position and watch as American flags or other memorabilia changed hands. All the Marines

MARINES CATCH UP ON THE NEWS DURING BREAK IN ACTION NEAR GIO LINH, 3 MILES SOUTH OF DMZ.

Figure 6.4
Circa May 20, 1967. Digging trenches and filling sandbags was an unending chore, participated in by all who manned Gio Linh. There was no more welcomed sight to a frontline Marine, Soldier or Sailor than a recent edition of Stars and Stripes, except for a letter from home. Reprinted with permission, Stars and Stripes.

CRANE DIGS TRENCH LINE WHILE MEN REPAIR CP THAT TOOK A DIRECT HIT FROM ENEMY FIRE.

Figure 6.5
Circa May 20, 1967. Machines could dig, but only men could "fill" the sandbags. Each weighed about 25 pounds, and handling them daily gave the troops (and most of their officers) a good workout. There were no overweight men on the frontlines, despite the 6,000 calories in their daily C-rations (assuming they actually ate all of each meal, which they usually did not). Reprinted with permission, Stars and Stripes.

MAJ. AL GREY (LEFT), POSITION COMMANDER, SITS WITH HIS STAFF NEAR COMMAND BUNKER NEAR GIO LINH.

Figure 6.6
Circa May 20, 1967. Maj Gray uncharacteristically permitted himself to be the subject of a picture. Also note the plush seating – it appears to be the same chair mentioned in the New York Times article! Of course, you might also see that Al Gray's "deception plan" is in effect – note the spelling of his name. Reprinted with permission, Stars and Stripes.

A 175MM GUN BELCHES SMOKE AS IT HURLS A SHELL INTO A DISTANT NORTH VIETNAMESE POSITION IN SUPPORT OF U.S. TROOPS BATTLING THE REDS ALONG THE DMZ.

Figure 6.7
Circa May 20, 1967. The 175mm gun was the largest, longest-range weapon in the U.S. artillery arsenal. It could fire a 174 pound shell distances up to 33 kilometers. Manned by troops from the Army's 2nd Battalion, 94th Artillery Regiment, the guns were first brought north to assist in the defense of the Marine outpost at Khe Sanh. The Marines heartily welcomed the help! This particular picture, while accurately showing the 175mm gun, was probably not taken at Gio Linh, note the absence of sandbags around the firing pit. Reprinted with permission, Stars and Stripes.

were happy to have the Soldiers and their 175mm guns, their Dusters and all the other capabilities they brought to northernmost I Corps.

More than just newsmen, grunts and artillerymen visited Gio Linh. Several generals, including the MAF Commanding General Lew Walt and the division commanding general periodically dropped in on the outpost. Such stopovers were never simply courtesy calls. There was a keen, ongoing interest in the situation north of the DMZ, and commanders were all making personal assessments of the position and its strength and viability; the continuous propaganda campaign waged by the North Vietnamese left no doubt of the communists' interest in taking Gio Linh. Of course, as any field Marine or Soldier knows, there are dramatic differences between those doing the fighting and those assigned to various headquarters. As has been noted, one of Al Gray's favorite sayings for many years was: "Your next higher headquarters is your natural enemy."[30] During one VIP visit, Gray was reminded why he thought as he did.

A senior officer flew in one afternoon. He was new to Vietnam and, of course, wanted to see why Gio Linh was the focus of so many goings-on. By the time Major Gray arrived at the helipad to greet the newcomer, he was already rebuking the Marines nearby about their lack of personal hygiene, having learned that they were not brushing their teeth regularly. It turned out that the division was putting particular emphasis on dental hygiene as the result of a rash of illnesses associated with tooth decay and worse. The officer, having just received the introductory lecture, was intent on doing his part to remedy the situation. Gray approached the officer and asked to speak with him privately. It took only a few moments for the Major to inform the newcomer, whom he knew well, that Gio Linh lacked sufficient water supplies, and that given the choice between his men brushing their teeth and keeping extremely clean, or having enough drinking water, he chose to provide drinking water. The officer climbed back aboard his helicopter and flew to a different position after receiving a detailed briefing on activities. Like other leaders, accomplishing his mission was always priority one, though caring for his men was surely priority #1B. However, Gray was never a martinet who was a slave to personal appearances given the circumstances that often existed in the field. When confronted by the difficult state of affairs associated with getting water into Gio Linh, he hardly was relaxing personal hygiene standards; rather, he was accepting the cards he was dealt while trying to maintain both morale and discipline. Interestingly, that officer was the only important visitor that Gray could remember who did not recognize the resupply situation.

Amongst the parade of dignitaries who came through the artillery outpost, perhaps the most important was someone well known to Al Gray, Lieutenant General Victor Krulak.[31] The Commanding General, FMFPAC, visited in May 1967. Undoubtedly Krulak was personally evaluating the effect that McNamara Line – or Wall, as some called it – was having. He and General Walt remained steadfast opponents of tying Marines to fixed positions, though General Westmoreland was an unabashed believer in the defensive alignment espoused by the Secretary of Defense. Major Gray, when asked his opinion, strongly supported his Marine seniors, though in 1967 the opinion of any major carried little significance. His view was noted, however.

When Tom Buckley of the *New York Times* reported, "Major Gray at Gio Linh supported the construction and maintenance of the electronic defensive barrier south of the DMZ," there were many raised eyebrows among the staff at Krulak's Headquarters in Hawaii. Fortunately for Gray, General Krulak knew him well, had visited him at Gio Linh before the Buckley report, and correctly surmised that the Major had been misquoted. Gray also got support in Saigon from Brigadier General John Chaisson, USMC. General Chaisson was the brilliant Director of the COC at MAC(V). One of the most professional officers in the service, Chaisson had been the G-3 of the 3rd Marine Division; he knew Al Gray very well and spoke up for the younger officer.[32] Although Buckley erred on that occasion, the many reports he filed in 1967 were largely positive, and contained no indication of an anti-war bias that by then had consumed the reporting of other media members. He was, however, an advocate of the McNamara Line and favored extending it all the way to Laos.

Years after leaving Gio Linh, General Al Gray would become known as one of the leading advocates of Maneuver Warfare. The Marine dispositions in northern I Corps in 1967 represented the antithesis of the way Gray wanted to fight.

LEAVING GIO LINH, REPUBLIC OF VIETNAM, JULY 1967

Al Gray's second six-month extension of his current tour in Vietnam started in April 1967. The Major had had several discussions about future assignments when he extended for a third time. He had been in Vietnam continuously since October 1965. Characteristically, Gray's first choice for a future assignment was to join an infantry battalion. Everyone knew of Gray's choice, and one, the Commanding General of the 3rd Marine Division, Bruno A. Hochmuth, indicated that an infantry assignment was forthcoming. But General Hochmuth could not dictate Gray's next posting. Nothing ever trumped the needs of the service.

General Bruno Hochmuth invited Major Ernie DeFazio, Sergeant Major Neal King and Major Al Gray together to his headquarters. Hochmuth thought it would be a nice touch to have the three former reconnaissance platoon comrades together to receive Vietnamese Crosses of Gallantry; indeed, Vice President Nguyen Cao Ky was at the 3rd Division Headquarters to award the medals and make the occasion memorable. After the ceremony, Hochmuth invited Gray to stay for lunch. The General told Gray that his decision to send Gray to an infantry battalion had been usurped by III MAF's need to improve its intelligence function. Gray recalled his disappointment at the news, but also fondly remembers that Bruno Hochmuth gave him a Marine tie clasp as a memento of the lunch. Like every Marine who knew the General, Al Gray had the deepest respect for his Division Commanding General. The luncheon would mark the last time Gray had occasion to speak privately with the General, who was killed in a helicopter crash the following November.

General Cushman decided that the special intelligence portion of his command needed to be significantly upgraded. There had been a big expansion of the Radio

Figure 6.8
At a ceremony arranged by Maj Gen Bruno Hochmuth, Commanding General 3rd Marine
Division, Maj Ernie DeFazio, Sgt Maj Neal B. King, and Maj Al Gray, the three former
recon platoon compatriots from 1951, received Vietnamese Crosses of Gallantry from Air
Marshal Nguyen Cao Ky. Gray met Air Marshal Ky several times while in Vietnam and
had great respect for the Vietnamese officer. The occasion also marked the last time Gray
was to see Gen Hochmuth before that officer's untimely death in a helicopter crash.[33]

Battalion assets in I Corps during the period 1965 through early 1967, but the host of
intelligence issues facing not only III MAF but also Military Advisory Command
(Vietnam) had never been greater. Production of useable intelligence products
needed upgrading. Indeed, there was no other aspect of staff work needing improvement more than intelligence. Having worked with Al Gray dating back to their time
at HQMC in the early 1960s, General Cushman knew exactly whom he wanted to
help fix his problem, and Gray would be reassigned in the summer of 1967.

Earning the respect of senior officers was always gratifying, but the respect that Al
Gray earned from the Marines meant more to him than anything. Gray always made
an impact on his men, and some of them long remembered him for it. In May 1986,

writing in the *St. Petersburg Times*, guest columnist M.Y. Keith wrote an open letter to his son, who had just joined the Army. Keith, a Vietnam veteran, wrote in part:

> *"...If you go into combat I expect you to do your job well and I give you my word when you come back home I'll see you get a welcome win, lose, or draw.*
>
> *It's a matter of keeping faith, it's as simple as that.*
>
> *Of course during my war I had the profound luck to be led by a major named Gray, he's now a three-star general in the Marine Corps. If you can find such a man in the Army, he'll get the job done an bring you home..."*
>
> *St. Petersburg Times Guest Column, May 1986*

Less than a year after the Keith column appeared, another Gray admirer, former Army Lieutenant Doug Beard, wrote an approval letter to Secretary of the Navy Jim Webb. Beard, who was then teaching school in Ohio and had not seen or heard from Al Gray for nearly 20 years, had read of Gray's selection to be Commandant of the Marine Corps. The former Army officer picked up his pen and wrote to the Navy Secretary indicating his support for the nomination, and saying Webb could not have made a better choice. Yes, Al Gray elicited many responses from his men, and usually all were very positive.

In retrospect, Al Gray's time at Gio Linh represented the last instance during his long service that he was exposed to intense, protracted, combat operations. Certainly, he endured more shelling, and it was not the last time that he faced imminent danger from armed foes before leaving South Vietnam for good, but at Gio Linh he faced severe, incessant fighting for nearly four months. Was his experience at Gio Linh the stimulus for his metamorphosis, only a few years later, into the Marine Corps' leading advocate of maneuver warfare? If it wasn't, it surely must have been a contributing, even leading, factor. It is difficult to conceive of circumstances that would cause General Al Gray, the father of FMFM-1 (*Warfighting*), to place Marines in a static location where they would be pummeled day after day, week after week, and month after month by mortar, artillery and rocket fire.

NOTES AND REFERENCES

1. Major Gray retained his S-3 assignment until 17 April 1967 when he was relieved by Lieutenant Colonel Willis Gore. Gore was a veteran artillery officer who served with distinction at the Chosin Reservoir and was widely respected by the artillery community.

2. Interview with Lieutenant General Richard Trefry, April 2008.

3. Author telephone interview with Colonel William R. Morrison, USMC (Ret), 2008.

4. There are many websites that Vietnam veteran's organizations have developed and maintained where veterans can trade memories and honor those who never returned. 2nd Battalion, 94th Field Artillery has one such website: http://www.2ndbattalion94thartillery.com/Chas/inwork.htm.

5. Pribblenow, 201.

6. A listening post is normally placed some distance outside a defensive position, along possible avenues of attack. Listening posts provide early warning of such attacks.

7. From General Gray's private collection.

8. 2nd Battalion, 94th Field Artillery website: http://www.2ndbattalion94thartillery.com/Chas/inwork.htm. Accessed 02-19-2012.

9. 2nd Battalion, 94th Field Artillery website: http://www.2ndbattalion94thartillery.com/. Accessed 02-19-2012.

10. The Soldiers of 2/94 did spoil the day for some North Vietnamese mortarmen on one occasion, however, by using their 175mm gun in a direct fire mode against an NVA mortar crew that was attacking Camp J.J. Carroll from a range of about 2000 yards. The Army artillerymen bore sighted their big gun toward a small structure behind which the mortars were being fired. About 8 rounds from the 175's completely obliterated the structure and put an immediate end to the mortar attack. The Marine artillerymen at Camp Carroll offered their unabashed and highly enthusiastic vocal support to their Soldier compatriots during the brief engagement.

11. D/2/94 was actually Task Force Bravo (TFB), 6th Battalion, 27th Field Artillery Regiment (TF B/6/27). TF B/6/27 was an augmented 175mm four gun firing battery that was originally stationed at Phouc Vinh about 50 miles north of Saigon and part of MAC(V). TFB equipment arrived at Dong Ha by boat early October (2-3) 1966 as the first Army artillery unit assigned to I Corp. TFB convoyed to Camp J J Carroll and became fully operational about 6 October 1966. The battery operated under direct control of the Marine Regimental Command at Dong Ha for several weeks. 2nd Battalion, 94th Field Artillery (2/94) arrived on JJC in late October 1966. One battery (A) of the 2/94 was sent to another Marine location so 2/94 only brought two firing batteries to Camp Carroll. Within a couple of weeks of the 2/94's arrival, TFB was attached operationally to 2/94 and assigned the designation D/2/94 for ease of operations. TFB was never reassigned organizationally to 2/94. In late March (24, 25, 26) 1967, D/2/94 (TFB) displaced from Camp Carroll and relieved B/2/94 at Gio Linh. D/2/94 remained at Gio Linh until late May 1967, when it was relieved by C/2/94 and displaced to Dong Ha for refitting, and then returned to Camp Carroll in early June 1967. D/2/94 (TFB) was present for the famous (infamous) April 27, 1967 shelling. Interview by author with Colonel Larry Vinyard, USA (Ret) on August 31, 2008. Then 1st Lt. Vinyard was the Fire Direction Officer for TFB.

12. Email correspondence with Lieutenant Colonel Andrew Tenis, U.S. Army (Ret), February 2011.

13. While General Gray is an unabashed Marine, he really does honor all services equally. The author has been privileged to attend many "Wallows" with the General. The Wallow is the annual convocation of the Military Order of the Carabao. The Marine Band plays a medley of service songs, and typically those present stand for "their service's song." As is custom at such events, guests take their cue from the host. We (General Gray's guests) were stunned to see him standing immediately; even before the first song (usually the Army's *The Caisson Song*) started, General Gray was standing at attention. Of course, we (his guests) jumped up. Looking around the room (in 1993 or so) very few, if any, Marines stood for the Army song. Fast forward 15 years: almost all active duty Marines stand for all the services' songs. It is just another testament to General Gray's leadership. http://www.carabao.org/index.php?. Accessed 02-19-2012.

14. Author interview and email correspondence with Douglas Beard, 2008-2010.
15. Commandant Lieutenant General John Lejeune introduced Marine Corps Order No. 29 in 1920, which states, "Young Marines respond quickly and readily to the exhibition of qualities of leadership on the part of their officers.… The relation between officers and enlisted men should in no sense be that of superior and inferior nor that of master and servant, but rather that of teacher and scholar. In fact, it should partake of the nature of the relation between father and son.… The provisions of the above apply generally to the relationships of NCOs with their subordinates and apply specifically to NCOs who may be exercising command authority."
16. 2nd Battalion, 94th Field Artillery website: http://www.2ndbattalion94thartillery.com/ Chas/inwork.htm. Lt. Smith's quotation is from the "1st Campaign."
17. 16 May 1967 article in the *Washington Star*.
18. Inscription in book Jim Lucas presented to Major Gray at Gio Linh, May 14, 1967. Book is entitled *Dateline Vietnam* by Jim G. Lucas, New York: Award House, 1966.
19. Statement of Captain E.L. Cody, Jr., 082225/0802 concerning the actions of Major A.M. Gray, Jr. on May 14, 1967.
20. More than 30 years after leaving Vietnam, General Gray still has occasional fragments that work their way out of his head. General Gray is officially credited with three Purple Heart Medals. In addition to the wounds on May 12 and 14, Gray was again hit by artillery on June 27. One reason for being quiet about his wounds involved his parents. They had, despite his best efforts to prevent it, been notified about the incident on May 12 and Gray certainly did not want them fretting over his health. The primary reason he did not mention the wounds, however, was because he did not want to be sent out of the war zone.
21. Author telephone interview with Douglas Beard, October 2008.
22. Marine 105mm howitzers are "towed" behind trucks, thus they are not "self-propelled."
23. Prior to his selection to General, Johnston had served as Aide-de-Camp to General Robert Barrow, the 27th Commandant of the Marine Corps, and then Johnston commanded the 8th Marine Regiment in the 2nd Marine Division, under then Major General Al Gray. As a Lieutenant General, Johnston commanded the Joint Task Force in Somalia is 1992.
24. Author telephone interview with Lieutenant General Robert B. Johnston, USMC (Ret), January 2011.
25. Statement of Sp5 John F. West RA14844780 USA, "A" Battery, 1st Battalion, 40th Field Artillery, USA concerning the actions of Major A.M. Gray, Jr. on 27 June, 1967.
26. Statement of Captain Robert B. Johnston, 083412/0302 USMC, Commanding Officer, "M" Company, 3rd Battalion, 9th Marines, concerning the actions of Major A.M. Gray, Jr. on June 27, 1967.
27. Author interviews with Colonel Charles Beale, 2008-2010. Charlie Beale was serving as General Walt's legal officer in Da Nang. Beale often asked about Gray in discussions with the operational staff and even the Commanding General, who well knew of Gray and Beale's close friendship. Almost all of General Walt's comments herein were gleaned from interviews with Colonel Beale.
28. From the *New York Times*, May 14, 1967. *New York Times*. All rights reserved. Used by permission and protected by the Copyright Laws of the United States. The printing, copying, republication or retransmission of this Content without express written permission is prohibited.
29. Used with permissions from *Stars and Stripes*. © 1967, 2010 *Stars and Stripes*.
30. Of course, during his final tour as Commandant, he was forced to alter this expression, or at least direct it outside the Marine Corps!
31. General Krulak visited Gio Linh on 6 May 67 according to the Command Chronology.
32. Lieutenant General John A. Chaisson served in Vietnam continuously for 29 months from February 1966 to June 1968; he was promoted to Brigadier General and sent to

Saigon after being G-3 of the 3ʳᵈ Division. His time there overlapped with Al Gray, and the two met numerous times. General Gray fondly remembers General Chaisson, a Yale graduate, as a brilliant American warrior.

33. From General Gray's private collection.

CHAPTER 7

SIGINT AGAIN
VIETNAM WAR, 1967

SIGINT AGAIN

Major Al Gray was up late. That was hardly unusual for a man everyone knew to be a night owl, given to surviving on only a few hours sleep each day. Nights, except when there was significant enemy activity to monitor, provided the peace and quiet needed to do detailed analyses of past enemy actions and try to align them with intercept logs maintained by the Radio Battalion cryptologists. For years, up to 3,900 signals intelligence/electronic warfare specialists from all the American military services and the National Security Agency, both inside Vietnam and in Thailand, had been attempting to find and exploit the North Vietnamese and Viet Cong tactical voice circuits, but to no avail. Only long-range weather communications from inside North Vietnam had been exploited to date.

Finally, in September 1967, the Marines had found where in the frequency band the North Vietnamese Army/Viet Cong tactical chatter was happening, but the codes that they were using yielded no hints as to what kind of communications was being passed between and among units. Gray and his analysts, augmented by some of National Security Agency's best crypto-linguists, were stymied. But the former college mathematics student was intent on solving the puzzle, no matter how long it took him. Gray, with the help of Lieutenant Colonel John Kelly, had undertaken a retrospective operational analysis. It involved aligning intercept transcripts with past North Vietnamese Army/Viet Cong operations. And on this night in early October, Gray finally hit the Powerball jackpot, apocryphally speaking.

The crypto-linguists had long understood the simple words they heard, usually the Vietnamese term for a vegetable or basic food, but had no idea of the context for the words. Gray's analysis revealed that the foods mentioned probably were a reference to numbers, which then equated to times. With that revelation, the entire codeword structure was revealed, and within a few weeks, the Americans and their South Vietnamese Army allies, could exploit the North Vietnamese Army/Viet Cong tactical communications with a degree of confidence. The breaking of the code had far-reaching implications, and it significantly affected the coming events of the war.

Al Gray was successful because he was able to use his knowledge of operations to complement his expertise in signals intelligence. Perhaps even more important was Gray's professionalism; he simply never quit working the problem. He attacked it from every angle. Al Gray was never a slave to a stovepipe approach to signals intelligence; he fused all-source intelligence and, thereby, the Marine Corps and the entire American war effort benefitted greatly.

9ᵀᴴ MARINES COMBAT OPERATIONS CENTER, DONG HA, JULY 1967

Knowing that that he would be assigned to the III MAF Headquarters instead of the infantry, Major Al Gray decided to go home on leave. He had not been home since early September 1965, nor had he taken Rest & Recuperation Leave since his arrival in country. He returned to Dong Ha intent on going back to the States and then returning to his former haunts in Japan on Rest & Recouperation Leave. But before he could leave, the new Commanding Officer of the 12ᵗʰ Marines, Colonel Edward Schick, had a vexing problem that needed fixing. The senior lieutenant colonel responsible for running the Fire Support Coordination Center, a vital part of the COC at the 9ᵗʰ Marines Headquarters, had fallen ill and was evacuated. Schick knew that he had several senior field grade officers who would soon be joining the Regiment, but right then he needed a stopgap, and he knew he could count on the former S-3 to more than adequately serve as a temporary replacement while awaiting the new arrivals. Gray's leave would have to wait a while longer.

The 9ᵗʰ Marines were responsible for manning the Forward Command Post and the very large COC in Dong Ha. The 3ʳᵈ Division's Command Post was still back in Phu Bai. The situation in Dong Ha had deteriorated, and the 9ᵗʰ Marines Commanding Officer had requested that the 12ᵗʰ Marines send someone over to assist; after all, the 12ᵗʰ Marines knew a lot about how to run COCs.

When sent to investigate the situation and recommend changes, Gray encountered poor leadership, low morale and a total atmosphere of fear, with personnel too afraid to leave the bunker complex. Indeed, close examination of the COC revealed that many people there left its safety for absolutely nothing. Aside from the inevitable stench resulting from men eating and sleeping in the close quarters of the bunker, a cursory inspection revealed that a contributing source of the odor was human waste. The first thing Gray recognized he had to do was exhibit positive leadership; and for Al Gray and many other Marine officers that normally meant showing an example.

Dong Ha was often subject to rocket and artillery attacks like those frequented on Gio Linh, where Gray had recently commanded all U.S. and Free World Forces assigned to the outpost. The attacks against Dong Ha, which is about eight miles south of Gray's former artillery firebase, were not quite as violent, given the greater range the NVA had to fire. Still, the attacks were nothing to be ignored nor discounted. While Gray was there going over the procedures in place and asking questions of those on duty, another NVA strike against the area took place.

Major Gray went outside the COC to see where the rounds were impacting and to check for casualties and damage. It was a large area to cover, and when he looked around for help no one else had left the bunker. Gray angrily ordered the men outside to see if anyone had been wounded. When those in safety balked at the order, Gray became furious and started throwing people outside. The overall effort paid off and drove home the point when one of Gray's teams found two badly wounded Marines a couple hundred yards from the bunker; their quick evacuation undoubtedly minimized their wounds and perhaps even saved their lives. For the men who had been in the bunker, the lesson could not have been timelier, or more obvious.

In short order, the large operations center was functioning superbly well, with the officers and Staff NCOs demonstrating leadership and professionalism expected in the Corps. Gray also took time to implement General Lejeune's dictate that officers be teachers. He shared as much as he could of his accumulated knowledge of the enemy activities, the operational area and factors affecting the war in northern I Corps as a way to educate everyone. Gray always tried to keep the men as informed as he could, and he always realized what big dividends General Lejeune's concepts paid every time they were followed.

Let there be no mistake; Al Gray was not impervious to fear. No one in his right mind could withstand months of incessant, accurate artillery barrages and remain fearless; but Marine leaders know it is their duty to set the example for the more junior personnel who keenly observed every action.

He was well aware of that incoming artillery and rocket fire could terrify the brave warriors caught without cover or relegated to open foxholes and trenches. He also knew the chasm that could develop between officers and men who spent their time in the relative safety of bunkers and those who remained outside, in foxholes or trenches under dangerous conditions. By making the officers in the bunkers get out and check the safety of their men that gulf was reduced, mutual respect increased, and basic leadership restored. As a young artillery forward observer in Korea, he had seen these conditions first hand and made a mental note of effects of artillery fire on men who stayed in bunkers too long.

It was a very happy Al Gray when in July 1967 he finally was able to leave northern I Corps and hop on a big bird back to the *Land of the Big PX* – as the troops in those days called America.

VISITING POINT PLEASANT BEACH, JULY 1967

Lucky II, Al Gray's faithful companion, had been boarded at a professional handler's training facility for the previous 22 months, prior to Gray's return to Vietnam in September 1965. While Gray served abroad, he would periodically get pictures and a report card detailing Lucky II's performance in various hunting events. But Gray was anxious to pick up his big Labrador; he flew into Kansas City and drove to the kennel located in southern Missouri in the Ozarks. Upon arrival Gray found many dogs, mostly Labs but including a variety of Retrievers, assigned to large, spacious dog runs – but there was no Lucky, nor was there anyone home.

Finally, the owners returned; Gray introduced himself. Lucky II had been shipped out to Missouri and Gray had never met the owners. He said that he was there looking for Lucky, while expressing his dismay that he did not see his old friend in any of the kennels. "Oh," replied the kennel owner, "Lucky lives in the house with us." Sure enough, Lucky, the dog that had long charmed Sailors and Marines from the Far East to Hawaii to Northern Virginia and New Jersey, had earned the love of a family of professional dog handlers and trainers.

Gray loaded the large, but strangely subdued, dog into his rental car. Having collected Lucky, there were other, far more somber actions awaiting Gray's attention. The reunited pair had traveled about 60 miles down the road when Lucky, finally realizing who it was that had picked him up, bounded into the front seat of the car and gave his owner a real Labrador Retriever welcome. Gray had to pull off the road and take time to enjoy a reunion with Lucky before continuing on his personal mission.

During the time Gray has been in Vietnam he had lost several men who were killed in action while serving in billets close to him. Gray always tried to make personal calls on the family of each of those who gave the ultimate sacrifice. After a week crisscrossing Kentucky, Ohio, and Pennsylvania he returned to New Jersey. He knew that he would be leaving to return to the war zone very soon, and while in his hometown he arranged for one of his closest friends, Bob Moore, and Moore's son, Bobby, to care for Lucky. It turned out to be a fine arrangement for everyone. The Moores loved hunting with Lucky in southern New Jersey, and the big dog thrived on the personal attention he received. After less than two weeks in Point Pleasant Beach, however, the Gray Ghost was gone, back to the Far East.

SAKATA, JAPAN, EARLY AUGUST 1967

Before returning to the war zone, Al Gray had decided to take advantage of the offer of Rest & Recuperation Leave in Japan; the Rest & Recuperation Leave would permit him to visit his old friends in Sakata. Gray's time in Sakata during 1956 and 1957 was among the most satisfying duty he ever had. Away from any supervision by senior Marine or naval officers, he had built a small electronic eavesdropping station from almost nothing.

While carrying out the myriad duties associated with constructing a new base, then Captain Al Gray had lived in town with his first Labrador Retriever, Lucky I. Now, more than a decade later, Gray rode the train from Tokyo north to Sakata not knowing what to expect on his arrival. He did not take time to advise anyone of his arrival; indeed, he did not know who might still be around even if he had wanted to give the Japanese a heads up regarding his holiday.

Despite the years that had passed, Gray, even without Lucky, was recognized at the train station. By the time he had reached the center of town and the hotel that Lucky and he had used as quarters during their first stay, news that "Gray-san" was back in town had spread far and wide. Young men and women who had been children, and who likely received candy or chocolates from then Captain Gray, wanted to practice their English or just say hello. Older townspeople, who recalled Gray's negotiations with the local government, the communist trade unions, the Japanese war veterans, or who just remembered him, clamored to shake his hand or simply touch him.[1]

Al Gray spent four days in Sakata. He paid for no meals, his hotel bill showed a zero balance and he never ate alone. When he finally made the walk to the train station to depart for Yokosuka and return to the war, he was showered with gifts of all sizes, shapes and value. The presents were far more than he could ever carry. Indeed, he could have used a boxcar to load them, but even then what would he do with them upon his arrival at his port of embarkation? True to form, he begged off taking the trinkets, mementos, pens, cards, snacks, chocolates, and other assorted paraphernalia and insisted they be passed to the children of the city. The warmth of the welcome, the breadth and depth of the reaction to him, and the animated nature of the Japanese with whom he interacted amazed Al Gray. These were hardly the proud, but generally reserved and stoic people he had first encountered in 1956.

It was last time that Al Gray ever visited Sakata. But the Japanese language skills he had practiced and polished there in the 1950s, the same skills he already put to use to help save his life in on Tiger Tooth Mountain in 1964, would be employed several more times in the years to come. And the circumstances when Gray needed those skills, when speaking Japanese was essential, were more serious and fraught with much more difficulty than his carefree holiday in 1967.

SUB-UNIT #1, RADIO BATTALION, III MAF, SEPTEMBER 1967

Al Gray returned to Vietnam with his batteries fully charged, with his focus renewed and with a single purpose – help the United States win the war in Vietnam!

The 1st Radio Battalion was part of FMFPAC, and both the Battalion and FMFPAC had their Headquarters on the island of Oahu, Hawaii. However, the number of Marine SIGINT/EW/SIGSEC personnel permitted in Vietnam was capped at about 200, so the entire Radio Battalion, which usually numbered a little under 400, could not be sent to the war zone. Thus, for administrative purposes, the SIGINT/EW unit in South Vietnam was identified as Sub-Unit #1; in reality, it was the 1st Radio Battalion (-).[2] The Commanding Officer of Sub-Unit #1 reported directly to the Commanding General, III MAF, as an attached unit, though the G-2 (Intelligence) had staff cognizance of special intelligence activities and the III MAF G-3 monitored EW matters. Signals Security matters fell under the III MAF G-6 (Communications Electronics Officer).[3]

By agreement between the Chief of Naval Operations and the Commandant of the Marine Corps in 1956 (and supported by the NSA), each Radio Battalion could be augmented by officers and 136 enlisted specialists from the NSG (then the Navy's Service Cryptologic Element). Later this agreement was modified to include cryptologic personnel, civilian or military, under control of NSA. Gray had been directly responsible for developing this concept and their integration into the war and contingency plans in the early 1960s. This modus operandi is still in effect today. Prior to the arrival of Sub-Unit #1, and even after it had been established inside Vietnam, individual cryptologists and special communicators were also in country working with SIGINT units from other services. When Al Gray took command in August 1967, he found the organization had a total of 12 officers and 218 men, which included many Sailors working in special communications.

The mission of the Radio Battalion was to provide SIGINT, EW and SIGSEC support to all forces operating in the I Corps Tactical Zone. Because of the nature of the conflict, the major effort was devoted to the cryptologic mission of providing SIGINT and other Special Intelligence support to the overall effort.

Captain John Hyatt led the first detachment of Marine cryptologists to Pleiku in early 1962. That was followed by Major Al Gray's contingent to Tiger Tooth Mountain in 1964. In between and after those deployments, there were Marines who helped to establish and then were assigned to the United States Army's 8th RRU located near Phu Bai, just southwest of Hué City. In 1965, the Marine Support Battalion established its Company "L" at the 8th RRU facility. The 8th RRU would be one of the last American units to leave Vietnam. However, Marines working there were not part of Sub-Unit #1, and did not report directly to Major Gray.

Many of the Marine cryptologists assigned to Vietnam – either in Sub-Unit #1 or at 8th RRU – during the period 1962 through early 1965 were there on Temporary Additional Duty from the Marine Support Battalion, which had companies located in Japan at Kami Seya, in the Philippines at San Miguel, and on Okinawa. Others were Temporary Additional Duty from Hawaii and 1st Radio Battalion, and a few came from other duty stations around the world, such as the NSA. The system was working exactly as Al Gray had envisioned during his assignment at HQMC earlier in the 1960s. Gray had stayed in cryptology for nearly 10 years, even as many influential senior officers suggested he had done enough and needed to get back into combat arms. Gray had confidence that his work organizing and staffing the Radio Battalions and the Marine Support Battalion would save Marine lives on the battlefield. He did not envision that such reality would come to pass so soon, however. By September 1967 the majority of the Radio Battalion was, in fact, in South Vietnam and working hard to contribute to the war effort, and they were as valuable as any infantry battalion. Still, it would not be until 1968 that the 1st Radio Battalion Headquarters was officially moved to South Vietnam.

Gray was well prepared to take command for many more reasons than his earlier history in the cryptologic business. From the time he arrived in Vietnam, he had monitored the cryptologic effort. First, he served as an unofficial intelligence advisor to General Kyle when that officer required Gray's presence at the 3rd Division Commanding General's staff meetings. Later, even while he was at Gio Linh, first General Lewis Walt and then General Robert Cushman would send their aides to visit him so Gray could comment on various intelligence reports and analyses that had been developed within III MAF. For example, his skewering of the Army proposal to jam ground communications targets was but one case of Gray keeping abreast of SIGINT/EW while serving in the artillery. Gray was also largely responsible for establishing the Radio Battalion detachment adjacent to the 12th Marines Command Post at Dong Ha. Several former cryptologists reported sharing a meal with Major Gray, including then Staff Sergeant Gale N. Monda. Staff Sergeant Monda was well aware of Major Gray's background, and the quiet curiosity exhibited by the artilleryman greatly influenced Monda. In fact, when he learned that Gray had extended in Vietnam and would likely be the new Commanding Officer of the Radio Battalion, Monda likewise extended simply so he could continue to serve with the Major.[4] But Gray's influence extended past Dong Ha; while still with the 12th Marines Gray had a prominent role in the establishment of Radio Battalion sites at Camp Carroll, Khe Sanh and Chu Lai.

While SIGINT, and other aspects of intelligence gathering, had achieved some modest successes, General Cushman had major intelligence challenges by the middle of 1967. The North Vietnamese were operating with large units in northernmost I Corps, attacking using long-range artillery and rockets from inside North Vietnam. It was a situation Al Gray was intimately familiar with because of his time in the 12th Marines and at Gio Linh. 3rd Marine Division outposts at Khe Sanh, Gio Linh, Con Tien and Camp Carroll and everywhere in between faced relentless enemy activity. Southwest of Da Nang, the 5th Marines, part of the 1st Marine Division, were deployed near An Hoa and they were in a prolonged multi-year battle against VC battalions and regiments who were trying hard to keep NVA infiltration routes open. The U. S. Army's American Division had been attached to III MAF and was operating near Chu Lai, having grown into division status from Task Force Oregon, the first major Army force assigned to I Corps and III MAF. While the South Vietnamese political situation had largely stabilized under the leadership of President Thieu, General Cushman knew about intelligence functioning well enough to realize that the MAF's intelligence production needed upgrading.

In 1963, then Major General Robert E. Cushman was the G-2/G-3 at HQMC. Lieutenant Colonel Charles Beale and Major Al Gray, part of AO2F, were in General Cushman's G-2 organization. The Gold Dust Twins – as Cushman referred to them – briefed the General several times a week, so Cushman well knew the personality and capabilities of Al Gray. Colonel Beale told the story that one day General Cushman stopped him in the passageway, saying, "Hey, Charlie, I need to talk with you." "Yes, sir, what can I do for you," replied Beale. "Well, that spook, when I ask him 'what's going on, spook' he just keeps walking and says 'everything is on track, General' or 'everything is fine, sir.' Now, Charlie, I'm the G-2 and I need more information than that!"[5] Of course, the spook that General Cushman was referring to was then Captain Al Gray. Less than five years later, newly promoted Lieutenant General Cushman would again be asking, "what's going on, spook?" It is doubtful that, while in Vietnam, Major Al Gray ever shrugged and told him simply, "Everything's on track, General."

When Al Gray took command of Sub-Unit #1 the unit was spread throughout I Corps at five major installations and many small detachments. The southernmost major site was at Chu Lai, which supported the Army's American Division that operated in that area. The other significant Radio Battalion sites were on Hill 55 southwest of Da Nang; at Dong Ha, inside the 12th Marines artillery position; Khe Sanh, where a major buildup of NVA was occurring; and at Camp Carroll, another of the artillery firebases about halfway from Dong Ha to Khe Sanh. Also supporting Marine operations was the U.S. Army site at Pleiku, which although located in II Corps area nonetheless provided assistance; also helping was the large 8th RRU at Phu Bai, where, as mentioned earlier, Marines of Company "L" and on Temporary Additional Duty from various Pacific Naval Security Group Activities.[6]

While Gray did not change the locations of his remote units, he nevertheless immediately took steps to modify the way his unit operated. As he had shown in every billet he had ever held, Al Gray was a body in motion; and compatible with the laws of physics, he tended to stay in motion. He enhanced the capability at every field site; fewer men remained at the Headquarters area, and more were deployed throughout I Corps. Processing information was also stressed and modified.

Another thing that Gray emphasized was increasing the direct support that SIGINT provided to subordinate commanders at the battalion and regimental levels, and Gray visited nearly all those commanders and staffs. He increased the use of mobile direction finding units at places like Gio Linh and Khe Sanh. He sent such mobile detachments into the field where they often accompanied infantry battalions; only when the cryptologists were close to enemy targets could the enemy's low-power, short-range radios be exploited. The grunts welcomed the increased support, and the commanders, operations and intelligence officers gained a much greater appreciation for the use of SIGINT/EW. Indeed, Gray's visits to every regimental commander and almost all battalion commanders in both divisions not only permitted him to ensure those commanders understood the capabilities and limitations of SIGINT, but also provided Gray the opportunity to solicit ideas about how things could be done to improve operations.

Each of the five primary SIGINT outposts emphasized direct support to the locally-supported unit. However, all information was also passed up to the Sub-Unit Headquarters in Da Nang, where it was again culled for unique data and data linkages to other information. From Da Nang, the information was then shared with all U.S. cryptologic efforts in I Corps and, when authorized on a selected basis, with ARVN and other Free World Forces. The Da Nang product was pushed onward to the NSA and to 1st Radio (Rear) in Hawaii. The cryptologists not deployed to Vietnam performed a second-echelon analysis that effectively refined the production of the Marines that had been performed in the war zone.

Another of his primary actions was to establish a SIGINT/EW Coordination Center. He could do that within the framework of the Radio Battalion without requiring the concurrence of the G-2, other intelligence activities (like Counter-Intelligence, photography or Force Reconnaissance) or even the Commanding General. It would mark the first time, but certainly not the last, that Gray sought to integrate SIGINT within the framework of general intelligence, reconnaissance and surveillance operations. While the Coordination Center lacked the formal name, to the best of his ability Gray ensured that it became the focal point for all intelligence information available within III MAF. And he ensured that his men did not simply collect information, but also that they distributed it to those who needed to know. The flow of SIGINT to Pleiku and the II Corps staff increased, as did the amount of noteworthy data passed to the MAC(V) staff in Saigon.

When Gray established a new certified Critical Communications Center in the III MAF Headquarters, the processing and distribution of SIGINT data became much more effective. The new communications center provided a window into the entire worldwide NSA network. The high-speed Critical Communications capability was a first for the Marines in a war zone, and it not only reduced the burden of the communicators, but it also gave General Cushman almost the same Special Intelligence/Special Communications capability that the Commandant enjoyed at HQMC. Intercepting enemy communications was important, but Al Gray never forgot that enhancing, securing and speeding up his own communications systems were also essential. In every billet, Gray emphasized communications up, down and throughout his unit.

Usually, SIGINT organizations are "stove-pipe" organizations. That is, they collect information; they then pass it up through their internal lines of communications where the collected information is processed. After being processed, information becomes intelligence that the traditional SIGINT community then reports back down the internal chain of command to various subscribers. Gray immediately modified that process and significantly altered the information flow.

Information was still passed up the chain of command inside Sub-Unit #1, but it was also, when appropriate, passed immediately to the supported unit. Thus, for example, if the SIGINT detachment in Dong Ha learned something that they knew would be important to the 12th Marines, that information was given to the 12th Marines without having to go to the Sub-Unit #1 Headquarters in Da Nang, being processed, and then being passed back down to the 12th Marines. As a result of this change, which emphasized that the SIGINT Marines were in direct support of the unit to which they were attached, a closer bond between the cryptologists and the supported unit developed. With that came increased credibility for the cryptologists. Cryptologists spend a lot of time in bunkers surrounded by rolls of concertina wire, which define areas into which 99% of Marines were specifically prohibited from entering. Now, instead of the leadership of supported unit asking what those guys were doing, they knew. As a result, the relationship became that of mutual respect and support.

Since most of the SIGINT action occurred at night, when the VC and NVA were most active, Gray's days were free for him to move about. He had access to a variety of helicopters from III MAF that were available to him on short notice, and

Figure 7.1
Al Gray had tremendous respect for Barney Prosser, and the two remain
lifelong friends. Note the signage for 1st Radio's Headquarters in Da Nang.[8]

he used them. Thus, it was not at all unusual for the Gray Ghost to drop in unannounced at any point in I Corps. Then Master Gunnery Sergeant Barney Prosser, who as a Gunnery Sergeant and later Master Sergeant had served with Gray both in Hawaii in the 1950s and at HQMC in the early 1960s, used to try to give the outlying detachments a heads-up that the Gray Ghost might be inbound. But even the wily veteran Prosser, the unit's Operations Chief and as well versed in the ways of his boss as any Marine alive, could not always warn his Marines to be on the look out for the Gray Ghost's impending arrival.[7]

Not that Gray's Marines were unhappy to see him. Nothing could be farther from the truth. Indeed, Gray's primary motivation for his travels was to ensure he was well aware of what was happening throughout I Corps and how he might improve all-source intelligence throughout the mission area. A major secondary reason, however, was to make sure his Marines saw him, knew he was interested in their welfare, and realized that he was doing everything he could for their well being. It is safe to say that Al Gray never had a group of enlisted Marines who did not love his leadership. Gray was always teaching; he was always questioning his men, searching for better techniques and procedures that he could spread throughout his command. And, of course he always shared his knowledge not only of cryptology, but also of operations and general intelligence everywhere he went. Those cryptologic Marines were among the best and brightest the Corps had to offer; Gray knew he could and should expect much from them, and they did not disappoint him. Indeed, to a man they would have been very embarrassed to let down their hard charging, highly professional and enormously respected Commanding Officer.

In addition to changing the way detachments passed information to the units they supported and with whom they were collocated, Major Gray made one other momentous modification to the way his SIGINT unit operated. Dating back to World War II, there are at least two schools of thought about how SIGINT information should be processed. One school thinks SIGINT should stand-alone. That number included not only most Navy officers of the day, but also many Marine cryptologic professionals. They believed SIGINT-derived information should remain separated from other sources of intelligence in order not to be diminished or contaminated in any way. For example, if an enemy unit is identified based solely on SIGINT information, then there is no chance that the SIGINT database of the enemy order of battle could become tainted. If, however, as Al Gray believed, SIGINT should be quickly and fully integrated with other forms of intelligence, then the SIGINT order of battle might be corrupted, because some other intelligence might be wrong and misidentify the enemy unit. Of course, it is often the case that the SIGINT identification of an enemy unit is also wrong. But all that did not matter to Al Gray; he wholeheartedly believed in all-source intelligence and he quickly moved to ensure that his SIGINT information complemented, reinforced, made use of and was in every way joined together with the human intelligence, counter-intelligence, regular intelligence, sensor intelligence and photographic intelligence collected within III MAF. His establishment of the SIGINT/EW Coordination Center reflected Gray's long-held beliefs.

In his quest to amalgamate intelligence, Gray was fortunate that he served with other exceptional professionals whose views coincided with his own. Lieutenant Colonel Bev Veal was the Counter Intelligence Officer at III MAF. The Combat Intelligence Officer was Lieutenant Colonel John Kelly, and Gray also spent time helping the III MAF Reconnaissance Officer, a young Major named Tim Geraghty.

All remained close friends throughout the years. Besides those officers, the MAF G-2 (Intelligence) was then Colonel Kenny Houghton. Colonel Houghton knew Al Gray when he was an enlisted from his amphibious recon days, and then when Captain Gray was at 1st Composite Radio Company in Hawaii in the late 1950s. Before joining the MAF staff, Houghton had recently commanded the 5th Marines during a portion of their nearly war long struggle to pacify the An Hoa area southwest of Da Nang. While leading his men in *Operation Union II*, Houghton had earned a Navy Cross. In addition to knowing Al Gray, Colonel Houghton knew the intelligence business inside out. They all made a fine team.

Veal, Kelly and Gray would meet each evening to discuss the day's events, compare notes, ask questions and generally ensure that each knew in detail what the other was up to. Those evening confabs would very quickly bear extremely important fruit.

As late as September 1967, there was one glaring hole in the picture the Marines had about their enemy. Most military organizations, at least in the 1960s, relied on radiotelephone communications to coordinate their activities during operational events. Tactical communications in those days were plain voice (just like the spoken language) and usually used frequency modulation (FM) in the range of 25 to 54 megahertz. The frequencies used by military communications are governed by international conventions. However, the radios that were used usually extended outside the band assigned to the military frequencies. It might come as no surprise to learn that on many occasions non-American military units did not limit themselves to that portion of the frequency spectrum to which they were assigned. Thus, Marine cryptologists, despite routinely and ad infinitum searching for VC and NVA voice circuits, had not found them. It was an enigma to all involved.

One late September evening Bev Veal, at his meeting with Kelly and Gray, passed on a note about a captured VC agent. The agent was found with receipts for all the purchases that he had made – the VC were very conscientious about saving their receipts in order to prove that they had properly spent the money given them. When questioned by the Counter Intelligence operatives, the VC agent explained that he had been buying batteries for tactical radios, batteries that were available on the black market. The Marine officer trio quickly deduced that if the VC were buying batteries for the new standard PRC-25 radios used by all U.S. forces, then certainly they were talking on tactical circuits. Gray ordered renewed emphasis on searching for VC tactical communications. He personally went out to the SIGINT site on Hill 55 and directed that all the intercept equipment and antennae be optimized. Further, he expected rigid, proper search techniques be employed.

While watching the search operators, Gray noticed that they would routinely stop searching when they reached 54 megahertz. After all, that is the frequency where military communications are supposed to end; indeed, American, South Vietnamese, South Korean and all allied military organizations took place below 54 megahertz because back home, in both the United States and in Korea, television and FM radio stations use frequencies above 54 megahertz. The military, loath to interfere with commercial television or radio, simply chose not to operate on those frequencies. Gray ordered the search to be expanded to the limits of the radio (25 to 74 megahertz). Sure enough, at about 70 megahertz, they found the VC chattering away to their hearts content.

The first part of the mystery had been solved, but there remained a very significant challenge. Though the Americans could understand the plain voice Vietnamese language, it made no sense to them. All they heard was a series of simple foods being named, as though the enemy was transmitting a grocery store shopping list – salt, pepper, rice, etc. Thrown in randomly were words like "meet me, meet me" and "antenna, antenna." Clearly the VC/NVA was using some form of low-level code to confound their enemies and prevent their communications from being exploited. Gray personally spent hours listening to the tapes of the new found communications, trying to discern a pattern. He could tell that the local dialect was different, but little else.

With the communications found, Gray knew that he now needed the best crypto-linguists he could find. As it turned out, an enigmatic NSA civilian was in country, and he was the best linguist NSA had. Because of his refusal to bow to military customs, Berkeley Cook was not highly popular in Saigon. Cook had an unconventional approach to his duties, and his services were made available to Sub-Unit #1 as soon as the requirement for a linguist for I Corps became known. Gray gave the inscrutable civilian some Marine Corps utilities and sent him out to the intercept site on Hill 55 to find out if, indeed, Cook had the language skills necessary to exploit the newly found VC/NVA chatter.

Thanks goodness Cook had some very skilled linguists helping him. When Cook first put on the headphones to listen to the local communications, he did not even recognize the speech as Vietnamese. Cook, and all American linguists, was trained in either the North Vietnamese (Tonkin) dialect, or the South Vietnamese (Cochinchina) dialect. There was a noticeable difference between the two, one even foreign-trained linguists could discern. But what Cook heard on Hill 55 was neither; it was unrecognizable, at least to him. Gray, though, had listened to the some of the live intercept, as well as some tapes, and recognized local words that he was familiar with from his time on Tiger Tooth Mountain. However, Cook's training in the new language was left to others.

Two ARVN linguists, Master Sergeant Hoa and Sergeant Tinh, explained to Cook that the dialect that flummoxed him was the language of Central Vietnam, formerly known as Annam.[9] The team set about applying crypto-analytic and traffic analysis techniques against the enemy chatter. The Annam dialect – much different than those found around Saigon or Hanoi, was used from the area south of Quang Nam province all the way north into the southern reaches of North Vietnam. It was the first dialect that Major Gray was exposed to during operations around Tiger Tooth Mountain.

Hoa and Tinh were part of a highly trained and carefully screened ARVN crypto-logic unit. While they never composed a large group, the ARVN intercept operators were very, very good; and they gave Berkeley Cook an intensive course in Central Vietnamese. With their help, Cook soon learned to distinguish the radio transmissions of interest.[10] The Americans referred to the ARVN operators as "dancers." The dancers' dedication and capabilities earned them the ongoing respect of their American counterparts. By 1967 the dancers were part of ARVN's Unit 15, their American liaison was an NSA civilian named Ralph Adams, the same Ralph Adams that Gray had first met in 1964 when he had been an Army language specialist. Unit 15 was, by then, performing so well that its cryptologists often flew airborne missions against the enemy. In addition, because there were few limitations on where and what the ARVN could do, Unit 15 personnel, sometimes accompanied by Adams or Cook, manned listening posts atop mountains overlooking the Ho Chi Minh Trail. Neither Adams nor Cook ever doubted the loyalty of the dancers.

But Berkeley Cook was having little success breaking the code Al Gray needed to exploit. He listened, and listened some more for days on end; Major Gray checked with him at every opportunity and continued to listen to the tapes personally. However, nothing was revealed and the Marines remained frustrated in their quest to exploit their enemy's prattle.

While Cook never formally briefed Al Gray, he did formulate some interesting opinions of the Commanding Officer of the Radio Battalion. In Cook's view, the only thing that Gray demanded was that each person – Marine, civilian, or "dancer" – executed his job. And when Gray asked about that job, the person had to be sure not to try to embellish on any results or analysis. In Cook's mind, blowing smoke was the worst thing that anyone briefing Al Gray could do. The NSA linguist reported

Figure 7.2
Barney Prosser poses with three "dancers." Note the high ground, terrain that the Signals Intelligence practitioners favored as they tried to intercept line-of-sight enemy communications.[11]

that until he met Al Gray, Cook had no idea "how to listen." As he observed the Marine officer, Cook became conscious of how intently Gray listened to others as they made reports, analysis or observations, and how Gray followed up with keenly accurate questions that amazed the NSA civilian. Berkeley Cook was indeed happy to just 'talk with Major Gray," he had no need, or desire, to formally brief the intensely professional commander. Another Vietnamese linguist of that time, who also worked closely with Cook during the war, was Master Sergeant Joseph Satterthwait. As a Staff Sergeant, he had joined Gray's mission to the old French resort at Dong Bac Ma in 1964, and he shared Cook's view of their commander. Al Gray, proclaimed Joe Satterthwait, is the smartest man he ever met.[12] Nonetheless, even the best officer cryptologist the Marines had, supported by the best linguists and the ARVN dancers, needed a fresh approach to breaking the VC code.

With the help of Lieutenant Colonel John Kelly, and other staff officers in both the G-2 and G-3 shops, Al Gray undertook a retrospective analysis of all the enemy's operations during the past month, hoping to align the intercepted communications with actual events. It was extremely tedious, detailed, time-consuming work, but sure enough, again the integration of SIGINT and general intelligence resulted in cracking the code. Pepper was equal to the number zero, salt was one, and so forth. Thus, the sequence "salt, salt, pepper, pepper, meet me, antenna" meant "call me on the radio at 1100."

It turned out that the enemy was much more straightforward in their radio procedures than the U.S. forces were. For example, instead of using forward observers to adjust artillery fire, the VC would send them to a position ahead of time. When the firing occurred, the observers would report back where the rounds landed and what damage was done. They also would invert coordinates upside down as a low level cryptographic measure. It took Gray, his Marines, Berkeley Cook, and the dancers, all with NSA support, a few more weeks to recover the complete code. The enemy code was amazing in that the VC had memorized the entire system of names that meant different things. Nothing was written. When the code was broken; the result was a major leap forward for the Marines. SIGINT alone probably could not have solved the code challenge for many, many more months, if ever.

It turned out that the VC code was a derivative of one used initially by the Viet Minh against the French. The French education system had almost ended the fluency of the native Vietnamese in their own language. As a result, North Vietnamese documents that revealed their desire to mask their communications showed that they started by using very rudimentary words – words the professional class of Vietnamese leaders had nearly forgotten.

Al Gray's old friend at NSA, Dave Gaddy, did his initial professional work against the Viet Minh; Gaddy had documented the Viet Minh's attempts to improvise a secret schema, but Gaddy's work was not broadly available and was unknown to linguists like Cook until well after the war.[13] Though the VC code system was highly effective, at least as far as Gray and the Americans initially were concerned, the VC's absolute trust in it was not justified. Happily, the VC never changed their codes and that failure cost them dearly, at least while the Americans like Berkeley Cook, Joe Satterthwait and Art Kidd were in country working to exploit their communications.

Figure 7.3
Hilltop positions were not only favored by the 1st Radio detachments, but by all Marines in the field in Vietnam. This Barney Prosser photo gives a excellent example of such positions, though perhaps the photo does not reveal the depth and breadth of the mud![14]

The impetus for the breakthrough in exploiting the codes was an integrated approach to the problem rather than relying exclusively on SIGINT. Drawing from operational summaries as much as from intelligence permitted Al Gray and his Marines to achieve great success. In the coming years, there would be countless events that the Marines would exploit as a result. However, within just a month, the fact that the Marines had broken the VC/NVA code permitted the Americans to take advantage of their knowledge of enemy positions to shape one very important battle.

The Marines of the Radio Battalion, like all Marines in a combat zone, hardly worked normal hours. Normally, Sailors and Marines (and Soldiers and Airmen) who are performing SIGINT/EW types of duties are assigned to watch sections. The number of positions that required manning, for example, determined the number of intercept operators needed. If there five positions, and a four-section watch, then at least 20 operators were required. However, the best situation for Marines never exceeded a three-section watch, and it was generally closer to a two-section regime – or, as they say in the naval service, port and starboard. In combat, all that went out the window. It was not unusual for operators, and particularly analysts, to work straight through for 24 hours. The best operators and analysts were almost always on duty, spelled only to sleep and eat, and even then they often ate at their positions whenever enemy activity was happening.

Concurrent with the efforts to exploit the enemy's tactical communications, other improvements to the overall SIGINT effort were being implemented. For the first time in history, the NSA designated a military direct support unit as the "Collection Management Authority" for a specific area. That field activity was the Radio Battalion, and it was so designated for I Corps. That meant the Marines on scene decided how to attack the enemy communications, not people far away at Fort Meade, Maryland. It was a seminal point in the evolution of Marine SIGINT/ EW operations, and it thrust upon Al Gray the responsibility for directing the efforts not only of his Radio Battalion personnel, but also the people at 8th RRU, those at the Army's site at Pleiku who were working against I Corps targets, and the 138th Aviation Company. Ralph Adams recalled that whenever Al Gray visited the 8th RRU, excitement was generated and "the troops" knew something was going to happen – the Major simply had that effect on everyone, including the senior officers. But the Aviation Company was also particularly significant, and the joining of forces brought SIGINT to new levels of effectiveness in I Corps.

Figure 7.4
An unnamed Marine operates direction finding equipment at one of the forward detachments like those at Dong Ha or on Hill 55 outside Da Nang. Note the construction of his "bunker." [15]

In 1967, the Army unit flew its first generation of tactical SIGINT planes, the RU-6 Beaver and RU-8 Seminole. Both were two-engine, propeller–driven aircraft that were used for airborne intercept and direction finding. Gray had made it a point to coordinate with the Army unit, which was then commanded by Major Donald I. Hobbs, but after the Marines were granted Collection Management Authority for all I Corps, the relationship achieved even better results. The aircraft, operating high above the battlefield, could hear many more signals than could any single, or even multiple, ground intercept sites. In addition, by using pre-assigned flight patterns, the Soldiers manning the aircraft could quickly fix the positions of targets. By rapidly and effectively integrating the Army capability with his own operations, Gray and the Army team demonstrated a model of effectiveness and efficiency never duplicated anywhere in Vietnam by other units of the 224th Aviation Battalion, to which the 138th was subordinate.[16]

TRAVIS TROPHY, OCTOBER 1967

The NSA annually presents an award named the Travis Trophy. Named for the first Director of the United Kingdom's Government Communications Headquarters, Sir Edward Travis, the award was first given for excellence in athletic competitions and chess among subordinate commands. In 1964, Lieutenant General Gordon A. Blake redesigned the award to make it reflect the subordinate command that most contributed to NSA's mission during the year. Among cryptologic units, it remains a big deal.

The event that, perhaps, best signified the maturation of Marine SIGINT/EW occurred in October 1967 at the Headquarters of the NSA. The Marines of 1st Radio Battalion were awarded the Travis Trophy. It represented the culmination of the long hours the men like General Wallace Greene, General Herman Nickerson, Jim Quisenberry, Barney Prosser, Jim Hatch, Murray Sklar, Herman Nickerson, Art Kidd, Charlie Beale, Howie Alberts, and a host of others had invested in order to reconstruct and then implement a SIGINT/EW capability for the Marine Corps. Spearheading the effort directly and from behind the scenes through all those trying years had been Al Gray. When notified that the Marines had been selected for the honor, General Cushman decided to send Major Gray to personally accept it.

Gray had been selected for promotion to lieutenant colonel in September 1967. He arrived back in Washington on a Tuesday, and reported in to HQMC on Wednesday. While there, the Commanding Officer of the Headquarters Battalion quietly promoted him. He merited promotion because he was serving in a lieutenant colonel's billet at III MAF, and because the Marines wanted him to receive the Travis Trophy wearing silver leaves instead of the gold leaves of a major.

Figure 7.5
Capt Ralph Cook, who would soon be promoted to Rear Admiral as Commander, Naval
Security Group Command, poses with the Travis Trophy and Lt Col Al Gray.[17]

On Friday newly frocked Lieutenant Colonel Al Gray went to Fort Meade and picked up the hardware signifying the best cryptologic unit of the year. Al Gray's Marines in Vietnam were very thankful for the support from both 8th RRU and the airborne assets, but it remained for the Marines to put the SIGINT picture together, allocate resources, identify primary and secondary targets, and ensure the effort was fully integrated. They did that task so well that, for the first time ever, a tactical SIGINT unit, not a permanent fixed station, was awarded the trophy. Though he assembled a book full of awards and achievements in the course of his long and illustrious professional life, having the Marines honored by NSA remains one of Al Gray's proudest moments.

The Travis Trophy also meant, in Al Gray terms, that Marine SIGINT had reached the status of the National Football League. The silent but superb efforts of

Figure 7.6
Lt Gen Victor H. Krulak, the Brute, admires the Travis Trophy. Gray had stopped in Hawaii
on his way back to Vietnam to show the Commanding General, Fleet Marine Forces, Pacific,
the award. Gen Krulak was in his final months on active duty; there was no more reso-
lute supporter of Marine Signals Intelligence/Electronic Warfare than Brute Krulak.[18]

the Marines of the Radio Battalion, the Marine Support Battalion and the NSG
were recognized at the NSA as pros. Their achievement also reflected the importance that SIGINT had on Marine operations throughout I Corps. Al Gray's vision
as a young captain in the Pacific and as a very junior major at HQMC had, in fact,
been fulfilled. SIGINT successes in combat had proven the organization worthy of
the 1,000 Marines that had been assigned to the SIGINT/EW MOS. They made
a difference on the battlefield, and they saved the lives of other Marines. Never
again would Marine Corps generals question the value of linguists, crypto-analysts,
special intercept operators, processing and reporting analysts and the other specialties that comprise the SIGINT/EW professional field.

But Gray also received private praise, and from a much less known source. Dan Buckley was one of the cryptologic Marines who accompanied Gray to Tiger Tooth Mountain in 1964. In November 1967, while stationed at NSA and obviously working in proximity to another veteran of Tiger Tooth, the civilian linguist Harry Williams, he typed a short letter to his old boss. Buckley knew that Al Gray was back in Vietnam. The letter reads (in part):

> *"I wasn't surprised at all to hear that you had been promoted... I was surprised that they had let you go back there, isn't there some kind of limit on you? ... Whenever Harry Williams looks sad (most of the time), I just say 'Al Gray' and he smiles again. Your name has a great deal of influence around here. If there is anything that you need in the way of office supplies, etc. let me know and I'll send it out disguised as courier material... Stay alive. You are still the standard by which most Marine officers are judged and we would all miss you. Semper fi, Buckley"*[19]

The men who performed their work with such dedication, expertise and professionalism in Vietnam paved the way for the expansion of intelligence throughout the Marine Corps. Without their efforts, and especially their successes, it is doubtful that the Corps would continue to enlarge the resources and commitments in manpower and equipment as time moved forward into the 21st century.[20]

KHE SANH OR CAMP CARROLL? 27 NOVEMBER 1967

Earlier in 1967, the first battle of Khe Sanh had been fought; the enemy, attacking in great numbers, had been repulsed by the Marines, aided to a large degree by repeated, massive Air Force B-52 strikes, and by artillery fire from the Army's 175mm guns of 2nd Battalion, 94th Artillery and other units of the 12th Marines. It was a fight that Al Gray had observed almost daily while flying as an aerial observer out of Dong Ha and Gio Linh. Though the NVA had withdrawn, no Marine, Army or ARVN commander throughout the chain of command thought the battle was over, especially not Al Gray.

After having visited all the remote locations that held Radio Battalion assets, Gray had focused his attention on Khe Sanh. Located down Route 9 from the village of Khe Sanh, the Marine base surrounded a small airstrip. Khe Sanh had long been an important position in the far northwest corner of South Vietnam. It was the largest American base close to the Ho Chi Minh Trail, whose tentacles ran only a few miles to the west. Further, the base's location at the base of many tall and surrounding hills made it an attractive target for the communists. Gray thought that the area could use more support from a forward collection site and perhaps another

Figure 7.7
Lt Col Gray conducts an informal awards and promotion ceremony. Note the
"sidewalks" constructed to avoid the omnipresent mud during the rainy season.[21]

direction finding team. Already there were Radio Battalion detachments attached to the infantry at Khe Sanh; indeed, in order to get closer to the enemy's low power communications, the SIGINT troops often manned positions at the very edges of the Marine lines. But Gray wanted to improve the direct support offered by his men.

As he was wont to do, the Commanding Officer asked his Operations Chief, Master Gunnery Sergeant Barney Prosser – his comrade from HQMC and other assignments – if he felt like taking a tour of the northern SIGINT facilities. Prosser, well aware of his boss's proclivities, nonetheless indicated he would be happy to go along. Armed with M-16s and little else, the pair with a driver headed up to Gio Linh, then went west to Cam Lo and Camp J.J. Carroll, before continuing to Khe Sanh – which was by then home to the 26th Marine Regiment.

Traveling in a single jeep with just a lone driver as security was excitement enough for the gritty Prosser. But soon after their arrival at Khe Sanh, Gray asked Prosser if he minded taking another jaunt, "with something that would be along soon?" Prosser had no idea what Gray meant, but sure enough a pair of Marine Huey's (UH-1) helicopters soon landed. Gray told the jeep driver to remain at the base while he and Prosser went to look over some hilltops to evaluate their suitability as SIGINT intercept sites. Gray explained to the pilots that they would not have to land, just hover while he and Prosser jumped out. The pilots could return in an hour or so and pick up the pair. Prosser could tell that the pilots were none too happy about the mission. After all, there were no Marines on the hills where Gray wanted to land (Hill 880 and 881) and there was no other air support in the area. Nonetheless, the pilots finally agreed and off they went. They flew over both hills, the tops of which were bare from artillery and air strikes, though neither had a suitable landing zone. Lieutenant Colonel Gray picked one of the possible sites, and sure enough, the helos dropped down low enough for him and Prosser to jump off; the pilots agreed to return in an hour or so.

The two Marine cryptologists scouted the mountaintop and fairly rapidly concluded that neither would be acceptable as a location for their men. The hills were not defendable by less than a company of Marines, and the intercept team would number less than 10. By this time, Barney Prosser was getting nervous. He trusted Al Gray implicitly, but this was the middle of indian country and Prosser was not sure the cavalry (i.e., the helicopters) would return. He could only imagine the possibility of walking off the hilltop back to Khe Sanh.

But, to Prosser's everlasting happiness, the Hueys did return on schedule and pick up the duo. They were dropped off to their waiting driver and made the return trip to Dong Ha without incident. But, the short trip burned forever in Prosser memory the field attributes of Al Gray, Marine. Gray believed in checking things out personally, even if the reconnaissance was slightly unconventional. Few lieutenant colonels conducted personal reconnaissance outside the wire anywhere in South Vietnam, and they were much less likely to do so in the rugged hills around Khe Sanh. But Al Gray never asked anyone to do anything he was not prepared to do himself – and his men's respect and loyalty were his just reward. Although he did not find a site that would serve his purposes, Gray did not divert his attention from the old coffee plantation that had become a Marine combat outpost.

By late 1967, Marine, Army and South Vietnamese intelligence began seeing the signs of another substantial buildup of NVA forces around the DMZ and to the region north and west of Khe Sanh. U.S. Army Brigadier General Philip B. Davidson, Jr., the head of MAC(V) Intelligence in Saigon, the NSA analysts, the Army Security Agency people at 8th RRU in Phu Bai, and nearly everyone else in the intelligence community predicted the place for the next NVA push would be at Camp Carroll, east of Khe Sanh. Indeed, the 3rd Marine Division, located in Phu Bai near the 8th RRU operation, had bought that Army unit's analysis hook, line and sinker. Camp Carroll's location was not quite as remote as Khe Sanh, but the

NVA artillery and rocket fire had, for several weeks, seemed to be targeting Camp Carroll first and foremost. There was one dissenting voice that thought Khe Sanh would again be the target; that voice was Al Gray and the 1st Radio Battalion.

Using SIGINT and every other form of intelligence to predict future enemy actions is certainly an art, never a science. Until there is a clear indicator of enemy intentions, the process of predicting is cumbersome and full of doubt. In World War II, when the code breakers were finally able to tell Admiral Chester Nimitz that Midway Island would be the target of Admiral Isoroku Yamamoto's huge task force, that result was known only after a carefully implemented deception plan confirmed the Japanese code. But as late as November 1967, less than six weeks before the anticipated start to the NVA winter offensive and the Têt holidays, there was no smoking gun pointed one way or the other.

Gray, of course, was collocated with III MAF and enjoyed a special relationship with the three of the most important officers at that Headquarters. He had served with General Cushman many times, and he was able to speak from his experience as an artilleryman with the 12th Marines and at Gio Linh. General Cushman believed whole-heartedly in his Radio Battalion commander. The G-2, Colonel Kenny Houghton, had seen Al Gray rise from a recon sergeant to the Corps' leading practitioner of SIGINT. And Gray spoke the language of the Colonel Fred Haynes, the G-3. No intelligence gobbledygook would sway Haynes; but since he was presented information in terms of combat operations, with examples of how the enemy had operated in the past, Haynes became a ferocious supporter of Al Gray. Thus, the III MAF Headquarters pointed toward Khe Sanh, while everyone else concentrated on Camp Carroll.

General Davidson, seeking to once and for all settle the issue, decided to hold an intelligence conference at Phu Bai at the 8th RRU facilities. Every intelligence analyst who knew anything about the debate was invited and attended. From Air Force photo interpreters in Thailand, to Army airborne SIGINT officers and technicians, to NSA, CIA and MAC(V)'s best, all descended on Phu Bai in late November. The conference was an oft times heated, daylong affair, with the resolution in doubt; finally, late into afternoon, Lieutenant Colonel Gray was handed a scribbled note by one of his Marines who had been in the facility communications center.

Marine analysts had been tracking through intercept, traffic analysis and direction finding a major who commanded an enemy reconnaissance company. At about 1700, a new intercept revealed that the major had reached his objective. The map coordinates he passed, confirmed by the use of direction finding, put the location of the radio used at a stream near Khe Sanh. Gray knew that the unit NVA major

Figure 7.8
Lt Gen Robert Cushman awards Gray his third Bronze Star with Combat "V" for his heroism in the minefield at Gio Linh in June 1967. Al Gray highly respected the fine intellect of the officer who would become the 25th Commandant of the Marine Corps.[22]

commanded was part of the 29th NVA Regiment and that unit was leading a fourth NVA division into the fight. The evidence was more than enough to tilt the debate in Gray's favor. General Davidson congratulated the Marines on their fine efforts and returned to Saigon.

The night of November 28, Colonel Houghton and Lieutenant Colonel Gray returned to III MAF Headquarters at about 2230 and briefed General Cushman. It was a wide-awake Commanding General who immediately ordered the 3rd Division to send three more infantry battalions to the area in and around the airfield at the old coffee plantation. In late December 1967 and early 1968, the entire world would learn of, and follow, the Battle of Khe Sanh. What remained largely unknown except to intelligence professionals was the role of Al Gray and his men of Sub-Unit #1. SIGINT had provided the Commanding General with a three-week advanced warning of the attacks.[23]

But that was not the only night that General Cushman went to bed only after speaking with Colonel Houghton and Lieutenant Colonel Gray. He usually made a point of dropping by the SIGINT/EW Coordination Center to learn if his cryptologists had any forecast of coming events. Not that he thought them soothsayers, but Cushman relied on the Radio Battalion – perhaps more than any Marine general up to that time.

Unfortunately, another general in Vietnam who knew and relied on Al Gray to a great extent was gone. Major General Bruno Hochmuth, the officer who promised Gray an infantry battalion if he extended to stay in the war zone, had been killed in a helicopter crash on November 14. The highly respected and much loved Commanding General of the 3rd Marine Division died with everyone else aboard the helicopter, and the news deeply saddened Gray. The entire Marine Corps had lost one of its stalwarts.

The Khe Sanh episode is perhaps the best example of why Al Gray was such a superb cryptologist. By 1967, he had been interacting with the NSA experts almost continuously for 12 years, and Gray was far more involved with the technical details related to cryptology than almost any other Marine officers were. Gray was able to not only contribute meaningfully, but also lead the efforts in the technical minutia related to traffic analysis, crypto-analysis, direction finding, and collection operations and all areas of processing and reporting. Putting all the technical skills required in cryptology to use in analysis is particularly challenging; still, Al Gray's biggest advantage was that he understood combat intelligence and combat operations. In almost every case when his Radio Battalion technicians were able to predict future events, it was because of the final correlation made by their Commanding Officer. Gray was able to take the technical details and envision what they meant for future enemy operations; it is a skill most cryptologic officers simply do not have because they lack a background in combat intelligence and operations.

Gray's natural affinity for languages endowed him with another major benefit. On a practical basis, for example, his skills permitted him to help decipher Korean when some analysts were incorrectly reporting that Chinese was the language being intercepted. A person's ability to learn languages degrades as one ages; though there are exceptions, and clearly Al Gray was an exception. "Mastering" a language after a person reaches his or her mid-twenties is rare. Gray had learned Korean and Japanese while still in his 20s; however, he was not exposed to daily Vietnamese until 1964, when he was 36. Al Gray's familiarity with a variety of foreign languages was but another fascinating aspect to a very complex man.[24]

His analysis associated with Khe Sanh represented, arguably, his finest hour as a cryptologist.

CHARLIE RIDGE, NEAR DA NANG, NIGHT OF 20-21 DECEMBER 1967

Every Marine unit at and above the battalion level prepares a monthly Command Chronology. Command Chronologies are not meant to be literary gems, and most surely are not. The Command Chronology is designed to give the highlights of the unit's past month, to note important and significant events, give brief analysis of the current situation and highlight any trends. The Chronology also gives facts and figures regarding the unit's personnel, equipment, casualties, enemy casualties inflicted by the unit's operations, etc.

The December 1967 Command Chronology for the III MAF contained the following item:

> *d. The enemy's attempt to attack the Danang area by use of rockets was thwarted when a squad from D/1/7, on the night of 20-21 December, ambushed a large column of VC carrying 122mm rockets toward the Danang Area, killing 17 VC and capturing two 122mm rocket tubes, one with sights and tripod, as well as 1 LMG and 4 rifles while suffering 2 KIA.[25]*

As Paul Harvey used to say, now comes the rest of the story; and there is a lot more to tell.

With the breaking of the low level codes, the idea of finally exploiting the NVA rocket attacks had begun rolling around in Gray's mind. Certainly he knew a lot about the timing of such attacks, the operational tempo that preceded them and the general indicators that such an attack might be forthcoming; in any case, he had been on the receiving end of such incidents dating back to soon after his arrival in Dong Ha with the 12th Marines in mid-1966. He knew that American reaction to the strikes was often quite successful and that the American response made the NVA and VC especially wary about the timing of their attacks. Now, with the low level codes broken, the Marines could be alert for anything that would offer advance notice of the enemy's rocket plans.

In mid-December the cryptologists began picking up chatter that they thought might be associated with another attack, this one against the airfield at Da Nang. It appeared that the NVA were planning something spectacular, something that involved a coordinated attack from at least two different firing points. While the Marines were not exactly sure where one position would be, the other was a long-time favorite setting for VC/NVA troublemaking – Charlie Ridge.

Charlie Ridge lay southwest of Da Nang toward An Hoa and the Liberty Bridge complex. The area was the scene of countless attacks, ambushes and nighttime activity on both sides. But since the Americans were fighting from fixed positions in and around Da Nang, and since Charlie Ridge overlooked vast areas of the region, the vicinity of the ridge was the scene of many enemy provocations; the Marines used the area primarily for ambushes designed to deny enemy passage or intercept VC units that were intent on making mischief, or worse.

By December 20, Lieutenant Colonels John Kelly and Al Gray had formulated a plan to meet the impending rocket attack. Kelly, an infantryman serving a tour in intelligence, had many useful insights into how the enemy operated and devised a brilliant scheme to counter the looming attack. And, consistent with all tactical plans that Al Gray had any part in concocting, it involved deception. Gray insisted, however, that the mastermind behind the plan was John Kelly, and Gray was more than happy to simply help out while adding some embellishments.

Nearly all VC night-time attacks occurred early enough in the evening to permit them to fall back into safe havens before daylight; or if the plan was for an actual assault where the VC intended to overrun and hold a position, then it would take place in the hours between midnight and dawn, when confusion among the target's defenders would be highest. A rocket attack was not going to be the latter type, so Gray and his Marines figured the launch times for the rockets would be about 2300, give or take an hour. The VC would need several hours of marching in near darkness to reach their firing positions, though the launching of the rockets would only take mere minutes, leaving the enemy force time to withdraw safely.

By December 1967, Gray and the rest of General Cushman's intelligence apparatus had the respect of the entire III MAF Headquarters. The G-3, Fred Haynes, the resolute veteran of Iwo Jima, knew both Kelly and Gray from his days at HQMC. Haynes and Houghton, the G-2, were all the support Kelly and Gray needed to implement a deception plan designed to fool the VC rocketeers in concert with planned ambush by Delta Company, 1st Battalion, 7th Marines.

It was thought that the best way to successfully ambush the attackers who would be using Charlie Ridge as a launch point was to make them rush to reach their firing position. Thus, working with the Air Wing, Kelly and Gray had several 55-gallon drums filled with jet fuel; the engineers also set off several loud explosions about 2130 on the night of 21 December. As the blasts sounded throughout the Da Nang tactical area of responsibility, the 55-gallon drums were ignited. To observers as far away as Charlie Ridge it appeared that rockets had slammed into the airfield, which was exactly what the Marines wanted the other VC contingent to think. With the enemy leader confused as to the time of the attack, the VC rocket unit rushed pell-mell toward their objective.

Lying in wait was one of the ambushes placed along likely routes of ingress and egress by D/1/7. Here is an excerpt from the 1/7 Command Chronology for December 1967:

> *Significant operations conducted. During the evening of 20 December 1967, the 1ˢᵗ Battalion, 7ᵗʰ Marines was able to prevent a rocket attack on the Danang Vital Area. The Battalion was alerted to the strong probability of coordinated ground and rocket attacks within the I Corps Area through a series of intelligence reports and during a special intelligence briefing conducted on the afternoon of the 20ᵗʰ by members of the 1ˢᵗ Marine Division Staff. During the evenings of the 20ᵗʰ squad patrol activities were deployed on all likely avenues of approach to the rocket belt within the Battalion's TAOR. At about 2300H a squad ambush patrol from Company D observed a column of approximately 100 NVA/VC moving east out of the Happy Valley complex and into the rocket belt. Immediately other patrols and a platoon-sized reaction force was maneuvered into position to intercept the enemy column. At approximately 2400 the patrols and reaction force engaged the enemy force with small arms, artillery and 81mm mortars. During the next four hours the units in the field had almost continuous contact with the enemy force, and the Battalion Command Post came under heavy mortar fire. The forces in the field attacked to the west and overran an enemy machine gun position and a complete 122mm rocket launcher tube and its tripod and sight. By 210430H the enemy had fled from the battlefield, and the reaction force and patrols had accounted for 17 confirmed enemy KIAs while sustaining 2 USMC KIAs and 5 USMC WIA. During the morning of the 21ˢᵗ the friendly forces searched the area of the battle and found an additional 122mm rocket launcher tube, enemy weapons and other assorted equipment.* [26]

The Marines of 1/7, led by Lieutenant Colonel William J. Davis, had been operating in the area for some time, and their knowledge of the terrain undoubtedly assisted them not only with their initial planning, but also when it became apparent that more than a single squad would be needed to engage the much larger enemy force. The capture of the 122mm rockets and their tripod was the first such seizure of the war. A young 2ⁿᵈ Lieutenant, Michael I. Neal, earned a Navy Cross for his actions during the ensuing firefights, and the air base and adjoining town were spared the wrath of incoming fire. It was a fine night for the Marines of 1/7 and for Marine cryptology, though the cost of the two Marines restrained any celebration.[27]

There was one other conclusion made as the result of the capture of the documents and paraphernalia that night. Back in April 1966, when the sapper attack against A/1/11 led to the appointment of Al Gray as the 12ᵗʰ Marines S-3, Gray had analyzed the motive for the attack. He had conjectured that the enemy had the intention of turning the guns and pointing them toward Da Nang, then firing on the American air base. The self-proclaimed intelligence professionals at the Division and III MAF roundly rejected his conclusion, however. And with little tangible evidence to dissuade them, Gray permitted the matter to drop. Fast forward to the night of December 20, 1967; one of the bodies of an officer carried the paperwork for some sort of award that the deceased had been given for the sapper attack on A/1/11. When the Marines were able to locate the complex that had been attackers base camp, they found a full mock-up of a 105mm howitzer, complete with artillery sights, and the plan to attack Da Nang. Of course, very few in the 1967 Marine intelligence operation knew of Gray's earlier involvement with the analysis of the April 1966 attack, since most had rotated home. But for the former recon sergeant-turned artillerist-turned infantryman-turned spook, it was very satisfying to know he had been right.

LEARNING OF THE COMING TÊT OFFENSIVE

By January 8, 1968, when Lieutenant Colonel Al Gray left Vietnam to return home following the death of his father, Gray was sure that the Marines knew everything the NVA and their VC counterparts were going to do in I Corps. Intelligence given to General Cushman and the South Vietnamese commander provided a multitude of details, excepting only the precise time for the attack.

Throughout Vietnam such was the case. In Saigon, General Westmoreland had convinced the South Vietnamese high command to cancel the cease fire originally planned for *Têt*, and he also asked and received confirmation that ARVN units would not permit too many soldiers to take leave over the holidays. In every Corps region, American commanders knew well in advance that something big was going to happen. However, there was a problem; the American generals could not believe that the communists would try to implement such a poor plan, one that the Americans considered had no chance of success. Thus, rather than diligently and patiently awaiting the attack, some were inclined to discount the danger.[28]

Figure 7.9
Al Gray, Sr. (seated) with a fishing party the day before his untimely death.[29]

In I Corps, the Marines had details that included such small elements as the specific culverts under the exact roads the VC planned to use to infiltrate into populated regions. One particular piece of intelligence pointed to a significant enemy push toward the ancient capital of Hué. Hué was home to 1st ARVN Division and also marked the site of a large MAC(V) compound. Nevertheless, the city itself and the old Imperial Citadel were not heavily defended.

Extensive intercept of local communications indicated that the VC was constructing a very large and elaborate hospital in the area near Phu Bai. Such construction could only mean one thing: that the VC anticipated having a large number of casualties. VC and NVA medical facilities, their quality of care for their wounded, injured and sick, and even their attitudes toward medicine were primitive compared to American standards. That such a large, carefully planned and constructed facility was being built certainly was a precursor for a large-scale attack. Gray knew that, and so did everyone else at the III MAF Headquarters and throughout I Corps.

Thus, despite the fact that intelligence reports warned of an impending attack, the 1st ARVN Division was surprised – at least it reacted as though surprised. No one knows why General Truong, the Commanding General whom Gray knew to be a fine officer, was unprepared for the communist assault. What is known is that the images of the Marines' vicious street fighting that eventually resulted in driving the communists from the Citadel, at a very heavy price in enemy KIA, WIA and captured had a terribly negative effect on American reporters and through them on public opinion.

When combined with the actions seen on video at the American Embassy in Saigon, it looked to the world that the communists had been stunningly successful, when in fact, they were badly defeated everywhere. If one wonders about the power of television to cause emotions, one only needs consider the *Tết Offensive*. Interestingly, for those in search of the "truth," the television images represented as attacks by "communist suicide commandos" do not square with the events on the ground. There was no evidence the dead communists shown on television, all of whom are seen lying outside the chancery building, were "suicide commandos." The video images were simply used – whether with malice of forethought or not – to drum up the emotions of the American viewers, and in that regard, they were most successful.

Of course, video and television could not convey the major enemy catastrophe of the *Tết Offensive*: namely, the failure of any Vietnamese peasants to rise up against the South Vietnamese and the Americans. That had been a major component of the communist plan, and it was utterly rejected by the South Vietnamese civilians. But, since that aspect of events did not lend itself to a sound bite or to a video clip, that piece of the *Tết Offensive* was largely unreported by the media.

Al Gray, on emergency leave looking after his mother in Florida, was stunned by what he saw reported, especially when he compared the intelligence reporting that he still had access to with the evening news. Though not in a position to change anything with respect to the public relations effort of the military, Gray certainly observed and learned from what he saw. And what he saw on television was enough to have him personally reject the reporting; he realized it was tilted strongly against the American effort. And Gray, like many others, declined to accept Walter Cronkite's evening tagline, "That's the way it is."

Al Gray, and other veterans, knew better.

Shortly after Gray left for home, Staff Sergeant Gale Monda arrived back in Vietnam to serve his six-month extension in Da Nang. Unfortunately for Monda, while he was on 30 days leave in Australia, prior to starting his extension, Lieutenant Colonel Gray had departed on emergency leave. Monda recalled discussing Gray with other members of the processing and reporting section, and how Gray would often quietly come around to discuss specific facts or conclusions with the analysts, especially the leading crypto-linguist, Staff Sergeant Gus Gutierrez. As the analysts came on duty, they would be greeted by stacks of intercepts, mostly from Marines but also from an Army aviation unit that flew out of Da Nang. Monda and Gutierrez supported the 3rd Division, and its direct support units, which operated mostly against NVA regulars; two other analysts, Sergeant Ted Gay and Staff Sergeant Fred McIntire supported the 1st Division and the Army's Americal Division, whose Tactical Area of Responsibility covered the southern portion of the I Corps Tactical Zone. The 1st Division and its supporting units operated primarily against indigenous VC, though after Têt in 1968 the number of VC units in the field dropped significantly. With the exploitation of the enemy codes, it was Monda and Gutierrez's, as well as Gay and McIntire's, responsibility to produce "spot reports" highlighting the NVA/VC activities. After some time, these reports provided very, very accurate insights into the enemy. Of course, the Operations Officer, Chief Warrant Officer-2 Murray Sklar, and the Operations Chief, Master Sergeant Jimmy Weeks knew Gray's ways very well, and neither had the slightest heartburn about Gray's circumvention of the chain of command to involve himself directly into the analysis phase of the production of intelligence. This was a team, and the chain of command was mostly for administrative issues; it did not stand in the way of matters related to winning the war.[30]

For Monda, and indeed every analyst, the work was highly rewarding, especially the direct support effort. Monda had returned to Dong Ha before returning home, and he recalled that on one occasion an intercept revealed that the big 120/140mm rockets would hit the sprawling logistics complex. The word quietly was passed to units around the base, and when the attack came the Marines were prepared, and suffered no casualties. For Monda, it represented the epitome of his analytical efforts.

WHAT MIGHT HAVE BEEN IN JANUARY 1968

Al Gray is not a man given to idle speculation regarding "would have, could have or should have" analysis of past events. When asked, however, if he thought his physical presence might have made a difference in late January and early February 1968, his musings, 42 years after the fact were interesting.

There can be little doubt that the Lieutenant Colonel Gray had unique access to and credibility among senior Marine officers, and even among the senior intelligence officials in Saigon and at the NSA. The Khe Sanh – Camp Carroll debate further raised his influence among the MAC(V) intelligence and especially General Philip Davidson, Westmoreland's highly influential G-2. And as anyone who has ever met Al Gray can testify, he is nothing if not persistent, mission-oriented and persuasive.

Thus, even though the American high command knew of the communist plans, the subject of what might have been had Al Gray remained in country prior to Tết is not one to be readily dismissed when future analysis in undertaken. James Robbins's book, *This Time We Win: Revisiting the Tet Offensive*, presents new data not seen in previous histories of the war; but even Robbins did not have the benefit of Al Gray's analysis.

At least part of the problem was that in the time immediately after Lieutenant Colonel Gray left Vietnam, January 8, until the time the *Tết Offensive* started, January 30, there was no senior officer up to speed with SIGINT. The Army generals in Saigon, II Corps and III Corps tended to dismiss the possible attacks, thinking (wrongly as it turned out) that the enemy could not be so stupid as to believe their plans for uprising could succeed. Al Gray was much more pragmatic; if the intelligence indicated that the VC and NVA would strike soon, then he would have been a strong advocate for taking immediate protective measures. Remember that General Cushman had moved three battalions of Marines to Khe Sanh well in advance of the enemy attacks there, based almost 100% on what the Radio Battalion analysis, presented by Al Gray, had showed. Undoubtedly the Commanding General would have followed Gray's warnings about *Tết* most seriously.

The officer who replaced Gray, then Lieutenant Colonel James Quisenberry, had been serving as the Force Psychological Warfare Officer in Phu Bai. Though Quisenberry was a fine officer, with a long background in cryptology dating to 2nd Composite Radio Company circa 1960, he did not have the in-depth knowledge of the target that Gray had. By January 1968 Gray had been in country 28 consecutive months, and 33 of the previous 46 months.

Of course, in I Corps the only failure by the defenders occurred in Hué City. Gray's ties to the 1st ARVN Division might well have changed that unit's alignment in advance of *Tết*. No one was more security conscious than Al Gray, but also few Marines had better professional relationships with the host country's military than did Al Gray. General Truong, the Commanding General, had known Al Gray since 1964; the pair often met in the course of their travels around I Corps. Truong was well aware of Gray's fondness for the South Vietnamese and his commitment to a successful conclusion of the war. It is difficult to imagine circumstances where Gray would not have seen, commented upon, been alarmed by or simply noticed that the defenders of Hué were not properly prepared to receive an attack. Clearly Gray knew that the presence of a new VC field hospital close to Hué, and that communist emphasis on the old Imperial capital meant that the walled city was in the attack's cross hairs. Arguably, no officer traveled throughout I Corps more than Al Gray. He not only would have noticed the defensive problem, but also he mostly likely would have done something about it.

There are many untold stories of the exploits of the Radio Battalion, especially when combined with the field craft exhibited by the Reconnaissance Battalions. Many involved Al Gray to varying degrees. For example, Sub-Group 44 was the enemy headquarters that controlled all NVA and VC units in I Corps and even parts of II Corps. Located in the mountains of western Quang Nam Province, Sub-Group 44 was an extremely high priority target for American activity, from bombers to artillery to SIGINT operations. And while Gray was in Vietnam, the Marines were extremely successful exploiting the enemy's communications, even those that the enemy thought to be secure. In the build-up to *Tết* not only the low level communications were thoroughly and completely exploited, but also the highest, most protected enemy links had been compromised. While Al Gray might not have been personally responsible for all that success, there is little doubt that as an intelligence briefer and advocate he had few peers, and his continued presence surely would have had a positive effect.

While it may be fanciful to suggest that one brand new Marine lieutenant colonel could have made a difference during the seminal event of the war, the convergence of so many factors hint that he just might have. SIGINT and captured documents drove the information that permitted the Allies to understand the enemy plan. No one in Vietnam had more credibility with respect to SIGINT than Al Gray. Few in I Corps had as much influence among ARVN officers. And few anywhere were as persuasive an advocate as the exceptionally proficient, hard working, intellectually gifted Marine professional.

VIETNAM WAR, 1967

WAR IN VIETNAM, 1967

In I Corps the tempo of operations increased in 1966 as the Marines moved elements of the 3rd Division north to Dong Ha and the DMZ to counter the NVA threat in the northern part of I Corps. Throughout 1967 both the VC/NVA and the Marines became increasingly aggressive; after all they shared a common goal – kill as many of the enemy as possible. As a result, the operational pace remained high and then increased into the early months of 1968. With it, the numbers of Marines in Vietnam, and the number of friendly and enemy casualties sustained also grew. While there are many differences between Marine combat in Vietnam and what the Marines faced just over 20 years earlier in the Pacific, or in Korea in the early 1950s, it would not be fair to characterize one as more difficult than the other.

Marines in World War II faced savage combat against a tenacious enemy, which was also the case Vietnam. Perhaps the biggest difference the men in the ranks experienced was that during World War II veterans stayed with their units for years, some for the duration of the war. In Vietnam, men rotated into the country on individual orders, stayed 13 months, and then, generally speaking, went home. Unless they reenlisted, veterans of Vietnam were unlikely to return to the war zone. However, that is not to say that among combat units – infantry, artillery, tanks – Marines in Vietnam saw less combat than their predecessors. In World War II, Marine divisions would be committed to campaigns that lasted, usually, a couple months or less; the division would then go to some area to rest and revitalize itself before starting another campaign. For most grunts and artillerymen in Vietnam, combat, or at least the threat of combat, was incessant. And while the big battles of Vietnam do not inspire the sacred memories associated with Guadalcanal, Tarawa, Iwo Jima, Okinawa, the Pusan Perimeter or Chosin Reservoir, it would be difficult to persuade veterans of *Starlite*, *Prairie*, Gio Linh, Camp Carroll, Khe Sanh, Hué City, Dai Do, the Rockpile, the An Hoa Basin or a hundred additional places that the "Greatest Generation" faced more challenging fights against more determined enemies a quarter century earlier.

Vietnam veterans also did not face the extreme weather brutality or enemy hordes that were seemingly more numerous than flies like their Korean War uncles did. But those in Vietnam fought a war without any front lines, and did so without the adulation and unequivocal support of their countrymen; and they were also under the continuous glare of the newest form of mass media – television. Vietnam was the first television war, and that was not always a good thing. Newsmen quickly learned that images were more powerful than words, and that images could influence public opinion in ways words never could. Regrettably, the television commentators of the day were more interested in manipulating public opinion than they were reporting objectively about Vietnam; it was a condition of reporting never encountered, or even imagined, by World War II or Korean veterans.

So in 1967 and into 1968 the Marines continued to expand their efforts, reinforced in I Corps by divisions from the U.S. Army. The Marine high command also remained committed to winning the hearts and minds of the Vietnamese people. Civic Affairs and the Combined Action Program (CAP) were given a much higher priority among the Marines than they ever got in the rest of Vietnam. While CAP related issues were largely positive, the rotation cycle played havoc with results. No sooner did the Americans earn the trust and respect of the locals than they were rotated, making consistency in execution very difficult; interestingly, and based only on anecdotal evidence, a higher percentage of Marines involved in CAP extended their tours in the war zone compared to grunts in line infantry units. However, having the Marines live, train and fight with the Popular Forces and Regional Forces, in effect serving as a force multiplier, was perhaps the most effective example of American-Vietnamese military cooperation of the entire war.[31]

Despite the Westmoreland strategy of *search and destroy*, even the Commanding General of the MAC(V), had to permit the Marines some latitude with respect to the conduct of the war in I Corps. Every level of the Marine Chain of Command, from the Commandant through the Commanding General of FMFPAC, to the Commanding General, III MAF in Da Nang believed that *clear and hold* was the appropriate strategy for the war. Westmoreland's view also became known as the *big war*. General Krulak, in Hawaii, was a particularly vociferous advocate of the Marine position – the *small war*. The debate was intense and passionate. The resulting compromise, while not detracting significantly from the big unit war advocated and demanded by Westmoreland, ensured that the small war would never achieve the critical mass necessary for success. At the height of the war there were about 79,000 Marines in Vietnam, with no more than 2,500 ever assigned to combined-action units.[32] More than simple numbers, however, too often Marine infantry units were not supportive of CAP units operating in close proximity. And there was a simple reason, Marine battalion commanders were tasked to seek out and destroy the enemy, not win the hearts and minds of the peasants.[33] There was no body count associated with winning hearts and minds.

Marine artillery, however, gave the CAP Marines a critical lifeline of support. Given the reactions by ARVN commanders, the effectiveness of the program paid excellent benefits in boosting the morale and combat effectiveness of Popular and Regional Forces; who knows what might have happened if the program was extended to all of I Corps?

Lieutenant Colonel William R. Corson, USMC, who had as much experience in Vietnam as any officer of any service, disliked the strategy of the big war and thought the small war could have, properly implemented and with long-term commitment, been effective. But even so bright and engaging an officer as Corson realized half measures would never be effective. Thus, while the development of the program at some level did reflect the Marines desire to secure population and make it safe from communist terrorism, it never had the resources and steadfastness of purpose to give it a chance for long-term victory. Nonetheless, where implemented, CAP was generally quite successful.

Not that there were many good examples of American/South Vietnamese military cooperation. As early as 1964, Major Al Gray had noted with skepticism the Americanization of the South Vietnamese Army. Already, at that early date, the ARVN had all the trucks, jeeps, and other extraneous items needed by an American fighting force in Europe, but not one fighting in Vietnam. One of the enduring images of the ARVN infantry is that of a young Vietnamese infantryman carrying a humongous backpack into a rice paddy. Who knows how long or how far that soldier could carry his burden? Certainly there are also images of NVA troops laden with heavy loads, but those were typically men toiling on the Ho Chi Minh Trail, carrying supplies into South Vietnam. NVA and VC troops did not carry large packs into battle.

But worse than molding the ARVN to fight like a North Atlantic Treaty Organization force, the American high command never actually trained or relied on the ARVN to take the fight to the enemy. Perhaps the best analogy of the situation was put forth by General Melvin Zais, U.S. Army, who likened the U.S. policy to college football players sent to coach a high school squad. Instead of coaching the young guys, the college players simply injected themselves into the game.[34] At some point the Americans had to permit the ARVN to take care of business, but while the U.S. still had major combat units in war, it never took such action. During 1967 and 1968, instead of actually training the ARVN to face the NVA threat while also encouraging the strengthening of local security forces, General Westmoreland remained intent on search and destroy missions using American troops. At that mission he was largely successful, especially in I Corps in 1967.

The Marines and Army forces in I Corps had a series of fierce battles with the North Vietnamese that resulted in a dramatic rise in the number of casualties on both sides. The convergence of Westmoreland's and the NVA's goals – both sought to inflict the maximum number of casualties on the other – resulted in nearly continuous combat for Marines along the DMZ and in places like the An Hoa Valley, and the ARVN participated fully in the fighting.

Usually, however, the ARVN were left mostly to their own ends and means, though American air power and artillery support were absolutely essential to ARVN operations. That reliance on American supporting arms would, in the end, prove fatal to the South Vietnamese, though that would be several years in the future.

AIR WAR, 1965-1968

As frustrating to Americans as the ground war in South Vietnam had become by 1967, the air war in North Vietnam was every bit as taxing in manpower, national treasure and military effectiveness. Lyndon Johnson, the principal architect of the air war, never figured out the purpose of his efforts. Sometimes he used bombing campaigns to punish the North for its aggression; other times he used it as a reward to get the South Vietnamese to improve either their government policies and operations or their military commitment. Still other times, LBJ seemed intent on cajoling the communists to join a peace process. Whatever his purpose, the air war suffered from a series of decisions made haphazardly without any understanding of conditions in North Vietnam.

Between March 1965 and October 1968, there were six phases of Rolling Thunder. There were seven halts to the bombing while LBJ gauged the communists' reaction, which in every case was the same. The North Vietnamese invariably used bombing halts to improve their defenses, gather new resources from the Soviet Union and China, collect supplies for shipment south, and generally made the most of their situation. More than anything else, however, the North Vietnamese were startlingly effective at using propaganda to inveigh against the American bombing attacks. Whether it was Harrison Salisbury of the *New York Times* reporting that Americans were committing atrocities by deliberately targeting civilians or, later in the war, Jane Fonda posing with anti-aircraft artillery, the communists were masters of influencing American public opinion. Indeed, there was one clear and unambiguous winner of the propaganda war – the North Vietnamese communists.[35]

The air war in Vietnam saw many innovations that were later refined, improved upon and then widely used during the more recent Gulf, Iraqi and Afghani wars. While the Global Positioning System had not yet been developed, precision bombing using television and electronic homing devices was introduced during the air war against North Vietnam. In fact, technologically speaking, the air war was characterized by a series of punches and counter-punches delivered by each side.

The introduction of advanced Soviet-made surface-to-air missiles caused heavy losses to American Airmen; the presence of the surface-to-air missiles also made the Americans change their tactics. While the ratio of surface-to-air missile launches to kills was relatively low, their presence forced Airmen to fly lower; that played into the hands of the communists, who significantly increased the number and effectiveness of their conventional anti-air weaponry to complement their surface-to-air missile capabilities. The fact was that optically controlled anti-aircraft artillery was more of a threat than surface-to-air missiles, particularly on clear days. The anti-aircraft artillery threat drove the aircraft even lower, where they were susceptible to small arms fire. An estimated 60% of American aircraft losses were the result of small arms fire, i.e., 12.7mm or smaller.[36]

The effectiveness of the surface-to-air missiles also caused the Americans to undertake aggressive, emergency programs to advance U.S. resources in both jammers and passive countermeasures. Jammers defeated the enemy radars by confusing or overpowering them; passive countermeasures gave flyers early notification of the presence of surface-to-air missile radars or the launch of missiles in their direction, thereby permitting pilots to take evasive action. Navy EA-6A Prowlers and during the later years its successor EA-6B aircraft made it suicide for communist forces to turn on their missile-guidance radars for any longer than a few seconds lest American bombs home in on their locations with devastating accuracy. Each side adjusted its tactics to confuse its enemy; and at various times each held the upper hand. By November 1967, jammer advances by the United States Air Force meant that, effectively, the Americans had free access over surface-to-air missile sites because the Americans could jam the uplinks of the communist system, thereby rendering the missiles useless. Unfortunately, it was a long time before the American planners realized their advantage.

By August 1967, the ability of the air war to bring an end to communist aggression was nearly at hand. The North Vietnamese were seriously hurting, even though LBJ never unleashed his forces to attack all military targets in the North. Indeed, by August the communist plan for a general offensive in the South (the forthcoming *Tết Offensive* of 1968) was in jeopardy because Ho Chi Minh's forces could not get enough supplies into South Vietnam. But, true to form, and not realizing the potential for success by maintaining or even increasing the pressure, President Johnson decided to call a halt to the bombing. The North Vietnamese quickly adapted and recovered; Johnson never did.

WASHINGTON, 1967

During World War II, Americans on the home front made countless sacrifices in order that the war effort would receive the benefit of most American resources. By 1967, the situation in Washington was radically different. In Southeast Asia, the American war effort continued to expand and more men and more equipment were committed to halting communist aggression. And one must not forget that throughout the 1950s, 1960s and even into the 1990s, America was deeply involved in an expensive and seemingly unending arms race with the Soviet Union. Indeed, the Soviets were the focus of the DoD budget, not Vietnam. Despite all the military requirements he faced, at the White House Lyndon Baines Johnson was in the fourth year of his Presidency and his top priority remained his Great Society initiative. The war in Vietnam continued to be just a troublesome distraction for the American President.

Johnson viewed himself as a worthy successor to Franklin Delano Roosevelt. Roosevelt had pushed through his "New Deal" during the depression years of the 1930s. By 1965, LBJ had formulated even more grandiose programs intended to reduce or eliminate poverty while improving race relations in the United States. Accordingly, he shepherded into law giant new spending plans associated with education, health care, urban recovery and transportation. The result of the combination of skyrocketing domestic spending with an ever-increasing defense budget was that, in macro-economic terms, LBJ attempted to provide both guns and butter. And like many plans where focus is diffused, he failed at both.

On the defense front, LBJ took more and more of the responsibility for the war in Vietnam. By early 1967, Robert Strange McNamara, the enigmatic Secretary of Defense had grown more and more skeptical of American ability to end the war there successfully. It is not clear which came first, the egg represented by LBJ's concentration of power in the White House or the chicken reflected by McNamara's growing diffidence toward events he had long dominated. Despite McNamara's evolving position towards Vietnam, the American public opinion towards the war in 1967 remained fairly strong.

On April 28, General William Westmoreland gave a 29-minute address to a combined session of Congress. The speech, during which the General gave an optimistic assessment of the conduct of the war, was interrupted by applause 19 times, hardly indicative of a Congress out of sync with the American commander.[37] And while television newscasts did not praise the American effort, during 1967 neither were they entirely negative about the war and its possible outcomes.

Perhaps the primary issue that drove a wedge between LBJ and McNamara was the President's lying both about his intentions for the war and the facts on the ground in Vietnam. LBJ simply could not bring himself to tell the truth to either the press or the country about expanding the war effort. Moreover, LBJ demanded that the Secretary of Defense and the Joint Chiefs publicly defend his stance.[38] Indeed, Johnson's public statements created a significant credibility gap for his administration.

As early as his presidential campaign against Barry Goldwater in 1964, Johnson was never forthright about his intentions in South Vietnam. By late 1967, Johnson's lack of candor was coming home to roost. In November Senator Eugene J. McCarthy of Minnesota, an avowed anti-war candidate, announced he would oppose LBJ and seek the Democratic nomination for the Presidency. It was McCarthy's surprisingly strong showing in the New Hampshire primary in March 1968 that eventually led to Johnson's withdrawal from the race, but not before LBJ further confused the policies related to the war.

When the bombing halt in August permitted the communists to again send military supplies, men and equipment south, the American diplomatic blunder committed in the early 1960s came clearly into focus. Ceding control of the border areas of both Laos and Cambodia to North Vietnamese occupation permitted the flood of supplies to be moved along the Ho Chi Minh Trail. It was the single biggest factor permitting the *Tết Offensive* of January 1968. While bombing of the Trail certainly had some effect, without troops on the ground there was never going to be a halt to communist domination of the area. South Vietnam and American ground forces ended up paying a heavy price for the foolishness with which American diplomats concluded the Geneva Accords on Laos in 1962.

Adding to the diplomatic miscalculation were the public relations efforts of General William Westmoreland. Westmoreland understood the significant damage that had previously been done to the North Vietnamese and had seen his forces inflict heavy casualties on the VC and NVA in South Vietnam during 1966 and 1967. Having given Congress an optimistic assessment in April, in November he forecast improved results in the near future. However, his remarks were obfuscated by the anti-war crowd, which claimed he had seen that there was "a light at the end of the tunnel in terms of ending the war." Westmoreland never publicly said that, though his television performances surely added to the growing disillusionment about the war only a few months later.[39]

SAIGON, 1965-1967

After a series of brief and largely ineffective governments, the South Vietnamese settled on Nguyen Van Thieu as its President in 1965. Thieu and Nguyen Cao Ky, the very effective and highly popular Air Marshall, put aside their ambitions and served together as President and Prime Minister. By 1967, the government was sufficiently composed to hold elections, with the Thieu-Ky team running largely unopposed. Like every election ever held in Vietnam (North or South) the contest in 1967 involved much fraud and was largely rigged. On the other hand, when in history has there ever been a free election inside a country that was defending itself from outside aggression and also was under significant internal strife? The answer is never.

Thieu had been a relatively obscure colonel before helping then President Ngo Dinh Diem put down a revolt in 1960. That action, and his conversion to Catholicism, placed him in a more prominent position, though he personally remained very cautious in his approach to politics. He obviously chose to rise through the ranks through the process of elimination as others put themselves in untenable positions. In 1963, however, he backed the overthrow of Diem and played no small role in that distressing event. After two years of coups and counter-coups, Thieu finally reached the pinnacle of power in 1965 through his partnership with Ky. The elections of 1967, largely symbolic and probably undertaken mostly to appease American sensibilities buttressed his position as the leader of the country.

Unfortunately, Thieu never achieved the stature that Diem held at the time of his assassination. Thieu lacked the ability needed to inspire his countrymen while also dealing with a superpower ally to hold off a determined aggression from North Vietnam. But Thieu, through Marshall Ky's security advisor, Nguyen Ngoc Loan, enjoyed considerable success in reducing violence and crime in and around Saigon, and even into the countryside. General Loan was a brilliant man, and surprising for one of the Vietnamese elite, steadfastly incorruptible. Nevertheless, Loan was immortalized by Eddie Adams's picture of him shooting a communist agent in the head. The picture made him appear a ruthless police figure when he was arguably more than justified in his actions. Living as though the country was subject to the civilian laws of the United States was hardly an option, and Loan was effectively stopping the communists until he ran afoul of the very people who should have supported his efforts the most – American diplomats and reporters. They created an uproar over Loan's methods and his seeming self-importance. That Marshall Ky remained somewhat a rival of Thieu exacerbated the situation.

In 1968 Loan, a brazenly brave leader who led from the front, was badly wounded while leading his men (and some American military policemen) against the remnants of the VC who remained in and around Saigon following the *Tet Offensive*. He was removed from power and soon left South Vietnam for treatment first in Australia and then the United States, a tragic figure. His removal further marginalized Marshall Ky, and made South Vietnamese security much more problematic. The whole, sordid Loan affair is illustrative of how not to aid and abet a friendly country struggling against both an invasion and an internal political uprising. The American diplomats and reporters then in Saigon should forever be ashamed of their treatment of General Loan.[40]

Among Thieu's many faults, perhaps his inability to select and retain effective high level, i.e., corps, commanders were his greatest. The South Vietnamese armed forces fought tenaciously, bravely and determinedly when well led. And at the division levels and lower, that was often the case. Lieutenant Colonel Al Gray and many other Marines considered the 1st ARVN Division to be a crackerjack outfit most of the time. It had a series of popular, professional and highly effective commanding generals. The independent ranger and parachute battalions, and South Vietnamese Marine battalions fought as well as any units in the war. The 2nd ARVN Division was also very good, though not quite at the level of the 1st Division.[41] But at the highest levels of the ARVN, generals were selected not so much for their fighting abilities, but for their loyalty to Thieu. And, of course, it must be noted that communists had infiltrated many ARVN staffs; as a consequence, it was nearly impossible for the ARVN to mount surprise operations against the VC or NVA.

At least President Lyndon Johnson had learned from the Diem debacle, and he was determined to support the South Vietnamese President every way he could. He dispatched advisors; he went to Vietnam himself, and at every opportunity Johnson stressed to Thieu his commitment to saving South Vietnam from the communists. Sadly, all the verbal support that Thieu was given created what would become a major problem for the South Vietnamese President: namely, he believed what he was being told. As a result, he never took the steps necessary to lay the groundwork for a South Vietnam capable of defending itself. And why should he have taken those steps? After all, Johnson was telling him, in effect, that America would be there forever.

Did the ARVN fight? You bet. By the end of 1967, South Vietnam had about 735,000 men in uniform and the country had absorbed nearly 48,000 killed in action; that was from a total population that never reached 20,000,000. Yes, the

South Vietnamese people were willing to defend their country. To compare the relative size and commitment of forces, the end of 1967 saw 385,000 Americans and 52,500 men from Allied countries fighting for South Vietnam. Americans killed in action at the end of 1967 numbered 6,644.

As 1967 closed, and 1968 unfolded, Al Gray was back in America for a new assignement. Heavy fighting remained ahead, particularly in northern I Corps, but for at least a while Al Gray was out of fight.

NOTES AND REFERENCES

1. Physically touching someone who is special or different, for example blonde, is widely accepted in Japan as a show of good feelings and warmth. Japanese reaction to such people is far different from anything seen in the United States.
2. The III MAF Command Chronology identifies the unit as Sub-Unit #1. However, other documents more rightly refer to 1st Radio Battalion (-), which indicates that less than the full radio battalion was deployed. For the purposes of this book, either designation is acceptable.
3. Though Sub-Unit #1 was an attached unit, the III MAF G-2, then Colonel Kenneth J. Houghton prepared Gray's reports during the period he was in command.
4. Author interviews with 1st Sergeant Gale N. Monda, USMC. 2009-2011.
5. Author interviews with Colonel Beale, 2007-2010.
6. Recall that the original agreement between Commandant Pate and CNO Burke permitted 33% of the 1,000 Marines to be withdrawn from Naval Security Group Activities for use by the Marine Corps when needed. The Marine Corps made full use of that arrangement, and such men were sent to work Marine targets at 8th RRU. It must also be noted that during the war many Sailors from the NSG worked at the III MAF Critical Communications Center, augmenting the Marines, who were happy to get the help.
7. From Major Bernand Prosser's private collection.
8. Extended interviews with Major Prosser, 2008-2010.
9. See Chapter 1 for an explanation of the languages of Vietnam.
10. Author telephone interview with Berkeley Cook, April 2011. During the interview, Cook revealed that he intended to visit Sergeant Tinh in Texas during May 2011. Tinh had made it to the United States, though General Gray indicated he thought Hoa did not.
11. From Major Bernand Prosser's private collection.
12. Email from Joseph Satterthwait to author, April 2011.
13. In the early to mid 1950s, the Viet Minh realized that some of their cryptosystems might be breakable, and they introduced an internal, "super-encipherment" of cover names to add an additional layer of security, difficult to exploit. Emails between author and David W. Gaddy, April 2011.
14. From Major Bernand Prosser's private collection.
15. From Major Bernand Prosser's private collection.
16. Letter of Appreciation from Major Donald I. Hobbs to Lieutenant Colonel Gray dated January 1968. From General Gray's private collection.
17. From General Gray's private collection.
18. From General Gray's private collection.
19. Dan Buckley letter to Lt. Col. Gray dated 28 November 1967. From General Gray's private collection.
20. From the two small Composite Radio Companies of the late 1950s, the Marine Corps of 2010 has three radio battalions and a Marine Cryptologic Support Battalion, all

carved from a total personnel count basically the same in 2010 as it was in 1965 when Gray's efforts at HQMC first took effect. Al Gray remained closely connected with NSA throughout his professional life, and long after retirement from active duty.

21. From Major Bernand Prosser's private collection.

22. Author interview with Major Prosser, 2009-2010. Prosser accompanied Al Gray to the ceremony and recalled that Major General Raymond L. Murray, the Deputy Commanding General, III MAF, remarked to Gray that the facts mentioned in the citation for his award would have been more appropriate for a Navy Cross. Awards, however, never were what mattered to Al Gray.

23. Author interview with Major Prosser, 2009-2010. Prosser recalled that Lieutenant Colonel Gray was focused on the target of the likely NVA attack, and that Gray personally directed most of the analysis. That Gray had previously seen the communist buildup in the area, while serving in the artillery and as an aerial observer, was a significant factor in the analysis.

24. The author attended the Defense Language School (Russian) when he was 25. The school had a variety of data that projected how well students would do, and age was a significant factor.

25. III MAF Command Chronology, December 1967; Part II, Narrative Summary, Section 3 Overall Evaluation. Note the spelling of "Danang." The Marines were hardly slaves to linguistically correct transliteration.

26. TAOR is Tactical Area of Responsibility. 2300H equals 11 PM; 2400 is midnight. 210430H also denotes the time: 210430H equals 21 December 04:30 AM.

27. Command Chronology, Headquarters, 1st Battalion, 7th Marines, 1st Marine Division (Rein), FPO San Francisco, CA 96601 dated 3 January 1968. The entire command chronology, as well as those for almost all other Marine units, is available online at http://www.recordsofwar.com/vietnam/usmc/USMC_Rvn.htm (January 2011). Included in the document are patrol overlays, including grid coordinates for each patrol that occurred the night of 20 December, and every other night that month. Unfortunately, Command Chronologies for Radio Battalion Sub-Unit #1 have not been declassified.

28. James S. Robbins has by far the best account of the American knowledge of the NVA plan for Tết: *This Time We Win: Revisiting the Tet Offensive*; Encounter Books, New York, 2010.

29. From General Gray's private collection.

30. Extensive email correspondence between author and 1st Sergeant Gale Monda (2009-2011).

31. For a complete understanding of the CAP program, see Peterson, Michael E., *The Combined Action Platoons: The U.S. Marines Other War in Vietnam*. Praeger, New York, 1989. A veteran of the Combined Action Platoons, Peterson provides a well-done history of the combined action program and how they were employed: their efficiencies, their triumphs and also their inevitable problems. In the end, Peterson proclaims himself a cynic about any chance of American success in Vietnam, and a person who "believes in peace." Who doesn't? Most likely Peterson is one of the many good guys brow-beaten into accepting academic and media orthodoxy.

32. Peterson, p. 123.

33. As a young lieutenant, the author was assigned to duty as the S-2 (Intelligence). Our Battalion, 2/4, was operating near the DMZ, and the battalion commander was relatively new to the war zone. Continuing a tradition long observed by military leaders, he would periodically ask the staff, during periods of inaction, questions about their views on various topics; and also in keeping with the tradition, he would require the most junior person to answer first, a tactic designed to ensure the views of the more senior officers did not influence what their juniors might say. The question one evening was, "What can the U.S. do to improve operations?" Being the only lieutenant present and the first to respond, my answer, based on personal experience months earlier, was that we needed to improve coordination between the Marines and USAID. That

organization handed out rice and other food to refugees, which we – the Marines – would then confiscate and remove back to our bases in order to prevent the food from falling into VC hands. The battalion commander pronounced me a "naïve idealist" and moved on to the next opinion. Clearly, his interest was entirely on how to kill the enemy more efficiently, perhaps rightfully so.

34. Willbanks, James H. *Abandoning Vietnam: How America Left and South Vietnam Lost Its War*. 2004, University Press of Kansas; p. 282.

35. See, for example, Footnote #42 in Chapter 5.

36. Interview with Dr. John Guilmartin, March 2011. John Guilmartin is an expert on all phases of the Vietnam War, but especially the air war over the North, where he flew Jolly Green Giant rescue helicopters.

37. Langguth, p. 443.

38. There are many sources that tell of Johnson's bullying ways towards his subordinates. Perhaps the best with respect to McNamara and the Joint Chiefs is McMaster. But also see Langguth or Karnow.

39. Langguth, p. 467.

40. James E. Robbins gives the best discussion of Nguyen Ngoc Loan. General Loan is a central figure in Robbins' account, which has a very interesting perspective on reporters and reporting of the war. The more traditional, that is to say dismissive and contemptuous, view of Loan and his career is reflected in Karnow's *Vietnam: A History*. Karnow's utter disrespect for the South Vietnamese patriot is clearly demonstrated in his three references to Loan. Of course, one must recall that the best source of Karnow's information about the South Vietnamese was Pham Xuan An, the communist agent who was so active among American and allied reporters. In A.J. Langguth's work *Our Vietnam*, Loan is not even important enough to merit description other than as part of the "Saigon Execution" photograph. The man executed, code-named Bay Lop, was in fact a communist assassin who killed several South Vietnamese before meeting his well-deserved fate. Any internet search of "Eddie Adams Loan Photo" will quickly bring up the photograph in question.

41. Major and then Lieutenant Colonel Al Gray had close and continuous interaction with both the 1st and 2nd ARVN Divisions during the period May 1964 through January 1968. Both impressed him. The effectiveness of the ARVN ranger, parachute and Marine battalions are widely known and reported upon.

BIBLIOGRAPHY

BIBLIOGRAPHY

INTERVIEWS

The author has had the privilege to interview and communicate with many military personnel and colleagues of General Al Gray in the process of writing Volume 1, and thanks these individuals for the use of their contributions in this work.

Lieutenant Colonel Howard Alberts (USMC) (2007 and 2008)

Ralph W. Adams (NSA) (2011)

Lawrence N. Bangs (USMC) (2008-2011)

Douglas R. Beard (USA) (2009-2011)

Colonel Raymond A. Becker (USMC) (2009)

Colonel Charles H. Beale (USMC) (2007-2010)

Colonel John A. Bicknas (USMC) (2007-2011)

Captain George Carnarko (USMC) (2008)

Berkeley Cook (NSA) (2010)

Barry DeVita (USA) (2011)

Captain Owen Englander (USN) (2007-2011)

Senior Executive David W. Gaddy (NSA) (2009-2011)

General Alfred M. Gray (USMC) (2007-2012)

Mrs. Alfred M. Gray (2007-2012)

Lieutenant Colonel John F. Guilmartin, Jr. PhD (USAF) (2007-2012)

Colonel John K. Hyatt (USMC) (2007)

Lieutenant General Robert B. Johnston (USMC) (2010)

Captain Arthur Kidd (USMC) (2008-2010)

Edgar Kitt (USMC) (2008-2011)

Colonel Donald Q. Layne (USMC) (2010)

Chief Warrant Officer-4 Donald C. Larson (USMC) (2008)

Albert Mason (USN) (2008)

Donald McIntyre (2012)

Senior Executive Robert S. Meck (NSA) (2009-2011)

Master Gunnery Sergeant Robert P. Merle (USMC) (2007)

1st Sergeant Gale N. Monda (USMC) (2009-2011)

Major General John E. Morrison (USAF) (2007)

Colonel William R. Morrison, USMC (Ret) (2008)
Lieutenant Colonel Jack Perry (USMC) (2008)
Major Bernard Prosser (USMC) (2008-2011)
Colonel James Quisenberry (USMC) (2008)
Master Gunnery Sergeant Joseph Satterthwait (USMC) (2011)
Gregory T. Smith (USA) (2011)
Lieutenant Colonel Andrew Tenis (USA) (2011)
Lieutenant General Richard G. Trefry (USA) (2008)
Colonel Larry Vinyard (USA) (2011)
Chief Warrant Officer-4 James Wiese (USMC) (2008)
Lieutenant Colonel Patrick D. Wilder (USMC) (2012)
Deputy Director Harry T. Williams (NSA) (2007-2011)

PRIVATE COLLECTIONS, PUBLIC ARCHIVES

Larry Bangs
Raymond Becker
George Carnako
General Alfred M. Gray
Dr. John F. Guilmartin
Dennis Jenkins
Arthur Kidd
Scott Laidig
Robert Meck
William Pedrick
Jack Perry
Pat Wilder
Harry T. Williams
General Alfred M. Gray Oral History, National Security Agency, 2010-2011
Author videotaped interviews with General Alfred M. Gray, 2009-2011.

BOOKS, ARTICLES

Berman, Larry. *The Incredible Double Life of Pham Xuan An,* Time *Magazine Reporter & Vietnamese Communist Agent.* New York: Collins, 2007.

Bernstein, Irving. *Guns or Butter: the Presidency of Lyndon Johnson.* New York: Oxford University Press, 1996.

Clancy, Tom, General Anthony C. Zinni, and Tony Koltz. *Battle Ready.* New York: G.P. Putnam's Sons, 2004.

Coram, Robert. *Brute: The Life of Victor H. Krulak, U.S. Marine.* New York: Little Brown & Company, 2010.

Davis, Colonel William J. (ed). *The Story of Ray Davis.* Varina, N.C.: Research Triangle Publishing, 1995.

Dickson, Paul. *The Electronic Battlefield.* Bloomington: Indiana University Press, 1976.

Drury, Bob, and Tom Clavin. *Last Men Out: The True Story of America's Heroic Final Hours in Vietnam.* New York: The Free Press, 2011.

Fall, Bernard. *Street Without Joy.* Mechanicsburg, PA, Stackpole Books, 2005.

———. *The Two Viet Nams*: A Political and Military Analysis (2ⁿᵈ Revised Edition). New York: Praeger, 1965.

Guilmartin, John F. *America in Vietnam: The Fifteen Year War.* New York: Military Press, 1991.

Halberstam, David. *The Best and The Brightest.* New York: Ballantine Books, 1969.

Hammer, Ellen J. *A Death in November: America in Vietnam, 1963.* New York: Oxford University Press, 1987.&

Karnow, Stanley. *Vietnam: A History.* New York: Penguin Press, 1997.

Kidd, Arthur. *My Life as a Marine.* Private Press, 2007.

Krulak, Victor H. *First to Fight: An Inside View of the United States Marine Corps* (Paperback). New York: Pocket Books, 1984.

Lansdale, Edward G. *In the Midst of Wars: An American's Mission to Southeast Asia* 1991. (Paperback).

Langguth, A.J. *Our Vietnam: The War 1954-1975.* New York: Simon & Schuster, 2000.

McMaster, H.R. *Dereliction of Duty: Lyndon Johnson, Robert McNamara, The Joint Chiefs of Staff, and the Lies that Led to Vietnam.* New York: HarperCollins, 1997.

McNamara, Robert Strange. *In Retrospect: The Tragedy and Lessons of Vietnam.* New York: Vintage Books, 1996.

Millett, Allan R. *Semper Fidelis: The History of the United States Marine Corps.* New York: The Free Press, 1980.

Millett, Allan R. and Shumlinson, Jack (ed). *Commandants of the Marine Corps.* Annapolis: Naval Institute Press, 2004.

Moyar, Mark. *Triumph Forsaken: The Vietnam War, 1954-1965.* Cambridge: Cambridge University Press, 2006.

Parks, W. Hayes "Rolling Thunder and the Laws of War," *Air University Review,* Vol. XXXIII, No. 2 (January-February 1982), 14.

Peterson, Michael E. *The Combined Action Platoons: The U.S. Marines Other War in Vietnam.* New York: Praeger, 1989.

Pribblenow, Merle L. (trans). Senior General Hoang Van Thai, et al, eds. *Victory in Vietnam: The Official History of the People's Army of Vietnam, 1954-1975*. Lawrence, KS: University Press of Kansas, 2002.

Robbins, James S. *This Time We Win: Revisiting the Tet Offensive*. New York: Encounter Books, 2010.

Sharp, U.S.G. *Strategy for Defeat: Vietnam in Perspective*. Novato, CA: Presidio Press, 1993 (Paperback).

Sheehan, Neil. *A Bright Shining Lie: John Paul Vann and America in Vietnam*. New York: Vantage Books, 1988.

Smith, Charles R. (ed). *U.S. Marines in the Korean War*. Washington, D.C.: History Division, United States Marine Corps, 2007.

Wicker, Tom. "Broadcast News." *New York Times* 26 January 1997. http://www.nytimes.com/books/97/01/26/reviews/970126.26wickert.html. Retrieved 2010-11-12.

U.S. Marines in Vietnam Series – All published by History and Museums Division, Headquarters Marine Corps, Washington, D.C.

U.S. Marines in Vietnam: The Advisory and Combat Assistance Era, 1954-1964. Captain Whitlow, Robert H., 1977

U.S. Marines in Vietnam: The Landing and the Buildup, 1965. Shumlinson, Jack; Major Johnson, Charles M., 1978.

U.S. Marines in Vietnam: An Expanding War, 1966. Shumlinson, Jack; 1982.

U.S. Marines in Vietnam: Fighting the North Vietnamese, 1967. Major Telfar, Gary L.; Lieutenant Colonel Roger, Lane; and Fleming, V. Keith, 1984.

U.S. Marines in Vietnam: The Defining Year, 1968. Shumlinson, Jack; Lieutenant Colonel Blasiol, Leonard A.; Smith, Charles R.; Captain Dawson, David A., 1997.

COMMAND CHRONOLOGIES

All Command Chronologies are available online at http://www.vietnam.ttu.edu/. Command Chronologies were published monthly by each unit during the Vietnam War.

III Marine Amphibious Force, 1965-1971

1st Battalion, 7th Marines, December 1968

1st Battalion, 12th Marines, 1965 through 1968

12th Marines, October 1965 through August 1967

2nd Battalion, 4th Marines, November 1965 through December 1968

INTERNET RESOURCES

http://www.2ndbattalion94thartillery.com/

Vietnam Studies, Riverine Operations 1966-1969, a monograph produced by the U.S. Army and available online at http://www.history.army.mil/books/vietnam/riverine/index.htm. Website checked March 2011.

http://www.time.com/time/magazine/article/0,9171,906068,00.html. *TIME Magazine*, June 26

http://www.afa.org/magazine/feb2007/0207tapes.asp, 1972.

http://www.tecom.usmc.mil/HD/PDF_Files/Pubs/Units/Brief%20History%20of%20the%2012th%20Marines.pdf. Smith, Charles R. *A Brief History of the 12th Marines.*

APPENDIX

APPENDIX

ABBREVIATIONS/ACRONYMS

I Corps	I Corps: South Vietnam was divided into four military zones- I Corps (prounounced "eye corps"), II Corps, and III Corps
1/7	1st Battalion, 7th Marines
2/3	2nd Battalion, 3rd Marines
2/4	2nd Battalion, 4th Marines
2/11	2nd Battalion, 11th Marines
2/94	2nd Battalion, 94th Artillery
AO2C	Intelligence Analysis Branch of the Intelligence Division at Headquarters, US Marine Corps
AO2F	Signals Intelligence/Electronic Warfare Branch of the Intelligence Division at Headquarters, US Marine Corps
APC	Armored Personnel Carrier
ARVN	Army of the Republic of Vietnam. Also referred to: South Vietnamese Army, Army of South Vietnam and Army of Vietnam
A/1/7	Alpha (Able) Company, 1st Battalion, 7th Marines
A/1/11	Alpha (Able) Company, 1st Battalion, 11th Marines
BOQ	Basic Overnight Quarters
B/1/7	Bravo (Baker) Company, 1st Battalion, 7th Marines
C/1/12	Charlie Battery, 1st Battalion, 12th Marines/ "C" Battery/ C Battery
C-130	A type of military cargo aircraft used by the Marines (Hercules)
CAP	Combined Action Program
CCP	Consolidated Cryptologic Program
CO	Commanding Officer
COC	Combat Operations Center
CIA	Central Intelligence Agency

CINCPAC	Commander-in-Chief, Pacific
CINCPACFLT	Commander-in-Chief, Pacific Fleet
COMSEC	Communications Security
D/1/7	Delta Company, 1st Battalion, 7th Marines
D/2/94	Task Force Bravo, 6th Battalion, 27th Field Artillery Regiment
DMZ	De-Militarized Zone
DoD	Department of Defense
DoN	Department of the Navy
Duster	M42 40 mm Self-Propelled Anti-Aircraft Gun
EW	Electronic Warfare
F/2/11	Foxtrot (Fox) Battery, 2nd Battalion, 11th Marines
FDC	Fire Direction Center
FM	Frequency Modulated
FMFM I	Fleet Marine Force Manual I
FMFPAC	Fleet Marine Forces, Pacific
G-1	Personnel Officer (on a general's staff)
G-2	Intelligence Officer (on a general's staff)
G-3	Operations Officer (on a general's staff)
G-6	Communications Electronics Officer (on a general's staff)
HF	High Frequency
HQMC	Headquarters Marine Corps
J-2	Intelligence Officer (on a Joint Staff)
J-3	Operations Officer (on a Joint Staff)
J-5	Plans & Policy Directorate Officer (on a Joint Staff)
J-6	Special Operations Officer (on a Joint Staff)
JCS	Joint Chiefs of Staff
K/4/12	Kilo Battery, 4th Battalion, 12th Marines
KIA	Killed in Action

MAF	Marine Amphibious Force
MAC(V)	Military Assistance Command (Vietnam)
MOS	Military Occupational Specialty
N-2	Intelligence Officer (on an admiral's staff)
NCO	non-commissioned officer
NSA	National Security Agency
NSG	Naval Security Group (Name has evolved to Naval Warfare Command, Cyberforces)
NVA	North Vietnamese Army
OCS	Officer Candidate School
RRU	Radio Reconnaissance Unit
S-1	Personnel Officer (on staff of a colonel or below)
S-2	Intelligence Officer (on staff of a colonel or below)
S-3	Operations, Plans and Training Officer (on staff of a colonel or below)
S-4	Logistics Officer (on staff of a colonel or below)
SIGINT	Signals Intelligence
SIGSEC	Signals Security
Staff NCO	Staff Non-Commissioned Officer
TAOR	Tactical Area of Responsibility
TFB	Task Force Bravo
TF B/6/27	Task Force Bravo, 6th Battalion, 27th Field Artillery Regiment
USAF	United States Air Force
USMC	United States Marine Corps
USMCR	United States Marine Corps Reserve
USN	United States Navy
VC	Viet Cong
VHF	Very High Frequency
VMCJ	Marine Corps's Composite Reconnaissance Squadron
WIA	Wounded in Action

MARINE AND NAVY OFFICER RANKS

Marine (Army/AF) Officer Ranks		Navy Officer Ranks	
Second Lieutenant	2nd Lt	Ensign	ENS
First Lieutenant	1st Lt	Lieutenant, Junior Grade	LT (jg)
Captain	Capt	Lieutenant	LT
Major	Maj	Lieutenant Commander	LCDR
Lieutenant Colonel	Lt Col	Commander	CDR
Colonel	Col	Captain	CAPT
Brigadier General	Brig Gen	Rear Admiral (Lower Half)	RDML
Major General	Maj Gen	Rear Admiral (Upper Half)	RADM
Lieutenant General	Lt Gen	Vice Admiral	VADM
General	Gen	Admiral	ADM

INDEX

INDEX